D1542784

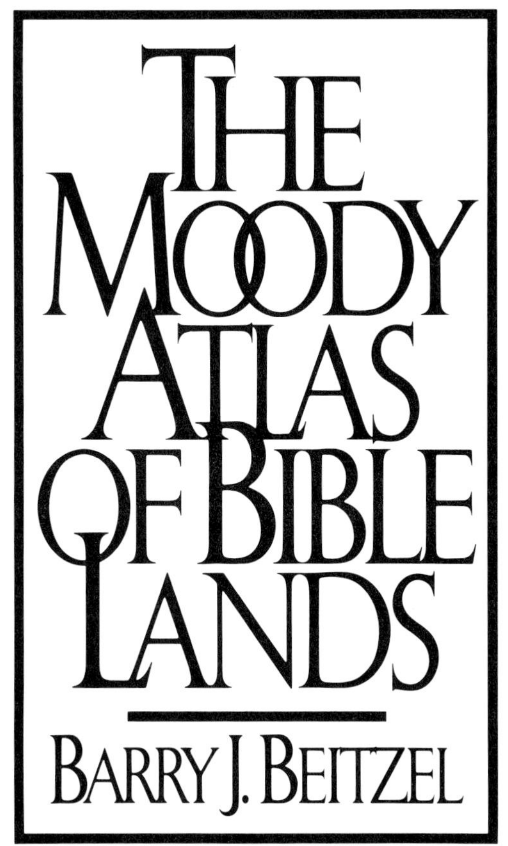
THE
MOODY
ATLAS
OF BIBLE
LANDS
BARRY J. BEITZEL

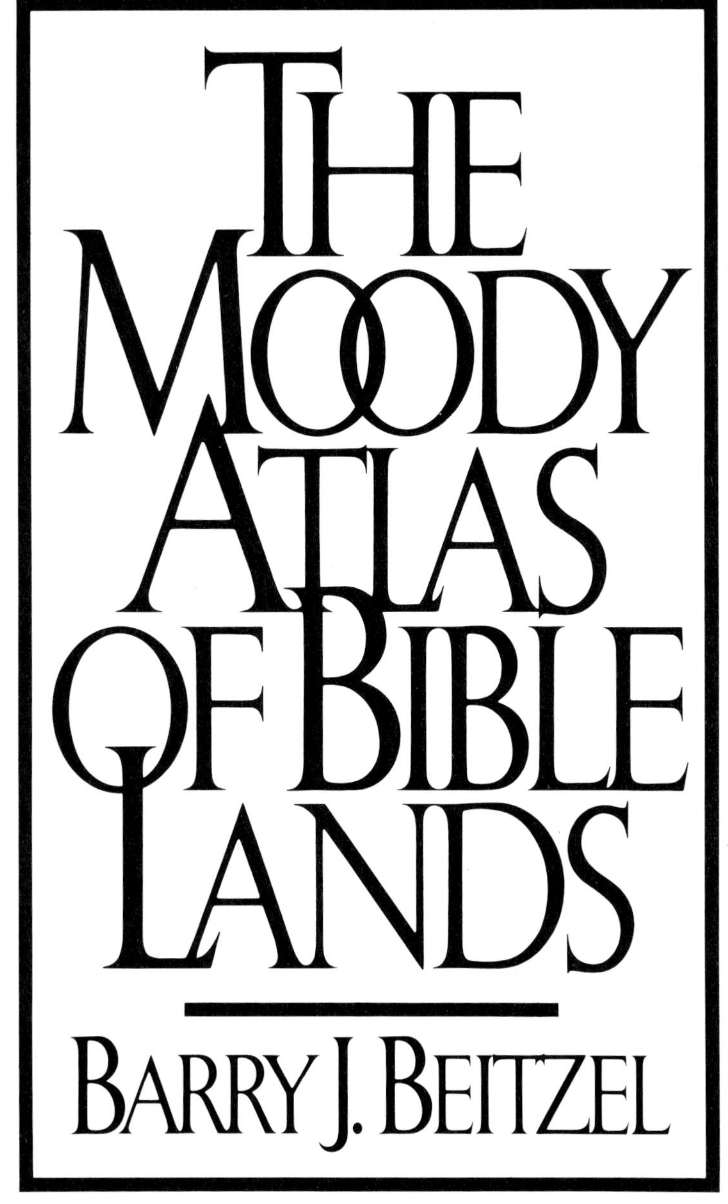

MOODY PRESS
CHICAGO

ACKNOWLEDGMENTS

All original maps have been compiled by the author and executed by the Donnelley Cartographic Services. Figure 2, rendered by Lloyd K. Townsend (Washington, D.C.), and Figure 25, rendered by Hugh Claycombe (Lombard, Ill.) were specially commissioned for *The Moody Atlas of Bible Lands.* All other figures are printed here with permission.

Figures 3-4, 10, 13, 15-17, 21, 23, 28, and 35 were kindly supplied by Richard Cleave (Pictorial Archive, Jerusalem). Pictorial Archive has made a special study of the biblical landscape, covering Israel, Jordan, and Egypt. Teachers of biblical studies and leaders of tours to the Holy Land are recommended to apply for additional information on the Bible Lands Exhibit as a set of posters and the various sets of transparencies, maps, and satellite imagery now available from Pictorial Archive (Near Eastern History), The Old School, P.O. Box 19823, Jerusalem.

Figures 8, 11, and 39 were supplied by the courtesy of the National Aeronautics and Space Administration (Washington, D.C.). Figure 27 was reprinted courtesy of the Westminster Press from *The Westminster Historical Atlas to the Bible* (rev. ed.), edited by George Ernest Wright and Floyd Vivian Filson; photo by David Singer. Figure 30 was included courtesy of the University Museum (Philadelphia). Figures 31 and 36 were courtesy of the British Museum (London). Figure 32 was reprinted courtesy of Oxford University Press from *A History of Technology*, edited by Charles Singer, E. J. Holmyard, and A. R. Hall; photo by David Singer. Figure 33 was included courtesy of the Harvard University Press; photo by David Singer. Figure 34 was supplied by the courtesy of the Newberry Library (Chicago). Figure 37 was reprinted courtesy of the Abraham H. Cassel Collection of the Bethany Theological Seminary Library (Oak Brook, Ill.) from *Itinerarium sacrae scripturae,* by H. Bünting. Figure 38 was reproduced courtesy of Kenneth Nebenzahl, Inc. (Chicago); photo by David Singer. Figures 1, 5-7, 12, 14, 18-20, 22, 24, 26, and 29 were supplied by the author. Figure 9 was supplied by the author; photo by David Singer.

Unless indicated otherwise, the Scripture translation used in this book is the author's own.

Library of Congress Cataloging-in-Publication Data

Beitzel, Barry J.
The Moody Atlas of Bible Lands.

Bibliography: p.
Includes indexes.
1. Bible—Geography—Maps. 2. Bible—History of Biblical events—Maps. I. Title.
G2230.B44 1985 912'.33 85-675158
ISBN 0-8024-0438-3

2 3 4 5 6 7 Printing/RR/Year 88 87 86 85

Printed in the United States of America

To Carol,
for her love, faith, companionship

CONTENTS

TABLE OF ABBREVIATIONS

(INCLUDING MAP ABBREVIATIONS)

Abel	F.-M. Abel, *Géographie de la Palestine* (2 vols.; repr.), Paris, 1967.
Aharoni	Y. Aharoni, *The Land of the Bible* (rev. ed.), Philadelphia, 1979.
AJ	F. Josephus, *The Antiquities of the Jews* (20 books).
AJA	*American Journal of Archaeology* (Baltimore).
Akk.	Akkadian.
ANEP	J. B. Pritchard, ed., *The Ancient Near East in Pictures*, Princeton, 1954.
ANET	J. B. Pritchard, ed., *Ancient Near Eastern Texts* (3d ed.), Princeton, 1969.
ARAB	D. D. Luckenbill, *Ancient Records of Assyria and Babylonia* (2 vols.; repr.), New York, 1968.
ARM	Siglum for the Archives royales de Mari.
BA	*Biblical Archaeologist* (Cambridge, Mass.).
BASOR	*Bulletin of the American Schools of Oriental Research* (New Haven).
B.B.	*Baba Bathra.*
BN	*Biblische Notizen* (Bamberg, West Germany).
Br.	Brook.
CAD	A. L. Oppenheim, gen. ed., *The Assyrian Dictionary of the University of Chicago* (18 vols.—presently), Chicago-Glückstadt, 1956-.
de Vaux	R. de Vaux, *The Early History of Israel*, Philadelphia, 1978.
EA	Siglum for the Tell el-Amarna Tablets.
EJ	C. Roth and G. Wigoders, eds. in chief, *Encyclopaedia Judaica* (16 vols.), Jerusalem, 1972.
Eusebius	Eusebius, *Onomasticon.*
Heb.	Hebrew.
Herodotus	Herodotus, *History* (9 books).
IDB	G. A. Buttrick, ed., *The Interpreter's Dictionary of the Bible* (4 vols.), Nashville, 1962.
IDBSupp	K. Crim, gen. ed., *The Interpreter's Dictionary of the Bible, Supplementary Volume*, Nashville, 1976.
IEJ	*Israel Exploration Journal* (Jerusalem).
J.	Jebel (Arabic word for mountain).
JAOS	*Journal of the American Oriental Society* (New Haven).
JCS	*Journal of Cuneiform Studies* (Ann Arbor).
JEA	*Journal of Egyptian Archaeology* (London).
JNES	*Journal of Near Eastern Studies* (Chicago).
Ket.	*Kethubboth.*
Kh.	Khirbet (Arabic word for ruins).
L.	Lake.
LXX	Septuagint.
Makk.	*Makkoth.*
Mt(s).	Mountain(s).
PEFQS	*Palestine Exploration Fund, Quarterly Statement* (London).
Pliny	Pliny, *Natural History* (37 books).
POTT	D. J. Wiseman, ed., *Peoples of Old Testament Times*, Oxford, 1973.
PTR	*Princeton Theological Review* (Princeton).
R.	River.

RA	*Revue d'assyriologie et d'archéologie orientale* (Paris).
Sheb.	*Shebu'oth.*
Simons	J. Simons, *The Geographical and Topographical Texts of the Old Testament*, Leiden, 1959.
Smith	G. A. Smith, *The Historical Geography of the Holy Land* (25th rev. ed., repr.), New York, 1966.
Strabo	Strabo, *Geography* (17 books).
T.	Tell (Arabic word for artificial earthen occupational mound).
W.	Wadi (Arabic word for intermittent water channel).
Wars	F. Josephus, *The Wars of the Jews* (7 books).
ZDPV	*Zeitschrift des deutschen Palästina—Vereins* (Wiesbaden, West Germany).

Table of Maps and Figures

Preface

The word *trivia* draws its origin from the realm of geography; it originally defined day-to-day discourse that took place at the intersection of three roads, usually by merchants who sold or bartered goods there, or by travelers who sought directions there. The word evolved in time to denote any conversation at that location, however commonplace or unimportant it might have been. Eventually, *trivia* came to designate anything at all viewed as trite or insignificant. It is singularly ironic, therefore, that geography itself is often perceived in the latter sense today.

But for one who believes that episodes described in Holy Scripture actually took place in the space of this world, such a perception is fundamentally ill founded. Quite to the contrary, geography must be seen as integral to the interpretative process. Jerome, who lived in Palestine for many years, wrote concerning geography's role in the enterprise of biblical interpretation: "Just as those who have seen Athens understand Greek history better, and just as those who have seen Troy understand the words of the poet Virgil, thus one will comprehend the Holy Scriptures with a clearer understanding who has seen the land of Judah with his own eyes and has come to know the references to the ancient towns and places and their names" (*Commentary on Chronicles*).

With this in mind, the *Moody Atlas* presents the geographical setting of the lands of the Bible, attempting along the way to establish the relevance of the study of geography in the elucidation of Scripture. The *Atlas* seeks to set forth and develop a central thesis: namely, that God prepared the Promised Land for His chosen people with the same degree of care that He prepared His chosen people for the Promised Land. The Promised Land might have been created as an environment without blemish; it might have exhibited ecological or climatological perfection. It might have been prepared as a tropical rain forest through which coursed an effusion of crystal-clear water; it might have been created as a thickly-carpeted grassy meadow or as an elegant garden suffused with the aroma of flowers and blossoms. It might have been—but it was not. As I will attempt to demonstrate, God prepared for His chosen people a land that embodied the direst of geographic hardship. Possessing meager physical and economic resources and caught inescapably in a maelstrom of political upheaval, the Promised Land has yielded up to its residents a simple, tenuous, mystifying, and precarious existence, even under the best of circumstances. It is an important and helpful insight to realize that God prepared a *certain kind of land,* positioned at a *particular spot,* designed to elicit a *specific and appropriate response.* God has been at work in both geography and history.

Geography is understood in the *Atlas* to define three separate, if somewhat overlapping concepts: physical geography (a description of those topographic and environmental features that impact upon the land), regional geography (a description of those political and regional subdivisions that comprise the land), and historical geography (a diachronic unfolding of those events that have transpired in the land, which are conducive to a geographic explanation). Chapter 1 of the book is an attempt to survey the entities of physical and regional geography. Chapter 2 presents an overview of historical geography. It is not my purpose in chapter 2 to supply a full and running commentary of the whole of the Bible narratives discussed, which would require a separate volume in itself, but only to provide a geographic sketch sufficient to elucidate a map. Some maps have no accompanying text beyond the explanatory boxes or Scripture citations found with them. To a certain degree, chapter 2 adheres to the axiom of Thomas Fuller: "The eye will learn more in an hour from a map, than the ear can learn in a day from discourse" (*A Pisgah-Sight of Palestine*). Chapter 3 briefly surveys the history of biblical mapmaking. Much detailed cartographic material covering long periods of time is available for the Holy Land, perhaps owing to its unique place among three monotheistic religions; it possesses one of the longest unbroken mapmaking records known.

Among the back matter, the reader will encounter three indexes (Map Citation Index, Index of Scripture, Index of Extra-Biblical Literature) and a Time Line. The Map Citation Index has been arranged according to map number; for a comprehensive list of maps arranged according to page number, refer to the Table of Maps and Figures found among the front matter. It should be stressed that the Map Citation Index is not a gazetteer (a comprehensive index of all geographic features of Bible lands, sometimes including information concerning the pronunciation of each entry, together with a description of its present location and name); inasmuch as gazetteers already exist in a variety of readily accessible versions, there seemed to be no need to reinvent the wheel.

Anyone today who wishes to write on Bible lands faces the vexing question of nomenclature, but this problem is perhaps most acute for the Bible geographer. Given the climate of contemporary Middle Eastern politics, it becomes almost impossible for a geographer to employ words like *Israel, Palestine, Jordan, Armenia,* or *Syria* without creating the impression that a certain political statement is being made or a particular ideology is being endorsed. Accordingly, I wish to state clearly at the outset to my readers—be they Christian, Jewish, or Moslem—that my intention is purely historical and that even when such terms are used in a postbiblical or modern context, they should not be construed as espousing any political opinion.

Someone may inquire: "Why write another atlas? Do not a wide array of atlases already exist?" My answer is twofold. First, the plethora of other atlases that presently exist is a bit of a misperception. Many atlases published in bygone days are presently out of print. Of those that remain in print, only a few have been written from an avowed evangelical Christian standpoint; and of those few, some employ outmoded mapmaking techniques, some embody very little accompanying text, some contain few or no historical maps, and none adequately addresses the subject of physical geography. I must emphasize, however, that there are some excellent sources for the modern-day Bible geographer, and I have listed a few of those in my bibliography. Second, as with the topics of dieting or counseling techniques, concerning which a number of books are available and yet new volumes continue to appear, new perspectives can be brought to the subject of geography, and no individual book is capable of incorporating the whole truth. In this latter regard, one must not naively imagine that the present *Atlas* represents forever the final word on this multifaceted subject of Bible geography.

It remains to discuss those technical and editorial procedures employed in the *Atlas.* The maps were produced by the Donnelley Cartographic Services in a five-step sequence, using a combination of manual and photographic techniques, carried out at reproduction scale on stable plastic film. Before any historical-geographical information could be mapped, a series of accurate base maps (showing shorelines, drainage, and elevation contours) at several scales were compiled and drafted, using information from a variety of source materials, primarily government maps.

Using these bases, artist-cartographer Lloyd K. Townsend created several pieces of art to portray the earth's surface. Some of these are in one color to show only the shape of the surface; other multitoned ones are designed to show terrain and drainage, and one in full color is intending to show the actual vegetation cover of Israel (see Map 15). All historical and geographical data (cities, features, roadways, boundaries, countries, and the like) were then compiled by the author and added to these newly created base maps, again at reproduction scale, on film overlays pin-registered to the bases.

Following general design specifications, the cartographers then drafted the maps from these compilations, creating color-separated film overlays (map "elements") to represent lines, colors (tints or tones), type, and symbols. Negative scribing was used to create the map linework—the framework to which all other information was fitted. This process involved the engraving (scribing) of light-transmitting lines on emulsion-coated opaque plastic materials. Computer-set type on an adhesive backing was cut out and hand-applied to overlays (word by word, sometimes letter by letter), while half-tone screens were photocomposed with certain other elements to create color and tones. Preliminary proofs, photocomposed in color, allowed editing and checking processes to take place.

Finally, the set of approved film elements created for each map (10 to 20 map elements per page) was photocomposed in sequence to create for the printer five pieces of film, one piece for each of the process colors (magenta, cyan, yellow, black, and a brown ink specially prepared for the *Atlas*). This film was retouched and a final proof was made. The final film was then exposed to light-sensitive metal printing plates, and the original maps were ready to be reproduced.

Beyond those common abbreviations found in the Table of Abbreviations, individual maps show abbreviations, symbols, and explanatory boxes in the legend and sometimes on the body of the map itself. The use of the question mark, traditionally shown on Bible maps to denote uncertain city locations, has been avoided in this *Atlas* because of irritation or possible confusion to the reader. By this, however, I do not wish to imply certainty where only probability or possibility exists. Instead of a question mark, I have uniformly used the symbol [○] for a city whose location is uncertain; it was thought that this symbol is both less conspicuous on a map and less susceptible to misinterpretation.

I have endeavored to treat spotting numbers

on maps in a consistent manner. Numbers that pertain to an appropriate passage in an accompanying text are printed in red; in those cases, corresponding red numbers will be found in the attendant text also. Numbers that pertain to matter found in the map legend or in a box superimposed over the map itself are printed in black, with one exception where diverse colors were demanded (Map 78).

A problem faced by any author of an atlas is the conflict between the area covered by a map and the scale at which it can be covered. If the area to be covered is large, then the scale must be small, or else the map will not fit on the size of a page. But this can make for an extremely vague and imprecise map. If a map is composed at a large scale, alternatively, then the area covered must be small, or again the map will be larger than page size. Now the map can be extraordinarily detailed but may lack the larger perspective or be without fixed geographic points. My effort in this *Atlas* has been to keep the scale as large as possible and yet to avoid cropping off an important section of a map and placing an arrow that pointed off the map towards a designated spot. On a few occasions, however, to have an arrow pointing to the margin of a page was unavoidable, even though that can be an irritating practice. Of similar practices, Plutarch once complained: "Geographers . . . crowd into the edges of their maps parts of the world which they do not know about, adding notes in the margin to the effect that beyond this lies nothing but sandy deserts full of wild beasts, and unapproachable bogs" (*Lives, Aemilius Paulus*). I trust that my readers will be more understanding. But my approach to this problem of area covered versus scale has necessitated that some map legends be positioned adjacent to, but not on, the map itself.

Complexities of phonetics between several writing systems used in the biblical world are profound, and a certain amount of inconsistency in the spelling of proper names was unavoidable. Nevertheless, a measure of systemization has been attempted. Names that have a well-known English form have been retained in the *Atlas* (e.g., Babylon, Carchemish, Jerusalem); names that are generally transliterated into English in a certain form (e.g., Akkad, Aleppo, Ebla) retain that customary form here, even though the transliteration may be slightly inaccurate; names not occurring in English are rendered phonetically in English script (e.g., Negeb, Wadi Fari'a, Kafr Bir'im), but without vowel length marks or diacritical signs (note that both length marks and diacritical signs *are* used when transcribing words that are not proper names). Arabic names normally have been spelled without the article *el-* (e.g., J. Magharah, not J. el-Magharah) except where the name involved was pertinent to an argument presented. Frequently cited reference points have been assigned a static spelling throughout the volume (e.g., Mediterranean Sea, not also Upper Sea, Great Sea, Western Sea, or *tâmtu elītu*; Sea of Galilee, not also Sea of Gennesaret, Sea of Chinnereth, Sea of Tiberias, Sea of Taricheae, or Sea of Galilea), even though such a spelling will be anachronistic on some maps.

Since color vision dysfunction is a particularly male deficiency, and since our product design studies indicated that three out of four users of a Bible atlas are males, selection of map coloration (tints and tones) has taken into account the special needs of color-weak or color-blind users, where this was feasible. But having said that, I must urge caution on two fronts. There are several types of color blindness, and one cannot eliminate all problems with color except by going exclusively to monochrone schemes, which would have made for an extraordinarily dull atlas. Second, in some cases an infinite number of color hues was required in order to fulfill the function of a map; in these cases, our sensitivity to user color deficiency had to be outweighed by the requirements of a map's function.

Finally, the *Moody Atlas* never could have become a reality without the diligent labors of a host of individuals, and my thanks to them is more than a mere accommodation to tradition. I wish to express my profound gratitude to the personnel of the Donnelley Cartographic Services, and especially to Barbara B. Petchenik (Sales Representative for Primary Project Responsibilities), Jeannine Schonta and David Stong (Project Coordinators). Barbara's supervision of a technical and aesthetic nature, and her personal commitment to the quality of our product, has provided impetus and encouragement to the author throughout the project. Jeannine and Dave were unstinting with their time, indefatigable in their labor, timely and courteous with their suggestions, and altogether professional in their sphere of expertise. Thanks and appreciation go to Sandra A. Smith (The Quarasan Group, Northfield, Ill.), who lent her proficiency to the design of the *Atlas*, and to Loretta Nelson (Joe Ragont Studios, Schaumburg, Ill.), who was tireless in her efforts of layout.

Lloyd Townsend (Washington, D.C.) was commissioned to draft the cross-sectional schematic of the Holy Land (Fig. 2) and Hugh Claycombe (Lombard, Ill.) labored diligently on the artistic aspects of the Jerusalem cross-sectional schematic (Fig. 25) and the Time Line. Photographs in the volume came from the University Museum (Philadelphia), the British Museum, the Newberry Library (Chicago), Harvard University Press, Richard

Cleave (Pictorial Archive, Jerusalem), David Singer Photography (Chicago), NASA, and the author (consult the copyright page for a specific figure).

I wish to express indebtedness to my two teaching assistants, Stephen Hall and Freddy Fritz, who invested long hours and concentrated energies in checking my work and in preparing the indexes. And to professors Douglas Moo, Perry Phillips, Walter Kaiser, and Davis Young, who read parts of the manuscript and offered helpful insight and counsel, I express sincere appreciation. Naturally, any remaining errors are my responsibility alone. Acknowledgement and thanks are due Jerry Jenkins (Vice President of Publishing, Moody Bible Institute), Dallas Richards (Production Manager), and Garry Knussman (Senior Editor/Academic Books) of Moody Press. Jerry initially offered the *Atlas* project to me and, through its course, has generously underwritten the cost of my ideas. Dallas and Garry were a constant encouragement in the project, and their care for the innumerable details created by such a volume must be thankfully recognized. To all of these I am profoundly grateful.

And finally, I will never be able to estimate fairly, much less to repay, the debt of gratitude that I owe my wife, Carol, and our children, Bradley, Bryan, and Kelly. Without their joyful sacrifices of time and money, and their patience and encouragement since its inception, this project never would have emerged from the study and light table.

For myself, the study of geography culminates in doxology: "The fulness of the whole earth is His glory" (Isa. 6:3*b*).

For the Lord is a great God,
  and a great King above all gods.
In His hand are the depths of the earth;
  and the mountain peaks belong to Him.
The sea is His, for He made it;
  and His hands formed the dry land.
O come, let us worship and bow down,
  let us kneel before the Lord, our Maker!
For He is our God,
  and we are the people of His pasture,
  the sheep of His hand.

(Ps. 95:3-7*a*)

1
THE PHYSICAL GEOGRAPHY OF THE HOLY LAND

General Introduction to Geography

ROLE OF GEOGRAPHY IN UNDERSTANDING HISTORY

Western civilization has commonly embraced the logic of Greek philosophical categories and has endeavored to describe cosmic realities in terms of "time and space." Individuals, ideas, movements, and even the course of nations are often interpreted precisely in accordance with those canons; hence, designations like *pre-*, *post-*, *intermediate*, *process*, B.C./A.D. or *east*, *west*, *oriental*, *occidental* are invariably employed in analyzing civilizations past and present. Christian theology itself has not escaped this encompassing mode of thinking: God may be described in terms that are corollary to time (*infinity*, *eternality*) or space (*omnipresence*). Christianity states that those attributes of deity were willingly relinquished by Christ through the drama of incarnation, when He became "locked in time and space." Accordingly, with even superficial reflection, one can comprehend something of the far-reaching significance of the temporal and spatial disciplines: history and geography respectively.

But beyond this, it is important to observe that history itself in many respects is inseparably bound by and subject to the limitations of geography. Geography is an impelling force that both initiates and limits the nature and extent of political history, what we might call geopolitics. Geologic formation and rock type have a decisive effect on altitude, manner and extent of erosion, location and quantity of water supply, and physical topography. These, in turn, have a profound bearing on certain aspects of climate, raw materials, soil formation, and land use, factors that may alternately repel or attract human settlement and, in any event, certainly influence the location, density, and socio-economic makeup of a settlement. Where settlements are founded, roadways are eventually opened and used by migrants, armies, or traders, and culture ultimately arrives at a particular location.

In short, factors of geography often dictate where and how geopolitics will occur. It is geographically significant that ancient civilizations emerged on the banks of rivers. Ancient Egypt owed its existence to the Nile; Mesopotamia drew its life sustenance from the Euphrates, Habur, and, beginning with the Seleucid period, the Tigris; the Indus valley civilization was located along the river by the same name; the Hittite empire rested astride the Halys; old Indian culture sprang to life in the Brahmaputra and Ganges valleys; ancient China had its Hwang-Ho and Yangtze; and European culture emerged on the banks of the Tiber, Danube, Rhine, and Meuse. Nor is it inconsequential that the Roman Empire was able to expand as far as the Danube and Rhine rivers, a boundary closely corresponding today to that of the Iron Curtain. Even in twentieth-century America, virtually all major commercial and industrial cities have outlets to rivers, oceans, or the Great Lakes network. Those few exceptions are themselves located at the hub of important interstate highways or airline routes.

Other factors of geography, earthquake activity, and volcanic eruption have played their parts in fashioning history. It is axiomatic that the face of much of western Asia and east Africa has been formed through seismic activity. A massive fissure in the earth's surface has been the single dominant factor in shaping the landscape of western Syria, Lebanon, Israel, Jordan, Ethiopia, Uganda, Tanzania, Mozambique, and the island of Madagascar. For western Asia, earthquake activity has always meant that certain areas were inhospitable to human occupation and that travel has been funneled into an essentially north-south axis. The seismic forces that produced the mighty Himalayan Mountain chain, on the other hand, have created what in antiquity was an impenetrable longitudinal barrier that caused culture to expand and traffic to flow in an essentially east-west axis. Vast badlands of congealed lava present to a potential settler a dreary terrain broken only occasionally by basaltic plugs or cinder cones, gaunt reminders of bygone volcanic activity. More important, however, is that this volcanic activity often rendered the soil totally unsuitable for human productivity and, in antiquity, always presented a cruelly hostile environment that was intolerably painful to the limbs of pack animals, and thus precluded any sort of arterial travel.

Volcanic eruptions could bring a segment of history to an abrupt conclusion. The effect Mt. Vesuvius's eruption had on Pompeii usually comes to mind in that regard. However, a more graphic illustration is the eruption of the island of Santorini, located in the southern Aegean Sea approximately midway between Greece and Crete. In the wake of a cataclysmic eruption that occurred there between 1520-1450 B.C., about 32 square miles of earth collapsed into a caldera approximately 2,250 feet deep. A gigantic tidal wave was created that was approximately 800 feet high at its apex. Within 20 minutes of the eruption, that wave, propelling massive amounts of toxic gases outward, catastrophically struck Crete at a speed of 200 miles per hour and a height of 200-300 feet. What is more, basaltic cores the size of a person's head would have been hurled like missiles from Santorini to Crete. A thick blanket of falling ash would have created an atmosphere of lethal air, thereby producing polluted water, rancid food, and diverse diseases. It is not difficult to understand how the homeland of the entire Minoan civilization instantly met a disastrous end.[1]

Mountains, deserts, caves, and oceans also have had their say concerning the location or nature of history. Were it not for the Andes Mountains, much of South America would be a blazing Sahara. It is instructive to note that the Assyrian, Babylonian, Persian, Greek, and Roman empires were all bordered in part by impassable mountain barriers or unnavigable desert wastelands. It is surely not mere accident that evidence for ancient cave dwellings found at Mt. Carmel, Shinadar, Çatal Hüyük, Jarmo, and Hassuna comes from precisely those areas of the Near East that receive an annual rainfall capable of sustaining the spontaneous generation of wild grains that could support human life.

From the demise of the Greek navy at the Battle of Salamis on the island of Cyprus (480 B.C.) until the defeat of the Spanish Armada (A.D. 1588), there existed a Mediterranean theater of history in which the northern and southern shores struggled for political and cultural superiority. But in the aftermath of the oceanic voyages of Christopher Columbus and Vasco da Gama, the sovereignty of the Mediterranean was challenged, the Renaissance and some of its important cities began to fade, and history moved westward.

Natural resources represent still another geographic factor that influences the location and nature of history. Much ancient documentation addresses the need to maintain sovereignty over the tin of Iran, the cedar of Lebanon, the silver of Assyria, the copper of Anatolia, or the gold and ivory of Spain. And who can doubt that the whole complexion of modern geopolitics has been altered permanently and dramatically by the OPEC cartel? Indeed, geography represents the stage on which the pageant of history is presented, without which history would wander aimlessly as a vagrant.

But the application of geography's effect on history transcends the practical level and extends also to the theoretical domain. Like the effect of environment on culture, geography actually establishes the boundaries within which history must operate. This is not to say that a people's history can be explained completely in terms of geography. Students of the effect of geography on history have made a most important distinction between its determining effect and its limiting effect. For example, where a frigid winter climate necessitates the wearing of heavy clothing, there is nothing in the temperature itself that decrees whether or not people shall wear seal skins or shetland wool; *but they must procure and wear winter clothing.* When a region unsuitable for agriculture becomes populated, very little in the environment predetermines which domestic animals shall be grazed or whether seafood will be secured with hooks, nets, traps, or spears; *but a nonagrarian society will certainly emerge.* It is geographically pertinent that certain plants and animals are peculiar to only one hemisphere or that writing arose where, when, and in the form that it did. Those facts all represent expressions of history that have been or continue to be subject to the limitations and indirect controls of geography.

Many of those limitations are discernable even in our modern technological world where deserts can be extensively irrigated or the effects of oppressive heat can be lessened by air-conditioning; where Landsat photography equipped with infrared capability can discover vast reservoirs of fresh water buried deep in the cavities of the earth's interior; where rampaging rivers can be restrained by huge dams and harnessed for hydroelectrical purposes; where formidable mountain barriers can be leveled, penetrated, or easily surmounted; and where air travel can put faraway places within quick and painless reach. One can imagine, therefore, how much more well-defined such geographic limitations would have been in a world that existed before technological advancement, one like the biblical world.

ROLE OF GEOGRAPHY IN UNDERSTANDING THE BIBLE

Included among the difficulties that vex a twentieth-century student of the Scriptures are those of "time and space." Modern students of the Bible live in a different millennium and most live on a different continent. The proclamations of Scripture, on the other hand, were occasioned and penned precisely from within their own distinctive settings in time and space. In our worthy desire to interpret and apply Scripture properly, therefore, we must ensure as much as possible that the enterprise is built knowledgeably upon the grid of the Bible's own environment. At the outset, it is imperative for one to see geography not as a superfluity that can be arbitrarily divorced from biblical interpretation. The Bible's portrait of Israel is painted on several levels, including the territorial level.

There is an acute consciousness of a national home, a definable geographic domain in which even the soil is divinely consecrated, what one may call the "holy land."[2] In fact, there exists an extraordinarily large body of biblical documentation devoted to geographical concerns: the locations of certain empires, countries, territories, cities, roadways, water systems, mountains, battles, miracles, and churches; the stations of itineraries undertaken or encampments made; and the meaning of geographical images and metaphors, with which the Scripture abounds. Oftentimes, it is precisely a geographical reference or allusion contained in a book of Scripture that enables scholars to assign to it a natural origin, as is the case of Amos (Israel's northern kingdom) and James (eastern Mediterranean basin).

It is moreover critical to observe the centrality of "land" contained in covenantal promises and eschatological expectations. There is in Scripture an umbilical cord that ties land to several aspects of theology. On the one hand, Old Testament faith especially was concerned with events that occurred in *this* world, the arena in which God acted on behalf of His people (e.g., call and covenant of Abraham, Exodus/Sinai, conquest, captivity, return, New Israel). Such actions of God, both discernible and theologically significant, correctly would have been understood to bear a direct and necessary relationship to bringing Israel into possession of a particular parcel of real estate, or later in restoring the nation to that land. In that sense, Old Testament faith would have exhibited a "here-and-now" essence. Perceived through the filter of New Testament theology, Israel's faith would appear to have possessed a "worldly" character, and the ascetic principle of 1 John 2:15-17 would have been largely absent.

It follows, however, that being in the land was a profoundly religious idea with theological overtones on a number of important fronts. Precisely by occupying the land of its inheritance could Israel expect to enjoy the fuller benefits of God's provisions. There existed a signal bond between the destiny of the chosen people and possession of the promised land. In fact, Israel's identity, security, and prosperity were all the direct results of *being in the land*. But when not in the land, Israel experienced a precarious existence described as that of a *sojourner* (e.g., Deut. 10:19; Gen. 15:13; Ex. 6:4; cf. Heb. 11:9, 13), *wanderer* (e.g., Num. 32:13; Hos. 9:17), or *exile* (e.g., 2 Kings 18:11; Ezra 1:11). These three terms share the connotations of aimlessness and estrangement. A *sojourner* was a resident-alien who could not settle down and enjoy the privileges customarily afforded the citizen, but who had to survive by other means. Unlike a New Testament pilgrim, a *wanderer* was someone en route to nowhere. He was not just between stops; somewhat like a gypsy, he was one who actually had no specified destination. Feeling altogether disenfranchised, an *exile* would have imagined that his whole world was shattered. Driven from his land, he would have sensed that faith itself had become meaningless, that even the promises and program of God had become invalidated.

There was therefore an inextricable and vital interconnection between landlessness and hopelessness. Alternatively, it was the whole notion of "land," and, more important, being in possession of it, that became at once a powerful medium to display God's mighty acts and through which His promises might be realized by Israel. Furthermore, monarchic, Messianic, and eschatological expectations cannot be dissociated from, and often find their context precisely within, the concept of "land."

But beyond all the preceding considerations, to appreciate the role of geography in understanding the Bible, one must have a special acquaintance with certain geographical realities of Israel and surrounding lands: physical topography, climatic seasons, prevailing winds, soil types, land use, and the like. Armed with such knowledge, one would be able to understand and appreciate, for example, biblical references to "the former and latter rains" or "the strong east wind"; the scorching effect of Israel's hot sun; the importance of dew for crop survival; the implications of no rainfall; the concentration of "Fertility Worship" in the land of promise; the nature of Egyptian, Canaanite, and Mesopotamian deities; the character of extrabiblical creation myths; the migrations of Abraham, Moses, and Nehemiah; the close correlation between the terrain Joshua's forces could conquer but over which the Philistines could not run chariots; the astounding success of David in eluding Saul's manhunt; the social psychology of the ministry of John the Baptist; the motivation behind Jesus' move from Nazareth to Capernaum; and the staggering distances undertaken by the apostle Paul.

Without such knowledge, one is faced with the prospect of foisting upon the Scriptures an alien, if modern, grid with potentially disastrous consequences. For example, since *north* functions as a compass point in the vocabulary of a modern Westerner, one might be apt to interpret those numerous passages that mention "the army of the north" or "the enemy of the north" to be referring to a compass point geographically north of Israel. At times, however, the Bible identifies such armies or enemies as Assyrians (e.g., Zeph. 2:13), Babylonians (e.g., Jer. 1:13-15; 6:22; Zech. 2:6-7), or even Persians (e.g., Isa. 41:25; Jer. 50:3), that is, people who hail from countries that lie northeast or due east, but *not north* of Israel. This fact may be explained geographically. Because of prominent geographical barriers, arterial traffic through Israel was forced into longitudinal routes. Even today, though the regions of Jerusalem and southeastern Iraq (land of ancient Babylonia) are separated by about 525 airline miles, and both are roughly situated at 32 degrees north latitude, they are not linked by a transverse highway. From Babylon travelers are required to follow a circuitous course for nearly 900 miles, through parts of Iraq, Syria, and Lebanon, before finally arriving at the *north* of Jerusalem. (The same thing could be said of ancient Babylonia: to prevent an invasion of individuals or tribes referred to in Babylonian sources as "westerners" [Martu, or Amorites], the Babylonians constructed a wall to their *north.*) Accordingly, the Bible's use of the expression "north" denotes the direction from which a foe would normally approach, and not the location of its homeland. The implications of this observation are especially important when interpreting some of the eschatological narratives within the Old Testament prophets.

Or again, because today the expression "a land flowing with milk and honey" is employed to connote lush fertility and abundance, one might be apt to infer from its application to the land of promise that the land was a veritable paradise, a luxuriant Garden of Eden that pulsated with life and fertility. But as will be shown later, such an inference would be in direct contradistinction to the Bible's own conception of the term—not to mention Israel's geographical reality.

Cultivating a geographic awareness is a necessary and valuable component in any serious study of Scripture. After all, the Christian faith is grounded and rooted in events that occurred in the "space" of this world. Like the Bible itself, faith is formulated precisely from within the spatial and temporal context of which it was a part. Hence the geographical discipline should become at once both the object and the vehicle of some of the Christian's most rewarding and enlightening study; it is clearly worthy of a detailed investigation.

Geographic Overview of Palestine

AS A COMPONENT OF THE FERTILE CRESCENT

Wrapped like a mantle around the Mediterranean, Black, and Caspian seas is a vast geologic formation of rugged mountains known as the Alpine-Himalayan chain. This chain stretches from the Pyrenees Mountains of northern Spain to the towering Himalayan chain of India, Nepal, and China. At its center are located the lofty Taurus, Kurdistan, Elburz, and Zagros ranges. On the other hand, across the Red Sea from Africa lie the burning sands of the Arabian Desert, bounded on the northwest by the hills of Palestine, Lebanon, and Syria, and on the northeast by the valley of the Euphrates River and the Persian Gulf. Hemmed in by these two natural barriers of mountain and desert is a thin, semi-circular strip of comparatively arable land, which arches from the southeastern corner of the Mediterranean Sea, near Gaza (cf. Acts 8:26), to the head of the Persian Gulf. That strip has been known since the days of James Breasted as the Fertile Crescent. In that crescent, mankind developed art, music, literature, mathematics, medicine, astronomy, and chemistry. There the human species learned how to domesticate animals, to cultivate grains and become a food producer, to cluster dwellings and build cities and civilizations, to work metals, and to write (first pictographically and later alphabetically).

At the risk of oversimplification, let me suggest that the Fertile Crescent may be divided into two topographic spheres, known respectively as the *Levant* and *Mesopotamia.* The western sphere, the Levant, consists of a narrow band of high hills and mountainous outcroppings that flank the eastern shore of the Mediterranean. Longitudinally segmented at two points, the Levant actually comprises a series of three such ranges that align with the seaboard. Beginning in the north near the Antioch basin and stretching as far as the so-called Tripolis-Homs-Palmyra depression, where lies the modern Syria-Lebanon border (the area of the el-Kabir River valley; see discussion below), is the Nusariya (Baryglus) mountain range. The Lebanon mountain range extends south of the el-Kabir valley as far as a deep gorge created by the Litani River (just north of Tyre). Finally, spanning the area between the Litani and southern Judah are the mountains of Galilee, Samaria, and Judah, what we will later call the "central mountain spine" of Israel. All three ranges are actually undulating limestone highlands, with steep rocky ridges and deeply furrowed wadi beds. They are devoid of surface water and are practically treeless—even the Lebanon range is all but shorn of its famed cedar forests.

Flanking the Levant's alignment of maritime mountains to the east and separating them from other high ranges farther inland is a deep, slender valley. In the north, the Nusariya mountains fall precipitously, more than 3,000 feet, into this chasm, known as the Ghab ("depression, thicket"). The Ghab is drained by the Orontes River, though in its northern stretches it descends to a depth of 650 feet below sea level, thereby

MAP 1 THE FERTILE CRESCENT

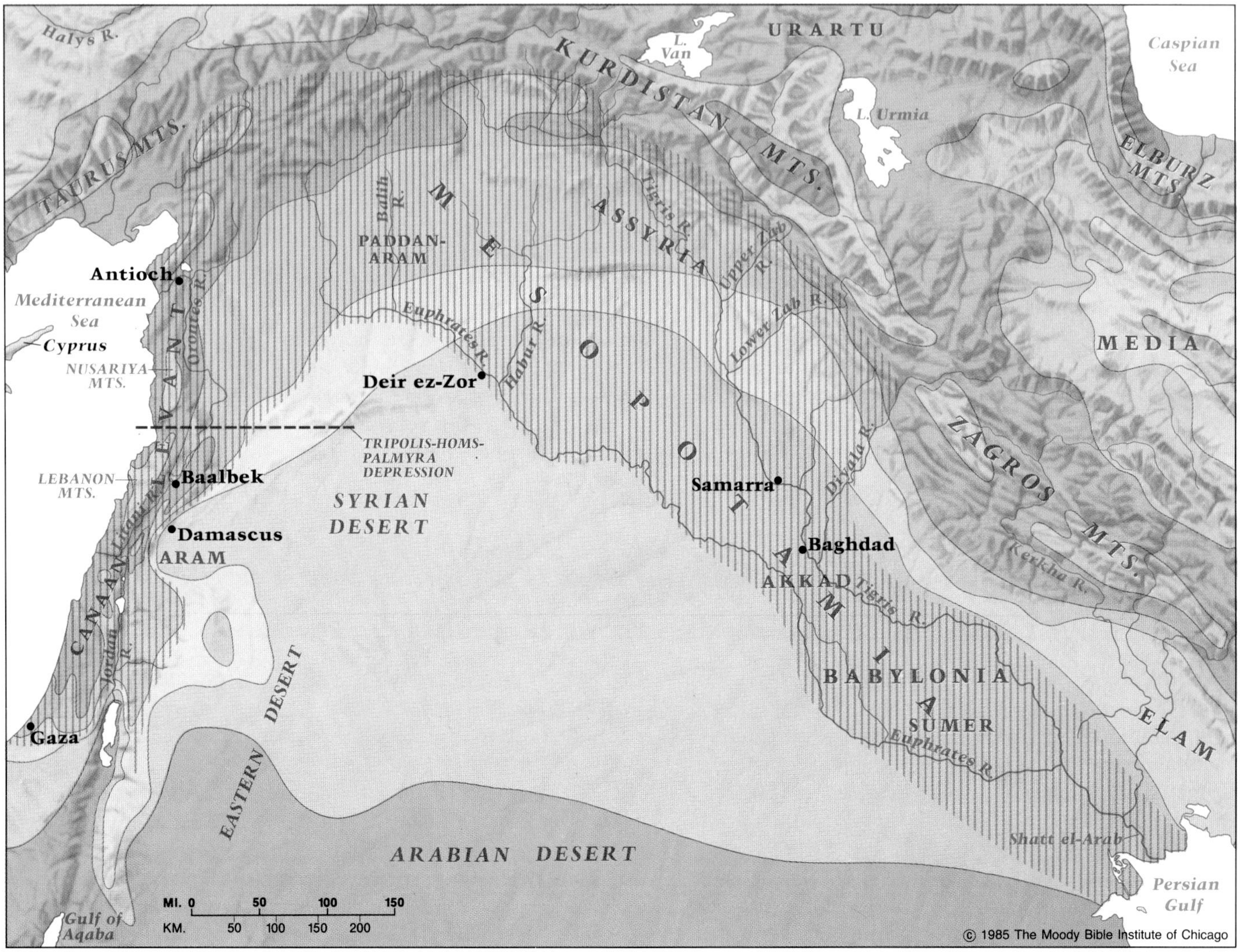

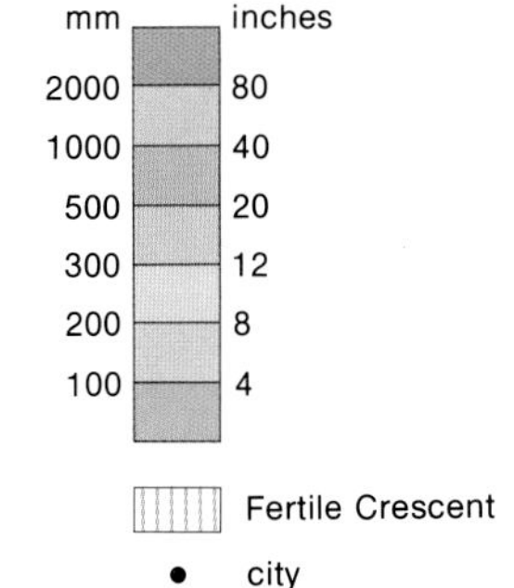

being inundated through the rainy winter months and remaining quite marshy throughout a large portion of the year. Opposite the Lebanon range this gorge is referred to as the Beqaʿ ("valley"). From the environs of Baalbek northward, the Beqaʿ is drained by the extremity of the Orontes River; south of that water divide the Beqaʿ is drained by the Litani River. Despite a watershed that rises at Baalbek to an elevation approaching 3,000 feet above the sea, the configuration of a deep depression remains readily apparent. The mountains of the Lebanon rise to heights in excess of 10,000 feet, while the Anti-Lebanon range, which lies immediately inland from the Beqaʿ and runs parallel to the Lebanon mountain, itself reaches 9,000 feet and also falls off steeply into the "valley." South of the Beqaʿ as far as the Gulf of Aqaba, this chasm is called the Arabah ("wasteland, desert-plain"), although the section between the Sea of Galilee and the Dead Sea may also be denoted as the Jordan Rift Valley (see discussion below).

The eastern sphere of the Fertile Crescent is known as Mesopotamia. A Greek term meaning "the land between the rivers," *Mesopotamia* was applied to a discrete cultural and political entity as early as Polybius, Josephus, and Strabo. They understood the term to denote the region enclosed by the Euphrates and Tigris rivers, north of modern Baghdad. Mesopotamia was introduced into

Christian tradition by the translators of the Septuagint (LXX), who employed it to designate the district from which the patriarch Abraham had emigrated, rendered by the Hebrew scribes as *Aram-naharaim* ("Aram of the two rivers"—Gen. 24:10; Deut. 23:4; 1 Chron. 19:6; in contrast, see Judg. 3:10). It is likely, however, that this latter expression should be understood to demarcate only the land between the Euphrates and Balih rivers, known also as *Paddan-aram* ("field of Aram," see Maps 1 and 22). Be that as it may, the term Mesopotamia is conventionally used today to denote the island of land bounded on the west and south by the Euphrates, on the east by the Tigris, and on the north by the outliers of the Taurus and Kurdistan mountains. The low-lying plain lies at an altitude of approximately 1,625 feet in some northern sectors and slopes gently toward the Persian Gulf.

Structurally, the 12-inch (300 millimeters) rainfall line differentiates Mesopotamia into a wet and dry steppe. The wet steppe receives more than 12 inches annual rainfall and is characterized by red-brown sediment, perennial grasses, herbs, and bushes, especially as one moves from west to east. This area between the Euphrates and the Balih rivers consists of low, stony hills, bare of vegetation except when watered in the spring. Between the Balih and Habur rivers the steppe is less arid and even relatively fertile in the springtime and early summer, as cuneiform texts from the Old Testament period applaud this region for its pasturage. Survival in this part of the steppe, however, depended upon numerous wells scattered throughout the terrain (cf. Gen. 24:11; 29:2), though it does not seem to have been heavily occupied or cultivated in antiquity.

The upper Habur River appears on the map to form the shape of an inverted triangle. In this "Habur triangle," the land flattens considerably. When combined with adequate rainfall and good soil, agriculture flourished in the triangle since high antiquity. The best grain in all of Mesopotamia was produced here in abundance. This area also provided lush grazing grounds for Mesopotamian shepherds who would migrate from their native areas south of the Euphrates during the spring and summer months. Flanking either side of the southern point of this triangle are mountainous outcroppings (Jebel 'Abd el-Aziz, Jebel Sinjar). The northern slopes of these ridges act as a retainer of the soil and mineral deposits washed down from the north. That region tends to remain grassy throughout even in the summer months and, accordingly, it provides permanent pasturage.

On the summit of those two outcroppings, especially on the more easternly Jebel Sinjar (more than 4,300 feet high), one can discover just about the only native timber available in Mesopotamia—pine, oak, terebinth, and pistachio trees. In modern times, though, poplar trees have been planted throughout much of Mesopotamia as windbreaks. In the southern environs of those mountains, however, the surface soil and rock contain large quantities of salt and gypsum, and wells are often saline. The barren steppe here provides only limited and seasonal pasturage.

Most of the dry steppe, by way of contrast, is characterized by gray gypsum desert soils, shallow-rooted seasonal grasses, scattered shrubs, and, where the soil is deep enough, marginal dry-farming of winter crops. Below the 8-inch (200 millimeters) rainfall line, only limited-scale irrigation farming is practiced. The flood plain of the middle Euphrates River, particularly in the area of Deir ez-Zor and south, which is in places as deep as 300 feet and up to 8 miles wide, has always offered ideal, but confined, possibilities for agriculture. The humus soil deposited there by the Euphrates and Habur rivers is especially conducive to that use; an entire network of settlements is known to have existed in the region throughout the biblical period. This same sort of agriculture has been practiced along a short section of the mid-Tigris, in the area surrounding Samarra, where the deposition of the Lower Zab and Tigris rivers has created a bed of rich alluvial sediments. On the other hand, the soil of south Mesopotamia is uniformly hard and nearly impenetrable. The landscape exhibits windblown formations and dunes, as sand is blown off the Arabian Desert. Since early antiquity, southern Mesopotamia has also had to contend with the problem of a high water table, which produced an ever-increasing soil salinization. Some authorities, in fact, share the opinion that the decline of the Sumerian civilization and the subsequent shift northward of the cultural center can be attributed to the salinization of the soil. Were this the case, the forces of geography once again would have dictated the terms of history.

The region between the confluence of the Tigris and Euphrates rivers and the Persian Gulf is known as the Shatt el-Arab waterway. Twice daily, the water level in this vicinity rises and falls by about six feet. Salt water from the Gulf penetrates inland, thereby creating a marshiness that severely restricts human settlement.

Even such a brief overview allows one to realize that the phrase "Fertile Crescent" is liable to create a misimpression. Actually, most of Mesopotamia can be called "fertile" only (1) by way of contrast with its arid desert neighbor, and (2) along the ribbons of greenery that flank the mighty Euphrates and Tigris waterways, their tributaries, and interlocking canal systems.

AS THE LAND PREPARED BY GOD

Theological borders. Even though Israel's borders are discussed in more than one biblical passage, significant questions remain with respect to three of its four borders. That these questions linger may be attributable to a combination of two factors: (1) an inability to pinpoint the location of certain perimeter cities and (2) an inability to achieve consensus on a number of interpretational issues. Bible atlases are often criticized for not attempting to make certain regions or borders more explicit. I will endeavor to make those as explicit as the evidence warrants, because I believe the risk of error is more than counterbalanced by the clarity and helpfulness that may ensue to the reader. In my judgment, one who believes the biblical narratives to be a reliable witness to actual historical events is bound to make some attempt at geographic specificity, even if all such attempts are necessarily tentative.

A proper starting point for a discussion of the boundaries of the Promised Land is the acknowledgement that they were set primarily at natural borders: the Dead Sea, the Sea of Galilee, the Mediterranean, at major mountains and rivers, and so forth. This means the lesser-known segments of border descriptions were also most probably established at fixed geographical points. The following discussion will include a study of fixed geographical points, less well-known but important points of reference, and the issues involved. Each segment will culminate with a summary of where, in my opinion, the evidence seems to point.

Western border (Num. 34:6; cf. Josh., various references; Ezek. 47:20). The western boundary happily presents no problem in identification: it extends to the great sea, to the Mediterranean.

Northern border (Num. 34:7-9; cf. Josh. 19:17-39; Ezek. 47:15-17; 48:1-7). We learn that the northern border diverged from the Mediterranean on a line that ran to Zedad, passing Mt. Hor and Lebo-Hamath. From Zedad the line ran via Ziphron to Hazar-Enan, where it turned toward the border of Hauran. Only two of those places may be identified positively, and both are situated on the edge of the Syrian desert: Zedad should be located at modern Sadad, about 40 miles east of the Orontes and 70 miles northeast of Damascus, just east of the present-day Damascus-Homs highway. Hauran refers to the plateau that extends east of the Sea of Galilee and is dominated by Jebel Druze (Mt. Hauran). The latter was an important military objective for Assyrian kings.[3] Owing to those identifications, one should seek the intermediate sites of Ziphron and Hazar-Enan along the perimeter of the same desert wastelands. Predicated upon the name Hazar-Enan ("village of a spring"), one searches for the site at nearby oases, a principal one being situated at Qaryatein, about 19 miles southeast of Sadad.[4] But beyond those two certain identifications, the precise course of the northern boundary becomes a matter of some uncertainty. A number of indications, however, combine to suggest that this border might have corresponded rather closely to a clearly established international border that was in existence before, during, and after the Mosaic era.

First, Lebo-Hamath, which refers to a site and not to the more-generic "entrance of Hamath" (cf. Amos 6:14, *millĕbô' ḥamāt*), is traditionally associated with modern Lebweh, a town located in the forest region north of the watershed that divides the Orontes and Litani rivers, some 15 miles north-northeast of Baalbek, along the Homs-Baalbek highway. Attested in Egyptian, Hittite, Assyrian, and classical literature as a city of some prominence located between Kadesh and Baalbek, Lebo-Hamath was situated in a territory that was commonly recognized in antiquity as a major boundary in the central Beqa' valley (cf. 1 Kings 8:65; 1 Chron. 13:5; 2 Chron. 7:8). Second, in the place of Lebo-Hamath, Ezekiel (47:16) refers to Berothah and Sibraim, cities customarily sought in the same part of the Beqa'. The former is located at modern Brital, just 6 miles southwest of Baalbek. Ezekiel adds, however, that they lie on the border between Damascus and Hamath. From another biblical passage dating from a period just prior to Ezekiel's (2 Kings 23:33; 25:21), one discovers that Riblah (modern Rablah), a town located along the Homs-Baalbek highway just north of Lebweh, was included as part of the Hamath territory. It appears likely, then, that Ezekiel is being inspired to describe this sector of Israel's northern border in a way that closely corresponded to an internationally-recognizable buffer zone that existed in his own day.

The book of Numbers marks the northern border between Lebo-Hamath and the Mediterranean at Mt. Hor, a site that cannot be specifically located but that doubtlessly refers to one of those summits within the northern Lebanon range. There are a number of mountain peaks both inland ('Akkar, Makmel [Kornet es-Sauda], Mneitri) and along the coast (Ras Shakkah) that have been identified with Mt. Hor. Although any proposal is presently undemonstrable and provisional, I believe there are two reasons a strong case should be developed for identifying Mt. Hor with the area of Jebel 'Akkar.

First, the northern border, as already suggested, followed the line of an ancient and natural boundary. The western portion of that boundary

Borders of the Promised Land

MAP 2

extended westward from Homs through what has been called the Tripolis-Homs-Palmyra depression. This depression separates the Lebanon mountains in the south from the Nusariya mountains north of it (see above). From the Lake of Homs to the Mediterranean, this plain forms the boundary between the modern countries of Syria and Lebanon, just as it served a similar function in antiquity (see below). Running through much of the plain is the Eleutheros (Nahr el-Kabir) River, which empties into the sea just south of the modern hamlet Sumra (see Map 2). Juxtaposed to this plain at the northernmost extremity of the Lebanon range stands Jebel 'Akkar. It rises steeply to a tableland of 8,200 feet, with several peaks over 9,500 feet and one in excess of 10,100 feet. This mountain, then, unlike other candidates proposed for Mt. Hor, stands contiguous to the ancient and long-standing border.

Second, instead of citing Mt. Hor, Ezekiel (47:15; 48:1) made reference to the way of Hethlon, which, according to some authorities, may recall the modern town of Heitela, situated some 21 miles northeast of Tripolis, in the plain of the el-Kabir River and directly north of Jebel 'Akkar. Moreover, in the actual allocation of the land, Israel received territory as far north as Aphek and *the border of the Amorites* (Josh. 13:4). It is striking that the heartland of the Amorites (Amurru) extended northward from that same el-Kabir River to the southern Nusariya ridges,[5] which again emphasizes that Israel's allocation ran precisely to the river valley that flanked Jebel 'Akkar to the north. In fact, even Sumra, where the el-Kabir River empties into the Mediterranean, was itself a border; it represented the northernmost city along the Phoenician coast, which was controlled by the Egyptians during much of the biblical period.[6]

Consequently, I propose that Israel's northern border stretched to the edges of the Lebanon and Anti-Lebanon mountains. That is to say, the actual border followed the course of the el-Kabir valley from the Mediterranean to the vicinity of the Lake of Homs, then south to the outer flanks of the Anti-Lebanon mountains (area of Lebo-Hamath), then east to the Syrian desert (at Zedad), from where it essentially followed the fringes of the desert to the area of Mt. Hauran Jebel Druze.

There are certain passages in Scripture (Gen. 15:18; Deut. 1:7; Josh. 1:4; cf. Ex. 23:31; Deut. 11:24), however, which declare that Israel's border extended to "the great river, the river Euphrates." A problem in understanding this expression is in its imprecise application; it may be employed to describe the *northern* border (e.g., Gen. 15:18, "from the Euphrates to the river of Egypt") or the *eastern* border (e.g., Deut. 11:24, "from the Euphrates to the western sea"). Accordingly, some writers interpret the terminology as a kind of idealized border that anticipated the grandeur of David's or Solomon's monarchy when Israelite control, if not occupation, actually extended as far afield as the Euphrates (1 Kings 4:21; 1 Chron. 18:3; 2 Chron. 9:26). Other authorities regard the words "the great river" to be referring to the aforementioned Nahr el-Kabir River, to which an interpolation ("the river Euphrates") was added later.[7] After all, Nahr el-Kabir means in Arabic "the great river" and is a well-deserved name, as it drains the greatest area of Lebanon's coastal ranges. In Israel's later history, amid the political realities of the united monarchy, the words "the great river" would have assumed a double meaning, referring both to Israel's actual border and to its ideal border. In any event, the Euphrates terminology is excluded from those passages that specifically delineate Israel's borders, and so we regard this as a separate issue and define the northern border as seen on Map 2.

Eastern border (Num. 34:10-12; Josh. 13:8-13; cf. Ezek. 47:18). A determination of the eastern border will depend upon (1) the course one charts for the northern border and (2) the relevance one assigns the battles against Sihon and Og (Num. 21). Placement of all the locations mentioned in conjunction with the eastern border is a matter of conjecture, excepting of course the Sea of Galilee and the Jordan River. But it is precisely involving the Jordan that a major issue surfaces: Were the territories east of the Jordan River and occupied by the tribes of Reuben, Gad, and half of Manasseh *beyond* or *within* the land of promise? Or in other words: Did Israel's conquest begin at the crossing of the Jordan River or at the crossing of the Arnon River (Num. 21:13-15; cf. Deut. 2:16-37; Judg. 11:13, 18, 22, 26)? Most recent studies have answered these questions explicitly or implicitly with the former option, with the result that the eastern border of the Promised Land has generally been drawn along the Jordan River between the Sea of Galilee and the Dead Sea.[8]

The weight of certain biblical data, however, leads me to suggest the alternate hypothesis: the eastern border should be extended east to the fringes of the Syrian desert wastelands, roughly approximating a line that could be drawn from the region of Mt. Hauran (end of the northern border) to the wilderness of Kedemoth, the place from which Moses dispatched messengers to Sihon, king of Heshbon (Deut. 2:26; cf. v. 24—immediately the environs of Arnon). The place was later allocated to the tribe of Reuben (Josh. 13:15-23). Such a hypothesis, I submit, is supported by three lines of argumentation.

(1) Deuteronomy 2-3 rehearses the victories gained over Sihon and Og and the territorial allocation of their land to the two-and-one-half tribes. According to 3:8, the allocation included terrain from the Arnon to Mt. Hermon, taking in the lands of Mishor, Gilead, and Bashan as far as Salecah and Edrei (cf. 4:48; Josh. 13:9-12). That land, we are informed from the text (3:18), was given to the two-and-one-half tribes as an inheritance by God (cf. Ps. 136:19-22). Deuteronomy 2:12 declares that just as the Edomites had destroyed the Horites in order to gain a possession, so Israel dispossessed other people to gain its inheritance. The wording here is unequivocal and logically requires that the passage be interpreted in one of two ways; either it is a historical description of those victories gained over the Amorite kings of Sihon and Og, or it is a post-Mosaic insertion added in historical retrospect to describe what later took place in the biblical conquest (Joshua).

Now the question in Deuteronomy 2:12 is not whether post-Mosaic expressions exist, but rather whether it represents one such specimen. The whole of chapter 2 presents a rather sustained argument that seems to pivot on a sharp distinction between those territories excluded from Israel's inheritance (Edom, Moab, Ammon) and those included. In this regard, verse 12 seems to be asserting that both Edom and Israel have received their territory by sovereign prerogative and not military skill. Because of that, there is established a clear theological reason Israel must not conquer territories beyond its own perimeter (cf. Judg. 11:13-28; 2 Chron. 20:10; see also Deut. 2:20-22—an Ammonite and Edomite exodus?). If that is so, the verse would then form part of the fabric of the entire narrative and could not easily be dismissed editorially. But even if it were taken as a post-Mosaic expression, one is still left with a clear and similar assertion in verses 24 and 31, which normally have not been regarded as later additions.[9] If then the theme developed in verse 12 and rehearsed in verses 24 and 31 is best understood to be an integral part of the narrative as a whole, referring to those historical events which surrounded the defeat of Sihon and Og, verse 12 is a completely lucid and unambiguous statement regarding the eastern boundary of the Promised Land (cf. Josh. 12:6).

(2) At the command of God, due consideration was given the territory east of the Jordan River in the apportionment of cities of refuge (Num. 35:9-34; Deut. 4:41-43; 19:1-10; Josh. 20:1-9) and Levitical cities (Lev. 25:32-33; Num. 35:1-8; Josh. 21:8-42; 1 Chron. 6:54-81); in the latter instance, ten of the forty-eight Levitical cities were located in Transjordanian territory. So the situation obtains that whereas the tribe of Manasseh was split in its territorial allocation at its own request, Levi's territorial inheritance was split in accordance with divine prescription, a thought that is preposterous if the eastern territory were excluded from the land of God's inheritance.[10]

(3) The attitudes displayed by Moses (Num. 32) and Joshua (Josh. 22) fit with this thesis. Though Moses objected when initially confronted with the request for Transjordanian inheritance, it is crucial to understand the nature of his objection. It had been a *national effort* that brought about Israelite control of eastern territories; any lesser effort could weaken the resolve of the remaining tribes and lead ultimately to the judgment of God. Accordingly, Moses laid down a condition that the two-and-one-half tribes were to fulfill in order to receive Transjordanian inheritance: their armed men must join in the fight for Canaan. Now it is instructive to notice that Moses' concern was one of justice and potential faintheartedness, not one of irreconcilability with the plan and purpose of God. Later, when the two-and-one-half tribes' vow had been fulfilled and the land of Canaan had been secured, one sees that Joshua, by divine directive, dispatched those tribes to their rightful inheritance with the blessing and instruction of the Lord.

But one may object that this hypothesis is not in harmony with Numbers 34:10-12, where the Jordan River is clearly demarcated as the eastern border. Context demands, however, that the border of Numbers 34 must refer specificially to the land that remained unconquered but eventually would be occupied by the remaining nine-and-one-half tribes (note especially vv. 2, 13-15; cf. Deut. 1:7-8). An unrealized objective in the narrative, that perimeter stood in marked contrast to the already-vanquished territories previously controlled by Sihon and Og (Num. 21) but now given as inheritance to Reuben, Gad, and one-half of Manasseh (Num. 32). Numbers 34, therefore, is describing a territory *that was yet to be conquered*, in contrast to the entire territory divinely apportioned and destined for Israelite inheritance. So it seems that no discrepancy exists between this narrative, other biblical passages related to the placement of the eastern border, and a hypothesis that seeks to locate this boundary of the Promised Land along the frontier of the great Syrian desert.

Southern border (Num. 34:3-5; Josh. 15:1-4; cf. Ezek. 47:19; 48:28). When the issue of the location of the River of Egypt is decided, four known points along the southern perimeter—the Dead Sea, Wilderness of Zin, Kadesh-barnea,

River of Egypt—permit the southern boundary to be fixed with relative certainty; like the preceding, this border was primarily established in accordance with natural geographic boundaries.

Traditionally, the River of Egypt has been equated with the Nile or the Wadi el-Arish, a major drainage system in the western Negeb and southern Philistia that courses for some 145 miles before emptying into the Mediterranean approximately 50 miles southwest of Gaza.[11] Proponents of the Nile equation must labor under the weight of linguistic and historical difficulties: Scripture makes a clear distinction between the Nile (Heb., *ye'ôr miṣráyim*) and the River of Egypt (Heb., *náḥal miṣráyim*). (In Genesis 15:18, the expression *nĕhar miṣráyim* occurs, but we have already suggested that this verse may be describing idealized borders. However we see no reason to propose with Simons, the alternate reading *náḥal miṣráyim* in this verse.[12] Such a suggestion lacks textual support.) Moreover, cuneiform inscriptions from as early as Tiglath-pileser III (744-727 B.C.) and Sargon II (721-705 B.C.) describe Assyrian military victories at the River of Egypt (Akk., *naḥal muṣri)*. However, numerous historical factors argue conclusively that Assyrians did not come to control Egypt proper prior to the time of Esarhaddon (680-669 B.C.).

On the other hand, Wadi el-Arish seems well suited to form this boundary line. Geologically speaking, el-Arish is the most prominent natural feature south of the populated areas of Palestine, and it is sometimes described as being situated on the natural geologic border between the Negeb plateau and the Sinai. The book of Judith, moreover, describes how Nebuchadnezzar attempted to conscript an army in order to wage war against the Medes. The author supplies a detailed delineation of those places from which the Babylonian monarch sought support: Cilicia, Damascus, the mountains of Lebanon, Carmel and Gilead, Esdraelon, Samaria, Jerusalem. . .Kadesh, the River of Egypt, Tahpanhes, Ra'amses, the land of Goshen, Memphis, the land of Egypt, the border of Ethiopia (Judith 1:7-11). Clearly, the sequence of locations indicates that the text is proceeding in a southerly direction, thereby placing the River of Egypt *between* Kadesh (either Kadesh-barnea or Kadesh of Judah) and Tahpanhes (Tell Defneh), a city bordering on Lake Menzaleh between the Nile delta and the Suez Canal. Or again, the region around Wadi el-Arish is depicted on a map from the Byzantine period, called the Medeba Map (see discussion in chapter 3). In a portion of this map that describes the Sinai coast is found the following inscription: "border of Egypt and Palestine." This legend is written between the partially-restored city of Raphia (Rafah), where Sargon II gained his victory, and Rhinocorura, the Greek word for the settlement occupied today by the townlet el-Arish (cf. LXX translation of River of Egypt, Isa. 27:12). And so this geologic, inscriptional, and cartographic evidence favors the hypothesis that locates the River of Egypt at the Wadi el-Arish.

Along the western edge of the Negeb plateau are three important springs that have been associated in one way or another with the location of Kadesh-barnea: Ain Qadeis; Ain Qudeirat, located six miles to the northwest; and Ain Quseima, located another four miles to the northwest. Of those three springs, all are situated on the aforementioned geological border (within the el-Arish system), none is clearly eliminated on the basis of ceramic remains, and each offers a distinctive consideration when attempting to localize Kadesh-barnea. Ain Qadeis's candidacy rests on three points: the ancient border descriptions of Numbers 34 and Joshua 15 list Kadesh-barnea *before* (that is east of) Hazar-addar and Azmon, the site retains the namesake of the biblical city, and the site is situated on the edge of a large open plain capable of accommodating Israel's encampment. Ain Qudeirat offers the advantage of a copious water supply, by far the largest in the area. Ain Quseima is located at an important intersection of two roads that link the Negeb with Sinai and Egypt. It is not surprising, therefore, that each of those three sites has been identified as Kadesh-barnea at one time or another.

We infer from Scripture that Israel encamped at Kadesh-barnea for the greater part of forty years. Because for a number of reasons that entire area generally offers a hostile environment for human occupation, it seems reasonable to suppose that the whole region might have been required to accommodate Israel's encampment and therefore have been referred to accordingly. Nevertheless, largely for the sake of map facilitation, we will locate Kadesh-barnea at Ain Qadeis, Hazar-addar at Ain Qudeirat, and Azmon at Ain Quseima, even though this is all quite tentative (see Maps 2 and 15).

Again, we suggest that this southern border was set primarily in accordance with natural boundaries. The wilderness of Zin seems to be applied to that stretch of land, sometimes referred to as the high Negeb, which is flanked on its north by the three parallel mountains of extreme southeastern Judah (Rakhama, Hathira, Hazera) and on its south by the awesome Ramon upwarp. The wilderness of Zin extended as far west as the area of Kadesh-barnea, perhaps beyond, and bordered on Edom. So, in a kind of semi-circular arc, the boundary itself most likely extended in a southwesterly direction from the Dead Sea via the Rift Valley and Tamar to the environs of the Wadi Murra. Here it passed by the Hazera ridge and came to the Ascent of Akrabbim ("ascent of the scorpions"), which is normally affiliated with Neqb Safa. There the modern road from Beersheba, which crosses Jebel Hathira, plunges abruptly into Wadi Murra.

From that point, it is reasonable to infer that the border continued to follow the contour of the Wadi Murra in a southwesterly direction until eventually it arrived in the vicinity of a slender, diagonal corridor of Turonian limestone. That corridor extends some 29 airline miles from Mt. Teref to Mt. Kharif and separates the Ramon summit from the Eocene acreage to its north. After traversing the corridor to its opposite end, one is only 5 miles from the upper courses of the Wadi Kadesh (a tributary of the el-Arish drainage system), only 11 miles from Ain Qadeis, and only approximately 17 miles from Ain Qudeirat. From that point, the border simply would have followed the configuration of the wadi past Kadesh-barnea and the other points mentioned along the way before it arrived finally at the Mediterranean.

Historical terminology. In antiquity, Israel's inheritance was designated by a wide array of terms, but none of the terms should be understood to be completely coextensive with the dimensions of the Promised Land. In most cases, names previously employed to denote a god or a people (ethnonyms) were simply borrowed and reapplied to designate a geographic entity. Thus, many ancient examples exist in which geographic names derived from a dominant population group which came to settle in a given area. Frequently, in turn, the residents were named for a deity whom they adored and who was supposed to own and protect the land. For instance, the name *Palestine* derived from the term *Philistine, Canaan* owed its existence to the Canaanites, and *Hatti* designated the land of the Hittites, who themselves may have been named for the god Hatti.

Palestine. For reasons as yet unclear to us, much of the biblical world experienced a major political upheaval around 1200 B.C., largely stemming from a company of invaders referred to in Egyptian sources as the "Sea Peoples." Scholars have long pondered what occasioned their widespread migration to Asia and North Africa. Some have attributed the displacement to a climatic change that produced a famine, whereas others have connected it with the political turbulence that surrounded the Battle of Troy. Whatever the case, included among those insurgents was a group known as the Philistines. Before striking at the heart of Egypt, the Sea Peoples defeated the Hittites, bringing about the immediate collapse of that once-mighty empire. The Philistines also ravaged vast areas of Syria, Lebanon, and Israel, including the cities of Ugarit, Alalakh, Tyre, Sidon, Carchemish, and Hazor. We discover in Egyptian literature that the Philistines were repelled from Egyptian soil toward the northeast and that they came to inhabit the region known in the Bible as the Philistine plain.[13]

The place from which the Philistines emigrated has been much debated in the past, but without resolution. The biblical tradition that they came from Caphtor (Crete; Amos 9:7; cf. Deut. 2:23; Jer. 47:4) is unhelpful because it declares they were brought from Caphtor in the same way

Figure 1 Wilderness of Zin near Kadesh-barnea; Acacia trees in foreground.

Israel was brought from Egypt; that is to say, Scripture is not necessarily specifying the aboriginal home of the Philistines or the Israelites. Some have argued that the Philistines migrated from Greece. This assertion is based on Philistine material culture (stylized coffins, characteristic pottery, depictions of a feathered headdress) and on certain biblical words found in the Philistine narratives and alleged to have been Philistine (champion, lord, helmet, chest, concubine). Others have asserted that the Philistines originated from the seacoasts of modern Turkey, based on other so-called Philistine words, Greek epics, and the LXX rendering of Caphtor in Deuteronomy 2:23 and Amos 9:7 ("Cappadocia"). But this all remains highly speculative because a Philistine language is still unattested in the modern world. Further, one learns from a number of sources that the Philistines began to undergo the process of cultural assimilation soon after their arrival in Canaan.

The word *Palestine* seems to have been applied to a discrete geographic entity as early as the time of Adad-nirari III (810-783 B.C.), who boasted that in bringing under his dominion all the territory from the Great Sea of the rising sun (Persian Gulf) to the Great Sea of the setting sun (Mediterranean Sea), he subjugated the banks of the Euphrates, the countries of the Hittites and Amorites, Tyre, Sidon, Israel, Edom, and Palestine.[14] We observe that Palestine is used to denote a specific terrain, but one in contrast to Israel. An inscribed Egyptian statuette from the twenty-second dynasty found in the nineteenth century seems to bear out both observations. Included in this inscription is the line: "Pade-East, commissioner of Canaan and Palestine."[15] Again Palestine seems to denote a distinct geographic entity, and this time in contradistinction to Canaan. We suggest, therefore, that the term *Palestine* served such a designation as early as 800 B.C., and most likely signified the Philistine coastal lands.[16]

In the sixth century B.C., Herodotus used *Palestine* for the entire eastern Mediterranean coastlands, known otherwise as the Levant. But in the aftermath of the second Jewish revolt (A.D. 132-35), Hadrian began to apply Palestine to the land of the Jews in order to eradicate the name *Judea*. In that sense, use of the term *Palestine* would have excited political animosity among disenfranchised insurgents, thereby creating a situation painfully similar to the contemporary one.

Canaan. The earliest attestation of the term *Canaan* is found in a document from Mari (eighteenth century B.C.), though it is reported to be extant in the Ebla tablets. If the latter is true, the term would have to be traced back into the third millennium B.C.[17] The term is frequently cited in the clay tablets from Alalakh, Nuzi, Boghazkoy, and Tell el-Amarna (sixteenth-thirteenth centuries B.C.), and it is employed consistently in Egyptian writings from the time of Amenophis II (1438-1412 B.C.) onward.[18] To judge from its usage in Egyptian literature, Canaan appears to have been the conventional term used during much of the second millennium B.C. to designate Egypt's southern holdings in Asia. This is in contrast to the terms *Amurru* (Amorite land north of the el-Kabir River) and *Upe* (inland territory of the lower Beqa' valley, including the area of Damascus).[19]

Accordingly, Canaan's boundaries can be marked out with a degree of specificity and certainty. According to the Papyrus Anastasi III, written during the time of Ramesses II, Canaan extended from Sile (located near the lower reaches of the eastern delta) to Upe. That location agrees with another document from the same period (Papyrus Anastasi I). The latter epistle discusses some of the main roads through Canaan at the time: the text begins in the north at the town of Sumur (located at the mouth of the el-Kabir) and describes a southward journey that culminated at "the end of the land of Canaan," where the towns of Raphia and Gaza were introduced. The clear intimation of the passage is that those two cities in some sense formed Canaan's southern boundary. In any event, one discovers from Egyptian documentation of the eighteenth and nineteenth dynasties that Gaza was part of Canaan.[20] Archaeological evidence discovered at the site demonstrates that it represented an important provincial capital throughout Egypt's New Kingdom period, which began around 1570 B.C. and continued until approximately 1100 B.C. The Egyptians, therefore, understood the term *Canaan* to denote the land that stretched form Gaza in the south to Upe and Amurru in the north.

Now the northern and eastern perimeters of Canaan are further clarified from cuneiform literature. One observes, first of all, that the aforementioned geographical distinction between Amurru and Canaan receives full confirmation from a study of the linguistic characteristics of the two regions, most especially in what linguists mean by the expression "Canaanite shift."[21] On top of this, one discovers that King Idrimi of Alalakh reported that he had sought refuge in the *Canaanite* town of Ammiya. From its use in the el-Amarna texts, Ammiya must have been located along the Phoenician coast, perhaps not far from Tripolis.[22] On the other hand, Canaanites were clearly regarded as foreigners at Ugarit and Alalakh.[23] The Amarna tablets indicate furthermore that Canaan referred to Egypt's southern holdings *exclusive of Transjordan*. The general picture that emerges, therefore, is that Near Eastern and biblical literatures bear a remarkable similarity in their delineation of Canaan (see earlier discussion of northern and southern borders of Promised Land; cf. Num. 13:29; 32:32; 35:14; Josh. 11:3).[24] And this assertion, we believe, carries far-reaching consequences regarding the antiquity and historicity of those biblical narratives containing such geographical descriptions and delineations.

Prior to the discovery of Nuzi, the word *Canaan* was generally thought derived from a verb meaning "to bend, to bow down, to be low." Partially inspired by biblical citations (e.g., Num. 13:29; Josh. 5:1; 11:3; Isa. 23:11), the word was related to the "lowland" occupied by the Canaanites in contrast to the hill country of the Amorites.[25]

But at Nuzi the word *kinaḫḫu* referred to a red-purple substance extracted from murex seashells and used in the dyeing of fabric, especially wool. Ancient literature is replete with references to the great esteem given one who was clothed in purple, and murex dye, being natural and not manufactured, was highly prized because it never faded.[26] Now that extensive and extremely lucrative enterprise was concentrated along the Mediterranean coast, north of Acco, where an abundant supply of murex shells constantly washed ashore. A large number of the shells have been found on the site of an ancient dye factory near Tyre. An indication that murex dyeing was an economically pivotal industry is that some of the Canaanite cities associated with it were themselves named for it. Zarephath comes from a verb meaning "to dye," and Zobah derives from a verb denoting the dyeing of cloth. In the Bible, even the word *Canaanite* itself was sometimes used to mean "trader, merchant" (Job 41:6; Isa. 23:8; Hos. 12:7 [Heb., v. 8]; cf. Prov. 31:24; Zeph. 1:11; Zech. 11:7, 11 [LXX]; 14:21).

We discover from later Greek literature that the cultural heirs of that inclusive dye industry were referred to as Phoenicians, a Greek word from *phoinix*, "purple." In fact, there is evidence both from within and without the Bible that the people called Phoenician by the Greeks still referred to themselves as Canaanites in the late first millennium B.C. (Matt. 15:22, Canaanite woman; Mark 7:26, Syro-Phoenician woman; cf. Acts 16:14, Lydia, a seller of purple goods). According to the theory, then, the word *Canaan* means "(the people of/land of) purple." Canaan differs from Phoenicia only in that the former is a Semitic word, whereas the latter is of Greek extraction. Originally designating the color of the dye, Canaan came to be applied to the people involved in the dyeing process. Eventually it came to refer to the land of those people, at first only to the Canaanite coast and later the entire province in which they were a dominant population group. Given Egypt's economic interest in Asian natural resources and its close association with a number of Canaanite ports, one can easily imagine how such a linguistic evolution could have occurred. I believe the pendulum has rightly shifted in favor of this viewpoint, though it is not without some lingering problems.

Land of Aram/Syria. The land of Aram (Greek Syria) is most frequently used in Scripture to describe the Arameans. From the beginning of the first millennium down until the Battle of Qarqar (853 B.C.), the Arameans represented a dominant population whose territories stretched from the Balih River to the Mediterranean, and from the Taurus mountains to near the Sea of Galilee. Their principal city-states included Arpad, Hamath, Zobah, and Damascus, thereby including territory within the land of promise.

Israel. The name *Israel* ultimately derives from the patriarch Jacob whose name was changed (Gen. 32:28). It was the honorific title adopted by the patriarchal descendants while living in Egypt (e.g., Ex. 1:9, 12; cf. Ezra 2:2; John 3:10; Phil. 3:5). Later, the name came to be applied to the kingdom of Ephraim, in contrast to the southern kingdom of Judah (e.g., 1 Kings 12:17-18; 1 Chron. 5:17); still later, after the collapse of Ephraim, Israel was used to denote the kingdom of Judah (e.g., Jer. 10:1). And so it becomes difficult to identify a biblical passage in which the word Israel is used to denote a specific stretch of geography. Admittedly, the expression "land of Israel" occurs (e.g., 1 Sam. 13:19; 1 Chron. 22:2; 2 Chron. 2:17 [Heb., v. 16]; Ezek. 40:2; 47:18), but it is always linked to the terrain occupied by some or all of the people of Israel, and its extent fluctuates accordingly. This same difficulty is met when investigating those extrabiblical citations of Israel. In the Merneptah stele, the word is qualified in such a way that it is the people of Israel rather than the land that is being referred to. References in the Moabite stone and Assyrian literature are specifically denominating the Northern Kingdom (e.g., a monolith of Shalmaneser III mentions that 2,000 chariots and 10,000 soldiers were contributed by *Aḫabu Sir'ilaya* [Ahab the Israelite]). Nevertheless, the term *Israel* cannot be divorced from a discussion of the dimensions of the land of promise, and thus it is included here.

Miscellaneous terms: Retenu, Djahy, Ḫurru, Ḫatti. Aside from the terms in the Scripture employed to designate Israel's inheritance, a number of extrabiblical expressions are found that denote this land mass, though their precise geographical limitation is difficult to define. In the aftermath of the Hyksos' expulsion from Egypt, a number of pharaohs carried out military expeditions against Syro-Palestine. Thutmosis III (1490-1436 B.C.), in particular, was responsible for reclaiming much of that territory for Egypt. He converted his gains into an Egyptian province that he called *Retenu*, a term which, though used throughout Egyptian literature beginning in the twentieth century B.C., remains enigmatic both with respect to its meaning and to the territory it defined.

But if Thutmosis III borrowed the term *Retenu*, he seems to have been the first pharaoh to have used two additional terms—*Djahy* and *Ḫurru*—to describe Syro-Palestine. Obscurity enshrouds the exact meaning of Djahy, but it is normally understood to be a synonym for Canaan. What can be stated is that a stele of Seti I describes how that sovereign dispatched troops to fight a battle at Djahy. Two days later those troops returned victoriously from Mt. Yarmut, located in the Galilean highlands. Alternatively, Rameses III claims to have checked the southward movement of the Sea Peoples at Djahy, interpreted to be somewhere along the Canaanite coastline. Ḫurru, on the other hand, was the term increasingly employed by Thutmosis's successors to define Syro-Palestine, no doubt due to the growing importance of a Hurrian group on Canaanite soil, a fact evidenced in the personal names found in the Tell el-Amarna tablets.

Another term, *Ḫatti*, was originally applied to the homeland of the Hittite empire in Asia Minor. But after that empire's destruction by the Sea Peoples, the term came to designate the land between the Euphrates, specifically at Carchemish, west to the Amuq plain and south to the environs of Homs. No doubt it was applied initially to those neo-Hittite enclaves that continued to exist in that region at least until the time of Nebuchadnezzar. But as a geographical designation, Hatti came to be replaced by the expression "Beyond the River" (*eber nāri*)[27] for the Semites, while for the Greeks the term *Syria* emerged. Under the Semitic name, this stretch of land was known later as a satrapy of the Persian Empire. Chronologically speaking, therefore, it seems reasonable to suppose that many of the Hittite references in the Bible actually signify those neo-Hittite enclaves (e.g., 2 Sam. 24:6 [LXX]; 2 Kings 7:6; cf. Ezek. 16:3). In that sense Israel's border may be said to have extended as far as the land of the Hittites (Josh. 1:4). At any rate, Hittite kings were contrasted with those of Aram (1 Kings 10:29 and 2 Chron. 1:17), a distinction that shows an appreciation of the political and ethnic divisions represented in the land surrounding the neo-Hittites early in the first millennium B.C.

Geopolitical districts. Before engaging in an extended discussion of the natural topographical features of Palestine, it is necessary to define and briefly delineate certain geopolitical terms used in Scripture to signify various subdivisions of the country. But to do this, one must first introduce two modern geographical terms that are sometimes used to designate the land of promise: *Cisjordan* ("this side of the Jordan") and *Transjordan* ("across the Jordan"). The Jordan Rift Valley has sometimes formed a political as well as a natural border. As indicated by the names' definitions, Cisjordan refers to territories west of the Jordan, whereas Transjordan may be used to specify the eastern regions.

Before proceeding, I must stress the provisional nature of the geopolitical boundaries we are about to delineate. It is axiomatic that the circumference of a particular district fluctuated over the centuries, and it cannot be precisely fixed for every period, given the scanty information sometimes available. This problem is especially aggravated when one attempts to fix borders of an area that continued to exist throughout a large segment of biblical history, at times remaining in existence for more than a millennium. Moreover, it is necessary to bear in mind that one and the same stretch of geography frequently bore dissimilar names in different periods.

Cisjordan. From a geopolitical perspective, Cisjordan was largely divided into four sections during most of biblical history: from north to south, these were Phoenicia, Galilee, Samaria, and Judea. *Phoenicia* should be defined in the Old Testament as the slender tract of coastland that stretched some 125 miles from Nahr el-Kabir to Mt. Carmel and was flanked on its east by the mountains of Lebanon and Galilee. By New Testament times, however, Mt. Carmel had fallen into the hands of monarchs from Tyre,[28] and so Phoenicia extended south into the plain of Dor. The Phoenician region played more than a trivial role in biblical history. Solomon's policy of economic and commercial expansionism hinged largely on Phoenician cooperation; the Phoenicians supplied the raw materials and technology for both his extensive building program at Jerusalem and his merchant fleets that sailed the Mediterranean and Red seas. But Phoenician ideology itself was imported through the marriage of Ahab and Jezebel (1 Kings 16:31-33); the worship of Baal would henceforth become a more prevalent reality of biblical history. Phoenicia was the site of two biblical miracles: it was at Zarephath that Elisha revived the dying son of a widow (1 Kings 17:8-24); and in the region of Tyre and Sidon, Jesus healed the Syro-Phoenician woman's daughter

OLD TESTAMENT DISTRICTS

MAP 3

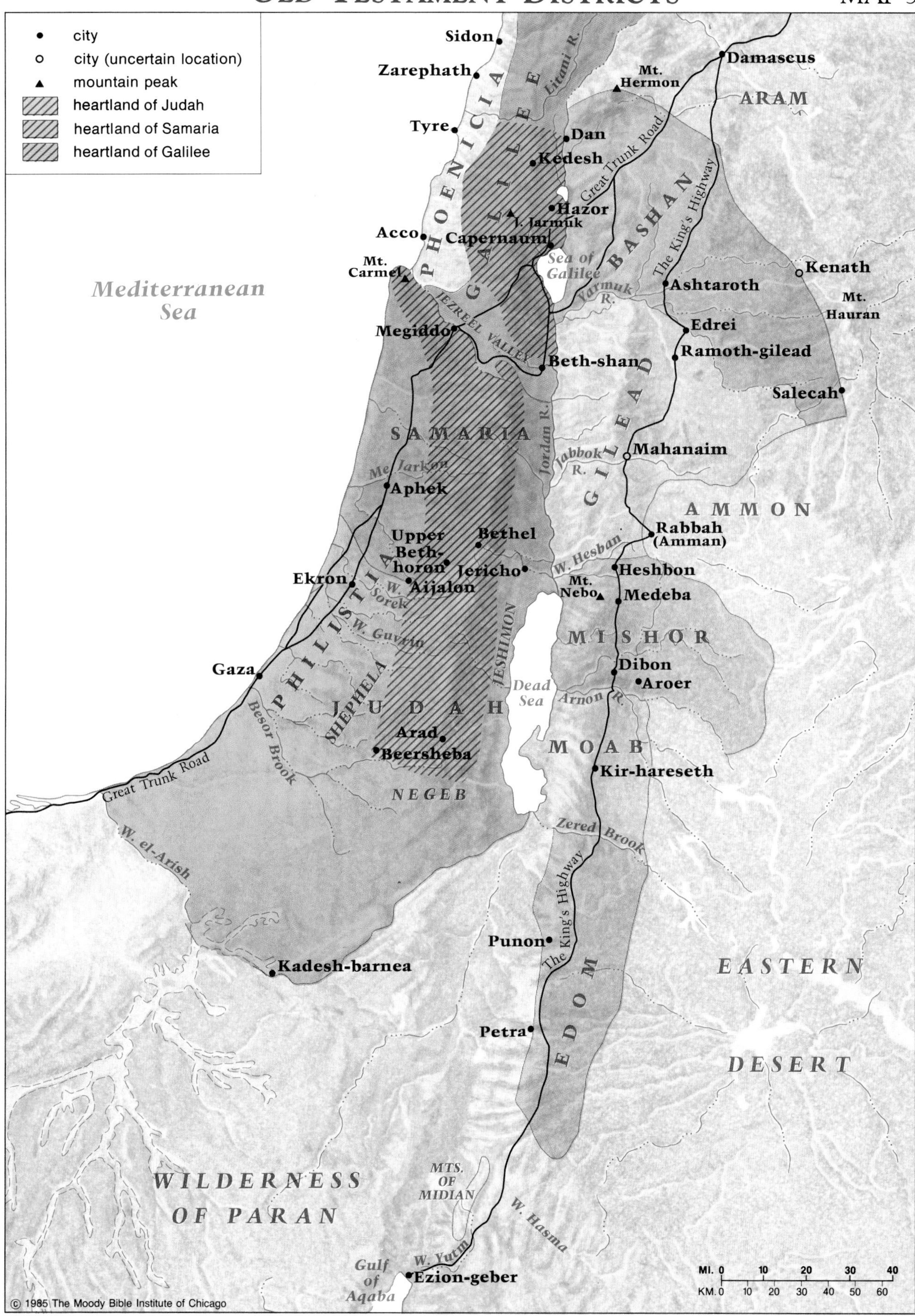

(Mark 7:24-30; cf. Matt. 15:21-28). The region also was prominent as a host of apostolic travels.

Just inland from the southern ranges of Phoenicia was the Galilean district, the northernmost territory actually occupied by ancient Israel. When used in the Bible as a proper name, *Galilee* referred to the mostly mountainous terrain that was bordered on its east by the Jordan valley, on its south by the mountains adjacent to the southern edge of the Jezreel valley (Esdraelon), and on its north by the Litani River gorge. To set the northern border, however, is extremely problematic. In Old Testament times it may not have extended beyond the reaches of Mt. Harun and Mt. Amal, on a line roughly connecting Kiryat Shmona and Tibnine; that is, as a contiguous Israelite region, Galilee may not have stretched north of the mountains that are more than 3,000 feet tall. (The city of Kedesh, located north of the aforementioned line, must have been in Israelite hands, as it was included among the cities of refuge [Josh. 20:7] and Levitic cities [Josh. 21:32; cf. Judg. 4:9-10; 2 Kings 15:29; 1 Chron. 6:72, 76].) This latter certainly describes the northern limits of Galilee as an administrative district under Roman rule. The Jewish historian Josephus states that Galilee extended from Xaloth (Chesulloth), a city on the great (Esdraelon) plain, past Bersabe (in the Beth Kerem valley), to Baca, perhaps located just west of Jebel Jarmuk.[29] Elsewhere he declares that Galilee stretches as far as Thella, a village sought in the Hula basin some 10 miles south of Kiryat Shmona (see Map 95 for Kiryat Shmona).

Galilee, therefore, measured no more than approximately 50 miles north-south and 25 miles east-west. The district was at all times divided laterally into upper and lower Galilee by a slender valley (Beth Kerem valley), which follows a fault line that extended east from Acco (Ptolemais), past Karmiel and Parod, to Rosh Pinna. The differentiation here is geographic and not administrative (cf. Judith 1:8, "higher Galilee"). Lower Galilean peaks remain below 2,000 feet, whereas most of upper Galilee's rugged, virtually impassible terrain lies in excess of 3,300 feet, with part of its central region boasting the highest altitude in all of Cisjordan: Jebel Jarmuk is nearly 4,000 feet above sea level. Most biblical references to Galilee, and all New Testament references, are to lower Galilee. Because of its northerly location, Galilee was more vulnerable to cultural (Isa. 9:1 [Heb., 8:23]; Matt. 4:15; cf. 1 Macc. 5:15) and military (e.g., 2 Kings 15:29) absorption. Accordingly, though inhabited in the Old Testament by the tribes of Naphtali, Issachar, Zebulun, and perhaps part of Asher (1 Kings 9:10-13), from the time of the Babylonian captivity onward, actual Israelite population in Galilee was but a minority among the dominant Gentiles. Therefore, the district was suspect ideologically (John 1:46; cf. 7:41, 52) and linguistically (Matt. 26:73). Notwithstanding, Galilee became very important to Jew and Christian alike. The city of Tiberias gradually became the center for Jewish Talmudic scholarship after the destruction of Jerusalem in A.D. 70; here the Sanhedrin last sat, here the Mishna was edited, here were centered the families of Ben Asher and Ben Naphtali (of Masoretic tradition), and here remains the tomb of the sage Maimonides. Christians too have realized the significance of Galilee: it was here that Jesus spent His boyhood in the sleepy village of Nazareth, headquartered His adult ministry in the strategic center of Capernaum, and, most interesting, performed most of His public miracles.

To the south of Galilee lay the third historical province—*Samaria.* Known earlier as the Hill Country of Ephraim (e.g., Josh. 17:15; 19:50; Judg. 3:27; 4:5; 1 Sam. 1:1; 9:4; 1 Kings 4:8; 2 Kings 5:22; Jer. 31:6), in contrast to the Hill Country of Judah (see below), the district of Samaria eventually drew its name from the third and final capital city of the Northern Kingdom. In general, Samaria's borders corresponded to the region of Palestine's central hill country. It stretched to the edge of the Esdraelon valley in the north, to the vicinity of Jordan River in the east, and to the interior of the coastal plain in the west. Its southern boundary followed a natural topographic line that extended from Jericho, via the Wadi Makkuk, to Ophrah (see Maps 11 and 28 for Wadi Makkuk). From there the border proceeded past Bethel to Upper Beth-horon, where it began to descend through the Wadi Aijalon (cf. Josh. 10:12) and broke out into the coastal plain opposite Gezer. Through this physiologic border passes a modern road that somewhat circuitously links Jericho and Tel Aviv (cf. Map 19). Samaria encompassed, therefore, an area approximately 40 miles north-south and 35 miles east-west. From Josephus's description of Samaria,[30] we infer that New Testament Samaria was slightly reduced in its southern precinct. Josephus states that Samaria extended only as far south as Acrabbene, a hamlet located only 6 miles southeast of Shechem. As he does with Galilee and Judea, however, Josephus extends New Testament Samaria west to the Mediterranean.

The natural geographic center of Samaria was at the city of Shechem, located in the vale between Mt. Ebal and Mt. Gerizim, and immediately adjacent to the modern town of Nablus. Here intersected the principal road coming from Jerusalem and the lateral roadway coming in from the

Mediterranean via Wadi Shekhem. Not unexpectedly, therefore, Shechem witnessed periods of protracted occupation as far back as 4000 B.C. During much of the early second millennium B.C., according to the Execration texts and those from Tell el-Amarna, Shechem vied with Jerusalem for supremacy of central Palestine. It is instructive to recall that this city was related to Abraham's initial worship in Palestine (Gen. 12:6); it was here that Joseph's bones finally come to rest (Gen. 48:22; Ex. 13:19; Josh. 24:32), that Israel's first attempt at monarchy was launched (Judg. 9), that Jeroboam's political insurrection was headquartered (1 Kings 12), and that Jesus confronted the woman at the well (John 4). Although eclipsed by the city of Samaria during the divided monarchy, Shechem's ascendancy was reasserted after the Assyrians brought about the end of the Northern Kingdom in 722 B.C. Captives from abroad were imported and settled in Samarian cities (2 Kings 17:24-34), and some of those refugees embraced a number of articles within Judaism and in time came to regard themselves as Jews (e.g., Ezra 4:2). Their bid for membership in the Jewish community was repudiated by post-exilic Jews, however, which set into motion a religious animosity that persisted throughout the remainder of the biblical period (Luke 9:52; John 4:9; 8:48). Nevertheless, Samaritanism has survived the centuries and currently numbers about 350 devotees, most of whom reside in a quarter of Nablus or in Holon, a sub-

NEW TESTAMENT DISTRICTS MAP 4

urb of Tel Aviv; they continue annually to celebrate the Passover atop Mt. Gerizim, their holy mount (cf. John 4:20; 2 Macc. 6:2).

The fourth major geopolitical entity of Cisjordan was *Judea*, referred to in pre-exilic biblical history as the Hill Country of Judah (e.g., Josh. 11:21; 15:48; 20:7; 21:11; 2 Chron. 21:11; 27:4; cf. Luke 1:65). According to 2 Kings 23:8, Judah extended from Geba, a strategic town located 5 miles north of Jerusalem, to Beersheba (cf. Zech. 14:10). So when taken with our earlier discussion, this conforms to the constantly recurring Old Testament formula "from Dan to Beersheba," which denotes the practical boundaries of Israel's territory (Judg. 20:1; 1 Sam. 3:20; 2 Sam. 3:10; 17:11; 24:2, 15; 1 Kings 4:25; cf. 1 Chron. 21:2; 2 Chron. 30:5). The Judean region may be specifically circumscribed on its lateral axis—it extends east as far as the precipitous descent into the Judean wilderness (Wilderness of Jeshimon, Num. 21:20; 1 Sam. 24:1) and as far west as the steep and rocky descent into a slender moat that divides it from the Shephela (see below). All of this means that the heartland of Judah took in no more than 50 miles north-south and only 15 miles east-west. A very small territory that was composed of large tracts of uncultivable land, that was isolated from international traffic, and that never experienced independent material prosperity, Judah was only rarely attractive to empire builders. George Adam Smith aptly describes Judah as a secluded land that promoted a pastoral life-style and was a place of fortresses, shrines, and villages.[31]

It must be admitted that Judah played only a negligible role in Israel's history prior to the time of David. But profound were the consequences of David's capture of Jerusalem (2 Sam. 5) and his bringing the Ark of God to the city (2 Sam. 6), thereby merging for the first time in Israel's history its political and religious capitals. Indeed, it is not an overstatement to suggest that, beginning with the Davidic monarchy, the history of Old Testament Jerusalem is tantamount to the history of Judah itself (cf. Map 46).

The province of Judea denotes the dimensions of the Jewish state, beginning in the post-exilic period (e.g., Ezra 5:8; 9:9; Matt. 2:1; cf. Tobit 1:18). In the time of Josephus,[32] Judea extended as far north as Anuathu-Borcaeus, normally affiliated with Berkit, a hamlet located about 9 miles south of Shechem along the road to Jerusalem. Thus the northern perimeter of New Testament Judea was expanded slightly from that of the Judean monarchy. But in Josephus's description of the southern frontier, Judea was said to have stopped at the Arabian frontier, near a place called Yardan in the local dialect. That site should be identified with Arad, a fortress town located near the edge of the biblical Negeb, 16 miles south of Hebron and again on a line with Beersheba. Although New Testament Judea theoretically extended westward as far as the coast, it always excluded the territory of Ashkelon and at times did not encompass the districts of Gaza, Azotus (Ashdod), and Jamnia.

In addition to the four major geopolitical entities of Cisjordan, the province of *Idumea* played a secondary role in post-exilic and New Testament politics. Idumea is the Greek name for Edom applied specifically to Edomite refugees who had fled north in order to avoid the growing pressure from their Nabatean neighbors. Though constantly fluctuating, being alternately detached from and reannexed to Judea, Idumean territory eventually stretched from Beth-zur (near Hebron) to Beersheba, and from the Dead Sea to the edge of the Philistine plain. Idumea was eventually subjugated by Maccabean rulers. One of those, Alexander Janneus, appointed an Idumean chieftain, Antipater, over the region. Ironically, however, it was from the loins of Antipater that Herod the Great emerged, one who as "king of the Jews" (Matt. 2:1) was not so disposed to decentralized authority.

Transjordan. The term *Transjordan* defines specifically that stretch of geography between Mt. Hermon and the Gulf of Aqaba (some 250 miles), and from the Jordan Rift Valley to the fringes of the eastern desert (between 30 and 80 miles). Now the geopolitical history of this region is actually much more complicated than that of its Cisjordanian neighbor, and to attempt to address both Old and New Testament Transjordania in a single discussion is only partially possible and certainly open to the possibility of inaccuracies. But the present purpose, we recall, is merely to supply approximate location of geopolitical terms used in Scripture and throughout this volume, so I offer a single, if more simplified, discussion of Transjordan.

Old Testament Transjordania was a composition of five geopolitical entities. From north to south those included Bashan, Gilead, Mishor, Moab, and Edom. Scripture declares that *Bashan*, a word meaning "a fruitful or smooth plain," applied to the territory that Israel's forces wrested from Og's control (Num. 21:33-35). It included sixty walled cities (Deut. 3:4-5; 1 Kings 4:13) and was assigned to half of the tribe of Manesseh (Deut. 3:13). Bashan stretched 35 miles from Mt. Hermon (e.g., Josh. 12:5) down to the Yarmuk River),[33] and extended as far east as Kenath

(Num. 32:42) and Salecah (Deut. 3:10), cities located on Mt. Hauran. The district is associated occasionally with that of Argob (e.g., Deut. 3:4, 13; 1 Kings 4:13; 2 Kings 15:25), and the exact relationship between the two names is impossible to ascertain; Argob simply may be a synonym for Bashan, or it may refer to a sub-division of Bashan. If it were a sub-division, Argob probably defined the northeastern sector of Bashan and would have corresponded roughly to New Testament Trachonitis.[34]

During New Testament times, the region north of the Yarmuk consisted basically of the provinces that made up the tetrarchy of Philip, brother of Herod Antipas: Gaulanitis, Trachonitis, Auranitis, Batanea, and Iturea.[35]

The mountains that rise sharply just to the east of the Hula valley and the Sea of Galilee composed what was known in the Hellenistic period as *Gaulanitis,* the Greek transliteration of Golan (Deut. 4:43; Josh. 20:8). This name has survived the centuries into the contemporary setting, where it is applied to the same region, known today as the Golan Heights. Located at the other end of what in the Old Testament had been Bashan were the provinces of *Trachonitis* and *Auranitis.* Trachonitis can be defined in general terms; according to classical sources,[36] the district was contiguous with Batanea and Auranitis, most likely located to their north or northeast, and was not far from Damascus (see Map 4). These data, when combined with the meaning of the Greek word itself ("stony ground"), have led scholars to seek Trachonitis in a large volcanic plateau covering about 350 square miles, beginning approximately 26 miles south of Damascus, known today as el-Leja ("the refuge").[37] For that matter, inscriptional evidence exhumed from two towns in the Leja would seem to support that assumption. The Leja texts, which date from the Roman period, speak of some important cities in the Trachon (cf. Luke 3:1).

Auranitis, on the other hand, is the Greek reflex of Hauran used in the LXX (Ezek. 47:16, 18) and in the New Testament world. Clearly therefore, the heartland of Auranitis was Mt. Hauran (Jebel Druze), located to the south-southeast of el-Leja. Historical sources record that between the second century B.C. and the second century A.D., the district of Auranitis suffered repeated conquest. It was governed in turn by Maccabeans, Nabateans, Romans, Nabateans, and Romans. Auranitis was coveted by the Romans because its fertile soil was capable of producing vast supplies of wheat, which rendered the district an important granary for Palestine and Syria (cf. Ps. 22:12; Ezek. 39:18; Amos 4:1). Nabatean interest in Auranitis would have been related to roadways they utilized in the transport of goods to points north and east. Therefore, the province probably extended west of Mt. Hauran, perhaps as far as the confluence of the Wadi el-ʻAllan and the Yarmuk River, thus including an area of rich soil and one through which a Nabatean transportation artery would have run.[38]

Batanea is the Greek form for Bashan; but as a province, it was distinguished from the other sectors of Philip's rule. We have seen already that Batanea was bordered by Trachonitis. A road by which Jewish pilgrims passed from Babylon to Jerusalem seems to have passed through Batanea,[39] and according to Eusebius,[40] the cities of Ashtaroth and Edrei were both part of Batanea. This leads one to suspect, therefore, that the province was situated in that intermediate plain between the more mountainous Gaulanitis and the rougher volcanic areas of Trachonitis and Auranitis.

Iturea, the final province of Philip's tetrarchy to be discussed, may also be the most problematic to locate precisely. Its name refers to some of the tribal descendants of Ishmael's son Jetur (Gen. 25:15; 1 Chron. 1:31), though they are called "Arabs" in some of the classical references. In the description of Strabo,[41] the country of the Itureans apparently lay in the Beqaʻ valley, extending no farther than the mountains that flanked it on either side. It would have encompassed the land between the province of Abilene (part of the tetrarchy of Lysanias, Luke 3:1) and the area of Mt. Hermon. In the first century B.C., Iturea probably extended from Damascus to the Mediterranean and certainly included areas south of Mt. Hermon, because Iturea bordered directly on Galilee.[42] From later first-century B.C. sources, the areas of Iturea and Trachonitis seem to have overlapped. Whether Iturea encompassed a larger area by colonization or migration, or for how long and to what degree, are questions that remain unanswered. It certainly seems to be their nomadic character that makes the Itureans' territory so difficult to define.

Transjordan's second basic geopolitical entity was *Gilead.* The probable meaning of the name itself ("rugged land"), in contrast to its neighbor in the north, Bashan ("smooth land"), and in the south, Mishor ("tableland, plateau") assists in the quest of delineating Gilead. The area is occasionally referred to in the Bible as the Hill Country of Gilead (e.g., Gen. 31:21, 23, 25; Deut. 3:12). Though used generically to denote all of occupied Transjordan (Deut. 34:1; Josh. 22:9), as a geopolitical entity Gilead specified a high, mountainous, oval-shaped dome that is in fact an eastern extension of the Samarian elevations. The Gilead dome rises just a few miles south of the Yarmuk and extends south more or less as far as the Wadi Hesban, a tributary of the Wadi Nusariyat system that joins the Jordan adjacent to Jericho. The eastern border of Gilead may only be defined negatively: it did not include the land of Ammon (e.g., Num. 21:23-24; Judg. 11:4-5; 1 Sam. 11:1-4), so consequently it did not extend to the desert in its southeastern quadrant. The Gilead dome was divided longitudinally by the deep gorge cut by the Jabbok River, which divided Gilead naturally into halves (cf. Josh. 12:5; 13:31—northern half; Deut. 3:12; Josh. 12:2—southern half). Thus defined, Gilead encompassed some 35 miles north-south and not more than 30 miles east-west. Northern Gilead was part of Manasseh's inheritance, whereas southern Gilead was given to Gad. The whole of the dome was effectively colonized by Israel, probably because its raised altitude allowed for sufficient rainfall to support some forestation (cf. 2 Sam. 18:6; Jer. 22:6; Zech. 10:10). The rainfall would have supported an agricultural enterprise that also would have contributed significantly to Gilead's survival; even today this area contains some extensive wheatlands. The medicinal balm of Gilead, whatever its exact character, was highly prized in antiquity (cf. Jer. 8:22; 46:11; cf. Gen. 37:25; 43:11; Ezek. 27:17).

In the aftermath of the death of Alexander the Great, many Greek cities were established throughout Palestine and continued to flourish in Ptolemaic and Seleucid times (see Map 71). Occupied largely by Greek-speaking immigrants, those cities formed the nucleus of opposition, even though largely unsuccessful, to the Jewish independence forged by the Maccabeans (Hasmoneans). But when Pompey's legions brought about an end to Hasmonean dominance, many of those Greek cities were restored to their Hellenistic compatriots, who in some cases found it necessary to band together into mutual protection leagues. One such confederation, known as the *Decapolis* in both the Bible (Matt. 4:25; Mark 5:20; 7:31) and in classical sources,[43] was composed of ten cities primarily situated along the trade arteries of central and northern Transjordan. In the New Testament era those cities included Scythopolis, Pella, Gerasa, Philadelphia, Hippos, Gadara (Umm Qeis), Dion, Canatha, Raphana, and Damascus.[44] The locations of all, except Dion and possibly Raphana, are firmly established and are positioned on or near strategic traffic lanes. Though the nature and purpose of such a loose confederation obviates attempts to define geopolitical frontiers clearly, one can conclude that the heartland of the Decapolis stretched across the Gilead highlands (see Map 4).

As with the two halves of Gilead, geographers sometimes discuss the two halves of *Moab*, divided by the gorge of the Arnon River but substantially the same in their topographic and pastoral makeup. Thus, northern Moab may be defined as the territory between the Wadi Hesban and the Arnon, whereas southern Moab refers to that terrain lying between the Arnon and Zered rivers. I prefer, however, to distinguish between the Mishor (northern Moab) and the heartland of Moab (southern Moab) for geopolitical reasons. The Mishor represented part of Israel's inheritance, occupied by Reubenites, whereas the heartland of Moab lay beyond Israel's perimeter. Now admittedly, the well-defined "plains of Moab" (e.g., Num. 26:3; 33:49; 35:1; Deut. 34:1) represented the comparatively fertile ten mile square situated immediately to the northeast of the Dead Sea. However, that representation may be only a reflection in the biblical tradition that the entire area had been controlled earlier by Moab. Numbers 24:17 uses Moab in a poetic passage that also has the parallel expression "sons of Sheth," an ancient term also found in Egyptian literature to denote part of Transjordan's nomadic populations. In any event, just prior to Israel's arrival, Sihon apparently drove the Moabites south of the Arnon and claimed the Mishor as Amorite territory (cf. Num. 21:12-26).

The *Mishor* ("tableland"; e.g., Deut. 3:10), as defined above, stretched in the north from Heshbon (Josh. 13:9) and Medeba (Josh. 13:16) about 25 miles south to the cities of Aroer (Josh. 13:9) and Dibon (Jer. 48:22), located just north of the Arnon's canyon and near the King's Highway. Also situated in the Mishor were the towns of Nebo (Jer. 48:22) and Beth-peor (Josh. 13:20), near to where Moses was buried (Deut. 34:6) and where Balaam uttered his untoward blessings (Num 23-24). Shittim, where Israelites entered into illicit sexual relations with Moabite women (Num. 25), and Bezer, the city of refuge (Deut. 4:43; Josh. 20:8), were also nearby.

Moab and Israel contested repeatedly for the Mishor, as early as the period of the judges (Judg. 3:12-30) and in the times of Saul and David (1 Sam. 14:47; 2 Sam. 8:2, 12). One of Solomon's many marriages, designed to cement political alliances, was with a Moabite princess (1 Kings 11:1). Even though during the divided kingdom the Mishor was controlled for a time by Omri, Ahab, and Jehoram, a Moabite contemporary (Mesha) of the latter two kings boasts that he conquered much of the Mishor, including the cities of Aroer, Dibon, Medeba, Nebo, and Bezer.[45]

In the thinking of Isaiah (e.g., 15:4-9; 16:8-9), Jeremiah (e.g., 48:2-5, 21-25, 34-36, 45), and Ezekiel (e.g., 25:8-11), the Mishor had been relinquished to Moabite control. Probably it was that political ebb and flow that explains why the Reubenites were unable to play a considerable role in Israel's later history, despite the prominence of Reuben, the eldest son of the patriarch Jacob (cf. Gen. 49:3-4).

The higher plateau extending from the Arnon to the Zered (southern Moab) represented the actual nucleus of Moab's heartland, with its capital city at Kir-hareseth (cf. Isa. 15:1).

Occupying the western segment of greater Moab in the New Testament era was the district of *Perea*, the Greek synonym of Abarim (cf. Num. 27:12; 33:47-48; Deut. 32:49; Jer. 22:20), which means "the region across" (cf. Isa. 9:1). The boundaries of Perea are generally discussed by Josephus.[46] The province extended north as far as the city of Pella, where the Christian community at Jerusalem fled just prior to the first Jewish revolt (A.D. 66). It extended south as far as Machaerus, a fortress city located just north of the Arnon gorge on the plateau overlooking the Dead Sea, where Herod is reported to have beheaded John the Baptist.[47] Josephus reports also that Perea extended from the Jordan River east as far as Philadelphia, and that its capital city was Gadara (Tell Gadur).[48]

Josephus's northern and eastern boundaries are puzzling, inasmuch as both Pella and Philadelphia were part of the Decapolis region. Perhaps his description should be taken to mean that the frontiers of the Pellan and Philadelphian city-states bordered on Perea. Modern geographers, in any event, tend to follow archaeological criteria and set the eastern border basically at a north-south line that extends from the upper Arnon to the vicinity of Jebel Munif, near modern 'Ajlun, and that runs west of Medeba and Geresa.[49] In attempting to establish Perea's northern boundary, some contemporary writers continue to follow the position espoused in the 1930s by Dalman, according to which Perea extended as far north as the Wadi Faqaris (known in modern maps as Wadi Kufrinja). That wadi flows out of the Gilead dome and connects with the Jordan River about 18 airline miles south of Beth-shan.[50]

But if, as assumed above, Josephus is declaring that the outer frontier of the city-state of Pella bordered on Perea, a stronger case could be developed for defining this northern border at the Wadi Yabis, a deep, narrow gorge that begins along the slopes of the Jebel Munif and flows in a westerly direction before emptying into the Jordan opposite Aenon; just 6 miles south of Pella, the Yabis is the one wadi system in the immediate proximity of Pella.

The northern border of Perea has excited controversy because it is thought to relate to a New Testament geographical issue: What was the route taken by Galilean Jews who desired to make religious pilgrimages to Jerusalem three times a year without becoming contaminated by having to set foot on "unholy sod"? Oftentimes it is suggested that certain sections of the Mishna (Sheb. 9.2; Ket. 13:10; B.B. 3.2) imply that the provinces of Galilee and Perea were contiguous, which if true would automatically eliminate Dalman's northern perimeter of Perea. But in my judgment, such debate is pure speculation. The Mishnaic passages in question are inexplicit, and Galilee's southern border was constantly fluctuating during the first century A.D. By the time of the first Jewish revolt, in any event, the southern border of Galilee ran along the northern edges of the Beth-shan valley, that is, it extended north of the city of Pella itself and so could not have been contiguous with Perea. Furthermore, Josephus flatly contradicts this sentiment in one passage, where he declares that Galilean Jews making their pilgrimages to Jerusalem preferred to pass through Samarian territory.[51]

Edom is the final geopolitical area of Transjordan to be enumerated. Sometimes known as Mt. Seir (e.g., Gen. 14:6; Deut. 1:2; 2:5), Edom designates the land and kingdom that was nestled atop the long, slender ridge of lofty mountains that extend from the Zered River to the Gulf of Aqaba. Though this region stretches a distance of 113 airline miles, the actual area encompassed by Edom was never gigantic, and only rarely was its influence significant.

The actual homeland of Edom extended southward from the Zered about 70 miles to Naqb el Ashtar, a plateau that overlooks the Wadi Hasma. That wadi was a massive sand-covered dissection in the earth that stretched in a southeasterly direction and represented the gateway to southern Arabia. Throughout the entire Edomite zone, the mountains rise in excess of 4,000 feet above sea level, and for more than half its distance, the ominous mountain terrain sustains a height above 5,000 feet. The highest peaks (Rujm Tal'at al-Jum'ah, Mubarak) soar to an elevation of approximately 5,700 feet above sea level. What is more, the forbidding landscape was plainly circumscribed on the west by the Arabah, a depression that actually continues the Jordan Rift Valley between the Dead Sea and the Gulf of Aqaba, and on the east by the lowlands of the Eastern desert. The summit, and thus Edom itself, ranges only about 12-13 miles east-west. Resting astride this

Modern Political Boundaries

narrow ridge was a series of fortresses and towns, basically aligning the King's Highway that traversed the ridge. Somewhere in Edom's northern precinct was the homeland of Eliphaz, the territory of Teman (Job 2:11; Jer. 49:7), a district that probably included the strategic Edomite centers of Sela (Sil', not Umm el-Biyara, cf. Judg. 1:36), a fortress city captured by Amaziah (2 Kings 14:7), and Bozrah (Amos 1:12).

Now the combination of natural and man-made fortification rendered Edom an impenetrable barrier to lateral traffic, with one possible exception: the pass at Punon. About 25 miles south of the Zered, a fault line has created in the mountains a canyon that fans eastward from the Arabah some 9 miles. At the foot of this remarkable wadi lies the site of ancient Punon, an important center for copper mining in the eastern Arabah and a spot where the Israelites camped en route from Kadesh-barnea to the plains of Moab (Num. 33:42). We recall from the Bible (Num. 20:14-21) how Moses requested that the king of Edom permit the Israelites to pass through Edomite territory to the King's Highway. But the king refused, thereby requiring the Israelite entourage to hike about 100 additional miles over arid terrain and through torrid heat just to skirt Edom (Deut. 2). That psychological defeat was surely related to the fiery serpent incident (Num. 21:4-9; 33:42-43), in which Moses lifted up a copper serpent in the wilderness (cf. John 3:14). At any rate, one can appreciate from geography why the king's refusal would have gone unchallenged, even though the Israelites may have outnumbered their antagonists. The gigantic cliffs and steep gorges of Edom, even from the more gentle slopes of Punon's pass, represented an inaccessible objective that at Edomite whim would continue to exist in splendid isolation (cf. Obad. 3, where Edomites live in *carved* dwellings).

Situated adjacent to the western Edomite mountains about 21 air miles south of Punon is a cavity-like canyon containing the impressive remains of Petra, the fabulous capital of the Nabatean empire, later occupied by the Romans. Though obscurity surrounds their ancestral roots, the Nabateans came to occupy Edom in the third century B.C., and by the first century B.C. their influence was felt from Damascus to Gaza and the interior of Arabia. Much of their power consisted of the control they inherited over part of a lucrative trade route extending at that time from the Saudi Arabian hinterland to the western Mediterranean. The site of Petra was approached through a one-mile corridor flanked on either side by high perpendicular cliffs that almost touch at a few points. The basin that actually housed Petra was itself surrounded by cliffs of colorful sandstone into which have been carved the structures and tombs of what in antiquity was a city laden with wealth.

Continuing south of Edom's heartland for about 40 miles, from the eastern interruption of the Wadi Hasma down to the Wadi Yutm, near the Gulf of Aqaba, is an extremely narrow wedge of impassable granite mountains rising to heights approaching 5,000 feet above sea level. On the crests of those mountains (sometimes described as the mountains of Midian), and those that continue south of the Yutm and east of the Gulf of Aqaba, have been discovered archaeological remains of a culture completely distinctive from that of its Palestinian counterpart, and thought to be Midianite in character. It is in that Midianite culture that some scholars believe Moses found asylum when he fled from the pharaoh, and there served his father-in-law, the priest of Midian (Ex. 2:15-17; 3:1).

Physical topography. A study of the topography of the land of promise must begin with a recognition of the land's small size. As defined above, the nucleus of Israel's inheritance actually encompasses no more than 10,330 square miles, meaning that it is approximately the size of Lake Erie, the state of Maryland, or the country of Belgium. (Cisjordan's heartland is approximately 6,000 square miles, whereas Transjordan takes in some 4,000 square miles.) In fact, on a clear day, it is possible to survey much of Cisjordan from any one of a several high vantage points.

The land is oftentimes described by the formula "from Dan to Beersheba" (e.g., Judg. 20:1; 1 Sam. 3:20; 2 Sam. 3:10; 1 Kings 4:25), defining respectively the northern and southern perimeters of Israel's heartland, which are separated by something less than 150 miles. Yet the east-west distances are still smaller. The western fringes of the Eastern desert range in distance from the Mediterranean between 80-105 miles; the Sea of Galilee is removed by only approximately 30 miles from the Mediterranean, while the Dead Sea is separated from the Mediterranean by a mere 60 airline miles. Added to its diminutive area, which was originally occupied by a native population no greater than that of some of the obscure tribes inhabiting the Philippine Islands today, the Promised Land was virtually devoid of prominent natural resources, was beleaguered for the most part by an inhospitable climate, and exhibited some of the earth's most forbidding landscape. At first blush, therefore, this stretch of geography would seem to be an unlikely candidate to become the center stage for a divine drama that would eventually affect all of humanity.

Upon closer examination, however, one discovers that this land mass is poised in an amazingly strategic position. Actually the Promised Land represents the only intercontinental land

MAP 6 FOREIGN INFLUX

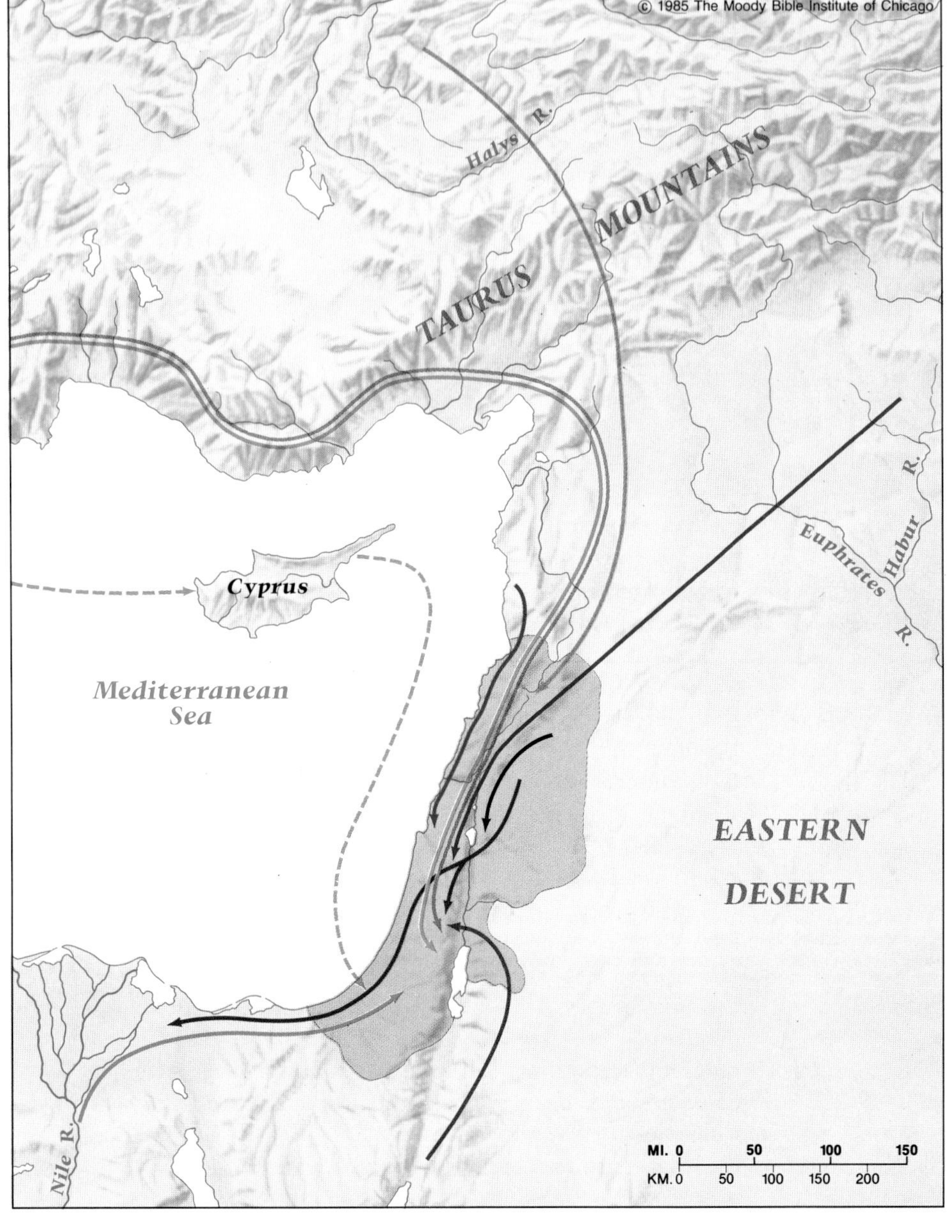

- Israel's promised land
- Amorite penetration
- Hyksos penetration
- Egyptian penetration
- Hurrian penetration (Mitanni kingdom)
- Israelite penetration
- Philistine penetration (part of Sea Peoples)
- Hittite penetration (neo-Hittite states)
- Aramean penetration
- Greek penetration
- Roman penetration

---

bridge that connects Africa with Asia and Europe, and that links the Indian Ocean, via the Red Sea, with the Atlantic Ocean, through the corridor of the Mediterranean. Since high antiquity, mighty powers with international political and economic aspirations have been positioned at either end of the bridge. What happened in Palestine was almost always a reflection of what was occurring or had just occurred in one of Israel's neighboring countries. It was on this land bridge that east met west. Israel became a "flashpoint" for international adventurism and imperialism, while it also represented a "fulcrum" for land and sea trade that ultimately linked India with Spain and Great Britain.

Unquestionably during the biblical period, the destiny of this tiny but strategic land was largely one determined by outsiders, be they Egyptians, Assyrians, Babylonians, Persians, Greeks, or Romans. In that context, it is instructive to observe that the Philistines and even the Israelites themselves must be regarded as foreigners. The same trend of foreign influence has continued in post-biblical history with the Moslem caliphs, the Crusaders, the Mamluke dynasts of Egypt, the Ottoman-Turks, and the British mandataries. Across this bridge have marched the armies of Thutmosis III, Seti I, Ramses II, Merneptah, Shishak, Necho II, Shalmaneser III, Tiglath-pileser III, Sargon II, Sennacherib, Esarhaddon, Ashurbanipal, Nebuchadnezzar II, Cambyses, Artaxerxes III, Alexander the Great, Ptolemy I, Antiochus III, Antiochus IV, Pompey, Vespasian, Titus, Saladin, Richard the Lionhearted, Napoleon, Allenby, and Begin, together with a host of lesser-known generals (see Map 6; consult Maps 58 and 62 for Assyrian and Babylonian penetrations; cf. Map 52).

Consequently, someone living in this land unavoidably was faced with a combination of geographic and military hostility. Possessing meager physical and economic resources and being inescapably caught in a maelstrom of political upheaval, one residing in these surroundings, even under ideal circumstances, might have been able to eke out the barest of existence. Life in this land would have been simple, mystifying and precarious. In the final analysis, survival in such terrain depended upon neither military prowess nor environmental ingenuity. For one to survive here depended ultimately upon cosmic forces that lay beyond the sphere of human control. The Canaanites believed that those forces could be humanly manipulated through what we shall later describe as the "Fertility Cult." For the Israelites, on the other hand, the Source of those forces could only be worshiped. In a word, this was a land that fostered faith.

The preceding background discussion leads to the formulation of a hypothesis that is central to the remainder of this chapter: namely, that God prepared the Promised Land for His chosen people to the same degree that He prepared His chosen people for the Promised Land. Although various biblical accounts and theological statements rightly describe how God set about preparing the Israelites to become the special benefactors of His grace by reason of inheriting the land, the following discussion will underscore that it was a *certain kind of land* that was selected and prepared by God, positioned at a *particular spot*, and designed to elicit a *specific and appropriate response*. In fact, God's craftsmanship has been vividly manifested both in the character of His chosen people and in the characteristics of His chosen land. He has been at work in both history and geography. A most helpful insight is lost for one who fails to realize that the Promised Land itself has been the object of careful divine crafting.

God's handiwork has specifically taken shape under the dominant force of geology, and the land of Israel is best described in terms of four parallel longitudinal zones. From west to east, these are the coastal plain, the central mountain spine, the Jordan Rift Valley, and the Transjordanian plateau. These regions, though parallel, actually display an exceptional variety in altitude, terrain, and rock formation, further fracturing the already small area and giving it a mosaic-like quality.

Coastal plain. In scope, the maritime plain defines that low, flat coastal strip extending from the Wadi el-Arish some 190 miles north to Rosh HaNiqra, where a finger of the Galilean highlands juts out to meet the Mediterranean and naturally bisects the narrow flatlands on either side. Historically known as the "ladder of Tyre" situated 100 furlongs (about 12 miles) north of Ptolemais (Acco),[52] the cliffs of Rosh HaNiqra have served as a political boundary in both ancient and modern times. They represented the northern perimeter of Simon Maccabeus's domain (1 Macc. 11:59) and functioned as the modern boundary between Israel and Lebanon until the 1978 war.

Simply stated, a discussion of the coastal plain could be pared down to the plain's three most apt characterizations: "low, fertile, and open." Those refer respectively to its topography, geology, and history. However, though the coastal plain is topographically similar—that is to say, uniformly low in altitude—it is geologically dissimilar and can be historically distinct. Those differences have a profound bearing upon biblical history, and therefore a more detailed discussion of the plain will be necessary.

The coastal plain was internally segmented by three natural barriers (Mt. Carmel promontory, Crocodile swamplands [Nahr Tanninim], Yarkon River), thereby creating four distinct plains. Moreover, for geographical reasons to be explained below, it is desirable to divide in two the northernmost of those plains. Included, therefore, in the coastal plain from north to south are the following: (1) the Asher plain (extending from Rosh HaNiqra to the city of Acco), (2) the Acco plain (the crescent-shaped bay reaching between Acco and Mt. Carmel), (3) the Dor plain (stretching from Carmel to the Crocodile marshland), (4) the Sharon plain (ranging from the swamps to the Yarkon) and (5) the Philistine plain (extending from the Yarkon to el-Arish).

The *Plain of Asher*, which is a geographic and not a tribal designation inasmuch as that tribe's territory seems to have extended as far south as the city of Dor (Josh. 17:11; 19:26), differs from the *Plain of Acco* in a number of significant ways. Hugging the entire coastline of the coastal plain is a series of higher ridges (100-120 feet in elevation). These ridges, called "kurkar" ridges, have been formed as sand dunes somehow came into contact with calcium-lime solutions, thus solidifying the dunes into a cement-like substance. On the one hand, these ridges prevent the day-to-day sand deposits from inundating inland soils. On the other, they present little obstruction to adequate drainage, except where the constant flow of perennial rivers produces an excessive volume of water, creating inadequate drainage and causing marshiness. Here is where there is a noticeable difference between the plains of Asher and Acco: only wadies traverse the Asher plain whereas two rivers (Na'aman, and Kishon) attempt to disgorge their waters only 6 miles apart into the Acco bay. Accordingly, swampland is rather widespread throughout the Plain of Acco, as Sisera was loathe to discover (Judg. 4:13-16; 5:21). But adequate drainage, combined with the heavy layer of rich topsoil across the Asher plain from erosion of the Galilean highlands, has made the plain a region of plenteous agricultural productivity. Towns in the Asher plain are located either atop the kurkar ridges or along the eastern foothills, because the

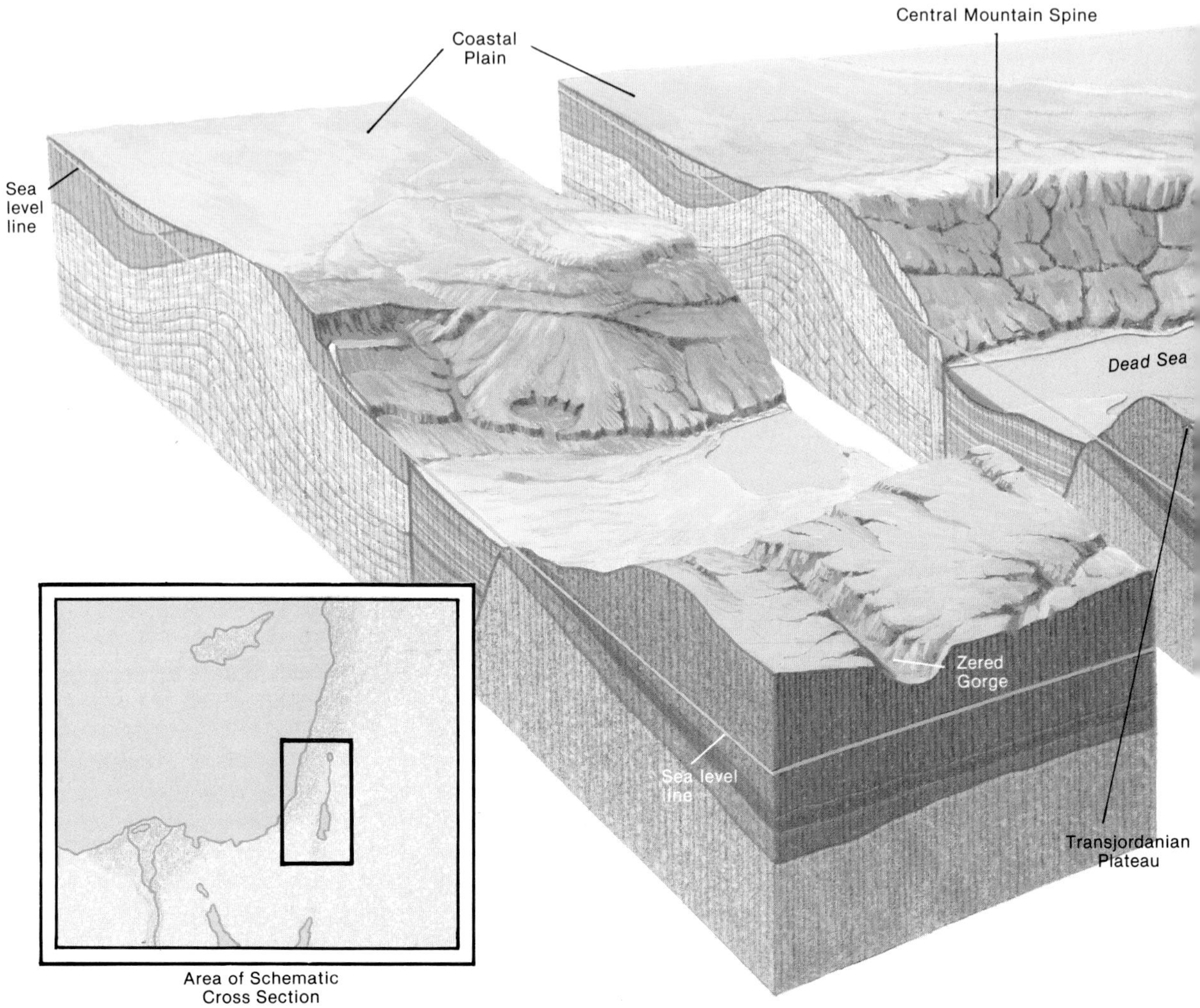

Central Mountain Spine

Coastal Plain

Sea level line

Dead Sea

Zered Gorge

Sea level line

Transjordanian Plateau

Area of Schematic Cross Section

Figure 2 Cross-Sectional Schematic of Palestine.

Figure 3 Mountains of Galilee plunge to the Sea of Galilee at Taricheae, Magdala, and Tiberias.

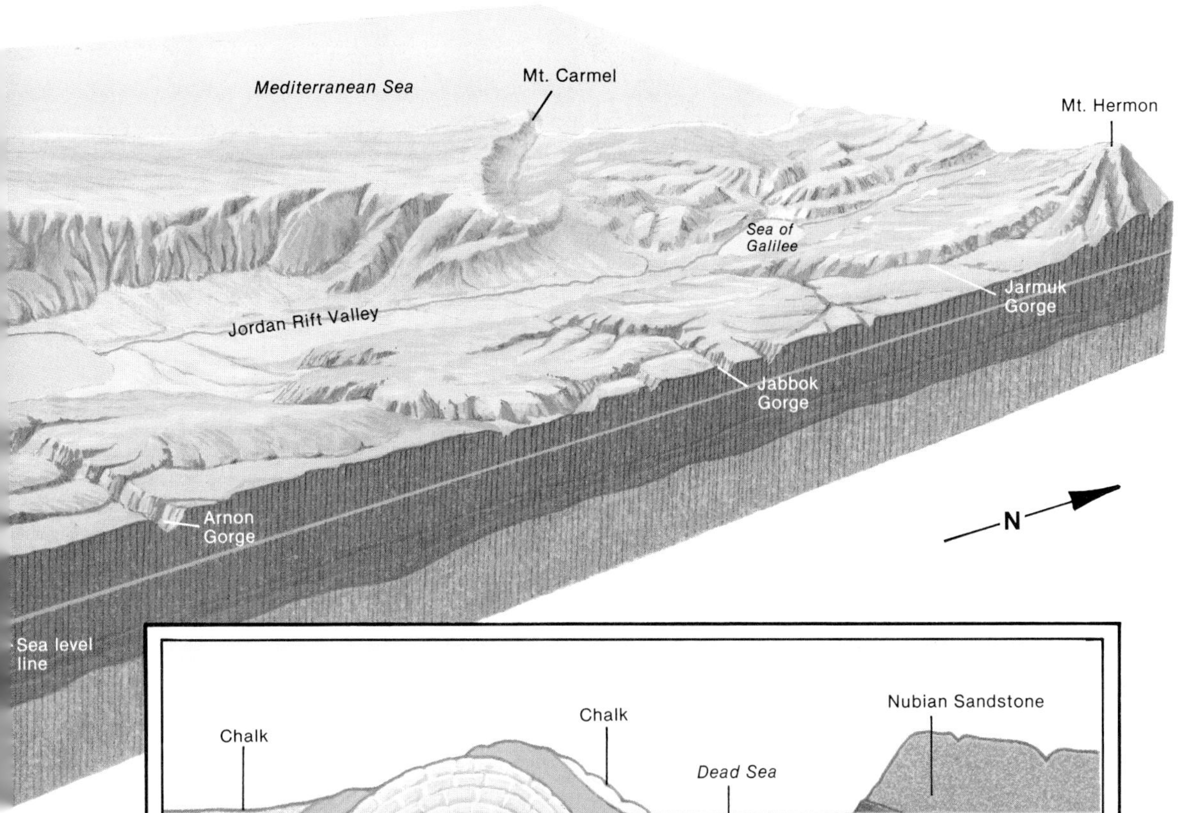

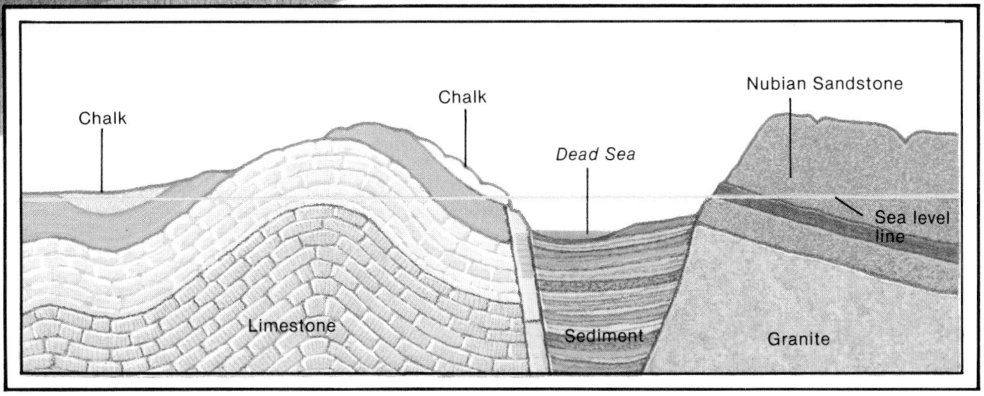

Figure 4 Jordan Rift Valley with the mountains of the Transjordanian Plateau towering in the background.

rich soil cannot be consumed on or by human occupation (cf. comparative richness of Gen. 49:20; Deut. 33:24).

Greatly constricted by a narrow hinterland, the Carmel barrier, and the Crocodile swamps, the *Plain of Dor* played almost no role in biblical history. Moreover, it was apparently blanketed with a thicket-like forest in antiquity (so described in Crusader literature). The supplication of the tribe of Manasseh (Josh. 17:15-18) to occupy additional territory in the "forest" of the Canaanites probably included the Plain of Dor, as well as those of Sharon and Jezreel (Esdraelon). In any event, the city of Dor was the only important settlement of this plain mentioned in the Old Testament.

If the Dor plain was enclosed horizontally, the *Sharon plain* was hemmed in vertically, owing to the presence of a red-brown "Mousterian sand," which predominantly covers the landscape. One of the properties of this sand is its tendency to gather and hold water only about six feet underground, thus worsening the situation of an already high water table and producing a generally marshy quagmire. Even the name Sharon likely should be translated "forested land" (so LXX, Isa. 33:9; 35:2), to be interpreted most likely as a kind of marshy thicket where scrubs and wild flowers may grow (cf. Song of Sol. 2:1, "rose of Sharon") and cattle may graze (cf. 1 Chron. 5:16; 27:29; Isa. 65:10). However, in antiquity agricultural efforts would have been futile and traffic would have been detoured in the Sharon. Described by ancient, medieval, and modern historians alike as a forest, large segments of the Sharon were still covered by trees and scrubs up until World War I, when they were destroyed in order to supply fuel for the Turkish railways. When the Jewish National Fund began acquiring this land in the 1920s, it was in part a malaria-infested swampland regarded as completely unsuited for agricultural uses. But as the Jewish settlers began draining the soil, a dramatically different picture began to emerge. They discovered that beneath and around the marshiness lay a combination of geographic ingredients that made the locale profitable for citrus growing. So it is today that hardly a segment of Israel is more intensively utilized for agriculture, and the Sharon forms the backbone of a flourishing citrus industry.

In the biblical era, the Sharon was part of the territory allotted to the tribe of Manasseh. Though Hepher, one of its cities, appears to have been temporarily captured by Joshua's forces (Josh. 12:17), the Sharon seems never to have been brought under Manassite dominion (Josh. 17:12-13; Judg. 1:27-28). None of the Levitical cities was located in the Sharon (Josh. 21:8-42; cf. 1 Chron. 6:54-66). Marginally controlled by David, the Sharon was eventually incorporated into the Israelite monarchy by Solomon, who placed the region (called the "land of Hepher," 1 Kings 4:10) under the rule of one Ben-Hesed and required it to furnish provisions to the royal court for one month out of the year (1 Kings 4:27). Later, in the wake of Herod's building program at Caesarea (see below), the Sharon took on a degree of prominence. It came to represent a link between the Roman capital and landward points Shere the legions had to establish and maintain law and order.

South of the Yarkon, in the Philistine plain, the red-brown sand begins to disappear. Heavy alluvium sometimes mixed with loess (a sediment deposited by wind erosion) made travel less hampered and the soil exceptionally productive agriculturally. This means that the Philistine plain and its eastern neighbor, the Shephela, has been the theater of much biblical history (see below).

Now the entire coastal plain, as already mentioned, is topographically similar. As one proceeds in a southerly direction, this plain slightly rises and widens. More specifically, aside from a few inland slopes in southern Philistia near Sede Zevi and Bet Qana that rise to a level of about 650 feet, the whole of this plain remains below 330 feet. Much of it is lower than 150 feet above sea level. The Dor plain is constricted in the north to not more than a few hundred yards in width, and in the south to only 4 miles in width, whereas the Sharon plain widens to approximately 10 miles, while the Philistine plain is some 14 miles wide at Ashkelon and 20 miles wide at Gaza.

When a shoreline forms a smooth, almost straight line running parallel to principal mountain ridges (what professionals call a "concordant shore"), a land is normally rendered poor in promontories and deep bays; Israel is no exception. What is more, Israel's case is aggravated by the counterclockwise currents of the Mediterranean that carry vast amounts of sand from North Africa, Egypt, or northern Sinai and deposit them along Israel's already-shallow waterfront. And so, by the standards of Rotterdam or New York, Israel has never possessed a good harbor. In the Old Testament period, it struggled along by utilizing the shallow bay of Acco (Ptolemais, Acts 21:7), the basin of Joppa (Jonah 1:3), and the coves at Dor and Ashkelon. In the wake of the unsuccessful Maccabean insurrection, Caesar Augustus bequeathed the coastline hamlet of Stato's Tower to Herod the Great. Herod immediately undertook an ambitious building program to transform that town into a worthy seat for official Roman rule, renaming it Caesarea for his patron. As part of the building program, Herod oversaw the creation of an artificial harbor that included a sophisticated breakwater design; some of its enormous stone pilings can still be seen today. From an engineering perspective, Caesarea's harbor represented a pioneering work of significant magnitude. Its construction incorporated the first extensive use of hydraulic concrete and included an anti-siltation system.[53]

Under the Roman procurators, Caesarea became the capital of Palestine. The fifth of those—Pontius Pilate, judge in the trial of Jesus (Mark 15:1-15)—left at the seaport city the only extant dedicatory inscription that actually bears his name. Through that port, the apostle Paul sailed on his second and third missionary journeys (Acts 18:22; 21:8) and embarked on his trip to Rome (Acts 23:33).

Contrasted to the smooth shoreline near Caesarea is that of Phoenicia, the contour of which is determined primarily by fault lines, where mountains meet the Mediterranean and deep, natural harbors at Beirut, Tripolis, Ugarit, and Zarephath have always existed. As a result of this diverse geographic reality, Phoenicians became seafarers and Israelites became farmers and shepherds. Thus, Solomon needed Phoenician materials and technology to build a merchant fleet, but he was able to afford the whole enterprise simply by exporting much-needed agricultural products to Hiram (1 Kings 5:11; 2 Chron. 2:15; cf. Acts 12:20).

But the coastal plain was not only "low"; it was also "fertile and open." Geologically speaking, the coastal plain was relatively fertile because of benefits that derived from its being positioned next to the central mountain spine. First, extensive erosion of the limestone mountain produced a deep layer of rich soil ("terra rosa"), which was partially exploited in the biblical periods (Philistines, Israelites in the Asher plain) and completely exploited in the modern period. In the eastern sectors of the plain along some of the same fault lines responsible for the uplift of the mountain spine lay an abundance of fresh water springs. In antiquity, of course, these represented a mixed blessing in nature: they supplied much-needed nourishment, but they were also responsible for much swampiness of the land. The springs have also played a role in the high ground-water table, which promotes the widespread utilization of this stretch of geography in the modern setting.

The foregoing topographic and geologic combination has meant that the coastal plain sometimes experienced historical unity and sometimes disunity. It was uniformly "open," that is to say, it always lay exposed to and was consistently unable to restrain foreign intrusion. Now this is of crucial historical interest, because the only international transportation artery (the Great Trunk Road) that cut across Palestine and connected the two ends of the Fertile Crescent ran through the eastern sectors of the Sharon and Philistine plains. So although the land of promise as a whole may be described as an "intercontinental land bridge," south of Mt. Carmel it was really only the coastal plain that formed such a bridge. In that respect, the plain was confronted by a constant parade of exploiters. As a consequence, whereas the important cities in the plains of Dor, Acco, and Asher were normally unwalled and situated along the waterfront, large fortified cities such as Tell Burga, Socoh, Tell Zeror, Aphek-Antipatris, Gezer, Tell Muqenna' (Ekron), and Tell Jemmeh (Yurza?) sprang up at strategic points near the Great Trunk Road in the Sharon and Philistine plains.

But openness is also meant to connote relative mobility. It must be stressed that military conflict in the coastal plain during the biblical period included the dimension of chariot warfare (cf. Deut. 20:1). Unlike its neighboring mountain, this plain offered a terrain that was conducive to the use of chariotry, and lightning-fast strikes would have been unhampered by large boulders and hilly landscape. It is informative that the smooth terrain became a pretext by which the Israelites cut short their conquest (e.g., Josh. 17:16). In fact, a striking correspondence exists between the terrain over which Philistines could run chariots and terrain Israel did not conquer during the conquest. In the end, the Israelites had been successful in capturing much of the mountainous spine, where chariots represented no real threat, whereas the Philistines continued to maintain control over virtually all of the coastal plain. Alternatively, this may explain why the Philistines, in an "open" area and with a great many similarities with the Israelites, were unable to survive as an indigenous political entity throughout the biblical period, whereas the more secluded Israelites were able to perpetuate a sense of national identity.

Then again, it is of interest to observe that when the modern state of Israel was created by the United Nations partition plan of 1947, its coastland sectors corresponded rather closely to what has just been described as the perimeter of the Acco, Dor, and Sharon plains. When to this are added sections of the Philistine plain, together with the plains of Esdraelon and Hula, and the Sinai, inland regions of the new state also set uniformly at a lower altitude, one comes to recognize that the partitioning plan was in part drafted according to geographical realities. Or to put it differently, the terrain Israel was unable to capture in the biblical conquest because of Philistine chariots corresponds rather closely to the terrain it was allotted through the United Nations partition.

MAP 7 ELEVATION OF PALESTINE

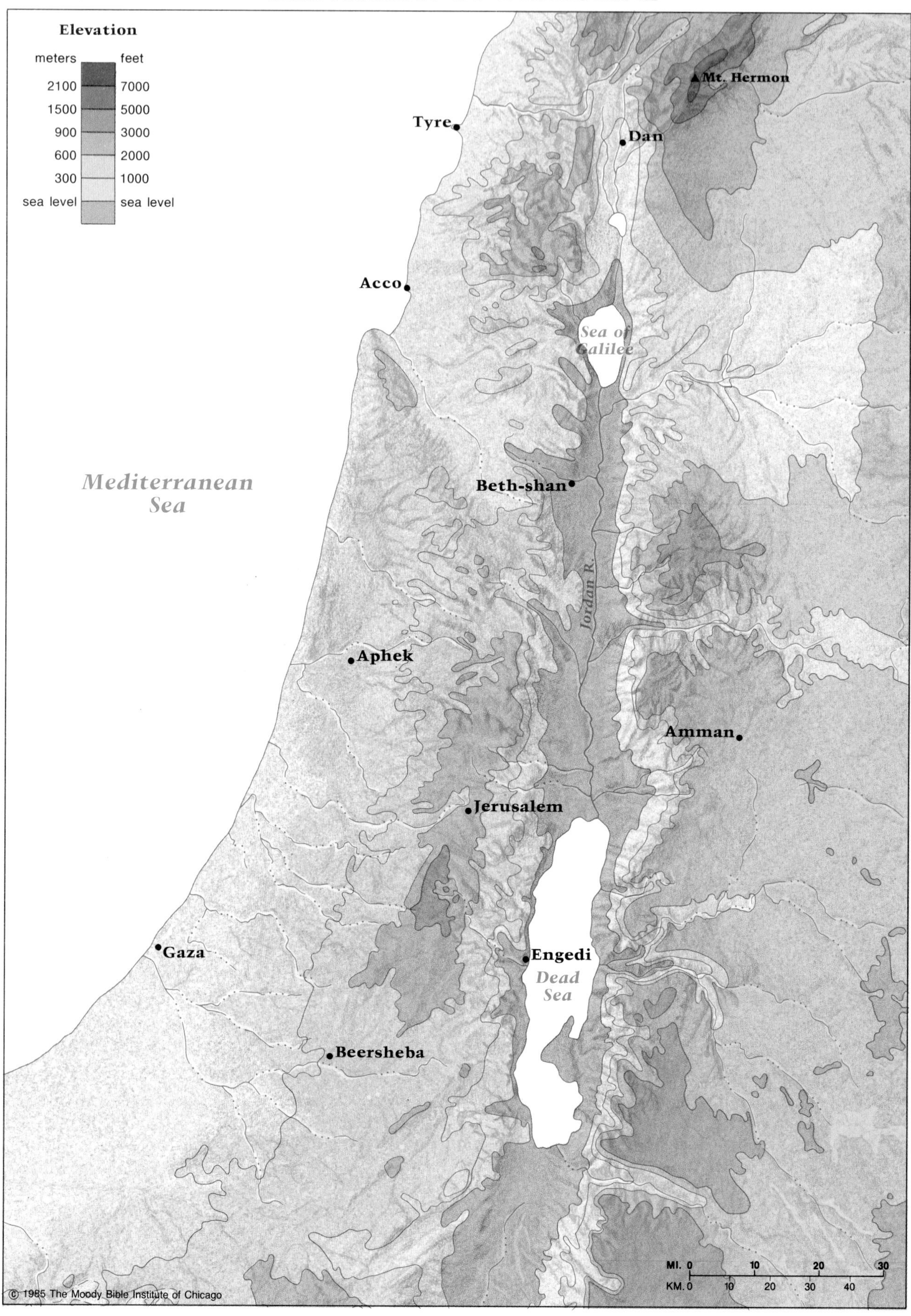

Alternatively, Israel was able to capture in the biblical conquest roughly the same territory west of the Jordan that it seized in the Six-Day War of 1967 (see Map 33; cf. Map 95). Some of the modern Israeli boundaries, therefore, seem to be an example of geographic determinism that transcends even thousands of years.

Central mountain spine. The second longitudinal zone, taking in the highlands of Galilee, Samaria, Judea, and the Negeb, is referred to as the central mountain spine. In character and topography, it is exactly the opposite of the coastal plain. If the latter was described as "low, open, and productive," the former must be characterized as "high, closed, and unproductive." If the coastal plain ascends to only 650 feet above the sea at its highest point, the central mountain spine is about 1,500 feet at its lowest point, with many segments of the mountain actually rising to heights in excess of 3,300 feet above sea level. Very often, this contrast in altitude is extremely pronounced; one might travel inland a distance of only 3 to 4 miles while simultaneously ascending in altitude more than a half mile.

Actually a series of interlocking ranges, the central spine stands as a natural impediment to lateral traffic, except where it is broken by the Jezreel (Esdraelon) valley. At some places along its undulation, it would be necessary for one to cross over as many as five distinct ridges, each separated by deeply-etched wadi beds, to pass from one side of the spine to the other. The spine is also closed, which means it was somewhat isolated and relatively unsusceptible to international adventurism or foreign assault. Only rarely has this zone proved to be attractive to empire builders. The spine is also unproductive; it is composed of hard limestone and lacks precious minerals or natural resources. On the face of things, therefore, it seems unlikely that this stone mountain, ranging in width from 10-30 miles, should ever have been viewed as a political asset. Yet it is precisely this central spine, below the Jezreel valley, which corresponds to what is dubbed today "the West Bank," a phrase that conjures the notion of vital political interest.

As an offshoot of the loftier mountains of Lebanon, Upper Galilee is a rugged mountainous limestone plateau with a most complex topography. Its Mt. Merom (J. Jarmuk) boasts the highest point in all of Cisjordan at 3,963 feet above the sea, though it is surrounded by other crests that ascend to more than 3,000 feet. Upper Galilee's difficult terrain and fragmented topography have rendered it less suitable for intensive settlement than some territories south, despite its more desirable climate, and the region has never possessed what could be called a large city.

Though segregated geologically, much of the eastern sector of Lower Galilee continues the rugged contours of Upper Galilee. One discovers there a large elevated limestone outcropping that drops off precipitously into the Sea of Galilee; included in that region are the heights of Mt. Tabor and of the Arbel, and the volcanic "Horns of Hattin." North of that is an extremely complicated series of tilted plateaus and deeply-cut valleys, the most prominent being that of the Wadi 'Ammud. Only in the last few years has that imposing topography been forded, with the completion of a modern road from Hula to Haifa. Central and western Lower Galilee, by way of contrast, is the most level section in the entire central spine. That area is composed of several parallel ridges running from east to west, between which are relatively level and open basins that become almost contiguous in the west. At no point do the rounded highlands of Lower Galilee exceed 2,000 feet in altitude, and the intermediate valleys are so flat that they lack proper drainage;

Figure 5 Cliffs of Arbel drop off sharply to the Sea of Galilee.

consequently, with plentiful water they are valuable for growing crops.

Between the heights of Galilee and Samaria there extends a valley linking the Jordan rift with the coastal plain at Acco. Shaped like an arrow that points to the Mediterranean just north of Mt. Carmel, that valley is known in the Old Testament as Jezreel ("may God sow") and in the New Testament era as Esdraelon (e.g., Judith 1:8; 3:9; 4:6; 7:3; cf. 1 Macc. 5:52; 12:49). The slender shaft of the arrow, stretching between the cities of Beth-shan and Jezreel, is hemmed in by Mt. Moreh in the north and the mountains of Gilboa in the south and is drained by the Harod River (see Maps 11 and 15). The area was the scene of Gideon's triumphant victory over the Midianites (Judg. 7:1) and of the humiliating defeat of Saul at the hands of the Philistines (1 Sam 29-31). The base of the arrow's head spans some 18 miles from Ibleam north to the hills of Nazareth, and from those two points it extends about 20 miles westward to its apex, which is near Harosheth-haggoim, where Sisera's chariot became lodged in the quagmire of the Kishon River (Judg. 4:16; see Map 36). The head of the arrow, sometimes called the plain of Megiddo (Zech. 12:11) is low, flat, and covered with an extremely thick blanket of black soil, more than 330 feet deep in places, which has been formed by the decomposition of Galilean basalts. It receives adequate rainfall to make it one of the most fertile regions in Palestine. Though topographically similar to the coastal plain, the strategic importance of the Jezreel during the biblical period was that it represented an interruption in the central spine, which made it inviting to international travel. And accordingly, it seems prudent to discuss the Jezreel valley in conjunction with the spine.

Figure 6 Remains of Megiddo overlook the Jezreel valley.

The plain of Megiddo had five gates. There was a western gate, at the point of the arrow, which led to the Acco basin and the Phoenician coastlands. A northeastern gate opened into the Kisslot basin of Lower Galilee. Through part of the year when the plain was dry, that gate was commonly used by arterial traffic headed for Syria or Mesopotamia (Great Trunk Road, see below). But during and after the rainy seasons, arterial traffic most frequently used an eastern gate, located between the cities of Shunem and Jezreel, which led toward Beth-shan and the Jordan River. The latter roadway offered immediate slopes on either side of the valley for travelers who needed to remain above the marshiness of the lowland. A southern gate past modern Jenin and Dothan would have been regularly employed by individuals who desired to journey southward toward Jerusalem. Finally, there were three southwestern gates formed by narrow valleys cut across the Carmel ridge and that emerged into the plain at Jokneam (W. Yokneam), Megiddo (W. 'Iron), and Taanach (W. Zavdon). The most important of the southwestern passes was the one at the city of Megiddo, for through it the Great Trunk Road passed to Egypt.

Actually, Megiddo may be the most strategic point in Palestine. From the late fourth millennium B.C. to the present day, Megiddo has been the scene of repeated military confrontations. The city's twenty archaeological strata reflect an almost continuous occupation from about 3500 B.C. to 350 B.C. Thutmosis III, the brilliant military tactician whose reign inaugurated the *Pax Egyptica* (peace of Egypt), and who is regarded by the historian Breasted as worthy to be ranked with Alexander the Great and Napoleon, fought a fierce battle at Megiddo. His inscriptions on the wall of a temple at Karnak vividly illustrate how geographical considerations often dictate battle plans that vary little over the millennia. There were three possible routes by which he could attack from the south (cf. the three southwest gates of the preceding paragraph). The most direct of those, the way of Aruna ('Iron), was also the most perilous. The wadi was so constricted in spots that troops had to pass single file. Had Thutmosis's enemies anticipated his passage through the narrow pass, they could have decimated his army or at least could have defended the city of Megiddo. But they anticipated precisely the opposite, and deployed their troops at the mouths of the two less treacherous passes. Thutmosis's gamble was a strategic success not unlike General Douglas MacArthur's decision to risk invasion of Inchon in 1950 during the Korean War, or General James Wolfe's resolution to scale the heights to the fortress at Quebec in 1759 during the French and Indian Wars.

When Megiddo collapsed before his forces, Thutmosis offered this verdict concerning its importance: "Capture it, and fortify it well; for to capture Megiddo is to capture 1000 towns!"[54] The same strategy was later employed by Pharaoh Necho II at the battle in which Josiah lost his life (2 Kings 23:29; 2 Chron. 35:22-24). And as recently as World War I, it was precisely the same strategy, now employed by the British forces of General Allenby, that broke the back of the Turkish army and brought the Ottoman period to an end. Recognizing the importance of the site, Alexander the Great solidified a hold on the city. The Sixth Roman Legion of Hadrian was stationed there (cf. the site was known as "Legio" in this segment of the Roman period [Map 73]; see also its provincial name in the Assyrian period [Map 59]). On that spot Crusaders clashed with Moslems; and in this century, Jews have waged two decisive battles against their Arab adversaries for control of the Megiddo terrain.

The apocalyptic language of Revelation 16:16 that mentions "Armageddon" has been interpreted in a bewildering number of ways. Although its exact meaning remains in doubt, it seems clear that the word was used as a symbolic term for a final decisive battle. In such a context, its paronomastic (word-play) relationship with Megiddo would have conjured in the minds of first-century A.D. individuals familiar with the geographic profile of the city images and impressions as profound as the combination of "Gettysburg," "Alamo," "Pearl Harbor," and "Bastogna" create for someone today.

South of the Jezreel lay the mountainous district of Samaria. In altitude, vegetation, and climate, Samaria is transitional between Galilee and Judea. Mt. Carmel, in the extreme northwest, was proverbial in antiquity for its beauty (Song of Sol. 7:5) and fertility (Isa. 35:2; Jer. 50:19; Mic. 7:14),[55] though it appears to have been even more famous as a religious shrine. It seems probable that the site was known to ancient Egyptians as Rosh-Kadesh ("holy cape").[56] Mt. Carmel served as the scene of Elijah's religious contest with the prophets of Baal (1 Kings 18:17-40) and elsewhere as a spiritual retreat for Elisha (2 Kings 2:25; 4:25). Its steep slopes and scrubland, especially on the Jezreel (north) side, rendered the Carmel range a rather isolated region throughout biblical history. Whether owing to its isolation or to its role as a holy sanctuary, Mt. Carmel yields the earliest evidence of human habitation within Palestine; skeletal and artifactual remains discovered in a series of caves along its lower western slopes, in the Wadi el-Mugharah, attest to a prehistoric, Stone Age occupation.

In the extreme northeast, the heights of Samaria are otherwise known as the limestone mountains of Gilboa. Other Samarian mountains, Mt. Ebal and Mt. Gerizim enclose the valley where lies the principal town of Samaria, Shechem. Those peaks and Baal Hazor, between Bethel and Shiloh, are the highest summits in Samaria.

Though mountainous, Samaria is interspersed with a number of small plains and open valleys, two of which are located near the juncture of the Carmel and Gilboa inclines, in proximity to the city of Ibleam. Here lie the plain of Dothan (from Ibleam west), the largest and most intensively cultivated basin, from where Joseph was sold into captivity (Gen. 37:12-28), and the plain of Sanur (from Ibleam south), which is extremely flat and remains inundated throughout much of the rainy season. A third trough, the long slender plain of Mikhmetat, which runs south from Shechem for about 7 miles before it is pinched off by Jebel Rahwat, rests astride the water-divide through which winds the central road to Jerusalem.

Laterally dividing western Samaria from the coastal plain near Socoh to Shechem is a low valley known as the Wadi Shehem. Similarly, dividing eastern Samaria is a major fracture known as the Wadi Fari'a, which ends near Tirzah. Those two valleys represent the lowest points of altitude in all of Samaria and therefore are the easiest ways to cross the central spine of Samaria.

Though there is no defined geological boundary separating Samaria and Judah, there is a marked difference in the topography of the two regions. Larger amounts of rainfall have contributed to much greater erosion and more-deeply furrowed wadies throughout Samaria. Judah remains more of a high plateau, on the other hand, less dissected because of its drier climate. As one proceeds south in Judah, the landscape becomes harsher and more rugged. Bare rocks and wide stretches of loose, broken stones, washed free of soil, are Judah's chief surface features. Only along the watershed in the vicinity of Ramah and between Bethlehem and Hebron do the soils of Judah permit intensive cultivation. Elsewhere, the harmful effects of shallow soils eroding in winter's downpours have prevented cultivation.

Only about 5 miles southeast of Jerusalem, the wilderness of Judah begins (Num. 21:20; 1 Sam. 26:1-2; Mark 1:4). This is a genuine desert: it is a solitary, howling, rough and rocky wasteland that is nearly devoid of plants and animals and virtually without rainfall (cf. Ps. 63:1). Even

Figure 7 Wilderness of Judah at the cleavage of En Avedat. People walking in the canyon floor are barely visible.

modern nomadic bedouin tend to avoid its aridity and rugged terrain. On its eastern edge, the wilderness plunges steeply as much as 4,500 feet into the Jordan valley. Between Jericho and the southern end of the Dead Sea there are more than 20 deep gorges that have been carved out by wadies. Yet those were all too narrow and tortuous to carry significant roadways during the biblical era, and Judah was naturally insulated on its eastern front. The prophet Isaiah heralds a time, however, when even the contorted and convoluted topography of the Judean wilderness will be made straight and flat, and when every rough place will be made smooth (40:3-4; cf. 41:18-20; 51:3; Baruch 5:7).

But the Judean mountain spine breaks off only slightly less sharply on the west. There a narrow, shallow trough (W. Ghurab, W. Sar) divides the heights of Judah from a distinct topographic region known as the Shephela ("foothills") (e.g., 1 Chron. 27:28; 2 Chron. 26:10; 28:18; Obad. 19). The Shephela region stretches from the Aijalon valley 30 miles south to a point east of Gaza; it covers an area about 6-8 miles wide and extends west to the edge of what were the Philistine cities of Gezer, Ekron, and Gath (cf. Map 42). Mainly composed of soft limestone with a rolling surface sloping westward and intersected by several important and fertile wadies, the Shephela was the scene of a number of episodes of economic warfare in the Old Testament period (e.g., Judg. 15:4-5; 2 Sam. 23:11-12), representing as it did a buffer zone between the spine (occupied by Israelites) and the plain (occupied by Philistines). Actually, it may be that most of the contention between the Philistines and Israelites was triggered precisely by a desire to dominate the rich valleys of the Shephela. Since that time, the Shephela has functioned as a buffer during the struggles of the Maccabean rebellion (cf. 1 Macc. 3:16; 4:14f; 7:39), the Jewish revolts against Rome, the Crusades, and even in the 1948 war of independence (for the Shephela marked out, see Map 42).

The Negeb ("dryness") originally denoted the barren wilderness south of Judah (cf. Josh. 15:2-4; 18:19; 1 Sam. 27:10; 2 Sam. 24:7; Jer. 2:6). But in its evolution, the word came to refer to a compass point in the direction of barrenness ("south"), and hence it came to designate "south" of almost anywhere (e.g., Negeb of the Sea of Galilee, Josh. 11:2; Negeb of Jerusalem, Zech. 14:10; Negeb of the Cherethites [Philistia], 1 Sam. 30:14; Ezek. 25:15-16). The region of the Negeb constitutes an adverse environment to human activity or extensive settlement. It provides only the barest of existence for bedouin, who either pass through or possess fixed settlements in the northern parts. The Negeb is entirely dependent on rainfall, always scant and uncertain, for its water supply, though the territory has a few wells in the vicinity of Beersheba (cf. Gen. 26:23) and Kadesh-barnea (where the Israelites encamped during their wilderness wanderings; cf. Map 25). The northern Negeb extends from the Judean plateau to the wilderness of Zin, where the land is partially arable when receiving sufficient rainfall, especially in the basins of Beersheba and Arad. After the 1948 war, the northern Negeb began to be intersected by roadways and even a railway line. Therefore the agricultural settlement (*kibbutz*) movement founded a number of towns there (Sede Boqer, Yeroham, Oron, Dimona), which were soon followed by some industrial installations. Acacia trees are also somewhat plentiful in the northern Negeb (cf. Ex. 25-27; Deut. 10:3).

The central Negeb roughly corresponds to what is called in the Old Testament the wilderness of Zin (e.g., Num. 20:1; 34:3; Josh. 15:1). This region is generally hostile to human activities, and not even bedouin flocks can find satisfactory grazing in its barren rocklands. The central Negeb remains basically unsettled today, except for one small development town of Mitzpeh Ramon. On the other hand, sections of the central Negeb attest to ancient efforts in farming, apparently from the third century B.C. down to the Persian and Moslem conquests of the seventh century A.D. It is still not known who those farmers were or what induced them to settle there. Whatever the case, extant remains of that enterprise consist of ruins of six towns (Avedat, Haluza, Mamshit, Shivta, Nizzana, Rehovot), provisions for collecting and storing water (dams, cisterns, canals), and man-made fields. Along the slopes of hills (never on the bottom of a valley) were arranged heaps of stones of similar size and shape (20-40 inches high, 50-60 inches in diameter), placed in straight rows down the slopes, spaced at intervals of 8-11 yards apart. Hundreds of thousands of those stones have been discovered and though their purpose remains unclear, it appears likely they represent an effort to remove obstacles from the slopes and thus to accelerate the soil wash and to increase the silting of the valley floor, where crops could be grown (cf. Ps. 126, which describes farming in the Negeb).

The southern Negeb, conforming more or less to the wilderness of Paran in the Bible (e.g., Num. 10:12; Deut. 1:1), is the most barren of all regions in this zone. Only the most saline vegetation intermittently occurs within its watercourses, and no useful minerals have been discovered until the present.

Jordan Rift Valley. The dominant geological forces that have sculptured the landscape of the whole of Canaan are most apparent in zone three: the Jordan Rift Valley. In fact, the story of this valley is much more extensive than even Canaan itself. For the Jordan Rift Valley is but part of one of the longest, deepest, and widest fissures in the earth's surface, otherwise known as the Afro-Arabian Rift Valley. A sunken block confined by two parallel geologic fault lines (see Map 8 and picture), this cleavage represents the most important continental rift system currently known to geologists; most likely it marks the splitting and slow separation of an underlying geological plate. The fault lines actually extend over a distance of 4,000 miles, beginning in the Amanus Mountains of southeastern Turkey and continuing southward through western Syria (the Ghab), Lebanon (the Beqa'), Israel (the Jordan Rift Valley), as far as the Red Sea. The fracture continues southward on a line that runs parallel to the Red Sea as far as Ethiopia, where it splits. An eastern rift separates the Arabian peninsula from the "horn of Africa"; a western branch begins a diagonal penetration of Ethiopia, Kenya, Uganda, Tanzania, Malawi, and Mozambique. Known in those parts as "the Great African Rift Valley," this geological gash has been responsible for creating most of the elongated lakes of East Africa (Rudolph, Albert, Edward, Kivu, Tanganyika, Nyasa), and is responsible for shaping Lake Victoria and for severing the island of Madagascar from continental Africa. Chiseled here into the earth's crust is one fault line that extends continuously over more than 4,000 miles, across 60 degrees of latitude, or 1/6 of the earth's circumference.

At its deepest point, which is in Israel near the shores of the Dead Sea, the rift descends below sea level to more than 24,000 feet. By this I mean that the unconsolidated deposits laid down by the Jordan River are estimated to overlay bedrock down to that sub-level. Were one to begin digging at some places along the shores of the Dead Sea, he would encounter only sedimentary alluvium down to 24,000 feet below sea level, where finally rock stratification would be met.

What is more, for Israel the Jordan rift represents only what might be called the "parent fissure." For fanning out in every direction from this primary fault line are scores of secondary fractures that virtually make a geologic mosaic of Israel. Some of those branches have themselves created lateral valleys (e.g., Harod, Fari'a, Jezreel/Esdraelon). According to seismographic registrations, between 200 and 300 tremors are recorded on a daily basis in Israel. The vast majority of those are humanly undetectable, but occasionally a devastating earthquake strikes this land. The medieval chronicler Nowairi recorded an earthquake said to have jolted Israel during the night of December 7-8, 1267, in which part of the cliff aligning the Jordan River collapsed at Damiya (located approxi-

MAP 8 FAULT LINE

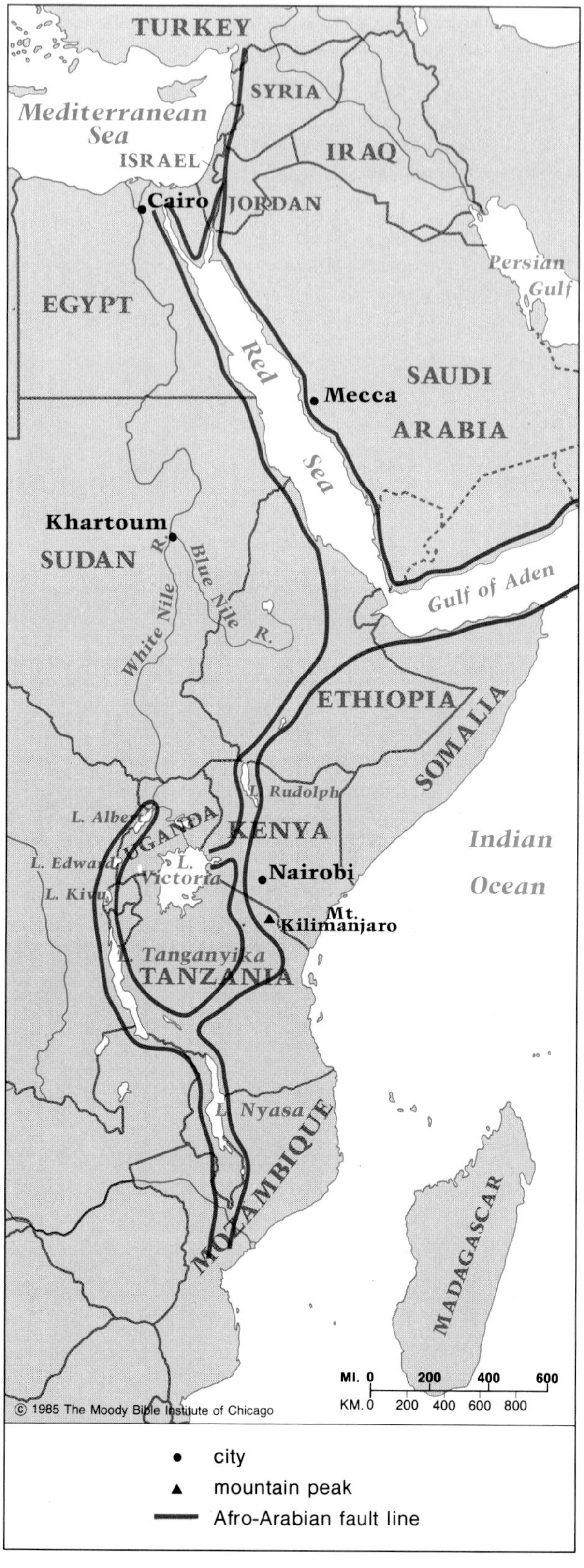

● city
▲ mountain peak
▬ Afro-Arabian fault line

mately 17 miles north of Jericho at the confluence of the Jabbok and Jordan rivers), damming up the Jordan for some 10 hours.[57] On January 1, 1837, a severe earthquake (i.e., one that registers the force of 9 or more on the Mercalli-Sieberg scale of 12 degrees) containing multiple epicenters struck Israel. In Galilee, 4,000 citizens of the city of Zefat were killed, with 1,000 casualties in the surrounding regions; the entire village of Gush Halav was destroyed. In central Israel, two streets of houses completely disappeared at Nablus (Shechem), and a hotel collapsed at Jericho, causing additional casualties. The two ends of what is known today as the Allenby Bridge were displaced. Even more than 100 miles away in Amman, much damage was reported from the quake.[58]

Another severe earthquake, also with multiple epicenters, occurred on the afternoon of July 11, 1927, at Kafr Kanna (4 miles northeast of Nazareth), Nablus, and Reina (near Bethlehem). Again, reports indicate the collapse of a 150-foot high wall of earth beside the Jordan near Damiya. That collapse carried with it the roadway and completely dammed up the river for 21 1/2 hours.[59] Parenthetically, it should be noted that the Jordan River was also said to have been "stopped" at the town of Damiya (Adam) during the days of the biblical conquest (Josh. 3:16). The last major quake to strike Israel occurred on September 13, 1954. Once again its multiple epicenters spread throughout much of central and south Israel, and it caused extensive damage in both Israel and Jordan.[60]

Those events are examples of geologic disturbance of catastrophic proportions. For instance, before its waters were harnessed earlier this century, the Jordan River discharged approximately 19.4 billion cubic feet of water into the Dead Sea annually. That is to say, the average annual flow of the Jordan was nearly half that of the Colorado River in the western United States. One finds it difficult to ponder such a magnitude of earth convulsion as to restrain such a huge volume of water over an extended period of time.

Having surveyed the Jordan rift as a whole, we now examine its several parts through which the Jordan River flowed. At an altitude of 9,232 feet above sea level, Mt. Hermon receives an annual precipitation of 60 inches and remains snow-covered throughout a great part of the year (cf. Jer. 18:14). Cascading from its side or percolating from its base is water from hundreds of springs that join to form three streams of the Jordan River's headwaters. Issuing from the western side of Mt. Hermon opposite the Lebanese village of Hasbiyya is the river Senir (Nahr al-Hasbani), rising near the foot of the biblical site of Dan is the river Dan (Nahr al-Qadi), and emerging from caves near the modern town of Banyas is the river Hermon (Nahr al-Baniyas). By the time it finally merges to form a single watercourse at Lake Hula, the water has already descended to an altitude of not more than 300 feet above the level of the sea.

A shallow marsh and papyrus jungle during the biblical epoch, Lake Hula would have represented a swampy obstruction to travel. When it was incorporated into the state of Israel as part of the 1947 partition plan, the Hula basin remained a malaria-infested swamp. But as it was drained and the water of the river was diverted along its western flank during the 1950s, an agricultural bonanza similar to that found on the coastal plain was discovered. The Hula today is a rich agricultural region—the soil there is capable of yielding up to ten crops per year at places. Recently it has been ascertained, however, that draining the Hula has created an ecological imbalance in the Sea of Galilee. Apparently the swampiness had acted as a sort of natural filter that strained out certain algae, as well as chemicals pumped up through the fault chasm.

The Sea of Galilee (e.g., Matt. 4:18; 15:29; Mark 1:16; 7:31; John 6:1), or as it is otherwise known, "Kinneret" (e.g., Deut. 3:17; Josh. 19:35), "Gennesar" (e.g., Luke 5:1; 1 Macc. 11:67; cf. nearby town called "Gennesaret" [Matt. 14:34; Mark 6:53]), "Tiberias" (e.g., John 6:1; 21:1), or simply "the Sea" (e.g., Luke 5:2; John 6:16), is a fresh-water inland lake measuring approximately 13 miles north/south, 8 miles east/west, and 165 feet in depth. The name *Galilee* is derived from the political territory contiguous to its northwestern shores, though the meaning of the name remains something of a mystery ("ring, artichoke, harp"). The Sea of Galilee is flanked by the highlands of lower Galilee and the Golan Heights, which drop off steeply to its shoreline. Actually, the Sea rests in the caldera or crater of an extinct volcano. In high antiquity, that volcano spewed its lava over the adjacent countryside, thereby creating the black basaltic rock characteristically found on the surface of the surrounding terrain. Situated at some 700 feet below sea level on the floor of this crater, the Sea of Galilee is the lowest body of sweet water on earth.

Figure 8 Africa and Saudi Arabia divided by Red Sea, with gulfs of Suez and Aqaba at top. Nile R. north of Khartoum in foreground.

The shores along the Sea must have been alive with activity throughout the biblical period. The international highway from Egypt to Babylon passed immediately along its western shores south of Capernaum, which points to an extremely early human occupation of the area, perhaps as early as 8000 B.C. It was in the Roman era, however, that the human utilization of the region reached a peak. The rabbis stated: "The Lord has created seven seas, but the sea of Gennesaret is His delight." It also delighted Herod Antipas, who constructed along its shore the city of Tiberias, with its castle, temple, bathhouses, and theaters. Then again, hot baths were constructed at Hammath, a hippodrome at Taricheae, a theater and acropolis at Gadara, together with a host of villas, many paved streets, and archways. In the time of Jesus, the region surrounding the Sea was thus experiencing relative affluence.

That affluence is reflected in some incidents of the gospels that took place near the Sea of Galilee. For instance, Jesus' parable concerning a rich fool who thought it advisable to tear down his barns and to build bigger ones was uttered along the shores of the Sea (Luke 12:16-21). Similarly, the parable of the wheat and tares was predicated upon the affluence of a householder who possessed barns and servants (Mark 13:24-37; cf. 1:20; John 4:47). As part of the Sermon on the Mount, Jesus addressed the subjects of giving many alms and of laying up earthly treasures (Mark 6:1-13). And Jesus' famous words spoken to the multitude in the vicinity of Caesarea-Philippi—"What does it profit a man to gain the whole world and to lose his own soul?"—were addressed to Galilean listeners, some of whom undoubtedly had experienced great gain (Mark 8:27-37; Luke 9:23-25).

Separating the Sea of Galilee and the Dead Sea are only 65 airline miles. Here the sunken rift, sometimes called the Ghor, varies in width from 2-4 miles, though it widens at the Beth-shan and Jericho basins. Within that distance, however, the Jordan River meanders for more than 200 miles, all below sea level, twisting circuitously through the Zor, a hollowed-out bed in the floor of the rift. Wrapped in a mantle of tamarisk, willow, cane, and oleander thickets, the Zor ("thicket") seems to have served as a habitat for beasts of prey during the biblical period (cf. "jungle" of Jordan, Jer. 12:5; 49:19; 50:44; Zech. 11:3); numerous passages suggest that it was infested with raging beasts (e.g., 1 Sam. 17:34-35 [by implication]; 2 Kings 2:24; 17:25; Job 40:15-18; Jer. 5:6; Amos 3:4; Mark 1:13; cf. Ezek. 34:25); many Arabic towns in the Jordan valley appear to bear names of beasts; the Medeba map depicts a lion on the prowl in the valley; skeletal remains of beasts have been found on the valley floor. Notwithstanding, and even though the Jordan has never been navigable and no sizeable city has yet been built on its banks, one must not suppose that the valley was never settled. Archaeologists have discovered ample evidence to the contrary, in the form of skeletal and occupational remains. Contemporary water conservation projects have rendered the Jordan no more than 60 feet in width, yet it would have represented in Bible times a formidable barrier, presumably crossed by swimming (passages in which the Jordan was crossed by this means include Judg. 3:28; 6:33; 1 Sam. 13:7; 2 Sam. 17:22; 24:5; Matt. 3:13).

Between the point where the river emerges from the Sea and the Beth-shan basin, the Jordan drops in altitude at the approximate rate of 40 feet per mile, thus contributing to its rapid acceleration and unattractive character. One prominent geographer describes the riverbed as follows:

> There are hardly less ugly mudbanks, from two to twenty-five feet high, with an occasional bed of shingle, that is not clean and sparkling as in our rivers, but foul with ooze and slime. Dead driftwood is everywhere in sight. Large trees lie about, overthrown: and the exposed roots and lower trunks of the trees still standing are smeared with mud, save where they have been torn by passing wreckage. There are, however, open spaces, where the river flashes to the hills above and an easy path is possible to its edge. But in the lower reaches this is mostly where the earth is too salty to sustain vegetation; and so it may be said that [the] Jordan sweeps to the Dead Sea through unhealthy jungle relieved only by poisonous soil.[61]

Some scholars have suggested that this swiftness of current may even be reflected in the name *Jordan* itself. According to this theory, the term derives from a verb meaning "to descend," and hence Jordan means "the descender, downcomer." In any event, more than one Christian, desiring to be baptized in the Jordan River like Jesus, have been happily rescued from the current some miles downstream. On the other hand, it is little wonder that Naaman objected so strongly to dipping in the Jordan, preferring the crystal-clear waters of the Abana or Pharpar rivers back in Damascus (2 Kings 5:11-12).

The Dead Sea measures some 53 miles in length and 10 miles in width, and it is divided into two basins by a 9-mile "Lisan" peninsula, which juts out from the eastern shore. The northern basin is larger and, at its deepest point in the northeastern sector, a water depth of approximately 1,300 feet has been measured. The southern basin, on the other hand, is much shallower, with a water depth fluctuating between 3 and 30 feet. With the recent lowering of the level of the Dead Sea, part of the floor of the southern basin now lies exposed, just as it was possibly unoccupied by water throughout a portion of the biblical period.

It is difficult to describe adequately the foreboding desolation and howling barrenness along the shores of the Dead Sea. It seems as if the very forces of nature have conspired against this torrid chasm, but we recall again that this is a land that has been delicately sculptured by a sovereign God who intended that its components should foster faith. To begin with, at 1,300 feet below sea level, this is the lowest point on earth. By way of comparison, the great Turfan depression in northwestern China is only 490 feet below sea level at its lowest point—beside L. Bojaite; the salt fields in the Qattara depression of the Sahara Desert plunge only to a depth of 435 feet below sea level; and Death Valley in California lies only at 282 feet below the sea. If there could be fixed in one's mind the image of the almost-painful sterility of the Sahara or of Death Valley, and then multiply that by a factor of four or more, one might come close to capturing the geographical reality to which he is exposed along the shores of the Dead Sea, or Salt Sea, as it is known in the Old Testament (e.g., Gen. 14:3; Num. 34:3; Deut. 3:17; Josh. 15:2; 18:19; see also the "Sea of the Arabah," Deut. 3:17; 4:49; Josh. 3:16; 12:3; 2 Kings 14:25; or the "Eastern/Former Sea," Ezek. 47:18; Joel 2:20; Zech. 14:8).

It has been calculated that the numerous wadies and four perennial rivers that feed the Dead Sea represent an average daily inflow of 7 million tons of water, yet the Sea possesses no outlet for this water except through evaporation. Because those conditions are coupled with relative aridity (it receives an annual rainfall of 2-4 inches) and enormous proportions of heat (the mercury sometimes soars as high as 125 degrees F.), there is regularly created an extremely high rate of evaporation and dense haze that on occasion is impenetrable to the eye.

What is more, most of the streams feeding the Dead Sea are unusually saline, flowing through nitrous soil and sulphurous springs. At the same time, openings in the floor of the Sea permit chemicals (sulphur, bromine, magnesium, potassium, calcium, iodine) to be pumped up from underlying fault crevices. Located on the floor of the Sea are extremely high concentrations of sodium chloride. It is estimated that the lower waters of the Dead Sea have been fossilized from the dense chemical content: those waters have remained permanently at the bottom of the Sea since before the beginning of biblical times. Along the Dead Sea's shores are extensive sulphur deposits and petroleum springs. In the southeastern corner, moreover, there is exposed a 300-foot-thick rock-salt ridge, which is only the tip of an estimated 4,500-foot salt plug that stretches for 5 miles.

All of those factors combine to produce a total salinity of 26-35 percent, which means that the Dead Sea is the earth's most saline water body. By way of contrast, the Great Salt Lake (Utah) is only 18 percent salt, and the average ocean salinity is a mere 3.5 percent. Obviously, the Dead Sea is devoid of all aquatic life, aside from a few bacteria and parasites that can survive there, and it undergoes an ever-increasing solidarity.[62]

There have been times throughout history, however, when the minerals in the Dead Sea have caused the surrounding real estate to increase in value. In antiquity, the Sea was sought out for its bitumen, a commodity prized for waterproofing properties and consisting of petroleum hardened through evaporation and oxidation. During the New Testament era, Dead Sea bitumen trade was apparently controlled by Nabateans, who also exported the product to Egypt, where it was used in embalming (the Egyptian word *mummy* originally meant "bitumen"). It has been suggested that Cleopatra's desire to govern the Dead Sea region was stimulated by her eagerness to regulate bitumen trade. The twentieth century has witnessed the emergence of yet another important mineral—potash (an essential element in the manufacturing of chemical fertilizer). Though two potash plants had earlier been constructed by the Israelis and subsequently seized by Jordanian forces in the war of independence, the state of Israel in 1952 decided to resume potash extraction. It founded the Dead Sea Works and undertook to construct a highway from Beersheba to the Dead Sea. This undertaking has signalled both a revitalization of potash production at the Sea and the erection of numerous settlements in the Negeb. In such a context, it may be stated that the Dead Sea is coming to life for the first time in modern history.

In antiquity, however, the ominous description of the Dead Sea chasm is reflected in the pages of biblical history. The events of Genesis 19, dealing with the destruction of Sodom and Gomorrah, transpired in vicinity of the Sea. Mt. Sedom, the previously-mentioned salt plug located at the southeast corner of the Sea, is quite likely a reflex form of the name Sodom. Though the exact nature of the destruction rained upon Sodom and Gomorrah has been variously interpreted either as a volcanic eruption or a spontaneous explosion of subsurface pockets of bitumenous soil, karstic salt pillars, known as "Lot's wife," are frequent phenomena in the Dead Sea area.

It is almost predictable that the howling wilderness surrounding the Dead Sea should provide a suitable refuge for the fugitive David (1 Sam. 21-

31), the contemplative company of Qumran Essenes, and the disenfranchised Jewish insurgents of the second Jewish rebellion. It was in barrenness like this that Jesus was confronted with His temptation (Matt. 4:1); perhaps such dismal surroundings contributed to the anguish He felt. On the other hand, Ezekiel (47:1-12; cf. Zech. 14:8) envisioned a time when even the brinish waters of the Dead Sea will be recreated afresh and the stark lifeless character of the water will issue forth in life.

South of the Dead Sea, the Great Rift Valley forms a rounded trough that narrows to the Gulf of Aqaba. There it begins to broaden again toward the Red Sea, and the Gulf is flanked by craggy slopes and high cliffs that rise in excess of 2,500 feet. Then again, there are places along the Aqaba not more than a mile from those cliffs where the water depth exceeds 6,000 feet.

Transjordanian plateau. The elevated plateau flanking the Jordan rift and the Arabah is designated in the Bible as "beyond the Jordan" (e.g., Gen. 50:10; Num. 22:1; Deut. 1:5; Josh. 1:14; 1 Sam. 31:7; 1 Chron. 12:37) and in modern history as "Transjordan." As a whole, the physical topography of Transjordan is more uniform in character than that of Cisjordan. The high tableland of Transjordan stretches about 250 miles from Mt. Hermon to the Red Sea, is between 30 and 80 miles in width, and rises to heights of 5,000 feet above sea level. It receives significant precipitation, creating deep gorges through which four important rivers flow: the Yarmuk, Jabbok, Arnon, and Zered. Overlaying a sandstone foundation that is exposed in those four cavernous ravines and in a few southern sections, the surface of the Transjordanian highlands is composed chiefly of limestone in the north, with a thin basalt covering north of the Yarmuk. The highlands continue southward by granite outcroppings that form the eastern wall of the Arabah. In the agricultural season, therefore, the northern regions are fertile, and the well-watered soil can produce large supplies of various grains, especially wheat (cf. Ps. 22:12; Ezek. 39:18; Amos 4:1). In the Roman period, this northern region served as a breadbasket for the Syro-Palestinian province. East of the watershed, which lies at a level of about 3,000 feet and at a distance of 15-40 miles from the Jordan rift, there develops a rather rapid transition from steppe to the eastern desert. Many parts of the western Gilead dome, for instance, are rich in brooks and springs with good drinking water, whereas east of the watershed, cisterns are the order of the day. The seasonal lushness of grain fields gives way to intermittent shallow grasses foraged by migrating flocks of nomads.

Geology. The broad outlines of Palestine's geological history can be reconstructed from rock formations that outcrop primarily in areas south of the Dead Sea and in eastern Sinai, in the walls of the Arabah, and in the canyons cut by Transjordanian rivers, and from rocks encountered through modern drilling efforts for water or oil, and through mining shafts, and in particular around Timna. This list suggests widespread activities of immense proportion and complexity, much too complicated to warrant full discussion here. Nevertheless, because part of the story of how God prepared the Promised Land for His chosen people is intricately linked to the creation of mountains and valleys (e.g., Deut. 8:7; 11:11; Ps. 65:6; 90:2; cf. Rev. 6:14), I offer a brief and simplified sketch of the geological processes by which Palestine's landscape appears to have been fashioned.

> Thou didst set the earth on its foundations,
> so that it can never be shaken.
> Thou didst cover it with the deep as with a garment;
> the waters stood above the mountains.
> But at Thy rebuke they fled;
> at the sound of Thy thunder they took to flight.
> The mountains rose, the valleys sank down
> to the place which Thou didst appoint for them.
> Thou didst set a boundary which they should not pass,
> so that they might not again cover the earth.
>
> Ps. 104:5-9

The entire region of Palestine lies along the shattered edge of an ancient land mass upon which rest Arabia and northeast Africa today. Over this basement platform of metamorphosed igneous (volcanic) rocks (i.e., granite, porphyry, diorite, and the like), there were deposited successive layers of sandstone formations. It would appear that Palestine's southern and eastern sectors were exposed to such depositions for lengthier and more frequent periods, as sandstone formations in southeastern Transjordan are measured in thousands of feet, whereas they are much thinner in the north and in Cisjordan.

Later, in what many geologists call the "great Cretaceous transgression," the whole region was gradually and repeatedly submerged in water from an ocean, of which the present Mediterranean Sea is but a vestige, and there began to be deposited several varieties of limestone formations (i.e., sedimentary strata laid down under water). This transgression (extension of an ocean over the land), actually a recurring series of transgressions, caused by slow movements in the earth's surface, produced the greater part of rocks exposed in modern Israel. These include Cenomanian, Turonian, Senonian, and Eocene deposits. (This identifying terminology is generally used, regardless of a geologist's acceptance or rejection of the geologic

GEOLOGY OF PALESTINE

MAP 9

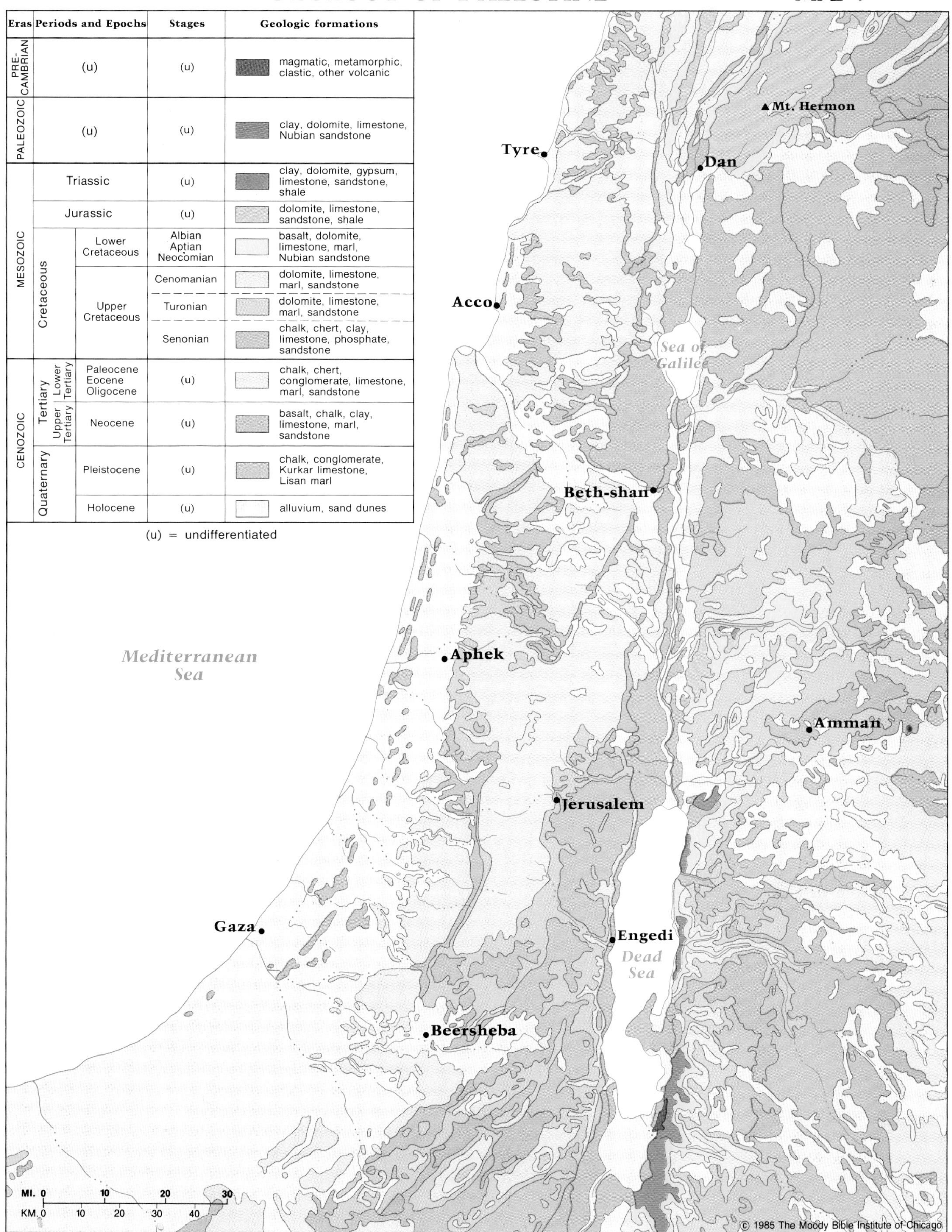

Figure 9 Rock specimens of Palestine: (1) Granite, (2) Cenomanian limestone, (3) Turonian limestone, (4) Eocene limestone, (5) Senonian chalk embedded with Flint, (6) Senonian chalk, (7) Sandstone, (8) Kurkar limestone, (9) Chert, (10) Basalt, and (11) Flint.

table.) The lower Cenomanian and Turonian deposits are the hardest (i.e., they contain greater concentrations of silica and calcium), and are therefore more resistant to erosion, impermeable to water (and are thus a source of springs and cisterns), and excellent for building purposes. Those hard limestones weather at an estimated rate of only one centimeter of surface rock per one thousand years into a deep, rich red soil (*terra rossa*). Its reddish hue is attributable to a minimal iron content of 10 percent, and terra rossa is quite porous and quick to absorb and hold precipitation. Unfortunately, however, this fertile topsoil erodes at a more rapid rate, and much of it has washed off the parent (mountain) formations into surrounding valleys. The more recent Eocene deposits are chalkier and mixed with layers of dark, hard flint, sometimes interlaced with thinly-bedded chert (almost pure silica) or coin-shaped fossils. However, where they exhibit a high calcium content, as in the case of the Shephela, Eocene limestones weather into a *brown alluvium* soil.

Though theoretically less rich than terra rossa, brown alluvium supports a wider range of crops and trees, is easier to till, is less affected by runoff, and thus has deeper and more heavily textured deposits. Accordingly, farmers generally prefer it to terra rossa (cf. the agricultural warfare waged between the Philistines and Israelites for control of the Shephela). Cenomanian uplifted formations are commonly framed on their flanks by narrow strips of Senonian rock, the weakest form of limestone. Senonian consists largely of clays, phosphates, and carbonated lime. It offers very little resistance to erosion, thus producing flatter and generally smooth landscapes. By comparing the geology and road maps, for example (see Maps 9 and 19), one can observe just how many of the Senonian valleys have provided roadways for Israel (e.g., West Hula to the Sea of Galilee; the ascent of Beth-horon; the Mt. Carmel passes of Jokneam, Megiddo, and Taanach; the moat separating the Shephela from the central spine; the diagonal trough from Shechem to Beth-shan). In a word, then, from Cenomanian and Turonian strata there emerge mountains, sometimes high and precipitous, making them attractive to masons and city-dwellers. Eocene formations can erode to form fertile valleys, attractive to farmers and vinedressers. Senonian deposits weather into flat valleys, which prove attractive to travelers.

The effects of this geologic transgression are more apparent in the north and west, suggesting a

Soils of Palestine

MAP 10

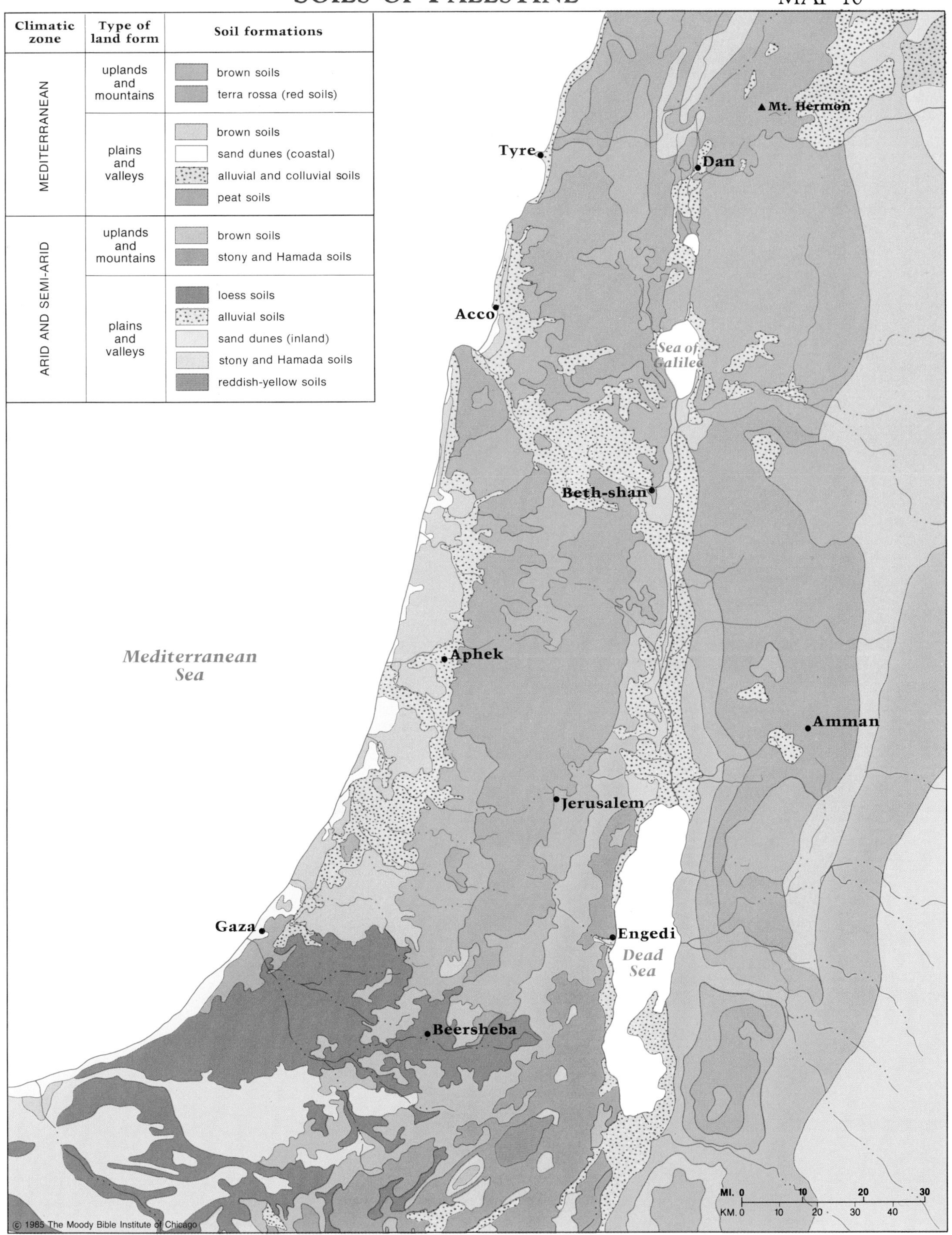

gradual, if periodic, receding of the ocean. For example, hard limestone stratification is as thick as 3,000-3,200 feet in northern Cisjordan (with even thicker deposits in Lebanon). The limestone is relatively thin in northern Transjordan, and it fades out altogether in southern Transjordan. Likewise, Transjordanian Eocene deposits are no more than 300 feet in thickness, whereas they range between 650-1,000 feet in the Jordan rift and at some points west.

In the next phase, a violent fracturing took place, which became the principal phase of mountain building in the country. The main activity took place along the Alpine-Himalayan chain, but especially in Turkey (Taurus and Pontus mountains) and Iran (Zagros and Urartu mountains), creating the Mediterranean, Black and Caspian seas. All of that activity was probably caused by the shifting of subsurface geological plates on which rests the continental basement stratification. At any rate, here is where the Jordan rift began to be sharply outlined, first in a series of three separate basins (Hula-Tiberias [from the foothills of Mt. Hermon down to the Jordan-Jabbok confluence]; Dead Sea; and Aqaba). Accompanying and following those continental pulsations was volcanic activity, which, in that instance, was responsible for covering the land around the Sea of Galilee and the Hauran dome as far northeast as Damascus with sheets of basaltic lava. It also created a basalt dam between the Hula and the Sea of Galilee, thus forming a fourth basin. It is probable that the mountain uplift that resulted from fracturing was also responsible for placing the Mediterranean coastline not far from its present location.

The final act of this geologic drama saw the creation of a large lake, called the Lisan, which inundated the terrain of the Jordan Rift Valley lower than 650 feet below sea level, that is to say, the area from the northern end of the Sea of Galilee to a point about 25 miles south of the present Dead Sea. Formed during a pluvial period (i.e., an era in which there were excessively heavy and extended rains), that brackish lake was responsible for laying down as much as 500 feet of the sedimentary strata found in the terrain it covered. During that time, the Transjordanian streams also carved out their deep, spectacular gorges. As the rains gradually diminished and evaporation lowered the level of the lake, thousands of thin (1 millimeter) salt-laden laminations (Lisan marl) were gradually uncovered. Alternately mixed with gypsum and dark calcite, those strata are the predominant characteristic of the southern rift and northern Arabah nowadays. During the pluvial period a thick accumulation of shale was deposited in the coastal plain, at some places totalling nearly 5,000 feet in depth, as were the so-called kurkar ridges, which today align the Mediterranean shoreline. Over those shale and dune layers in more recent times have been deposited soils of either alluvium (i.e., deriving from water erosion) or loess (i.e., deriving from wind erosion of desert dust), so commonly characteristic of the contemporary coastal plain.

Apart from properties of water storage and retention, Palestine's geologic structure yields little of value. Meager phosphates, sandstones, and gypsum may be found in certain localities, and the Dead Sea contains diverse salt solutions, including potash. But beyond those, Palestine's sedimentary layers are mineral poor and apparently lack petroleum supplies.

Hydrology. It is no accident that the chief deity of Egypt, Amon-Re, was a sun god, as was the head of the Mesopotamian pantheon, Marduk.[63] But the great god of Canaan, Baal, was a rain/fertility god. Herein lies a story with profound and far-reaching consequences for anyone wishing to live in Canaan, a story that controlled much of Canaanite life and society and at times even came to absorb Israelite thinking as well. The story is the direct reflection of certain hydrologic realities of the Promised Land.

Simply stated, it never needs to rain in Egypt or Mesopotamia. Each of those ancient lands was endowed with the rich heritage of a great river. From the Nile and Euphrates, Egyptian and Mesopotamian civilizations respectively drew their sustenance and life, irrigated their crops, and watered their flocks and herds. Each of those rivers offered a vast supply of fresh water, more than ever could have been consumed by the societies they fed and sustained. As long as there was sufficient precipitation hundreds of miles away in the mountains of Ethiopia and Uganda or in the rugged highlands of eastern Turkey, from which the mighty Nile and Euphrates respectively emerge, it never needed to rain in Egypt or much of Mesopotamia. In reality, it scarcely ever did! Survival in those parts depended upon nourishment from rivers that could be tapped and utilized in the greenhouse-like environment created along their banks by the warmth of the sun.

In Canaan, by way of sharp contrast, survival depended precisely upon rainfall. In the land of promise, there were no great rivers, and what meager river resources did exist were incapable of meeting society's needs. Certainly the Jordan River coursed through Canaan, but it lay at such a low altitude and was always so heavily laden with chemicals that its potential nourishment was lost to Canaanite society. Amidst the historical trend of civilizations that emerged along the banks of large rivers, the Jordan stands as a conspicuous

MOUNTAINS AND RIVERS OF PALESTINE

MAP 11

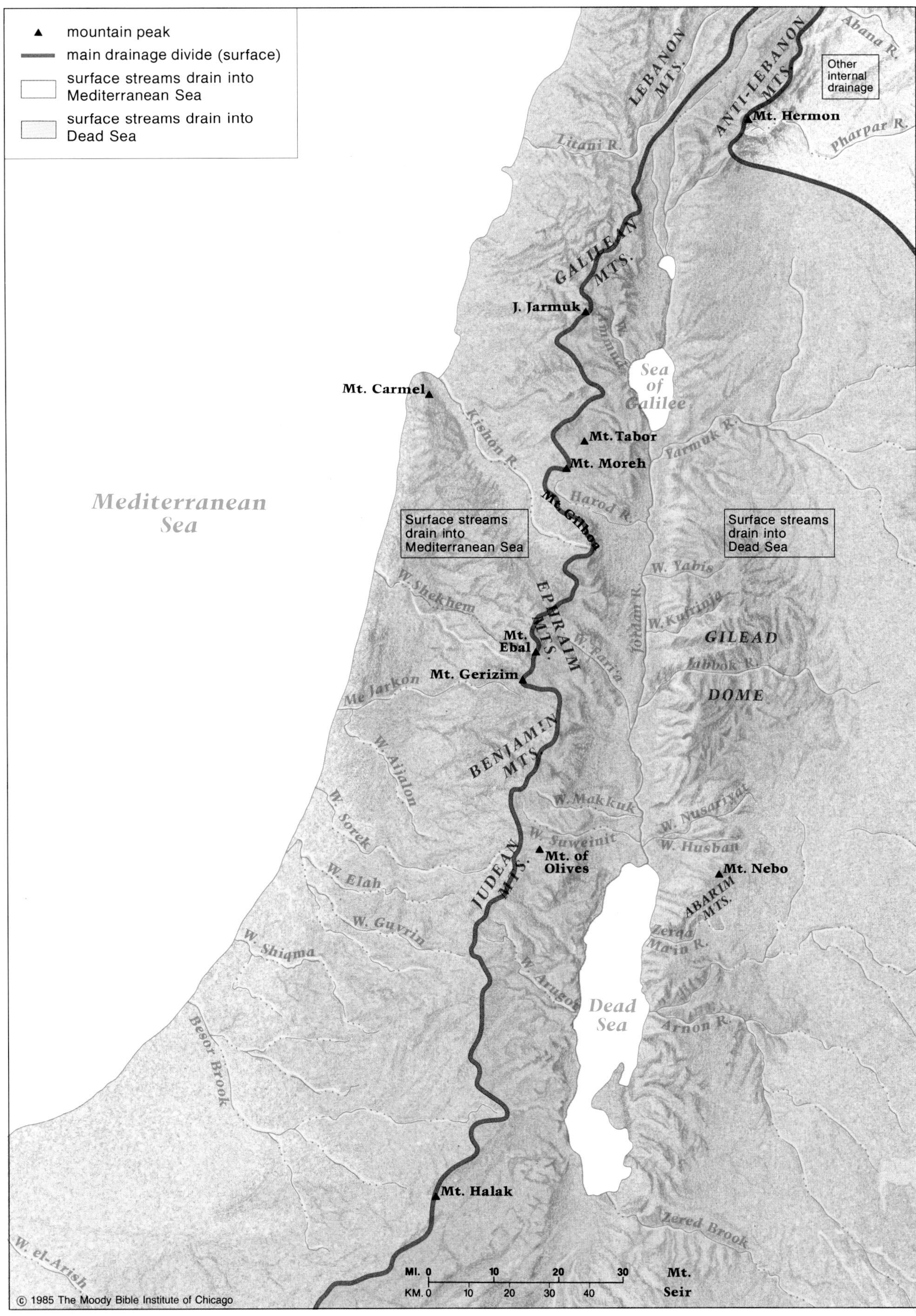

exception. But alas, beyond the Jordan, Canaan possessed only a trickle of river water. The Me Jarkon, which rises from springs near Aphek and flows into the Mediterranean north of Joppa, produced sufficient dampness in antiquity to force travel to its inland side, but not until the twentieth century were its resources finally tapped. The Kishon River, which drains part of the Jezreel valley before being emptied into the Mediterranean Sea at the Acco bay, is little more than a brook for much of the year. The Harod River, which enters the Jordan opposite Beth-shan, flows from a single spring at the foot of Mt. Gilboa.[64]

So it was that Canaanites, and even the covenant community of God itself, would in this land experience survival or death, crop success or failure, fertility or drought precisely as a consequence of storms that might deposit their rainfall upon a land that was otherwise incapable of sustaining human existence.

It is a recurring, even formulaic, pattern for the writers of Scripture to sermonize that faith produces blessing whereas disobedience results in condemnation. Perhaps at no other point than that of rainfall dependence is this pattern more forcefully underscored. For example, near to the inception of Israel's national existence at Sinai, the Lord instructed the nation concerning the consequences of faith: "If you . . . observe my commandments . . . then I will give you rains in their season, and the land shall yield its increase . . . but if you will not hearken to me . . . I will make your heavens like iron and your earth like brass . . . and your land shall not yield its increase" (Lev. 26:3-20).

Later, as the nation was about to embark on its mission of conquering the Promised Land, Moses' concluding exhortation to Israel included one of the most complete descriptions of the land's physical properties. There he said: "The land which you are entering to take possession of it is not like the land of Egypt, from which you have come, where you sowed your seed and watered it with your foot [referring either to a kind of water-lifting device operated by foot power or to irrigation sluice gates that could be raised by foot to permit water to flow into secondary channels], like a garden of vegetables; but the land which you are going over to possess is a land of hills and valleys, which drinks water by the rain from heaven, a land which the Lord your God cares for; the eyes of the Lord your God are always upon it, from the beginning of the year to the end of the year" (Deut. 11:10-12). The author then proceeded to contrast faith and fertility (vv. 13-15); his message was, in effect, that if the Israelites obeyed God's commands, He would send both the former and latter rains so that they could gather in grain, wine, and oil. But should their hearts prove faithless, in anger God would shut up the heavens and there would be no rain. It seems clear, then, that fertility became a function of faith, and that life itself in this particular terrain was imperiled by lack of rainfall, with its ensuing drought and famine.

Moreover, both of the above-quoted texts clearly sound a note that is echoed in many other passages, in each section and genre of biblical literature: namely, it is God who benevolently sustains life in the Promised Land by bestowing the blessing of rainfall (e.g., 2 Chron. 7:13-14; Job 5:10; 36:27-28; Pss. 65:9-13; 107:33; 135:7; 147:8; Isa. 30:23-26; Ezek. 34:26; Hos. 6:3; Amos 9:6; Zech. 10:1; Mal. 3:10; Matt. 5:45; Heb. 6:7), just as it is within His sovereign prerogative to withhold rainfall as a sign of His displeasure and judgment (e.g., 1 Kings 8:35-36; 17:1; Job 12:15; Isa. 5:6; Jer. 3:3; 14:1-6; Amos 4:7-8; Zech. 14:17). This theological reality was employed by writers of Scripture precisely because of the dynamic geographical implications that would have been all-too-evident to those attempting to survive in Canaan. Those passages plainly declare that fertility in Canaan must be attributed to a caring and benevolent God; for the ancient Israelite, then, rainfall was a providentially conditioned factor.

At certain times in Israel's history, in fact, God became so displeased with their behavior that He withheld from them both rain *and dew* (e.g., Gen. 27:39; 2 Sam. 1:21; 1 Kings 17:1; Hag. 1:10-11.[65] Certainly few North American or European farmers will experience crop success or failure owing to the presence or absence of dew. In ancient Israel where water was so scarce and unavailable except from the heavens, however, crop success in certain seasons depended precisely upon the formation of dew. That was especially true in the early autumn when the grapes and figs were ripening just prior to the start of the "former rains."

Some scholars have even asserted, and I believe with good reason, that the close interconnection between precipitation, faith, and life may best explain why Israelites living in the Promised Land could have so quickly and rather completely apostatized. No generation of Israelites before Christ experienced in a more convincing manner the element of divine miracle than did those individuals who participated in the conquest. Yet their children and grandchildren became so thoroughly enamored of Canaanite Baalism that their syncretism became the dismally recurring theme of the book of Judges. That later generation regrettably left Moses' exhortation unheeded, and they found themselves to be practicing Canaanites—people who sought to guarantee a sufficient rainfall through the practices of the Fertility Cult.

The key to understanding Canaanite Baalism, or the Fertility Cult, may be found in a central guiding principle: it was committed to a cyclical (i.e., not a linear) interpretation of history, in which the phenomenal world, namely the forces of nature, were personified. Because of that, proponents of Baalism could not appreciate that the seasons were rhythmic and mechanically regular; for them, such seasonal recurrence was seen in terms of cosmic struggles. Hence, when the dry springtime season commenced, with its ensuing cessation of rainfall and death of vegetation, they inferred that the god of sterility (Mot) had killed his opponent Baal. On the other hand, when in the autumn the early rains began to fall, so that seeds could be planted and crops later harvested, Baalism inferred that the god of fertility (Baal) had been resurrected and restored to prominence.[66]

Moreover, Canaanite Baalism's failure to perceive that seasonal variation was governed by the inevitability of natural law led it to believe that the outcome of those cosmic struggles could be humanly manipulated. Thus, if the Canaanites wished their deities to perform certain actions, they believed they could ensure the gods' response by performing the same actions themselves in a cultic setting, a practice known today as "sympathetic magic." To that end, the Canaanites sought to ensure the ongoing triumph of Baal, which for them would have been tantamount to an enduring fertility, by means of the sacred prostitute. The role of that sacred personage, either male or female, was thought integral to anticipate, induce, and participate with Baal's intercourse with the earth (rainfall was his semen). And when Baal triumphed, women would be fertile, flocks and herds would reproduce in abundance, and fields would be standing full of grain. So it was with Canaan's fertility worship.

It was precisely against the wholesale adoption of that abomination that Moses had inveighed (Deut. 4-26). Yet despite his injunctions, the impact of the hydrologic factors under discussion apparently led the Israelites to suppose that they too needed Canaanite rites to survive in a land that was so rainfall dependent (e.g., 1 Sam. 12:2-18; 1 Kings 14:24; 2 Kings 23:7; 2 Chron. 15:16; Jer. 3:2-5; Ezek. 8:14; 23:37-45). Moreover, Israel soon attributed the good gifts of the land to Baal, not Yahweh (Isa. 1:3-9; Hos. 2:5-13), and eventually the Israelites went so far as to call Yahweh "Baal" (Hos. 2:16). Accordingly, one is enabled to understand that the biblical theme of "playing the harlot" represented more than just a theological metaphor and that the degeneracy of Baalism in the end contributed to Israel's defeat and exile (cf. Jer. 2:7; 5:18-28; 9:12-16; Ezek. 6:1-7).

It is well to bear in mind that even the characteristic expression used in the Bible to describe the land of promise—"a land flowing with milk and honey"—addresses the issue of rainfall dependence and contrasts life in Canaan with that in Egypt (e.g., Ex. 3:8, 17; cf. Deut. 11:9-12; Ezek. 20:6; and other passages). Modern Westerners are apt to see in this phrase the connotation of lush fertility and abundance, of a veritable paradise or luxuriant Garden of Eden. But it is quite another picture the Bible is actually painting by using that expression. To begin with, the commodities involved were pastoral in character—goats' milk and probably bees' honey (Judg. 14:8; Prov. 24:13; cf. Isa. 7:15)—in contrast to the agricultural commodities known from Egypt, which included cucumbers, melons, leeks, onions, and garlic (Num. 11:5). This lends credence to the supposition that the expression should be understood as a *pastoral* metaphor, one that tells of the uncertainty and vulnerability of the life of a wandering shepherd or itinerant farmer. Life in the land of Egypt, contrariwise, would then be seen to represent the refuge and security offered a sedentary farmer.

So it is that *flowing* becomes the pivotal word in the expression. Canaan is described as a "flowing" land of milk and honey as God showers His blessing upon it in response to Israel's obedience and faith (e.g., Num. 14:8; Deut. 6:3; 11:9; Josh. 5:6; Jer. 11:5; 32:22), which brings us again to the intertwined notions of faith and fertility. Employing some of those same terms, the prophet Joel described how God's people would someday be restored: "In that day, the mountains shall drip sweet *wine*, and the hills shall *flow* with *milk*, and all the *stream beds* of Judah shall *flow* with *water*; and a *fountain* shall come forth from the house of the Lord and *water* the valley of Shittim" (3:18, italics added). Job used such terms as he reflected upon God's faithfulness in prospering him: "My steps were washed with *milk*, and the rock poured out to me *streams* of *oil*" (29:6, italics added). Conversely, when Zophar detailed the misery that awaited the wicked, he declared: "He [the wicked] will not look upon *rivers*, or *streams flowing with honey and curdled milk*" (Job 20:17, italics added). Accordingly, I share the opinion that to say the Promised Land will "flow" with milk and honey is to declare that it is a place that will experience fertility as a function of faith and as a consequence of obedience. It is to declare that showers from heaven will be responsible for creating a land that will "flow" with prosperity and fertility. It is to see once again that this land has been specially molded by a sovereign God.

MAP 12 # Rainfall of Palestine

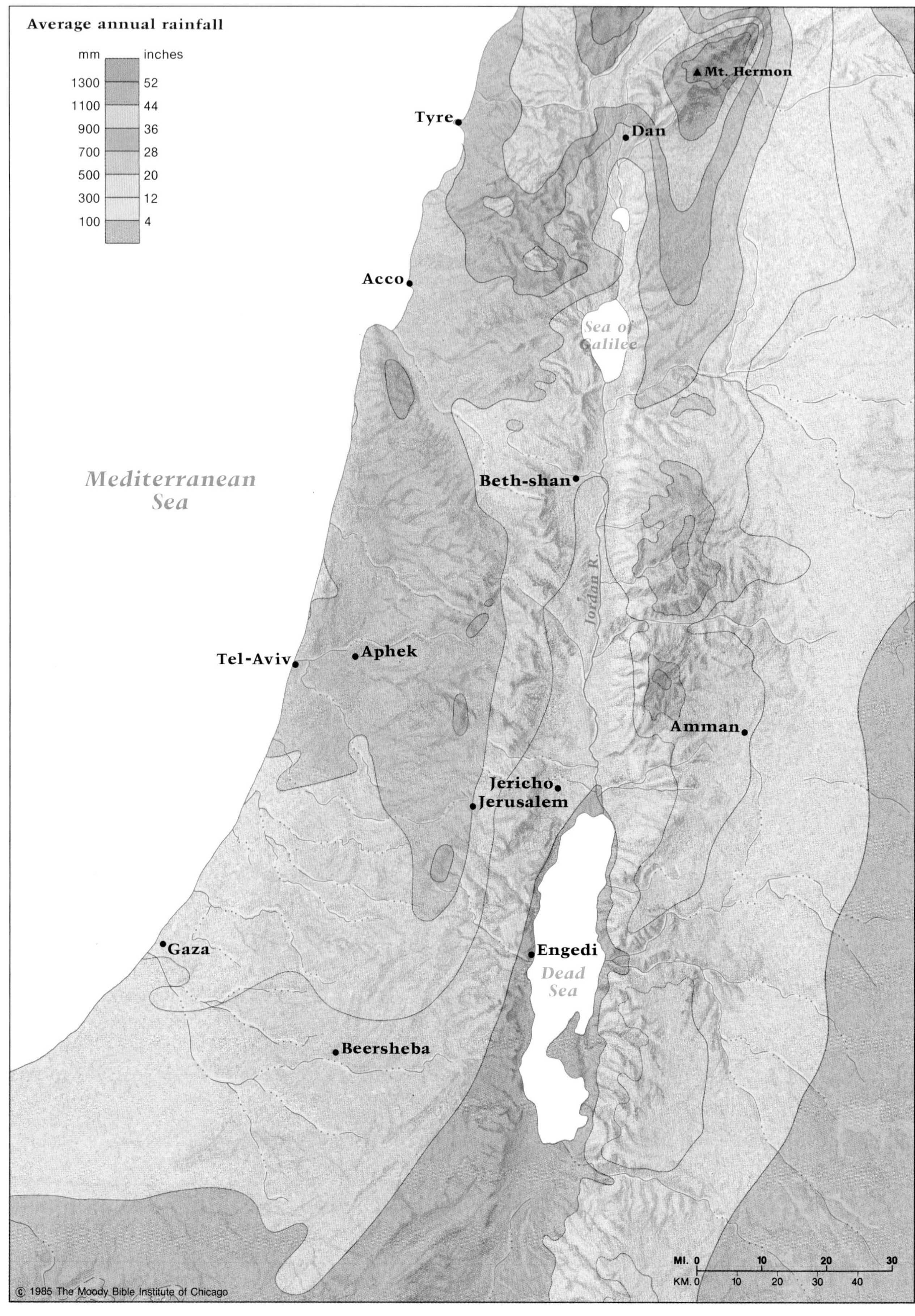

It is pertinent to point out here that the month of "former rains," the month Tishri (September/October), is related by several Semitic calendar systems with the beginning of the year, which indicates both that those calendars were agricultural in nature and that the former rains inaugurated a new agricultural beginning. In the Old Testament, the first day of Tishri was marked by a festival (Feast of Trumpets, Lev. 23:23; Num. 29:1), one that is known today as Rosh HaShana ("new year's").

In light of these harsh hydrologic realities, the need for conserving meager water supplies would have reigned supreme in Israel. So it is that the Bible is replete with references to wells (e.g., Gen. 21:19; Jer. 6:7; John 4:1-6), cisterns (e.g., 2 Chron. 26:10; Isa. 36:16), fountains (e.g., Lev. 20:18; Jer. 9:1), and springs (e.g., Gen. 16:7; Judg. 7:1; Prov. 5:15-16). On occasion, the need for water became a vehicle for conveying spiritual truth (e.g., John 4:1-26); elsewhere, writers of Scripture employed the imagery of water as a sign of blessing (e.g., Num. 24:6; Isa. 41:18-20; 44:3-5), joy (e.g., Isa. 35), delight (e.g., Ps. 1:1-3), or even eschatological perfection (e.g., Ezek. 47:1-12; Zech. 14:8; Rev. 22:1-2). On the other hand, especially eloquent in a torrid and parched land (Pss. 63:1; 143:6) would be the imagery of dried up rivers (Ezek. 30:12; Nah. 1:4), poisonous water (Jer. 23:15), clouds without water (Jude 12), springs turned to dust (Ps. 107:33), parched springs (Hos. 13:15), dry fountains (Jer. 51:36), polluted fountains (Prov. 25:26), wells that cannot produce water (Num. 21:22), empty cisterns (Gen. 37:24; cf. 1 Sam. 13:6; Jer. 41:9), and broken cisterns (Jer. 2:13). Again, in the realm of hydrology, our theme of God's sovereign preparation of a certain kind of land is shown poignantly.

Climate in the Promised Land. It is necessary at this juncture to address several facets of Palestine's climate, including rainfall. Like other places in the world, Palestine's climatological realities were and are largely determined by a combination of four factors: terrain configuration (including altitude, land cover, angle of relief, and so forth), locational relationship to large water bodies or continental land masses, direction and effect of principal air currents, and latitude (which determines the length of daylight). The Promised Land, situated between 29 and 33 degrees north latitude and dominated by prevailing westerly (i.e., oceanic) winds, has a climate marked by two sharply divided and well-defined seasons: a hot-dry period (summer), which runs approximately from mid-June to mid-September; a warm-wet period (winter), which extends between October and mid-April. In its sea breezes, desert winds, semi-desert terrain, maximum of solar radiation during most of the year, seasonal variations, temperatures and relative humidity, the Palestinian climate has close analogies with certain parts of California, as expressed in the following graph:

	Tel Aviv	*Jerusalem*	*Jericho*
California environmental analogue:	*Azuza*	*Davis*	*Palm Springs*
Mean temperature (coldest month—January):	55° F.	47° F.	57° F.
Mean temperature (warmest month—August):	81° F.	75° F.	88° F.
Maximum temperature:	115° F.	107° F.	120° F.
Minimum temperature:	37° F.	26° F.	36° F.
Precipitation (April-October):	1.7 in.	1.3 in.	0.6 in.
Precipitation (December-February):	15.3 in.	12.3 in.	3.8 in.
Precipitation (annual):	20.8 in.	15.9 in.	5.0 in.
Average relative humidity:	79%	69%	54%

The word that most aptly characterizes Palestine's summer season is *stability*. During summer, the jet stream (which allows for the depression and convection of air masses and produces storms) has been forced northward to the vicinity of the Alps by the equatorial movement of the sun toward the northern hemisphere. In the wake of that, there develop a stationary high pressure cell over the Azores and a monsoonal low over Iran and Pakistan, which results in basically north-south isobars (barometric pressure lines) over Israel (see Map 13). When that happens, a thermal barrier is created that (1) produces uniformly clear daylight conditions, with some morning haziness manifested near the Mediterranean, and (2) prevents the formation of rain clouds, even in the face of an extremely high relative humidity. A storm in summer is most unexpected (cf. 1 Sam. 12:17-18). That means the summer season features consistently fine weather, regular westerly breezes, daytime heat, and almost complete drought. Those summer air masses, slightly cooled and moistened as they pass over the Mediterranean, condense to form the aforementioned dew, which nourishes

MAP 13 ATMOSPHERE—SUMMER

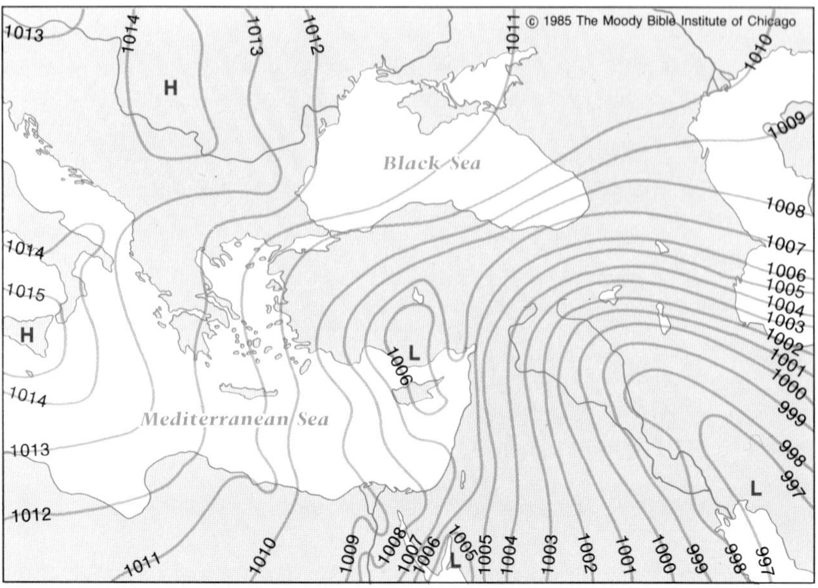

summer growth. The coastal plain south of Gaza, the central Jezreel valley (cf. Judg. 6:36-40), the heights of Mt. Carmel, and the western Negeb all experience about 250 dew nights annually.

The winter season is characterized by *instability*. As they take advantage of the equatorial path of the sun toward the southern hemisphere, winter upper air masses become infused with an extremely cool surge of polarized air. From that mixing of air masses there develop three dominant high pressure currents, any one of which can collide unpredictably with the air that meanders through a Mediterranean depression, thus producing an instability and irregularity in atmospheric conditions. The first of those air masses, a so-called central Asian high, is a direct flow of polar air of extremely high pressure—as high as 1,036 millibars—that covers Asia and at times parts of Europe. When that polar mass descends across the Urartian and Zagros mountains, it sometimes traverses the entire Syrian desert and strikes Israel from the east with a blast of freezing air and frost (Job 1:19; cf. Sirach 43:20). Then there is the Balkan high which, in the wake of a severe Mediterranean depression, can slide southward and strike Israel, usually with moister air from the west. This air system is generally responsible for snowfall on Israel (2 Sam. 23:20; 1 Chron. 11:22; Job 37:6; Ps. 68:14; Prov. 26:1; cf. 1 Macc. 13:22; Sirach 43:17). Elevations more than 2,500 feet usually receive a moderate amount of snow every year (it snows two years out of three in Jerusalem), though the lofty Mt. Hermon receives most of its precipitation in the form of snow. Thirdly, there develops a somewhat less intense Libyan high that, in the face of a deep Mediterranean depression, can be attracted into the Negeb, bringing dust storms that can turn into rain.

The Mediterranean trough itself is a stationary depression through which move about twenty-five cyclonic storms in an average season. Such an influx of warmer air takes about four to six days to cross the Mediterranean and collides with one of the fronts. That produces strong winds and rain, lasting usually for two or three days (Deut. 11:11; 1 Kings 18:43-45; Luke 12:54). When in the biblical period a great number of those depressions were deflected north by the Cyprus low, instead depositing their precipitation across eastern Europe, Israel began to experience drought that at times led to famine. The winter season, then, corresponded to the season of rain (Song of Sol. 2:11; Jer. 36:22; Acts 28:2; cf. Acts 27:12), which included both the "early and late rain" (Deut. 11:14; Ps. 84:6; Jer. 5:24; Hos. 6:3; Joel 2:23; James 5:7). The former rains, normally deposited

MAP 14 ATMOSPHERE—WINTER

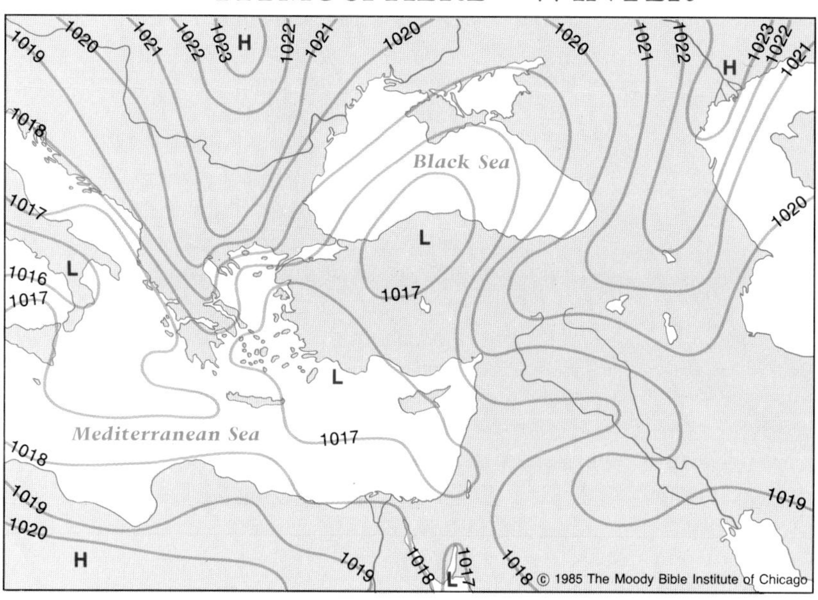

throughout October, gently soaked the ground and prepared it for plowing and planting; the latter rains of April were important for the ripening of certain crops (Amos 4:7). However, the days of heaviest rainfall coincided with the period of coldest weather in December through February (Ezra 10:9, 13; cf. 1 Esdras 9:6, 11), and precipitation might include snow and hail in those months. Generally speaking, precipitation increases as one proceeds north: Elat on the Red Sea receives 1 inch or less annually; Beersheba in the Negeb gets about 8 inches; Nazareth in the lower Galilean hills receives about 27 inches; J. Jarmuk in upper Galilee gets approximately 44 inches, and Mt. Hermon receives nearly 60 inches of precipitation annually (cf. averages for Tel Aviv, Jerusalem, and Jericho on the graph above).

At the turning of the seasons are found brief transitional periods: one between late April and early June and another between mid-September and mid-to-late October. In those times, a hot sweltering air mass, popularly known today as a sirocco (cf. Sirach 35:16), or "hamsin," reaches Israel from the Arabian desert. The sirocco produces torrid heat and parched dryness, not unlike the Santa Ana winds of California. Known in the Bible as "an east wind" (e.g., Gen. 41:6; Ex. 10:13; Job 27:21; Ps. 48:7; Isa. 27:8; Jer. 18:17; Ezek. 19:12; Hos. 12:1; 13:15; Jonah 4:8; cf. Jer. 4:11; 13:24) or "a south wind" (e.g., Luke 12:55), that wind condition sometimes persists for more than a week, withering delicate vegetation and causing irritation to men and beasts.

Forestation and land use. Where the land received adequate rainfall, ancient Palestinian forestation included standing woodlands (e.g., Deut. 19:5; 2 Sam. 18:6; 2 Kings 2:24; Eccles. 2:6; Isa. 10:17-19), though the land was more commonly covered by the thicket brush and shrubby plants (*maquis*) typical of the Mediterranean basin (e.g., Josh. 17:15; 1 Sam. 22:5; Hos. 2:14). In early antiquity, Palestinian forestation was most likely rather dense and sometimes impassable, except in those southern and southeastern regions that bordered on desert. Present evidence indicates, however, that there was an ever-increasing destruction of that forestation by the ravages of mankind, beginning as early as about 3000 B.C., but with three periods standing above all others as particularly ruinous: the Early Iron Age, the late Hellenistic and Roman periods, and the last 100-150 years. It is the first of those cycles of destruction that affects the biblical story of forestation and land use, and so we will focus our attention there.

Between 1200-900 B.C. (Early Iron Age), there was a truly massive and enduring encroachment by man upon the landscape of Palestine, triggered largely by a substantial wave of new immigrants and the introduction of iron implements. Palestine's woodlands thus began to disappear before society's domestic, industrial, and wartime needs. In the domestic realm, for instance, large tracts of land had to be cleared to make way for human settlement and for the production of food; vast amounts of timber would have been required in the construction and ornamentation of homes (cf. 2 Kings 6:1-2; Jer. 10:3; Wisd. of Sol. 14:1). It is moreover estimated that each household would have required one to two tons of firewood annually (Isa. 44:14-17; Ezek. 15:1-8; cf. Mark 14:54). The grazing of transient flocks of sheep and goats would have uprooted seasonal forestation that was succulent, but not deeply rooted.

Man's settlements in turn enlisted the support of certain industries, especially those that worked with fire, further aggravating Palestine's ecological imbalance. The mining, smelting, and forging of metals required vast wood resources, and sometimes entailed the damming of streams or the quarrying of mountainsides. Wood was burned in baking kilns or pits in the production and glazing of glass (cf. Job 28:2-11) and in the manufacturing of lime, plaster, bricks, terra cotta pipes and drains, baking utensils, and writing tablets (some writing was actually placed on *wood* tablets). Vast amounts of wood also were consumed through sacrifices at Palestinian temples. Then again, certain wood byproducts were industrially useful as water solvent, in tanning and dyeing, or in medicine. Finally, additional areas of forestation would have been devoured through war, both in producing military implements (cf. Deut. 20:19-20) and in wanton wartime activities (cf. Ps. 83:14; Isa. 10:15-19; Jer. 6:6-8).

The effects of deforestation were dramatic and permanent. There is considerable evidence that the accompanying disruption of Palestine's topsoils led directly to a greatly accelerated wind and water erosion, with a subsequent loss in potential fertility of the thinly-covered hillsides. Some soil conservationists estimate that more than three feet of soil and subsoils have been swept off the central mountain spine as a result of Iron Age deforestation. This means that soil has eroded down to bedrock on nearly half the central spine resulting from Iron Age encroachments. Once the topsoils were severely marred or destroyed, the predominantly unproductive subsoils were unable to regenerate forestation. So, although there seems to be no evidence for substantial climatic change within the period of Palestine's human history, this rampant deforestation, with a subsequent deterioration and displacement of fertile topsoils, has caused a gradual and inexorable degeneration of the land's natural environment. The landscape has been altered for the worst. Even modern reforestation efforts around Mt. Carmel and in portions of the Shephela have not yet proved successful.

Accordingly, the Bible's portrait of Palestinian forestation appears to show a lack of those hardwoods necessary for large architectural projects. There is only slight mention of oak, pine, fir, cedar, and cypress, and even those forests were often located elsewhere by the biblical writers, either in Bashan, Mt. Hermon, or in Lebanon (e.g., Ps. 68:15; Isa. 40:16; Ezek. 27:5; Zech. 11:2). To be sure, Lebanon's seemingly inexhaustible supply of timber was celebrated in antiquity; it was imported into Egypt as early as 3000 B.C., and rather consistently thereafter. Numerous Babylonian and Assyrian kings proudly boasted that their supreme accomplishment was scaling the heights of Lebanon and cutting down its massive timbers (cf. Isa. 14:8). On the other hand, Palestine's forestation was characterized by biblical references to olive, fig, sycamore, terebinth, myrtle, balsam, date-palm, almond, and pomegranate trees—trees of the vintage variety, whose species were more conducive to the marred soil conditions but were incapable of supplying hardwoods.

Because of Israel's lack of hardwoods, David found it necessary to conclude a treaty with Hiram, king of Tyre, when he undertook building projects in Jerusalem that required large stockpiles of hardwood (2 Sam. 5:11; 1 Chron. 14:1). Likewise, Solomon was obliged to ratify that pact when he began his numerous construction enterprises (1 Kings 5; 2 Chron. 2; 9:10-28). And just as they would later build a naval fleet for the Assyrians in southern Mesopotamia, so the Phoenicians supplied Solomon with both the raw materials and the technology to build his fleets (1 Kings 10:22; cf. Ezek. 27:5-9). Through one of those fleets the Jerusalem monarch imported, among other commodities, certain kinds of precious woods otherwise unavailable in Israel (1 Kings 10:11-12; 2 Chron. 9:10-11). Throughout the monarchy period, an entailment of construction on even a modest scale was the securing of hardwoods from outside sources, as Joash (2 Kings 12:12) and Josiah (2 Kings 22:6) discovered.

The availability of hardwood lumber had not improved by the post-exilic period. As part of Cyrus's decree to permit the Jews to return to their native land, the Persian granted a sum of money with which they were to secure timber and rebuild their temple (Ezra 3:7; cf. 1 Esdras 4:48; 5:54). It is suspected, however, that when that timber arrived in Israel, it was squandered instead for use on private dwellings (Hag. 1:8; cf. v. 4). Later, as Nehemiah sought to be released from his royal appointment in an attempt to improve conditions surrounding post-exilic Jerusalem, he requested Artaxerxes for letters to secure timber for the reconstruction of the city wall (Neh. 2:4-8).

Ironically enough, the activities of the Israelites themselves must have contributed significantly to the diminished capacity of Palestinian land resources. The period in view followed immediately on the heels of the Israelite conquest. Furthermore, the keystone of Israel's economic survival was its supervision of Canaan's "grain, wine and oil" (e.g., Gen. 27:28; Num. 18:12; Deut. 8:7-8; 11:14; 12:17; 18:4; 32:13-14; 2 Kings 18:32; 2 Chron. 31:5; 32:28; Neh. 5:11; 10:39; 13:5; Pss. 4:7; 104:15; Isa. 36:17; Jer. 31:12; Lam. 2:12; Hos. 2:5; Joel 2:19, 24; Mic. 6:15; Hag. 1:11; cf. commodities of export, 1 Kings 5:11; 2 Chron. 2:15; Ezek. 27:17). Ultimate peace and prosperity were envisaged in the recurring formula "everyone resting under his own vine and fig tree" (1 Kings 4:25; 2 Kings 18:31; Isa. 36:16; Mic. 4:4; Zech. 3:10; cf. 1 Macc. 14:12).

Cities: their location and identification. Urban settlements in Palestine and surrounding countries have been situated in accordance with a number of geographical/political factors. Because those factors were not mutually exclusive, more than one of them sometimes played a role in determining a city's exact location. Of course, it remains unclear just what factor(s) may have been operative in locating some cities. Generally speaking, however, there were five major factors that could determine the location of cities in Palestine: water accessibility, availability of natural resources, regional topography, local topography, and natural lines of communications.

Foremost among those was the question of *water accessibility*. Although it could be rightly argued that water was central to all settlement in an otherwise arid environment, some cities appear to have been positioned *exclusively* on the basis of water accessibility. Among those would be the cities of Capernaum, located along the shore of the Sea of Galilee; or Damascus, positioned at the eastern foot of the Anti-Lebanon mountain on a vast oasis fed by the effusive Abana and Pharpar rivers (cf. 2 Kings 5:12); or even Tadmor, a lush oasis in the Syrian Desert nourished by a generous spring. Owing to the inexhaustible supply of fresh water in those localities, settlements were built at each one long before the dawn of biblical history, and they represent some of the oldest continuously occupied settlements in the Fertile Crescent.

But cities were also known to have been positioned in close proximity to *natural resources*. A prime example here would be the city of Jericho, one of the earliest settlements in all of Palestine. Although it is true that Old Testament Jericho was built near an exceptionally large and prolific spring, it is likely the city was established at such an early date precisely because that spring was situated near the Dead Sea and its bitumen. Bitumen was a highly prized commodity in antiquity, used as a water solvent, fumigation agent, or in construction that utilized baked bricks. Bitumen from the Dead Sea was transported throughout Egypt and much of the Fertile Crescent because few other known sources of the commodity existed. Consequently, an economic motivation that brought into the area a colony of laborers also led to the eventual founding of a settlement nearby.

Also illustrative of the natural resource factor is the city of Ezion-geber, located near the head of the Gulf of Aqaba. A copper refinery foundry was positioned there to utilize the strong winds that swept across the Arabah, and to process metals mined nearby. The presence of the foundry best explains the settlement there. The site was hardly ideal as a port city, positioned as it was some distance from the waterfront, nor could it have been otherwise attractive to settlement, because it lay exposed to the torrid heat of the desert. The nearness of fertile soils, another natural resource, has also prompted the site selection for many cities, such as Ashdod, Ekron, and Gath (on the Philistine plain); of Jezreel (on the Jezreel plain); and of Dothan (in the Dothan Basin).

Cities were also situated in accordance with *regional topography*. We have already seen how Megiddo was positioned to dominate a strategic intersection at a pass in the Carmel range. Likewise, the city of Beth-horon was situated precisely where it was in order to govern the main approach from the west into the interior of the central mountain spine (cf. the strategic nature of this site is illustrated in Maps 19, 72). Other cities were situated in accordance with *local topography*; cities such as Jerusalem, Masada, and Samaria vividly illustrate this factor. Jerusalem was surrounded on every side except the north by deeply-carved valleys that plunge more than 200 feet; Masada was a lofty isolated mesa encompassed by precipitous rock cliffs in excess of 600 feet in height, where the first Jewish revolt was finally quelled in A.D. 73; and the city of Samaria straddled a 300-foot high isolated hill engulfed by two steep valleys. As a consequence of local topography, those three cities were commonly resistant to attacks, or they fell to opponents only after a protracted period of siege followed by a fierce assault. Jerusalem, for example, repeatedly resisted attack (see Map 52); Samaria thwarted a prolonged siege in the time of Elisha (2 Kings 6:25), withstood the mighty Assyrian hordes for three years, and held off the assaults of John Hyrcanus's army for one year; and Masada withstood a lengthy siege and all-out attack of the Roman Tenth Legion with numerous auxiliary forces for seven months.

Finally, urban settlements may have been positioned along *natural lines of communication*. The powerful urban center of Hazor was situated on a 200-acre tell 9 miles north of the Sea of Galilee. A heavily fortified emplacement, Hazor was the largest tell in the country, and during the Late Bronze Age, prior to the biblical conquest, the city appears to have served as a provincial capital (cf. Josh. 11:10). Hazor's location was dictated mainly by the course of the Great Trunk Road, and the city served as the port of entry for Palestinian locations and points south (cf. many extrabiblical citations of the city are found in trade or itinerary texts). Lines of communication also most likely determined how the cities of Gaza or Rabbah-Amman came to be situated in a particular spot.

Now, because the factors dictating localization remained rather constant, what I choose to call "geographic determinism," Palestinian towns usually experienced an amazing continuity of settlement. Even when a site was destroyed or abandoned for a long period, perhaps owing to famine, plague, or natural catastrophe, later settlers of the town were almost always attracted by the same factor(s) that determined the original choice of the site. The subsequent settlers were glad to make use of portions of walls still standing, or beaten earth floors, of fortifications, storage pits or wells, or at least to reuse the convenient supply of on-site building materials. And as succeeding settlements rose and fell, and towns were literally built one on top of another, the platform mound (tell) on which they rested (cf. Josh. 11:13; Jer. 30:18) grew ever higher, with steeper slopes along its perimeter, thus rendering a site increasingly defensible. When that pattern was frequently repeated, as in the case of Megiddo, Hazor, or Beth-shan, the occupational debris could reach heights of seventy feet or more.

This leads to the question of site identification, which is critical to the concerns of a Bible atlas. In spite of continuity of settlement, sound identification of biblical places is not possible in every case, due to insufficient documentary evidence and/or to a limited knowledge of ancient geography. Not every name has been preserved to the present, and even where a name has been retained or has been resurrected and applied to a site in modern times, attempts at identification may be fraught with problems. For example, there are cases in which a particular settlement has undergone a location shift. Old Testament Jericho is not at the same site as New Testament Jericho, and neither of those sites corresponds to modern Jericho. Location shifts are also known to have occurred at Lachish, Beth-shan, Tiberias, and else-

Cities of Palestine

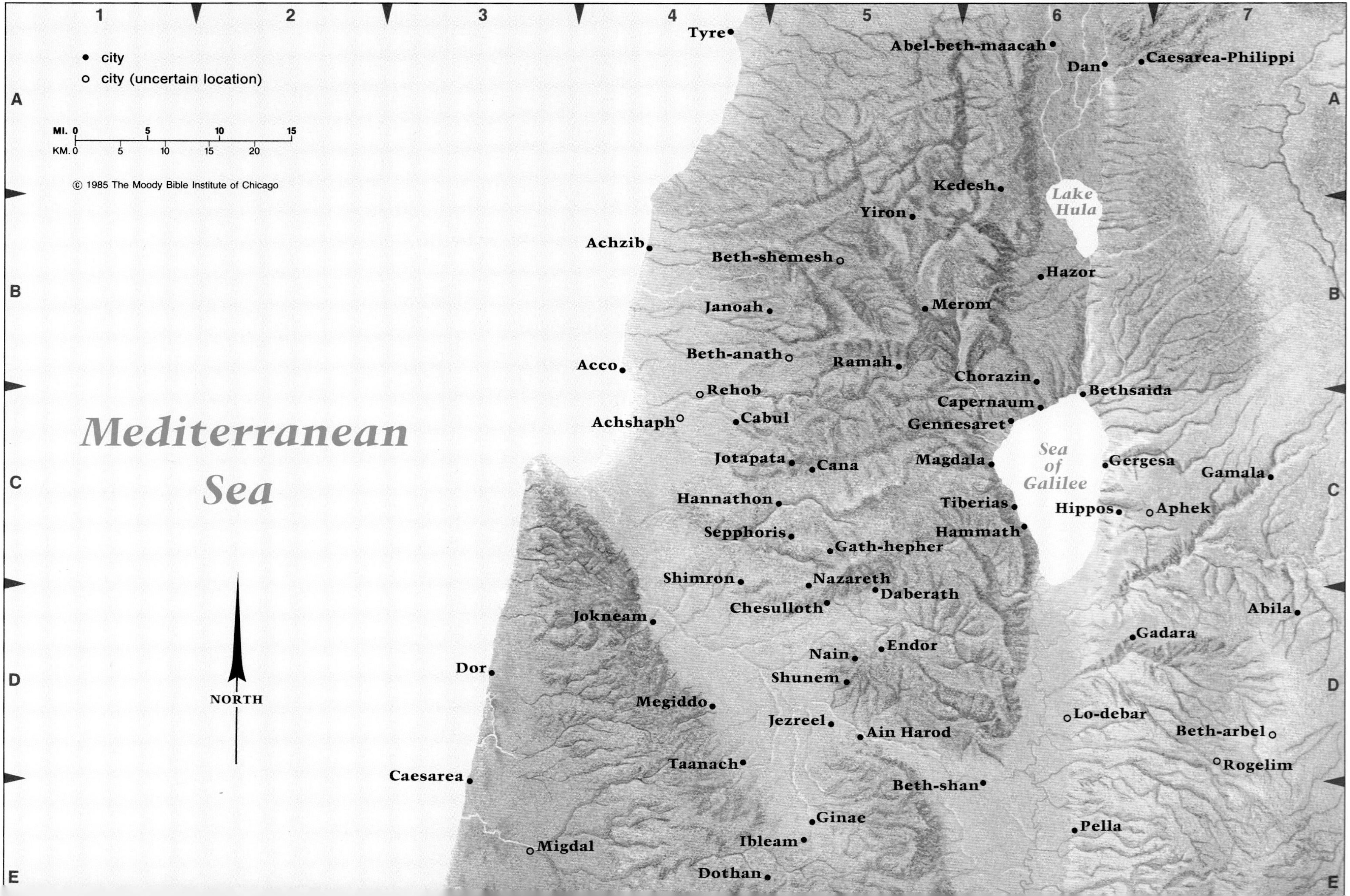

• city
○ city (uncertain location)

MI. 0 5 10 15
KM. 0 5 10 15 20

Mediterranean Sea

NORTH

Tyre
Abel-beth-maacah
Dan
Caesarea-Philippi
Kedesh
Lake Hula
Yiron
Achzib
Beth-shemesh
Hazor
Janoah
Merom
Beth-anath
Ramah
Acco
Chorazin
Rehob
Bethsaida
Capernaum
Achshaph
Cabul
Gennesaret
Jotapata
Cana
Magdala
Sea of Galilee
Gergesa
Gamala
Hannathon
Tiberias
Hippos
Aphek
Sepphoris
Hammath
Gath-hepher
Shimron
Nazareth
Daberath
Chesulloth
Abila
Jokneam
Gadara
Endor
Nain
Dor
Shunem
Megiddo
Lo-debar
Jezreel
Ain Harod
Beth-arbel
Taanach
Rogelim
Caesarea
Beth-shan
Ginae
Pella
Ibleam
Migdal
Dothan

Samaria
Tirzah
Zarethan
Zaphon
Gerasa
F
Sychar
Shechem
Succoth
Mahanaim
F
Pirathon
Penuel
Mizpah
Aphek
Ebenezer
Tappuah
Adam
Gath-rimmon
Lebonah
Joppa
Shiloh
Gilgal
Arimathea
Ono
Jogbehah
G
Timnah-serah
Beth-dagon
G
Jordan River
Gophna
Ophrah
Lod
Jazer
Amman
Modin
Bethel
Ai
Lower
Beth-horon
Gittaim
Beth-nimrah
Mizpah
Upper
Beth-horon
Gilgal
Shaalbim
Michmash
Jamnia
Jericho (OT)
Gezer
Geba
Gibbethon
Ramah
Jericho (NT)
Emmaus
Aijalon
Gibeon
Shittim
Beeroth
Gibeah
H
Kiriath-jearim
Beth-haram
Waters of Nephtoah
Heshbon
H
Timnah
Eshtaol
Baal-peor
Bezer
Ekron
Jerusalem
Beth-
jeshimoth
Ashdod
Zorah
Bethany
Beth-shemesh
Nebo
City of Salt
Jarmuth
Bethlehem
Medeba
Gath
Azekah
Socoh
Ashkelon
Adullam
Almon-diblathaim
Libnah
Tekoa
Moresheth-gath
J
Beth-guvrin
Keilah
J
Mareshah
Beth-zur
Jahaz
Dead
Sea
Ataroth
Lachish
Eglon
Kedemoth
Hebron
Gaza
Dibon
Aroer
Ziph
Engedi
Debir
Carmel
K
Mattanah
Ziklag
Eshtemoa
K
Gerar
1
2
3
4
5
Masada
6
7

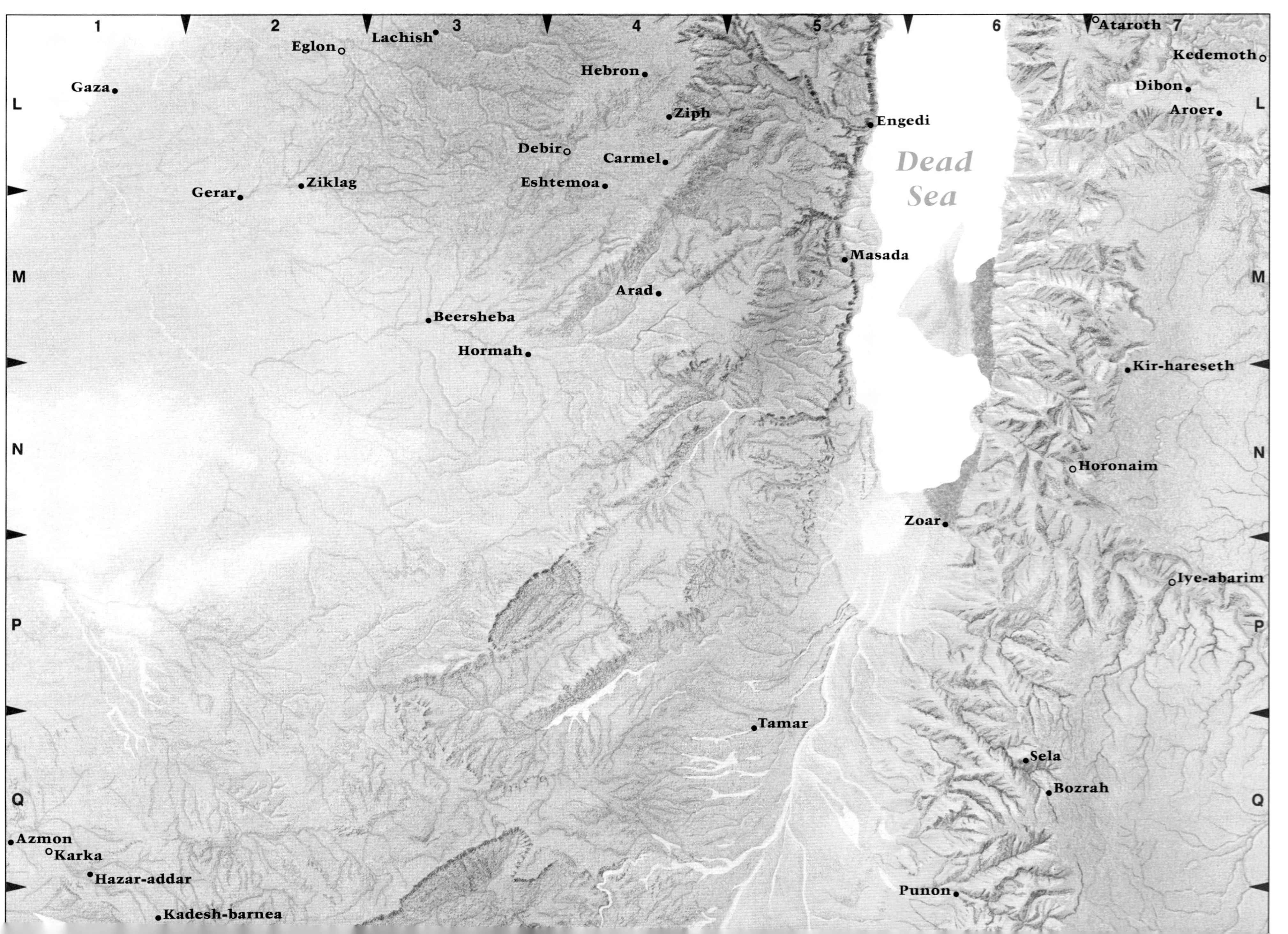
1
2
3
4
5
6
7
L
M
N
P
Q
Ataroth
Kedemoth
Dibon
Aroer
Eglon
Lachish
Gaza
Hebron
Ziph
Engedi
Debir
Carmel
Eshtemoa
Gerar
Ziklag
Dead Sea
Masada
Arad
Beersheba
Hormah
Kir-hareseth
Horonaim
Zoar
Iye-abarim
Tamar
Sela
Bozrah
Azmon
Karka
Hazar-addar
Kadesh-barnea
Punon

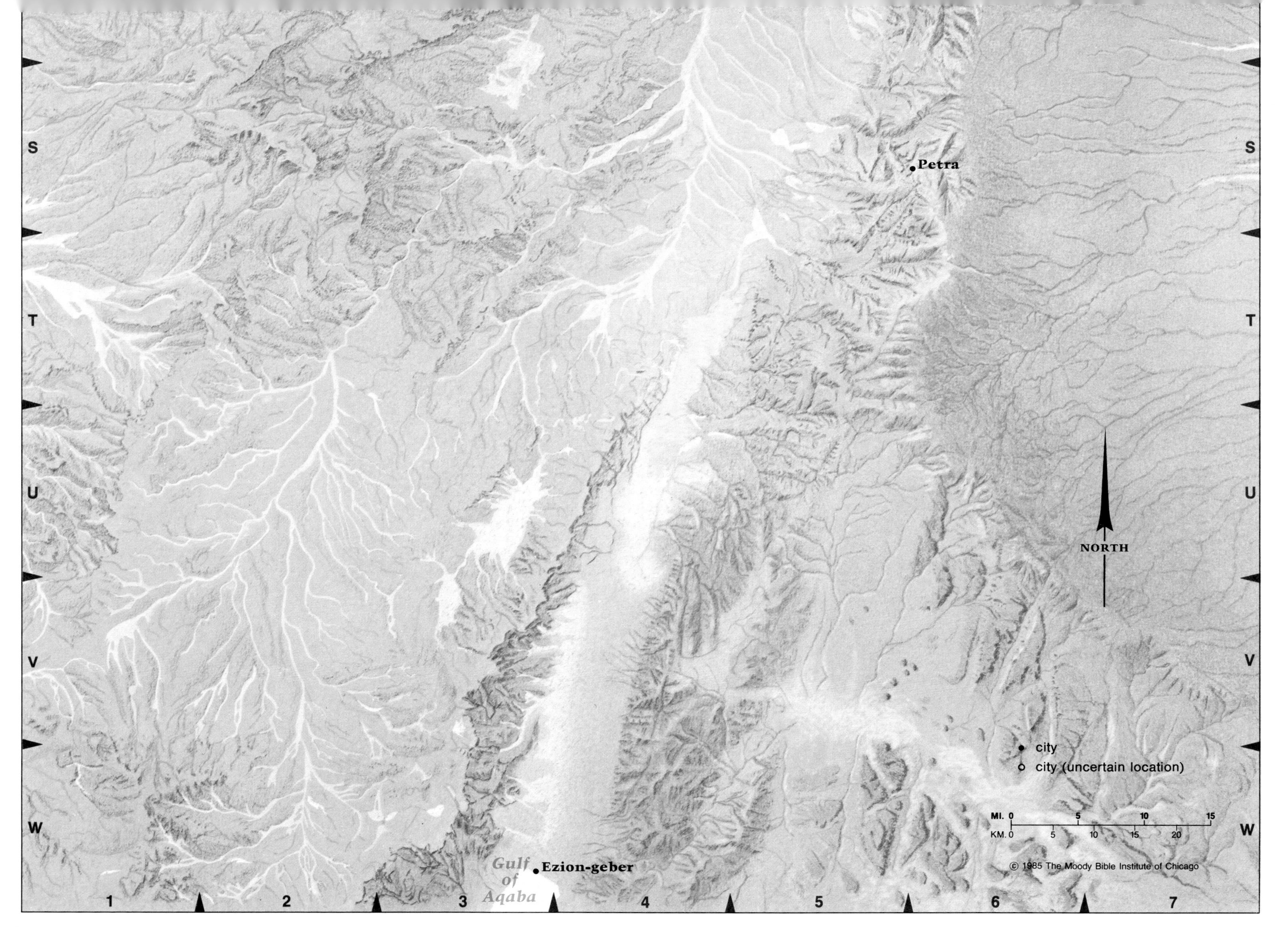

Petra
Ezion-geber
Gulf of Aqaba
NORTH
city
city (uncertain location)
MI. 0 5 10 15
KM. 0 5 10 15 20
© 1985 The Moody Bible Institute of Chicago
S
T
U
V
W
1
2
3
4
5
6
7

MAP 16 ARCHAEOLOGICAL SITES OF BIBLE LANDS

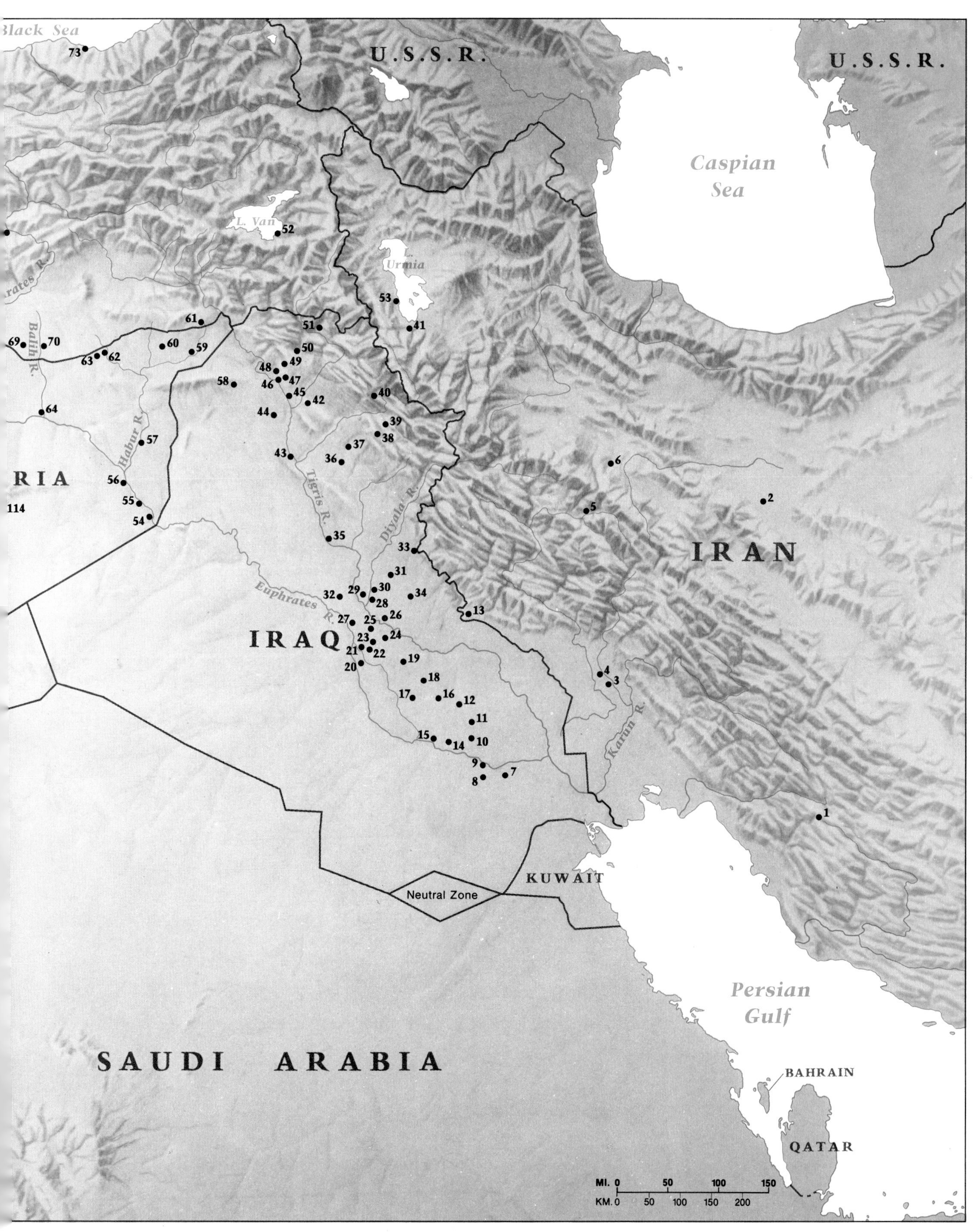
Black Sea
U.S.S.R.
U.S.S.R.
Caspian Sea
L. Van
L. Urmia
Balih R.
Habur R.
Tigris R.
Diyala R.
Euphrates R.
Karun R.
IRAN
IRAQ
KUWAIT
Neutral Zone
SAUDI ARABIA
Persian Gulf
BAHRAIN
QATAR
MI. 0 50 100 150
KM. 0 50 100 150 200

where. But there can also be a name shift from one period to another. Old Testament Rabbah became New Testament Philadelphia, which in turn became modern Amman. Old Testament Shechem became New Testament Neapolis, which evolved into modern Nablus. And then there are instances in which a name change occured *within* a Testament, examples of which include Luz/Bethel, Kiriath-Arba/Hebron, Kiriath-sepher/Debir, and Laish/Dan. Analysis of those cases demands an intimate familiarity with the cultural succession and linguistic interrelationships between several epochs of Palestinian history: even then, site identifications often remain inconclusive.

Then there is the problem of homonymy—more than one site may bear the same name. Scripture knows of an Aphek in the Sharon plain (e.g., 1 Sam. 4:1), in Lebanon (e.g., Josh. 13:4), in Galilee (e.g., Josh. 19:30), and in Golan (e.g., 1 Kings 20:26); there is a Socoh in the Shephela (e.g., 1 Sam. 17:1), in Judah (e.g., Josh. 15:48), and in the Sharon plain (e.g., 1 Kings 4:10). Other examples can be found in the Bible. For the most part, homonymy occurs because place names are frequently generic in meaning. For example, Hazor means "enclosure," Bethlehem means "granary," Migdal means "tower," Abel means "meadow," Gibeah means "hill," Kadesh means "cultic shrine," Ain means "spring," Mizpah means "watchtower," Rimmon means "pomegranate," and Carmel means "vineyard," and so on. Not unexpectedly, therefore, more than one of each of those names is attested in the Old Testament; it is conceivable, to cite but one example, that a "Bethlehem" could be found wherever a granary had existed in Palestine. The difficulty that vexes the geographer here is really twofold: (1) how to know when to posit another case of homonymy, and (2) how to ascertain in some contexts which homonymous site was envisaged by an author. Homonymy also occurs when one and the same name alternately refers to a town or a surrounding province or territory (for example Samaria, Damascus, Tyre, and Jezreel).

Despite the aforementioned problems, the scientific identification of biblical sites is generally based on three considerations: archaeological attestation, uninterrupted tradition, and literary/topographic analysis. The first of those, which is most direct and conclusive, identifies a city through an inscription excavated from the site. Although numerous specimens of that sort occur in Syro-Mesopotamia, they are relatively few in number within Palestine. Such documentation has been exhumed from the cities of Gezer, Beth-shan, Lachish, Taanach, Gibeon, and Dan.

Regrettably, most place names are not identified by inscriptional evidence. That means one of the other two considerations must be used. The first of those, name survival (uninterrupted tradition), applies where the name of a site has remained lexically the same and the identity of a site has never been lost. Into that category fall such notable cities as Jerusalem, Bethlehem, and Nazareth. Most modern sites with biblical names, however, cannot offer that kind of unbroken traditional support. Consequently, this raises the obvious question of just how valid such associations really are, given the location shifts and name shifts mentioned above. It needs to be stressed, first of all, however, that these transferences do not seem to have taken place in a random, willy-nilly manner. Where location shifts are known to have occurred, they appear to be confined within a narrow radius. The three Jerichos listed above, for instance, are all contained within an area of about 5 miles, and the same is generally true of other location shifts of which I am aware. Frequently, when name shifts take place, the original name of the site is preserved in a nearby geographical feature. To cite illustrations, the name of biblical Beth-shemesh (T. Rumeileh) is reflected in an adjacent spring (Ain Shems), and the modern wadi name Yabis is but a reflex form of the biblical site Jabesh-(gilead), which aligned it in antiquity. Moreover, where archaeological data has supplied irrefutable evidence for the biblical name of a given site, it is quite common for that name to be reflected in the modern name of the site. Biblical Gibeon, for instance, is known today by the name el-Jib, and biblical Taanach is reflected in its modern name of T. Tiʿinnik. And so, whereas name association does entail some risk, it can often provide identifications of the highest probability.

The third consideration used in site identification consists of literary and topographic analysis. Biblical passages often give a fairly reliable literary clue to the approximate location of a particular site. A case in point would be the location of biblical Ekron, one of the chief cities of the Philistine plain. Scripture positions Ekron along the northern frontier of Judah's inheritance between Timnah and Shikkeron (Josh. 15:11), though it was actually allotted to the tribe of Dan (Josh. 19:43). Now the sequence of towns in the latter passage is significant. Ekron is found between cities of the Shephela (e.g., Zorah, Eshtaol, Beth-shemesh) and others found in the vicinity of Joppa (e.g., Bene-berak, Gath-rimmon), which enhances the supposition that Ekron should be sought near the western border of the Shephela. We learn, secondly, that Ekron represented the northernmost city within the Philistines' sphere of control (Josh. 13:3), and that it was a fortified city (1 Sam. 6:17-18). We discover, finally, that Ekron was

ARCHAEOLOGICAL SITES OF PALESTINE

joined directly to Beth-shemesh by a road, and presumably separated from the other site by a distance of one day's travel or less (1 Sam. 6:12-16). Accordingly, even without the later testimony of Assyrian records, 1 Maccabees, Josephus, and Eusebius, biblical Ekron should very likely be sought at modern T. Miqne (Kh. el-Muqenna'), a tell situated where the Philistine plain and Shephela adjoin, and on the opposite end of the Sorek valley from Beth-shemesh (see Map 42).

Sometimes, however, the Bible does not supply sufficient data to identify a site. In those cases, the geographer must resort to an analysis of extra-biblical literary sources from ancient Egypt or Mesopotamia. Thutmosis III, for example, inaugurated the custom of compiling lists of cities and countries in western Asia over which he claimed domination. At least eight of his successors, down to Shishak I, also compiled such lists. Alternatively, site identifications are often enhanced by comments of classical writers on such matters. Of special prominence here is the geographical encyclopedia assembled by Strabo. A seventeen-volume treatise on the inhabited world at the inception of the Christian era, his *Geography* supplies much helpful information on the lands of the Bible. The works of Pliny the Elder, a military statesman under the emperor Vespasian before his untimely death in the eruption of Mt. Vesuvius, are valuable geographic resources. Pliny's extensive travels carried him throughout the biblical world. The Jewish historian Flavius Josephus was a contemporary of Pliny who deserves recognition. Josephus lived for more than thirty years in Palestine, and his active interest in Palestinian cultural affairs led him to compile much useful geographical data. And then there was the work of Eusebius, Bishop of Caesarea, whose *Onomasticon* (geographical index) contains the names of Palestinian towns, both biblical and those contemporary with the bishop, and distances between them.

But literary analysis must be coupled with topographic analysis. Taking into consideration whatever documentary evidence is available, one must then correlate that with known sites in the surrounding terrain and familiarize himself with the spectrum of tells in the area—tells that may serve as candidates for equation with the site. When a site identification is proposed, the geographer must ensure that the extent and character of the site fulfills the equation requirements. Moreover, he must ensure that the remains on the site date from the period(s) required by the equation. Nevertheless, at the end of the day when all these requirements have been met, site identifications made exclusively by topographic analysis must not be set forth definitively; they should be given only balance-of-probability credence.

Roadways and transportation. In a papyrus text dating from near the end of the thirteenth century B.C., an Egyptian official supplies eloquent details concerning the perils and the difficulty of roadways and transportation in Palestine. He declares:

> Behold, the ambuscade is in a ravine 2,000 cubits deep, filled with boulders and pebbles. . . . The narrow valley is dangerous with Bedouin, hidden under the bushes. Some of them are four or five cubits [from] their noses to the heel, and fierce of face. Their hearts are not mild, and they do not listen to wheedling. You are alone; there is no messenger with you, no army host behind you. You find no scout, that he might make you a way of crossing. You come to a decision to go forward, although you do not know the road. Shuddering seizes you, [the hair of] your head stands up, and your soul lies in your hand. Your path is filled with boulders and pebbles, without a toe hold for passing by, overgrown with reeds, thorns, brambles and "wolf's-paw." The ravine is on one side of you, and the mountain rises on the other. You go on jolting, with your chariot on its side, afraid to press your horse [too] hard.[67]

In all likelihood, this is a reasonably accurate reflection of travel throughout Palestine prior to the time of Rome. It was a difficult and hazardous business. To begin with, the context of the passage cited above makes clear that the Egyptian official was traveling through Palestine on the international transportation artery called the Great Trunk Road. If conditions on that major artery were so primitive and perilous, one can imagine that what I denote on Map 19 as regional thoroughfares and secondary roadways were actually narrow, trodden paths. To apply the word *highway* as commonly understood today would be a misnomer.

Perhaps these initial observations give a better appreciation to the implications of certain biblical terminology concerning roads.

> In the wilderness prepare the way of the Lord;
> make straight in the desert a highway for our God.
> Every valley shall be lifted up,
> and every mountain and hill be made low;
> The crooked shall be made straight,
> and the rough places smooth.
> And the glory of the Lord shall be revealed,
> and all flesh shall see it together,
> for the mouth of the Lord has spoken.
>
> Isa. 40:3-4

To "prepare the way" (cf. Luke 3:4-6) entailed the clearing of obstructions (Isa. 57:14) and the removal of stones or boulders (Isa. 62:10). The "way of the righteous" is described as a level and smooth path (Isa. 26:7; cf. Ps. 1:6). Such observations may help supply a context for some of Jesus' teachings ("Broad is the road that leads to destruction . . . narrow is the road that leads to life," Matt. 7:13-14; "I am the way," John 14:6).

In addition to walking, the usual means of overland travel in the biblical world was by way of donkey (e.g., Gen. 22:5; Num. 22:21; Zech. 9:9). That beast of burden was strong, even tempered, sure-footed, and inexpensive. Though less common, certain other animals were also used in transportation, including the camel (e.g., Judg. 6:5; 1 Kings 10:2; cf. Matt. 19:24), the horse (e.g., 1 Kings 4:26; Esther 8:10; Isa. 30:16; Acts 23:23; cf. Rev. 6:2-8), and the elephant (e.g., 1 Macc. 1:17; 6:30-47). At times people were transported by wagon (e.g., Gen. 45:27; Num. 7:3-8), chariot (e.g., Ex. 14:6-28; 2 Kings 5:9; Acts 8:28), or pallet (e.g., Mark 2:4-12; Acts 5:15).

Most overland travel in biblical Palestine likely sought to avoid the oppressive heat of the day. There is some evidence to suggest that especially noncaravan travel may have been nocturnal. Nighttime travel would have offered the added advantage of escaping detection by brigands and bandits. (One wonders, in fact, whether or not travel under darkness contributed directly to the ubiquitous nature of moon-cult worship, the most prevalent form of religion across the Fertile Crescent.) Most international travel was also undertaken by caravans, precisely to avoid the same threat of bandits. There is considerable textual evidence from Mesopotamia and Asia Minor indicating that caravans were generally quite large and almost always escorted by security guards. It was not uncommon for caravans to include 100 to 200 donkeys, and one extraordinary text from Mari refers to a caravan of 3,000 donkeys.[68]

Another obstacle of overland travel was the limited headway one could make per day. Now it is axiomatic that dissimilar terrain, different circumstances in travel (administrative, military, economic), and variation in season would dictate the actual distance covered in a single day. Nevertheless, we possess numerous texts and military annals from all parts of the ancient Near East: from Egypt, Babylonia, Assyria, and Asia Minor. Some of this evidence comes from the second millennium B.C., and other portions come from the first millennium. The evidence is uniform and mutually corroborating that one day's journey in the biblical world incorporated between 17-23 miles, with slightly higher average mileage when traveling downstream by boat. Moreover, those same averages are found in later classical and medieval literature from Egypt to Turkey. Even as late as one hundred years ago or so, some modern itineraries document the same sort of meager daily averages.

Such restricted travel is seen in a number of biblical narratives. Abraham cited Mt. Moriah on the third day of his trip from Beersheba (Gen. 22:24), and the two sites were separated by approximately 50 airline miles. Ezra led a Jewish caravan from Babylonia to Jerusalem. His company departed from the Babylonian frontier on the twelfth day of the first month (Ezra 8:31) and arrived in Jerusalem on the first day of the fourth month (7:9), which means that the journey itself took a little more than three-and-one-half months. Given the route traversed by Ezra and his compatriots, they traveled about 900 miles in a little more than 100 days. The same traveling distances pretty much hold true in the New Testament, too. On one occasion, Peter journeyed 40 miles from Joppa to Caesarea and arrived at his destination on the second day (Acts 10:23-24). The urgency of the apostle's mission implies that he took a direct route to Caesarea and made no intermediate stops. Cornelius later explained that his own ambassadors had journeyed round trip between Joppa and Caesarea in four days (Acts 10:30). Then again, it is estimated that New Testament pilgrimages between Galilee and Jerusalem (75-95 miles) would have taken about five days.

A methodological consideration must be expressed before we discuss the routes throughout Palestine and the ancient Near East depicted on the maps here. The routes pictured on the maps have been established in accordance with the principle of "geographic determinism." That means that in ancient Near Eastern geographical research, certain largely unchanging physiographic and/or hydrologic factors determine the routes followed by caravans, migrants, or armies. Those routes remained relatively unaltered throughout extended periods of time, except when things were temporarily disrupted by geo-politics. Deeply incised canyons cut by sometimes raging rivers were an impediment to travel to be avoided in all periods or, if unavoidable, to be forded at places offering a minimum of difficulty. The quagmire of disease-infested swampiness or the badlands of congealed lava were always to be shunned at any cost. Densely forested mountain slopes, oftentimes with twisting gorges, were consistently navigated at passes, however narrow those passes might have been. The need to commute between copious sources of fresh water through this stretch of land was required for travel during all periods. Accordingly, although we do not possess an ancient road map of the Fertile Crescent, the location of the roads can be inferred with a high degree of probability, especially when the principle of geographic determinism is augmented with ancient tablets that address aspects of travel.

What was unquestionably the most important international artery of the Fertile Crescent is known as the Great Trunk Road, an expression equated by some scholars, we believe mistakenly, with the Via Maris, a term originating in the Vulgate (Isa. 9:1). The Great Trunk Road began

MAP 18 TRANSPORTATION SYSTEMS OF BIBLE LANDS

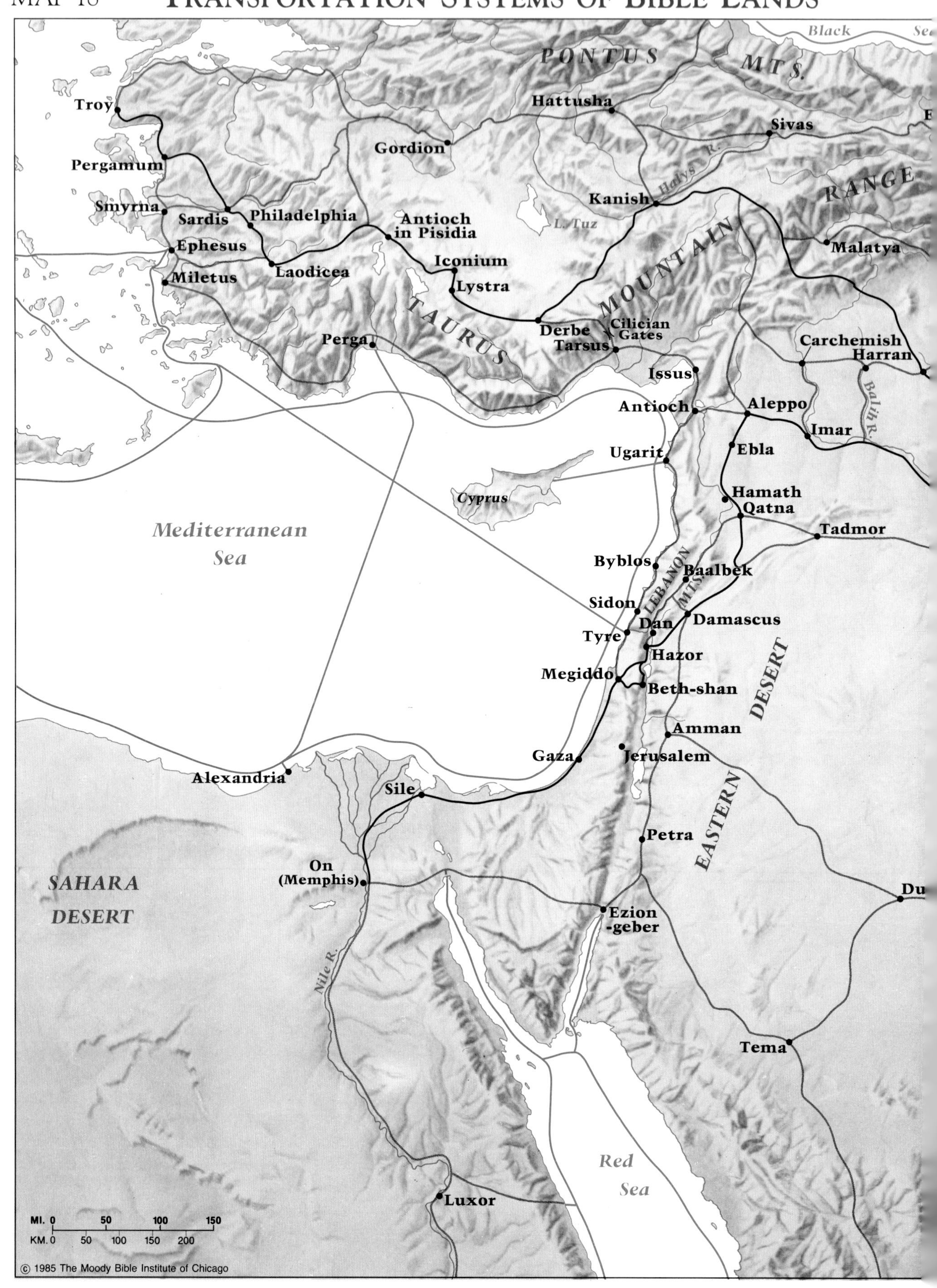

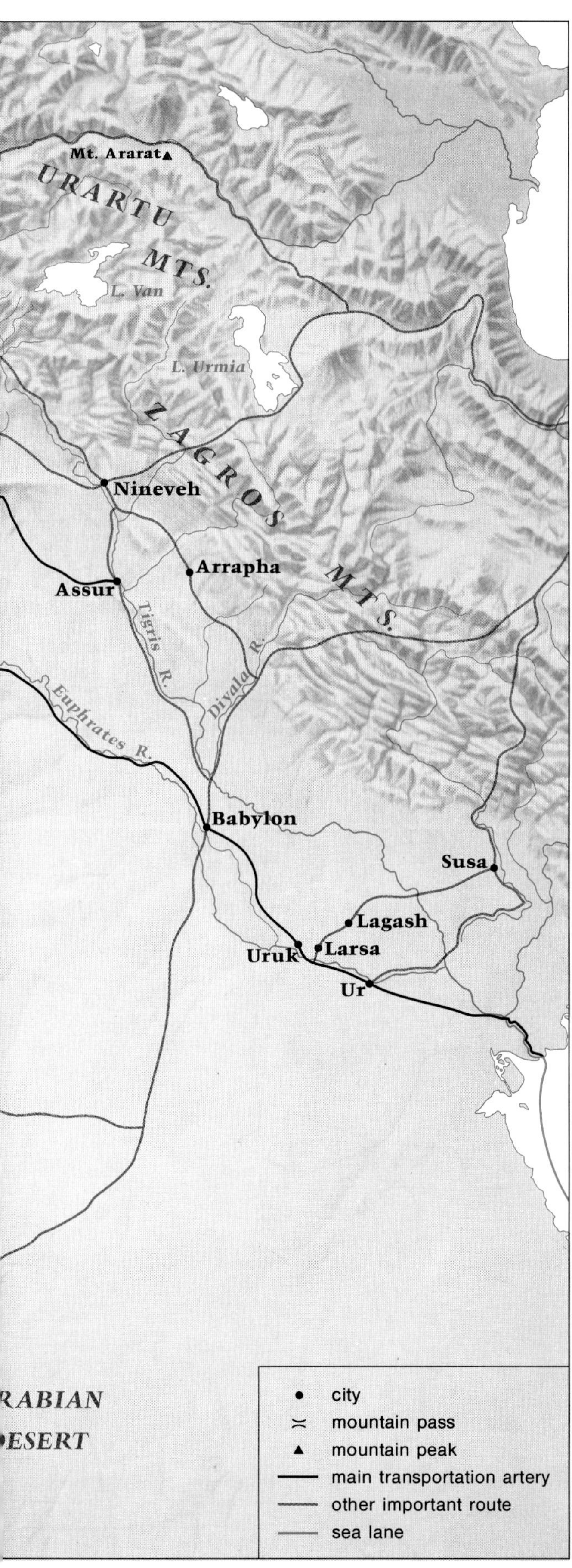

near Memphis and passed the cities of Ra'amses and Sile before arriving at Gaza. Gaza was a fortified emplacement on the edge of Canaan that was an important Egyptian provincial capital and that sometimes served as a launching pad for Egyptian campaigns through Palestine and Syria. From there the beltway stretched to Aphek/Antipatris, located at the springs of the Me Jarkon River; the effusion of those springs forced the Trunk Road to pass on its inland (east) side. Continuing in a northward direction and skirting the menacing sand dunes and seasonal marsh of the Sharon plain, the Great Trunk Road was inevitably confronted by the barrier of Mt. Carmel. It was normally through the main pass in the Carmel range, known as the Aruna pass (W. 'Iron), that the artery ran. The northern extension of that pass, where it opened into the Jezreel valley, was dominated by the installation city of Megiddo.

It appears that the Trunk Road had two branches between Megiddo and Capernaum. The first of those, what we believe to have been the principal one, turned eastward from Megiddo and followed the course of the northern flanks of Mt. Carmel and Mt. Gilboa before arriving at the strongly garrisoned city of Beth-shan, across from the mouth of the Yarmuk River. That section of the Road most likely ran along the edge of the valley during the dry season, but took to the higher ground during the winter months to avoid the marshiness of the lowlands. But at Beth-shan, the roadway veered northward and proceeded up the Jordan valley for about 15 miles, before it encountered the southern end of the Sea of Galilee. This branch of the Road then ran northward along the western perimeter of the Sea as far as Capernaum. On occasion, however, travelers crossed the Jordan at Beth-shan and made their way to Damascus via the Yarmuk valley and the Golan plateau.

The second branch from Megiddo stretched diagonally across the Jezreel valley, passed between Mt. Tabor and the hills of Nazareth, ran past the "Horns of Hattin," cut across the Arbel pass with its sheer cliffs, and finally burst onto the plain along the northwest shore of the Sea of Galilee. There it joined the main roadway from Beth-shan.

At Capernaum, the Great Trunk Road proceeded up the western flank of the Hula valley and approached the preeminent fortress city of Hazor, which guarded Palestine's northernmost sectors. From there, the roadway turned northeast in the direction of Damascus, hugging the outliers of the Anti-Lebanon range and attempting to avoid the basaltic land surface of the Golan and Hauran. A regional thoroughfare also extended northward from Hazor, navigating the entire Beqa'

MAP 19 ROADS OF PALESTINE

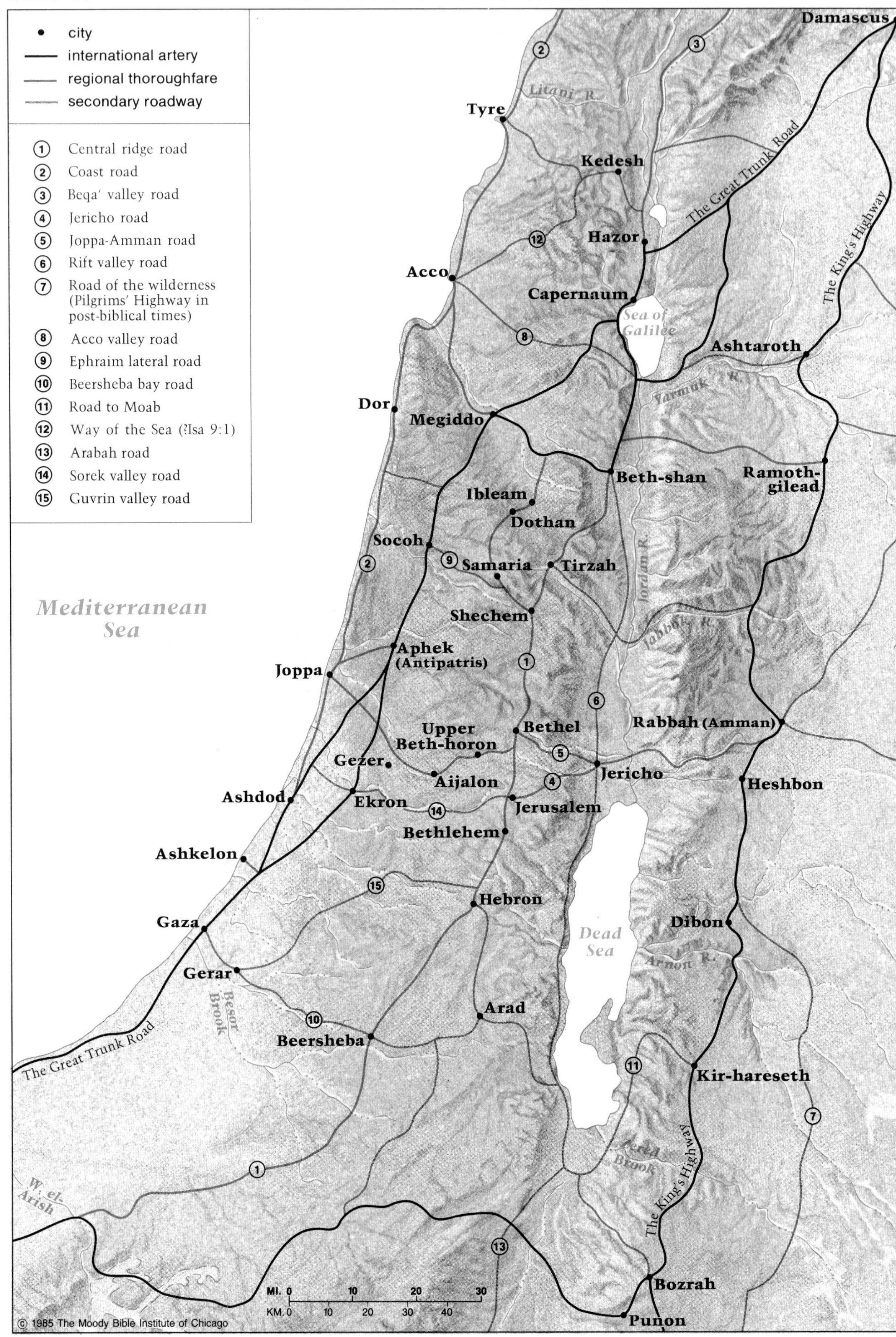

valley past Baalbek before merging with the Trunk Road at Qatna.

Along the way to the city of Qatna, a shortcut from the Great Trunk Road to the Euphrates could carry one past the oasis at Tadmor. From Qatna, the Trunk Road essentially followed the course of the Orontes River to Hamath, where it set off on a directly northern course, passing Ebla and arriving at Aleppo. There the Road curved sharply to the east and ran to the city of Imar, located on the western bank of the Euphrates River. The Road then followed the Euphrates flood plain past Mari to a point just north of Babylon, where the river could easily be forded. Continuing southward through Babylonia, the roadway trekked past Uruk and Ur, before finally arriving at the head of the Persian Gulf.

A second route of importance that intersected the land of promise is known in the Old Testament as the King's Highway (Num. 20:7; 21:22), and outside the Bible as the Sultan's highway or Trajan's highway (Via Nova Traiana). It was the emperor Trajan who converted this route from a track into a bona fide road in the second century A.D. This passageway stretched from the head of the Red Sea at Ezion-geber and essentially rode the watershed of Edom and Moab, past the cities of Bozrah, Kir-hareseth, Dibon and Heshbon, before coming to Amman. It made its way from Amman across the Gilead and Bashan plateaus to Damascus, where it joined the Great Trunk Road.

A third important international artery ran westward from the Assyrian capital city of Assur to the Habur River, where it followed the northwestward course of that valley past T. Halaf to a place near modern Samsat (where the Euphrates was easily crossed). The road then cut through a major pass in the Taurus mountain range, entered the Elbistan plain, and eventually came to the strategic city of Kanish. From Kanish, the roadway proceeded across the central Turkish plateau, past the cities of Derbe, Lystra, Iconium, and Antioch in Pisidia, before bending in the direction of the Aegean Sea. Along its descent to the Aegean, the roadway intersected Laodicea, Philadelphia, Sardis, and Pergamum. From Pergamum the road ran parallel with the northern coastline as far as the city of Troy, which was situated on the threshold of Europe.

Some of the more important regional thoroughfares and secondary roadways within Palestine are marked by name on Map 19. It is important to observe the cities through which those roads passed, and how the roads may have conferred additional importance upon otherwise rustic villages. In any event, one should correlate the information of the two road maps with various routes charted on maps in chapter two of this atlas.

Sea travel appears not to have varied much during the biblical period, though its description must be slightly modified in the New Testament era, owing to larger cargo vessels built during the Roman Empire. But throughout Phoenician and Punic ascendancy across the Mediterranean Sea it was normal for water travel to occur seasonally and in the daylight, and seaways were generally not far from the mainland. Sailors apparently always cast anchor at night, and the distance between one anchorage and another averaged approximately 40 miles. Although early seafarers required an inland area accessible to fresh water in order to found a settlement, they preferred promontories or islets lying off the coast in which to make anchor. The island was used as a breakwater and the inlet as a kind of harbor. Tyre, Sidon, Byblos, Arvad, Beirut, Ugarit, Carthage, and other coastal cities all exhibited this kind of characteristic topography. Modern archaeologists, knowing such facts, have had great success in discovering landing stages of ancient sea travelers, especially along North Africa.

Notes for Chapter 1

1. For additional reading on Santorini see D. L. Page, *The Santorini Volcano and the Destruction of Minoan Crete*, 1970; N. Platon, *Zakros: The Discovery of a Lost Palace of Ancient Crete*, 1971; M. Veber, "Voyage to Atlantis," in *The World's Last Mysteries*, 1982. A popular treatment is contained in R. Schiller, "The Explosion That Changed the World," *Reader's Digest* (November 1967).
2. *admat haqqōdeš*, Zech. 2:12; cf. *gĕbûl qodšô* ["his holy land," Ps. 78:54]; *'ereṣ bĕnê Yiśrā'ēl* ["territory of Israel," e.g., Josh. 11:22]; *'ereṣ Yiśrā'ēl* ["land of Israel," e.g., 1 Sam. 13:19]; *gĕbûl Yiśrā'ēl* ["area of Israel," e.g., Judg. 19:29]; *naḥălat Yiśrā'ēl* ["inheritance of Israel," e.g., Judg. 20:6]; *har Yiśrā'ēl* ["hill country of Israel," e.g., Josh. 11:16]). Moreover, the biblical concept of *hā'āreṣ* is used with great frequency to denote "the land of promise," in contrast to the world as a whole. Such geographical thinking continues into the pages of the New Testament (see, for example, *chōra tōn 'Ioudaiōn* ["the land of the Jews," e.g., Acts 10:39]; *gēn tēs 'epaggelias* ["the land of promise," e.g., Heb. 11:9]).
3. ARAB I, p. 243, §672; II, p. 314, §818; cf. I, p. 294, §821.
4. See Simons, pp. 98-102, for a discussion of Qaryatein -Hazar-Enan.
5. M. Astour, "Ugarit and the Great Powers," in *Ugarit In Retrospect*, ed. G.D. Young, 1981, pp. 9-10.
6. Aharoni, p. 75.
7. The same fluidity may be seen in Daniel 10:4, in which *nāhār haggādôl* ("the great river") explicitly denotes the Tigris River.
8. In my opinion, this view may be influenced greatly by Christian hymnology, as seen in the following examples: *Guide Me, O Thou Great Jehovah* ("When I tread the verge of Jordan, bid my anxious fears subside; bear me through the swelling current, land me safe on Canaan's side"); *On Jordan's Stormy Banks* ("On Jordan's stormy banks I stand, and cast a wishful eye; to Canaan's fair and happy land, where my possessions lie"); *He Leadeth Me* ("And when my task on earth is done, when by grace victory's won; even death's cold wave I will not flee, since God through Jordan leadeth me"); *I Won't Have to Cross Jordan Alone* ("When I come to the river at ending of day, when the last winds of sorrow have blown; there'll be somebody waiting to show me the way, I won't have to cross Jordan alone").

   Note how in the same way hymnology and not Scripture has presupposed Calvary to have been located on a hill: *The Old Rugged Cross* ("On a hill far away stood an old rugged cross, the emblem of suffering and shame"); *Grace Greater than Our Sin* ("Yonder on Calvary's mount outpoured, there where the blood of the Lamb was spilt"); *There Is a Green Hill Far Away* ("There is a green hill far away, outside the city wall; where the dear Lord was crucified, who died to save us all"); *I Walked Today Where Jesus Walked* ("I climbed the hill of Calvary, when on the cross He died").
9. Consult R. deVaux, *The Early History of Israel*, 1978, pp. 555-56, and literature cited there.
10. If there were prescribed only a total of six cities of refuge, and not nine, Deuteronomy 19:7-8 would represent a statement of unequivocal support for the boundary extending east of the Jordan River; cf. Mishna, p. 404 [Makk. 2.4].
11. N. Na'aman, "The Brook of Egypt and Assyrian Policy on the Border of Egypt," *Tel Aviv* 6 (1979): 68-90; "The Shihor of Egypt and Shur That Is Before Egypt," *Tel Aviv* 7 (1980): 95-109, has recently proposed that in Assyrian and biblical literature the River of Egypt should be identified with the Brook Besor, a stream that deposits its water into the Mediterranean five miles south of Gaza at Tell el-'Ajjul. According to him, the River of Egypt only came to be associated with Wadi el-Arish in the intertestamental period. For a cogent rebuttal, see A. Rainey, "Toponymic Problems," *Tel Aviv* 9 (1982): 131-33.
12. Simons, p. 96, number 272.
13. For additional reading on the Sea Peoples, including the fascinating account of how the city of Ugarit was summarily demolished by them, refer to M. Astour, "New Evidence on the Last Days of Ugarit," *AJA* 69 (1965): 253-58; V. R. Desborough, *The Last Mycenaeans and Their Successors*, 1964; E. T. Vermeule, *Greece in the Bronze Age*, 1964; T. Dothan, "The Philistines," *JAOS* 92 (1972): 447-59; Stuart West, "The Original Palestinians," *Dor le Dor* 10 (1982): 243-57.
14. See *ANET*, pp. 281-82 for translation, and refer to Map 58.
15. G. Steindorff, "The Statuette of an Egyptian Commissioner in Syria," *JEA* 25 (1939): 30-33 and pl. vii; cf. M. Gorg, "Der Name 'Kanaan' in ägyptischer Wiedergabe," *BN* 18 (1982): 27.
16. For a discussion of possible chronological problems associated with finding Philistines in patriarchal narratives, consult K. Kitchen, POTT, 56-57; cf. J. Heckelman, "Abraham and Atlantis," *Dor le Dor* 11 (1983): 189-93, who argues that the Philistines in the patriarchal stories are not out of place but represent the result of an earlier immigration into the Levant after the eruption of Santorini.
17. G. Pettinato, "The Royal Archives of Tell Mardikh-Ebla," *BA* 39 (1976): 48. See now Pettinato, *The Archives of Ebla*, 1981, p. 248.
18. Consult M. Gorg, *BN* 18 (1982): 26-27.
19. deVaux, p. 128.
20. Cf. H. J. Katzenstein, "Gaza in the Egyptian Texts of the New Kingdom," *JAOS* 102 (1982): 111-13 Aharoni, pp. 62, 172.
21. Cf. I. J. Gelb, "The Early History of the West Semitic Peoples," *JCS* 15 (1961): 42-44.
22. See especially EA 98.10-18; 102.20-23; cf. 104.10-11, 40-51; and most recently A. Altman, "Some Controversial Toponyms from the Amurru Region in the Amarna Archive," *ZDPV* 94 (1978): 100-102.
23. Cf. A. J. Rainey, "A Canaanite at Ugarit," *IEJ* 13 (1963): 43-45; Aharoni, p. 67.
24. Na'aman, *Tel Aviv* 7, p. 97, provides additional points.
25. A modification of this theory was recently revived by M. S. Astour, "The Origin of the terms 'Canaan,' 'Phoenician,' and 'Purple,'" *JNES* 24 (1965): 346-50, in which Canaan was interpreted as the place where the sun "bends" (i.e., sets); that is to say, Canaan means "west."
26. Cf. Pliny V. 77.
27. *CAD* E, 8.
28. Josephus *Wars* III.iii.1.
29. *Wars* III.iii.1.
30. *Wars* III.iii.4.
31. Smith, pp. 206-15.
32. *Wars* III.iii.5.
33. Note the location of Edrei.
34. Cf. Targumic rendering of Argob by Trachona; Simons, pp. 9, §21.
35. *AJ* XVII.viii.1, xi.4; XVIII.iv.6; *Wars* II.vi.3.
36. *Wars* I.xx.4; Ptolemy V.xv.4; Strabo XVI.ii.20; cf. *AJ* XVII.ii.1.
37. *AJ* XVII.ii.2, describes it as a place of bandits.
38. Cf. Bar-Kochva, "Gamla in Gaulanitis," *ZDPV* 92 (1976): 68, places the border of Gaulanitis at the Wadi el-'Allan.
39. *AJ* XVII.ii.2.
40. *Onomasticon*, s.v. Βαταναία; F.-M. Abel, *Géographie de la Palestine*, 1967, 2:155.
41. XVI.ii.16, 18.
42. *AJ* XIII.xi.3.

43. E.g., Pliny V. 74.
44. A list from the geographer Ptolemy (second century A.D.) adds other cities to the Decapolis, some of which should be situated in Gilead (e.g., Edrei, Abila), Bashan (e.g., Bosra) or at points north; cf. North, pp. 58, 39 n.35.
45. *ANET*, pp. 320-21.
46. *Wars* III.iii.6.
47. *AJ* XVIII.v.2; cf. Matt. 14:1-12; Mark 6:17-29.
48. *Wars* IV.vii.3.
49. This follows N. Glueck, *Explorations in Eastern Palestine* III, 1939, pp. 139-44.
50. G. Dalman, *Sacred Sites and Ways*, 1935, pp. 234, (map), 237.
51. *AJ* XX.vi.1.
52. So Josephus *Wars* II.x.2.
53. See R. L. Hohlfelder, J. P. Oleson, A. Raban, and R. L. Vann, "Sebastos: Herod's Harbor at Caesarea Maritima," *BA* 46 (1983): 133-43.
54. For the fascinating text in question, refer to *ANET*, pp. 234-38.
55. Carmel is praised for its fertility in the Melqart votive inscription (consult W. Beyerlin, *Near Eastern Religious Texts Relating to the Old Testament*, 1978, pp. 232-34, for translation); the same notion may be inferred from certain Tell el-Amarna texts (no. 288-90) (see *ANET*, pp. 488-89, for translation).
56. Refer to J. Simons, *Handbook for the Study of Egyptian Topographical Lists Relating to Western Asia*, 1937, pp. 111, 157, 165, for references to Rosh-Kadesh.
57. deVaux, pp. 386, 607; cf. *PEFQS* (1895): 253.
58. J. Garstang, *Joshua/Judges*, 1978 reprint, p. 137; *Atlas of Israel*, 3:4.
59. Garstang, p. 137; but see deVaux's pessimism, p. 607 n.45.
60. *Atlas of Israel*, 3:4.
61. Smith, p. 313.
62. The Medeba mosaic pictures fish in the Jordan River, but none in the Dead Sea. Obviously, this level of salinity produces great buoyancy, but Pliny's statement (V.72) that bulls and camels were able to float in the Dead Sea must have been hyperbole.
63. Marduk also played a magical function in Babylonian society.
64. Hydrologic realities are no different for modern Israel: despite sophisticated measures of cloud seeding that have increased Israel's annual rainfall by 15 percent, 95 percent of Israel's annual water supply is being consumed by its population. By contrast, just 1 percent of what the Nile disgorges into the Mediterranean is 350 times greater than Israel's entire annual water supply. Water that is available, even as far south as the Negeb, is being piped there by Israel's National Water Carrier, which collects the water of the Jordan before it empties out of the Sea of Galilee (or the modest amount that emerges from the Me Jarkon springs) and holds the precious commodity in a network of reservoirs, water channels, and pipe lines. In such a context, the importance of water for political security becomes immediately apparent; not unpredictably, therefore, water lines have become a prime target of modern warfare in Israel.
65. By the same token, the presence of dew became a signal of benevolence and blessing (e.g., Gen. 27:28; Zech. 8:12; cf. Sirach 43:22).
66. Note that as a common noun in Arabic, *bá'al* means "a place that is watered by seasonal rains" (cf. the Talmudic expression *sade bá'al/bêt bá'al,* "land irrigated by rain"); whereas *máwat* means "uncultivated soil.")
67. Translation adapted from *ANET*, pp. 477f.
68. Text B.590, the relevant section of which was originally published by A. Finet, "Adalšenni, roi de Burundum," *RA* 60 (1966): 24-28; cf. M. Greenberg, *The Ḫab/piru*, 1955, 18 (no. 15).

2
The Historical Geography of the Holy Land

Garden of Eden

God created a place to live for the first couple, a garden that included rivers, trees, and animals, and He called it "Eden." The high drama of this arresting account has fascinated young and old readers alike, has prompted sober and profound reflections for theologians, and has inspired many poets' pens and artists' brushes. But as soon as one attempts to reconstruct the geographical setting of the passage, he discovers that it remains shrouded in mystery at a number of levels.

To begin with, the verb from which Eden derives never occurs itself in the Old Testament; normally when that happens, it becomes virtually impossible to ascertain the precise nuance of a given noun, unless a cognate word is found in ancient Near Eastern literature outside the Bible. But with Eden the inability to develop from the text its exact meaning has given rise to a number of geographical misconceptions, the most prevalent being that the garden was some kind of a luxuriant "paradise." That notion originated with the Greek translation of the Old Testament (Septuagint), but it may bear no correspondence to the Hebrew word involved. It appears more likely that the word *Eden* may derive from a Sumerian root (*edinu*) that defines the steppe land of the Mesopotamian valley.

This word also appears in Ugaritic literature,[1] where it denotes a place that is fertile and well-watered, a connotation that Scripture sometimes attaches to it (e.g., Gen. 13:10; Ezek. 36:35; Joel 2:3). Given Canaan's water situation as discussed in chapter one, it is reasonable that the biblical writer should have borrowed a Mesopotamian water term to describe something that was alien to his own environment. Also from a Canaanite perspective, the garden was said to have been located "in [not of] Eden, in the East" (Gen. 2:8). Rather than to define its paradisiacal character, an initial observation suggests a possible *location* for the garden—somewhere in the Mesopotamian valley.

That observation is reinforced by the fact that the latter two of the four rivers in the garden—Pishon, Gihon, Tigris, Euphrates—are known to have coursed through this same valley. Fanciful attempts to locate the garden of Eden in Ethiopia, Australia, India, Mongolia, North America, or at the North Pole, therefore, need not detain us at all. No more plausible are those efforts that interpret the narrative to be a picture of four rivers which encircled the entire globe; such an hypothesis assumes that the passage is legendary in character and/or that the biblical author was ignorant of his world.

But if we accept a Mesopotamian locale, then it becomes very difficult to identify the first two rivers, Pishon and Gihon. These rivers are not attested elsewhere in ancient literature, aside from a passing reference in Ben Sirach (Ecclesiasticus) 24:25-27. Their names bear no resemblance to any river names known today, and the words themselves, meaning "to cascade" (Pishon) and "to bubble" (Gihon), suggest that they are descriptions of a river's movement, rather than rivers' names.

Attempts to identify these rivers on the basis of their assumed relationships with the descendants of Havilah and Cush are also frustrated (Gen. 2:11, 13). In the case of Havilah, Scripture knows of at least two such clans (Gen. 10:6, 29), neither one of which can be demonstrably located inside Mesopotamia. In the Bible, Cush normally designates a section of the Sudan (see Map 21), though in at least one passage (Gen. 10:8), the term may be referring to the Kassites, a dynasty of people who occupied a sector of Babylonia for much of the second millennium B.C.

The mention of gold and bdellium in Havilah does not aid in our geographical quest. Although gold in antiquity was also found in places far afield from Mesopotamia—India, Turkey, and Egypt—the metal was rather common throughout most of Assyria and was not isolated to any one region. As for bdellium, its translation remains in doubt; perhaps the word refers to a precious stone, such as a ruby or crystal, but it may also designate an apothecary aromatic, such as a kind of gum resin.

The map shows a northern (Urartian) and southern (Sumerian) Mesopotamian environ in which the garden might have been situated. One cogent argument in favor of each of these viewpoints can be put forth. The northern view is supported by verse 10, which states that a river watered the garden and then became four separate rivers. Part of the Tigris's headwaters and one of the main sources of the Euphrates (Murad Su) emerge from the Urartian highlands only about 1,100 yards from each other. In this same general region are also located the headstreams of the Araxes River, which eventually empties into the Caspian Sea, and of the Choruk River, which flows northward into the Black Sea. Proponents of a northern hypothesis will equate these rivers with the Pishon and Gihon.

A southern view may be favored by verse 12*b*, which speaks of an "onyx stone." As illustrated here, the word "onyx" in the Bible is regularly accompanied by the word "stone," which is otherwise rare for mineral terms. Now there was one mineral in the Sumerian world that also was regularly hyphenated with the word *stone*, and that

mineral is known today as *lapis-lazuli*, a deep blue stone commonly used for royal decorations in Babylonia. In this latter regard, it is instructive to note that the "onyx stone" is found in Exodus 25:7, where it formed part of the decoration of the high priest's ephod.

If the word translated "onyx" were actually specifying lapis-lazuli, a southern view would be enhanced, inasmuch as there was only one known source of it in antiquity: Afghanistan. Lapis was imported into Mesopotamia via established arteries of trade, which in this case would have included the Kerkha River.[2] In such an event, the Karun River would then constitute the most likely candidate for the fourth river of the garden.

This discussion obviously shows that a measure of hypothesis is required when attempting to pinpoint the location of the garden. Whatever the case, one cannot dismiss the southern view by saying that the ancient coastline extended farther north than the modern coast, such as is drawn on many maps of this region today. In fact, most recent geologic research says that the ancient coastline may have been farther south, and aerial photographs are thought to show traces of ancient habitation, now covered by a higher sea level.

TABLE OF NATIONS

Genesis 10, sometimes referred to as the "table of nations," has been the subject of countless studies and commentaries (cf. 1 Chron. 1); few passages from the Old Testament have been more widely analyzed. Nevertheless, significant and diverse questions remain concerning its structure, purpose, and outlook. What is clear is that the table may be subdivided three ways: (1) the descendants of Japheth (vv. 2-5, fourteen), (2) the descendants of Ham (vv. 6-20, thirty), and (3) the descendants of Shem (vv. 21-31, twenty-six). Each section concludes with a formula summarizing the preceding narrative in terms of families (genealogy), languages (linguistics), lands (territories), and nations (politics).

But how these respective terms are to be understood and what the various subdivisions represent have been interpreted in numerous ways. The sections have been classified according to biology,[3] climate,[4] apologetics,[5] ethnology,[6] mathematics,[7] socio-politics,[8] and geography.[9] Though a systematic interpretation of this intriguing biblical chapter lies beyond the scope of this atlas, we should underscore that the names in chapter 10 are presented in a dissimilar manner: the context may be that of an individual (e.g., Nimrod), a city (e.g., Asshur), a people (e.g., Jebusites) or a nation (e.g., Elam).

A failure to appreciate this mixed arrangement of Genesis 10 has led, we believe, to numerous unwarranted conclusions. For example, it should not be assumed that all the descendants of any one of Noah's sons lived in the same locality, spoke the same language, or even belonged to a particular race. A glance at the map shows the first of these conclusions to be untenable. Nor can the text be interpreted in a purely linguistic manner: the Elamite language (Shem) now appears to have been a non-Semitic language, whereas Canaanite (Ham) bears all the earmarks of a Semitic dialect. Attempts to trace all existing languages back to three parent groups are ultimately frustrated because the earliest written forms are pictographic. Such forms are not conducive to precise linguistic classification. Anthropologists have not yet achieved a consensus regarding what constitutes a proper definition of "race," thus weakening the conclusion about racial groups.

THE FOURTEEN DESCENDANTS OF JAPHETH

1. Gomer. Mentioned in cuneiform sources as Gimirraya and in classical texts as Cimmeria. According to the Greek historian Herodotus, they were displaced by the Scythians and eventually settled in the area of L. Van.[10] After being defeated by the Assyrian monarch Esarhaddon, they conquered Gugu of Luddi (or, Gyges of Lydia; cf. Ezek. 38:1) and colonized that area of Cappadocia.
2. Magog. Associated with Tubal and Meshech in Ezekiel 38:2 and with Gomer and Togarmah in Ezekiel 38:6; Magog is sometimes understood as *mā(t) gog(i)*, "land of Gyges," i.e., many have sought to identify Gog with Gyges, king of Lydia in the seventh century B.C. (refer to Time Line). The Jewish historian Josephus maintains that Magog is a description of the Scythians.
3. Madai. Kingdom of the Medes (2 Kings 17:6; 18:11; Isa. 13:17; 21:2; Jer. 25:25; 51:11, 28)
4. Javan. Probable reference is to the Ionian Greeks of the coast of Asia Minor; the name occurs frequently in cuneiform literature from the eighth century B.C. to designate the Greeks (cf. Isa. 66:19; Ezek. 27:13) and in Ugaritic texts from the thirteenth century B.C. (often in connection with Elishah).
5. Tubal. Attested in cuneiform documentation as the Tabali people, linked to the regions southeast of modern Caesarea (Mazaca) (cf. Josephus). Herodotus claims that Tubal is in Cilicia and that it formed part of the nineteenth satrapy of Darius I.
6. Meshech. Mushki, mentioned frequently in cuneiform and Egyptian literature, were part of the Sea Peoples; they came to be localized in eastern Cappadocia, northeastern Cilicia, and between the Black and Caspian seas. Josephus locates them in the area of Caesarea (Mazaca). Herodotus alleges that Meshech's territory was in Phrygia, and that it formed part of the nineteenth satrapy of Darius I (see Tubal).
7. Tiras. Uncertain; identified by some with the Etruscans (Tursenoi of Greek texts) whom Herodotus sought in the Greek parts of Asia Minor. Others have affiliated Tiras with the Turusha, a member of the Sea Peoples, with the Tyrrhenians, or the Thracians.
8. Ashkenaz. Mentioned in cuneiform literature as Ashkuza, in Persian as Saka, in Greek as Skythes, and by classical writers as the Scythians. In Jeremiah 51:27, the kingdoms of Ararat, Minni (located just

south of L. Van), and Ashkenaz were summoned to war against Babylon. Esarhaddon cites Manna and Ashkuza in the same context.

9. Riphath (Diphath in Chronicles). Uncertain; Josephus states that they were the Paphlagonians (located between the Black Sea and Bithynia, on southern edge of Black Sea). Others have connected them with the Tiphean Mountains (area of Erzerum) because of the attestation in the Cappadocian Tablets.
10. Togarmah. Attested in Hittite and Akkadian texts as both city and district (Tagarama/Til-garimmu), located on the border of Tubal, between the upper courses of the Halys and Euphrates rivers. Ezekiel 27:13 mentions commercial ties between Togarmah and Tyre.
11. Elishah. A place rich in copper and attested at Mari, Nuzi, Ugarit, Tell el-Amarna, and Boghazkoy as Alashiya. This doubtlessly refers to the island of Cyprus, though some recent authorities have sought to equate the name with Crete because the Cretan island supposedly is not otherwise mentioned (but see Caphtorim). Most of the copper deposits on Cyprus are in the central and western sectors.
12. Tarshish. (Refer to discussion at Map 47.) Tarshish is the area of southwestern Spain.
13. Kittim. Undoubtedly Cyprus (possibly Kition), an ancient city in the vicinity of Larnaca, though some biblical references denote a region or a people. Written *Kt(j)* in Phoenician inscriptions. Since Elishah equally well designates Cyprus, perhaps Kittim refers only to the Phoenician segments of the island.
14. Rhodanim. Dodanim in Genesis.[11] This is the island of Rhodes.

THE THIRTY DESCENDANTS OF HAM

1. Cush. Land of Nubia.
2. Seba. Uncertain. Josephus cites a Seba at Meror, the country between the White and Blue Niles. Strabo and a few other classical geographers refer to a Saba(i) along the African coast.
3. Havilah. Uncertain. A proverbial source of gold, possibly located along the African coast or along the coast of the Arabian peninsula (cf. Shemite Havilah).
4. Sabtah. Long standing theory is that this designates the Shabwat of Sabean inscriptions and Sabatah of Greek texts. This latter is located in the western Hadramaut region.
5. Raamah. Uncertain. On the basis of Septuagint translation (Regma), it may be possible to relate this name with Ragmah of Sabean inscriptions, the latter most likely situated in extreme southwest Saudi Arabia.
6. Sabteca. Unknown. Affiliated by some writers with the land of Nubia or Ethiopia.
7. Sheba. Famous Sabean kingdom of southwest Arabia (Yemen). It is the homeland of the Queen of Sheba (cf. Gen. 25:3) (cf. Shemite Sheba).
8. Dedan. Mentioned in Jeremiah 25:23 and 49:8 with Edom and other tribes of Arabia. In Ezekiel 25:13, Dedan borders on the land of Edom. Isaiah 21:13 speaks of the caravans of Dedan. Dedan most likely should be sought at the modern oasis of el-'Ela in northwestern Saudi Arabia.
9. Nimrod. Variously identified with kings or heroes from Babylonia: Sargon the Great (founder of the city of Akkad), Naram-Sin (warlike grandson of Sargon), Marduk (titulary deity of Babylon), Ninurta (Babylonian god of war), Gilgamesh (cunning hunter of Sumerian literature), or Nu-marad (which means "man from [the city of] Marad). Also identified with the Assyrian Tukulti-Ninurta I (distinguished monarch who captured Babylon and carried off statue of Marduk) and the Egyptian Amenophis III (referred to as *neb-ma-ri* in Amarna texts), and finally the Greek Orion (famous mythic hunter), or Ninos (folk hero). Whatever the case, a kingdom in the land of Shinar is ascribed to Nimrod, including the cities of Babel, Erech, Akkad, and Calneh. He is described, moreover, as the builder of the Assyrian cities of Nineveh, Rehoboth-Ir, Calah, and Resen.
10. Mizraim. Land of Egypt.
11. Ludim. Uncertain. This group is located somewhere along North Africa. Not to be confused with the Shemite Lud or Lydia.
12. Anamim. Unknown.
13. Lehabim. Uncertain. Located in the vicinity of Egypt, possibly related to modern Libya.
14. Naphtuhim. Uncertain. Because the Naphtuhim are located between Lehabim (Libya?) and Pathrusim (Pathros), schol-

MAP 21

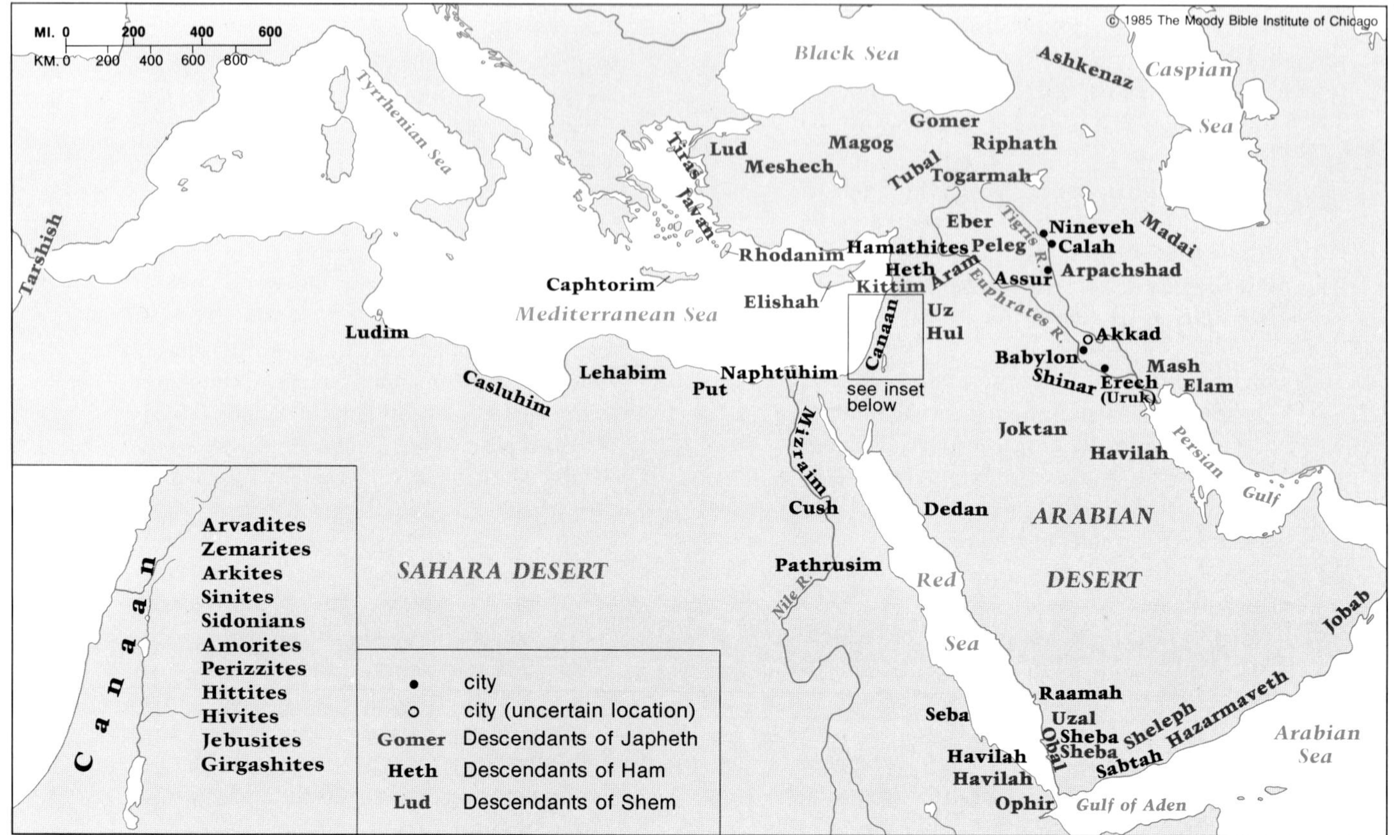

ars have tended to locate Naphtuhim in the delta region. Accordingly, the word may be a Hebraized form of the Egyptian *na-patoh + im*, "those of the delta."

15. Pathrusim. Land of Pathros (upper Egypt).
16. Casluhim. Uncertain. Because the Septuagint translates this word Chasmonim, some scholars have speculated that it designates the Nasmonim peoples who, according to classical Greek texts, lived in the area of the Gulf of Sidra (or Syrtis Major). The Casluhim also have been related to the Tjekker, a contingent of the Sea Peoples, though the origin of the Tjekker is presently unknown.
17. Caphtorim. Island of Crete.
18. Put. This is the Putaya of Old Persian inscriptions; it identifies the section of North Africa adjacent to the delta, and corresponds to modern-day Libya.
19. Canaan. Land of Canaan.
20. Sidon. Land of the Sidonians.
21. Heth. Land of the Hittites (i.e., neo-Hittite principalities in Syria).
22. Jebusite. Occupants of the Jerusalem area (Josh. 15:8; 18:28; Judg. 1:21; 19:10; 2 Sam. 5:6-9).
23. Amorite. Amurru of cuneiform and Egyptian sources. In the Old Testament, it designates the "hill country" of Palestine (Num. 13:29; Deut. 1:44; Josh. 11:3) as opposed to the lowlands of the Canaanites, although the term is also used to denote some of the occupants of central Transjordan (Num. 21:13; Deut. 1:4; Josh. 2:10; 9:10; 24:8; Judg. 10:8; 11:20).
24. Girgashite. Uncertain beyond general Canaanite localization. The name is attested in Phoenician texts and in an Egyptian text of Ramses II. It has been suggested that the name is related to Gergasenes (Luke 8:26, 37), and therefore situated in the region of the Sea of Galilee.
25. Hivite. People who occupied part of central Palestine (Gibeon, Josh. 9:7; 11:19; Shechem, Gen. 34:2), although Joshua 11:3 speaks of Hivites at the foot of Hermon. There is no justification for relating the Hivites with a place name (Ammiya) mentioned in the Amarna tablets, and at Alalakh, as this latter town should be located somewhere in the vicinity of Tripolis.
26. Arkite. Occupants of T. Arqa (12 1/2 miles north of Tripolis), known in cuneiform texts as Irqata and as Caesarea of

Lebanon during the Roman period.

27. Sinite. Siyannu, a city-state known from neiform and Ugaritic texts to have been situated along the Mediterranean seacoast between Ugarit and Arvad.
28. Arvadite. Ruad, an island city that is the northernmost Phoenician city to have preserved its name up to the present; it is attested in cuneiform, Egyptian, and classical sources.
29. Zemarite. Sumra, a city located between Arvad and Tripolis at the mouth of the el-Kabir (Eleutheros) River. This strategic city is frequently mentioned in cuneiform, Egyptian, Phoenician, and classical sources. It was the northernmost Egyptian stronghold in Canaan and was located on the border of Amurru.
30. Hamathite. Well-known city on the Orontes River, Hamath is the only inland city within the Phoenician group (i.e., the final five names of the Hamite list).

THE TWENTY-SIX DESCENDANTS OF SHEM

1. Elam. Famous country to the east of Babylon, having its capital at Susa.
2. Asshur. Land of Assyria.
3. Arpachshad. Uncertain. Variously identified with Arrapha (area of Nuzi) or Babylon (area of Chaldea).
4. Lud. Mentioned in classical sources as Luddi, this is Lydia in Asia Minor. Some scholars object to this equation because they believe that such a location does not fit with other Shemite locations, and they seek to relate Lud to the Lubdu peoples who are situated in the vicinity of Nuzi.
5. Aram. Land of Aramea, a territory between Damascus and the Euphrates River.
6. Uz. Uncertain. Josephus locates Uz in the area of Trachonitis (northeast Canaan).
7. Hul. Uncertain. Because Hul follows in sequence after Aram and Uz, it is possible that Hul should be situated in the Leja region. Josephus, on the other hand, locates Hul in Armenia.
8. Gether. Unknown. Josephus locates Gether in Bactria (northeast Afghanistan).
9. Mash. Uncertain. Josephus places Mash at Mesene, at the mouth of the Euphrates near Charax, in the immediate environs of other known Shemite locations. Others relate this name with Strabo's Mt. Masius, the Tur 'Abdin range, located between the Habur triangle and the Tigris River. To relate Mash with Carchemish is totally unjustified and based on a false etymology. Nor is it likely that Mash should be related to the Masha, a Sea Peoples group.
10. Shelah. Unknown.
11. Eber. Uncertain. This may be the origin of the Hebrews (Eberites); if so, Eber must be situated in the region of Ur of the Chaldeans, Harran, and Paddan-aram.
12. Peleg. Uncertain. A text of Tukulti-ninurta II refers to a Palga people who live near the Habur River. Later geographers have a Phaliga in this same location.
13. Joktan. Unknown.
14. Almodad. Unknown.
15. Sheleph. Uncertain. Attested in Sabean inscriptions and Arabic geographic treatises. Ptolemaeus places Sheleph at Salipeni, between Sheba and Hadramaut.
16. Hazarmaveth. Modern Hadramaut, located along southwest coast of Saudi Arabia, just east of Yemen. This name is frequently found in Sabean inscriptions and classical authors.
17. Jerah. Unknown. Perhaps this name should be related to a moon-cult center such as Tema (oasis in northwestern Arabian desert), based on its possible etymology.
18. Hadoraim. Unknown.
19. Uzal. Uncertain. Arabic tradition refers to Uzal (or Azal) as the pre-Islamic name for San'a, the capital of Yemen. Less likely is a possible relationship with the city Azalla, which is found in a campaign of Ashurbanipal.
20. Diklah. Unknown. The name translates "date-palms" and is suggestive of an area that was rich in this commodity. Some authors have suggested a linguistic relationship between Diklah and Nakhla, a town just south of Mecca.
21. Obal. Uncertain. Abil is a common rubric for certain sectors of Yemen; accordingly, Obal is often located near modern Hodeida.
22. Abimael. Unknown.
23. Sheba. See comments at Hamite Sheba.
24. Ophir. Most likely found in Somaliland (refer to Map 47).
25. Havilah. See comments at Hamite Havilah.
26. Jobab. Uncertain. Ptolemaeus mentions a Yobaritai in southeastern Saudi Arabia.

PATRIARCHS' JOURNEYS

The book of Genesis portrays both patriarchal migrations and patriarchal wanderings. The migrations disclose how Abraham and his offspring came to live in the land of Canaan, whereas the wanderings describe the manner in which they lived there.

Patriarchal migrations began when Abraham moved with his father's clan from Ur of the Chaldeans to the city of Harran. Since the archaeological work and publications of Leonard Woolley earlier in this century, it has been fashionable to equate "biblical Ur" with the famous metropolitan capital of the Third Dynasty of Ur (Mugayir), situated some 140 miles southeast of Babylon in the heartland of Sumer (but see Fig. 38). Initially, that view seemed logical because of the obvious name similarity and because both the Sumerian capital and Harran flourished in the early second millennium B.C. as centers of moon-cult worship. A form of moon-cult worship is clearly attested in patriarchal ancestry: the names of Terah, Laban, Milcah, and Sarah all are derivative of it (cf. Josh. 24:2).

Subsequent investigation, however, has brought Woolley's view into question. Uncertainty prevails, in the first place, concerning both "Ur" and "Chaldeans." The Bible never refers merely to "Ur," but always to "Ur *of the Chaldeans*" or "Ur *in the land of the Chaldeans*" (Gen. 11:28, 31; 15:7; Neh. 9:7; cf. Acts 7:4). Such a consistent qualification might suggest that the biblical writers were endeavoring to distinguish the place of Abraham's emigration from the famous city with the same name. In much the same way, a person from Paris, *Illinois*, might have to qualify where he lived, so as not to confuse his native town with the more famous French city.

The need to distinguish the name Ur is further strengthened as one grapples with the meaning of Chaldeans, any interpretation of which points to a *northern* location for the place involved. The word translated "Chaldeans" is written *kaśdîm* in Hebrew. Scholars tend to identify this word with "Chaldeans" either on grounds of phonetics[12] or phonology.[13] But in any event, there is no sure trace of the Chaldeans in southern Babylonia before the early ninth century B.C., long after the conclusion of the patriarchal era. Earlier than this date, one must look to northern Mesopotamia to find Chaldeans. Perhaps their presence there is documented as early as the time of Tiglath-pileser I (c. 1100 B.C.) or even Adad-nirari I (c. 1300 B.C.). On the other hand, if *kaśdîm* is related to the patriarchal ancestor Chesed (Gen. 22:22) and the phrase becomes "Ur of [the region of] Chesed," one is left with the same conclusion, for Chesed's descendants settled in Paddan-aram (northern Mesopotamia; cf. Gen. 24:10).

Moreover, where Mesopotamian cultural influences seem to be reflected in the lives of the patriarchs (e.g., levirate marriage, polygamy, genealogical inheritance, population makeup, etc.), northern Mesopotamia ordinarily provides the cultural parallel. Southern (Babylonian) influence, as far as we now know, is almost totally lacking in the patriarchal narratives (cf. trips of Eliezer [Gen. 24] and Jacob [Gen. 28] to Abraham's homeland near Paddan-aram). Mesopotamian literature does mention a "northern Ur," as attested in the archival materials at Alalakh, Ugarit, Hattusha and Ebla, although its precise localization remains elusive. The combination of all these factors leads us to place Abraham's Ur in the northern sectors of Mesopotamia.

A study of the patriarchal wanderings presents us with two overriding conclusions. The first is that the patriarchs lived in tents as pastoral seminomads on seasonal pasture land. The places in Canaan visited by patriarchs received between ten and thirty inches annual rainfall, which was ideally suited for the pastoral grazing of flocks and herds. However, the patriarchs did not normally settle in towns (Lot is an exception) and did not farm (Gen. 26:12 probably is an exception). Even when offered (e.g., Gen. 34:10), the patriarchs seem not to have owned land, except for the modest burial sites at Mamre (Gen. 23:2), Shechem (Gen. 48:22; cf. Josh. 24:32), and where Rachel was buried (Gen. 35:16-19).

The second conclusion is that the patriarchs must have arrived in Canaan during an era when the land was relatively free from external political control (see discussion with Map 25). This assessment coincides with the historical profile of Canaan during much of the Middle Bronze Age (2000-1525 B.C.). During that period, Canaan and Syria were vitally involved together and one might even say that they shared the same material culture. But in the Late Bronze Age (1525-1200 B.C.), the strong Egyptian domination—temporarily interrupted during the Amarna period—and the formation of larger political entities led to more cultural differentiation, which undoubtedly made free traffic and ethnic migration much more difficult.

There are several other features found in the patriarchal narratives that point towards a Middle Bronze Age setting. For example, the price paid for Joseph (20 shekels of silver, Gen. 37:28; cf. Lev. 27:5) represented the average price given for a healthy male slave during the Middle Bronze

Age (e.g., Code of Hammurapi §§116, 214, 252; ARM VIII.10 [1/3 mina = 20 shekels]). Admittedly, market prices for slaves fluctuated in antiquity depending on supply and demand; nevertheless, the average price of a slave had increased to about 30-40 shekels of silver in the first millennium B.C. and to between 90-120 shekels of silver by the time of the Persian Empire. Also fitting into Middle Bronze Age social patterns are a variety of patriarchal social customs (a man without sons could adopt his own slave [Gen. 15:2-6], a barren wife could provide her husband with a slave-girl by which to bear a son [Gen. 16:1-4; 30:1-8; cf. 30:9-13], the practice of granting birthright to the eldest son [Gen. 25:5-6, 32-34; 43:33-34; 49:3-4], the Hebrew term used for the eldest son [Gen. 25:23], the gift of a female slave as part of a dowry at marriage [Gen. 16:1-6; 30:1-13], a father's prohibition forbidding a prospective son-in-law from taking another wife [Gen. 31:50], the arrangement of marriage by a bride's brother, assuming that her father was deceased [Gen. 24:29-33, 50-61]).

In summary, though no individual mentioned in the book of Genesis is yet otherwise known from antiquity, the patriarchal narratives do present an accurate historical picture of the age about which they purport to speak.

ABRAHAM IN THE PROMISED LAND

In some respects, God's call upon Abraham carried with it many of the same consequences as did His curse upon Cain: each was directed to forsake every form of security known to his world. Abraham abandoned his heirdom (land, clan, family) at Harran in response to God's command and proceeded toward the land his descendants would eventually inherit (Gen. 11:31; 12:4-5). Upon arriving in the central highlands of Canaan, the great patriarch built an altar at the city of Shechem and worshiped God there (12:6-7). He then moved south to encamp near Bethel and Ai (12:8) **(1)**. Abraham also discovered a harsh reality about this land of promise: it was dominated by Canaanites (Gen. 12:6*b*) and was caught in the grip of famine (12:10). He was forced to migrate into Egypt, presumably via Hebron and Beersheba **(2)**. When the famine passed, however, Abraham and his entourage returned to his former campsite near Bethel/Ai and began to live there (Gen. 13:3-4) **(3)**. Before long, however, conflict arose between the clansmen of Abraham and Lot, a conflict that culminated in Lot's departure to live in the city of Sodom (Gen. 13:12; cf. 14:12) **(4)**. Abraham moved on southward and came to dwell by the oaks of Mamre, at Hebron (Gen. 13:18) **(5)**.

(The location of the cities of the plain, including Sodom and Gomorrah, remains very much of a mystery. Those cities are sometimes sought at the north end of the Dead Sea, where the Jordan River runs into it. Depending heavily on the wording of Genesis 13:10-11, this view infers that Sodom and Gomorrah must have been visible from the vicinity of Bethel. Others argue that the cities of the plain must been located toward the southern end of the Dead Sea, based on the fact that one of the cities [Zoar] is positioned in that region on the Medeba map and on a presumed name survival [Sedom]. Near the southeastern shore of the Dead Sea have been found many hundreds of graves containing thousands of skeletal remains, related by some writers to the events of Genesis 19.)

Some time thereafter, the five cities situated in the Valley of Siddim (Sodom, Gomorrah, Admah, Zeboiim, Zoar) rebelled against their Mesopotamian overlords (Gen. 14:1-4). Responding to this challenge, the Mesopotamian monarchs led their armies toward Canaan and assaulted the Transjordanian lands of the Rephaim, Zuzim, Emim, and Horites along the way (14:5-6) **(6)**. Passing El-paran, they turned toward Kadesh-barnea, where they subdued some Amalekites (14:7), before vanquishing the Amorites at Tamar (14:7) **(7)**. That cleared the way for the Mesopotamian kings to turn their attention to the real enemies: the cities of the Siddim valley (14:9-11) **(8)**. Because a Mesopotamian victory was swift and decisive, the cities of the valley were captured, along with some of their citizens, including Lot, who was taken as far as Dan (14:12) **(9)**. Having learned of the catastrophe at Hebron, Abraham immediately led his men in pursuit of Lot's captors, successfully overtaking them at Dan and routing them as far as the north of Damascus (14:13-15) **(10)**. As he returned from that mission past the Valley of Shaveh, Abraham was met by the king of Salem, Melchizedek, with whom Abraham shared the spoils of victory (14:17-24) **(11)**.

Abraham then journeyed toward the Negeb and eventually came to Gerar (20:1) **(12)**. During his years there, the long-awaited promise of a son was finally realized (21:2-3). But when a problem over water rights arose with the king of Gerar (21:25), Abraham moved farther inland to Beersheba (21:31, by implication) **(13)**. That location served as the patriarch's home until his death, when he was buried beside Sarah in a cave near Hebron (Gen. 25:8-10).

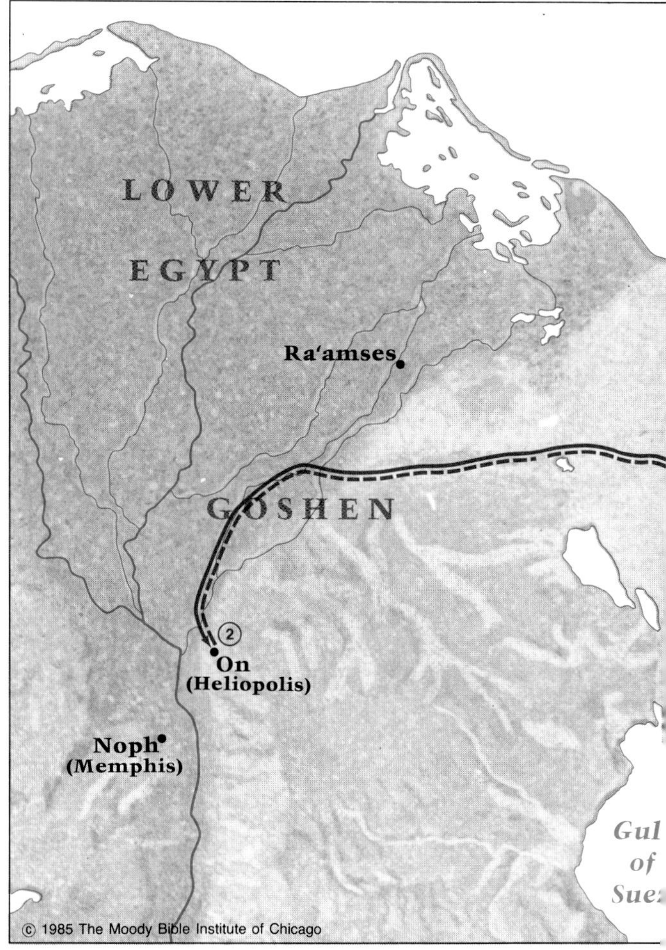

city
city (uncertain location)
mountain peak
Abraham's arrival in Canaan and migration to Egypt
Abraham's return from Egypt
Abraham's pursuit of enemy kings
Abraham's return from battle and final journey to Beersheba
Lot's departure from Abraham
course taken by enemy kings in Genesis 14
to Hobah
Damascus
Mt. Hermon
Dan
Hazor
Sea of Galilee
Karnaim
Ashtaroth
REPHAIM
Yarmuk R.
Megiddo
Ham
Jordan R.
ZUZIM
Mediterranean Sea
Samaria
Shechem
Jarkon
Me
Jabbok R.
Aphek
Bethel
Ai
Jericho
Ashdod
Ekron
VALLEY OF SHAVEH
Salem
Kiriathaim
Gaza
Hebron
Dibon
Dead Sea
Arnon R.
EMIM
Gerar
Besor Brook
Beersheba
Possible location of Sodom, Gomorrah, Admah, Zeboiim
Zoar
Zered Brook
W. el-Arish
AMORITES
VALLEY OF SIDDIM
Hagar fled here from Sarah —Gen 16:14f; Isaac lived here after Abraham's death —Gen 25:11f
Beer-lahai-roi
Tamar
HORITES
EASTERN DESERT
AMALEKITES
Punon
Kadesh-barnea
LDERNESS OF SHUR
Petra
WILDERNESS OF PARAN
El-paran
Gulf of Aqaba
MI. 0 10 20 30 40
KM. 0 10 20 30 40 50 60

PATRIARCHS IN THE PROMISED LAND

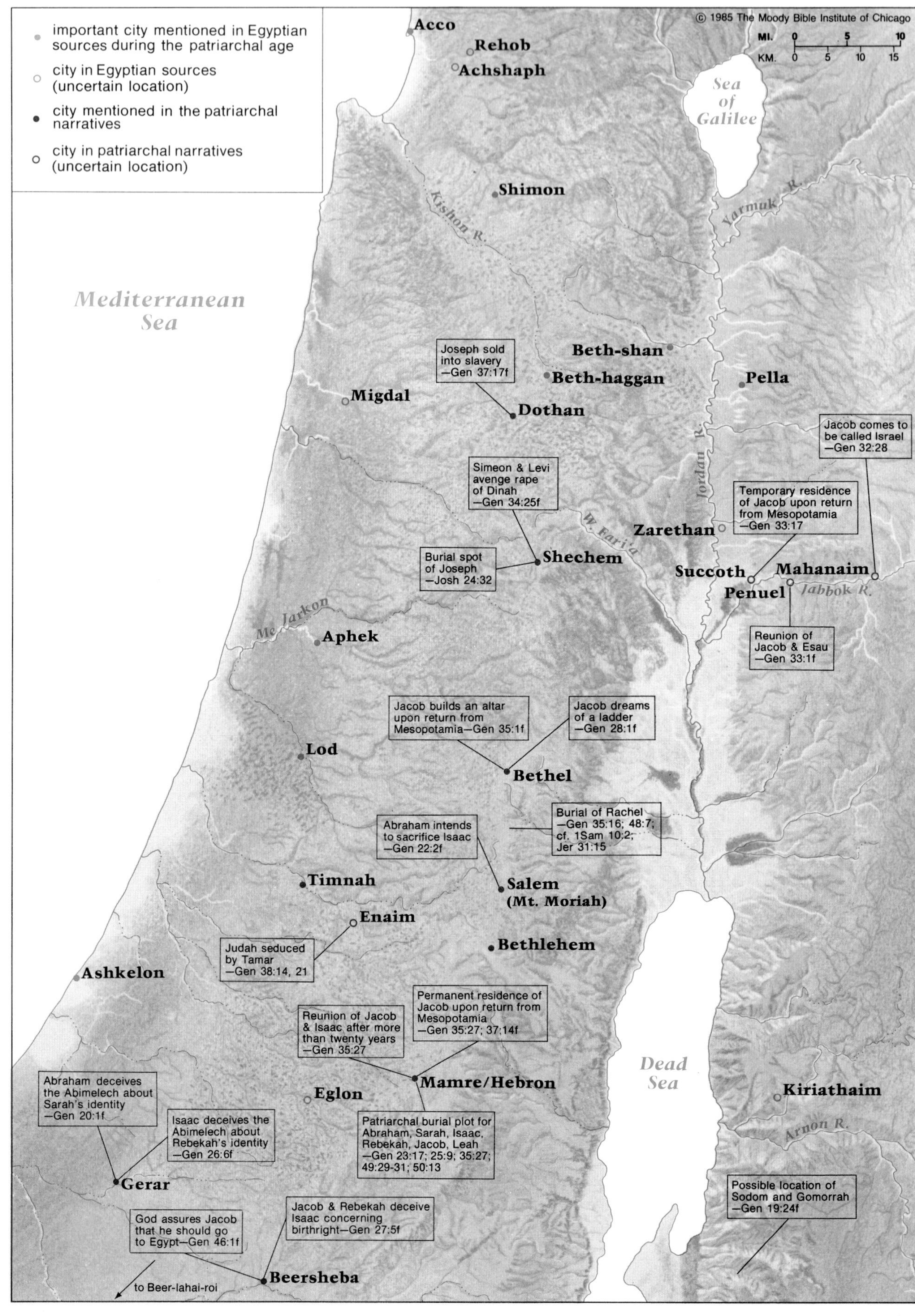

THE ROUTE OF THE EXODUS

There can be no doubt that an Israelite Exodus from Egypt occurred. However, a number of significant historical and geographical questions remain concerning events prior to and during the Exodus. On the historical side, one is prompted to ask, Who was the "new king" of Exodus 1:8 who "came to power in Egypt" and "did not know Joseph"? Was this new pharaoh Egyptian or Hyksos? What was the identity of the pharaoh who initially refused, but eventually was obliged to acquiesce to Moses' demand that the Israelites should be released from bondage?

In the geographical column are questions like the following: Where were located the cities of Ra'amses, Pithom, Succoth, and Etham, places through which God's people passed as they began their eastward trek toward the "Red Sea"? At which body of water was it that the Israelites passed through "on dry ground"? What were the logistics involved in such a crossing? Where were Mt. Sinai and Kadesh-barnea? And by what route(s) did the liberated Israelites cross the Sinai peninsula and approach the land of promise?

The list of geographical questions will receive the most attention here, but perhaps a passing historical footnote is also in order. Around 1720 B.C., a group of foreigners referred to in Egyptian sources as *heqa khoswe* (Hyksos, "rulers of foreign lands") invaded the land of the Nile, erected their capital at Avaris (Tell ed-Dab'a), and ruled Egypt in what is known historically as Dynasties 15 and 16. Though they penetrated Egypt at a time of political disintegration that had resulted in a proliferation of local rulers throughout Lower Egypt (the western delta had already seceded to form an independent kingdom), the success of Hyksos imperialism should be attributed largely to their exploitation of a number of Asiatic technological innovations. Those may have included the horse-drawn war chariot, the battering ram, and the composite bow. Soon after 1560 B.C., however, the Hyksos were expelled from Egypt by native princes, and the so-called New Kingdom period of Egyptian history was inaugurated. During that time, a concerted effort was mounted to rid Egypt of any trace of Hyksos influence. One illustration of that is found in the historical records of Thutmosis III. This sovereign appears to have launched at least twenty-one military campaigns against the Hyksos and their Asiatic allies (Amorites, Mitannians), and in a few of those he boasted that he even crossed the Euphrates River to rout the enemy and free Egypt from its influence.

In a word, it appears to me that the biblical, historical, and archaeological data are best served by theorizing that it was a Hyksos monarch before whom Joseph stood as an interpreter of dreams (Gen. 41:14-37) and who later ceded a choice parcel of land (Goshen) to Joseph's family (Gen. 47:6). According to such a theory, the "new king" of Exodus 1:8 would have been one of the native Egyptian monarchs of the New Kingdom who, as part of his Hyksos purge, resolutely refused to recognize the validity of the Goshen land grant. Discerning in the Israelites a multitude who might very well join with his Asiatic enemies in war, this new king moreover acted quickly to enslave God's people.

The above-mentioned theory also fits well with the historical profile attested in the book of Genesis. The patriarchs moved in and through Palestine for some 215 years (cf. Gen. 12:4; 21:5; 25:26; 47:9), seemingly with the greatest of ease, mobility, and freedom. Yet it is inconceivable that their movements should have gone unnoticed (e.g., Gen. 14:14). That bespeaks a political climate in Palestine that would have been free from any sort of national or international domination, which is most truly characteristic of that period between 1850 and 1550 B.C. The theory might also humanly explain how Joseph, a non-Egyptian, was able to rise to the position of grand vizier in a foreign land—the court itself would not have been Egyptian, but Hyksos.

This is obviously not the place for a detailed discourse concerning the date of the Hebrew Exodus. However, an interpretation of Exodus 12:40 does impinge upon our discussion, and it must be addressed at least briefly. Does the mention there of 430 years designate the amount of time that the Israelites spent *in Egypt* (so the Masoretic text) or *in Canaan and Egypt* (so the Samaritan Pentateuch and the Septuagint, though the order is inverted in the latter text)? Prior statements should make it clear that I have given historical and textual preference to the latter view (cf. Gen. 15:13; Gal. 3:17). And accordingly, I would advocate that the Israelite sojourn in Egypt took place between approximately 1660 and 1445 B.C. and that the patriarchal sojourn in Canaan encompassed approximately the dates 1875-1660 B.C. Thus, some 430 years lapsed while the early Israelites lived in Canaan and Egypt. This would mean that Joseph was promoted about 1670 B.C., in the middle of the Hyksos occupation of Egypt. But it is impossible to identify the individual before whom Joseph appeared, because the dating and succession of Hyksos kings remains undemonstrable today. In addition, the Bible provides virtually no clues for the length of time the Israelites suffered under Egyptian bondage, so it seems hazardous to speculate on the identity of the pharaoh of Exodus 1:8, aside from identifying him as a Hyksos monarch.

The biblical narrative locates the beginning of the Israelite trek at the city of Ra'amses (Ex. 12:37; cf. 1:11), from which they journeyed first to Succoth (13:20), then to Etham, to Pi Hahiroth (14:2, between Migdol and the sea, opposite Baal-zephon), and finally to the body of water where the actual miracle occurred (cf. Num. 33:5-8).

Of all those sites, it is the location of Ra'amses and Succoth that is established beyond reasonable doubt. Though earlier sought in the eastern delta at the site of Zoan/Tanis (San el-Hagar), Ra'amses must be placed at Qantir (Tell ed-Dab'a), some 17 miles to the southwest. Furthermore, it seems conclusive that that was also the location of the Hyksos capital, known in that period as Avaris. Excavators have discovered archaeological remains at Tell ed-Dab'a that indicate it was a large habitational site in the Hyksos era and into parts of the New Kingdom period. The artifacts dug up at the site (pottery, utensils, burial wares, etc.) do not conform to Egyptian typology, but rather to what is found in contemporary layers in Palestine. One prominent Egyptologist has commented: "Archaeologically, it is as if the site were actually in Palestine."[14] Just north of the tell a tile factory was found where glazed blue tiles were manufactured for use in the palatial estates of pharaohs. And in the environs of this installation were found certain ostraca that actually bear the name of Ra'amses.[15] This, then, was the locale from which the Israelites began their journey.

In the Wadi Tumilat of the southeast delta (the valley that forms the main route from the Nile to modern Ismalia) stands the site of Tell Maskhuta, which should be associated with biblical Succoth. From this site a series of monuments have been unearthed that repeatedly refer to the ancient city of Tjeku, which name merely represents the Egyptian phonetic equivalent of the Hebrew *Succoth*. Egyptian literature, moreover, relates something of the importance of ancient Tjeku by describing its fortifications and temple dedicated to the god Atum. An Egyptian story from the thirteenth century B.C.[16] bears a striking resemblance to the biblical account and tells of two runaway slaves who were being tracked down by an Egyptian official. It seems that he pursued the slaves as far as Tjeku, where he learned they had fled south. He then proceeded to a place called Htm where he was informed that the slaves had penetrated the fortifications north of Migdol, and so he abandoned the chase.

This Egyptian story is arresting for a number of reasons. First, on the assumption that Egyptian *Htm* corresponds to the biblical *Etham* (which is

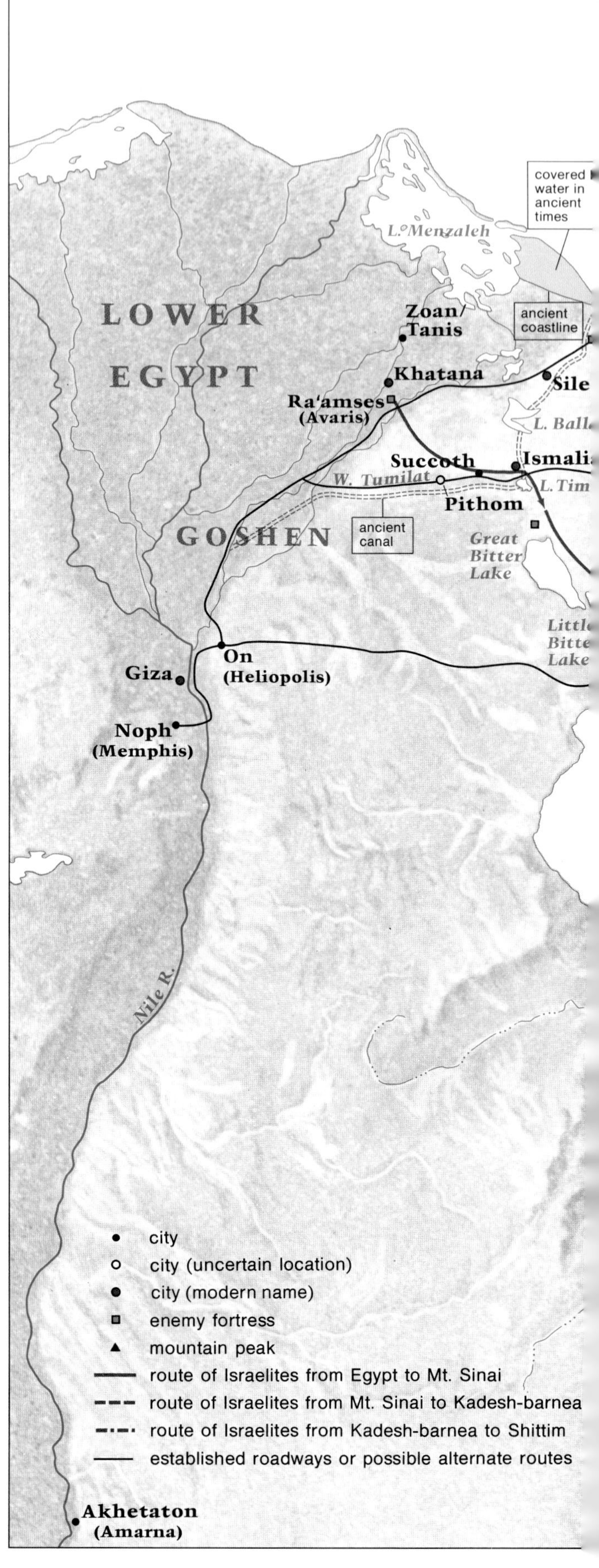

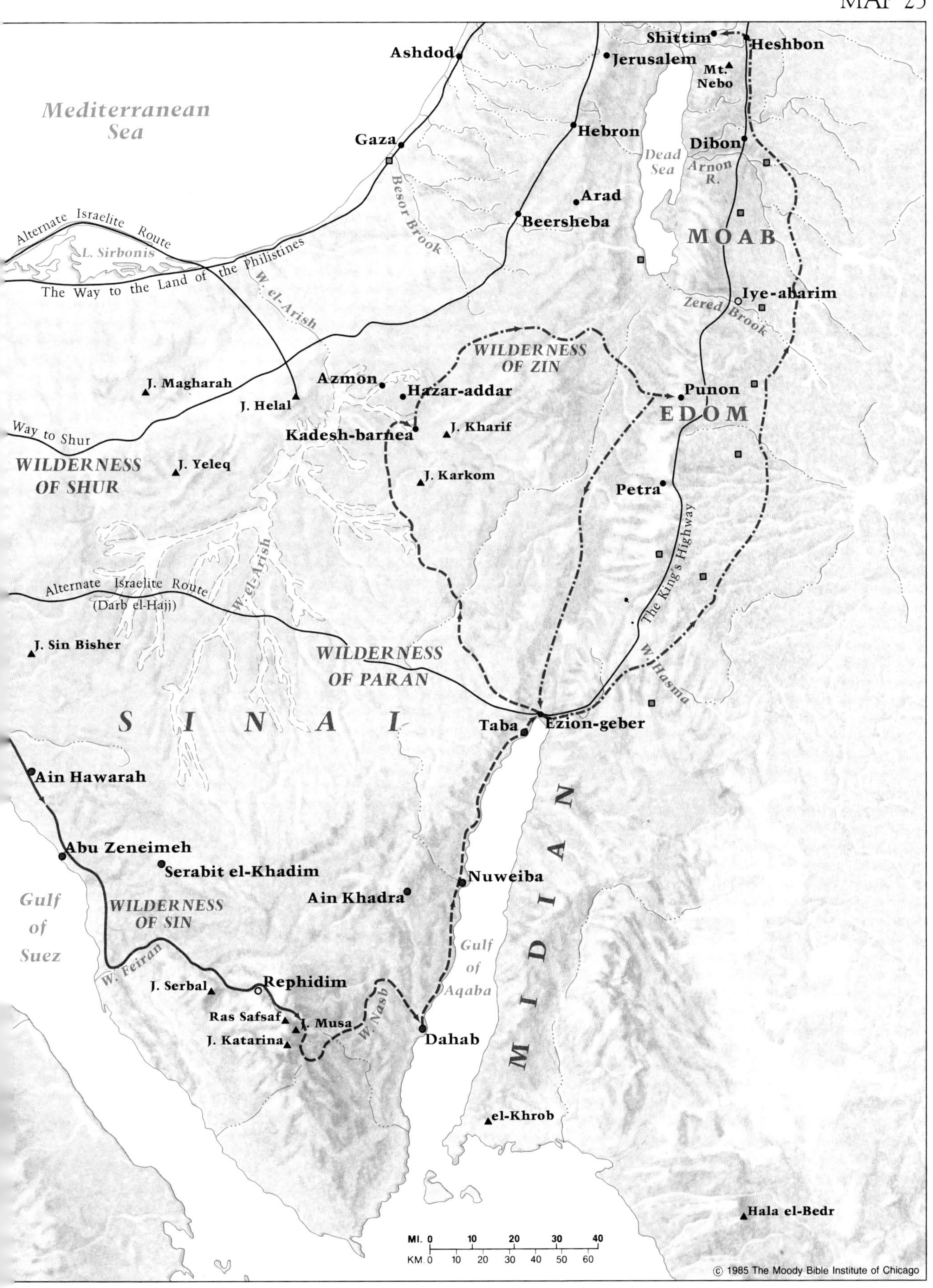

Mediterranean Sea
Ashdod
Jerusalem
Shittim
Heshbon
Mt. Nebo
Gaza
Hebron
Dibon
Dead Sea
Arnon R.
Besor Brook
Arad
Beersheba
MOAB
Alternate Israelite Route
L. Sirbonis
The Way to the Land of the Philistines
W. el-Arish
Iye-abarim
Zered Brook
WILDERNESS OF ZIN
J. Magharah
Azmon
Hazar-addar
Punon
J. Helal
EDOM
Way to Shur
Kadesh-barnea
J. Kharif
WILDERNESS OF SHUR
J. Yeleq
J. Karkom
Petra
The King's Highway
Alternate Israelite Route (Darb el-Hajj)
W. el-Arish
J. Sin Bisher
WILDERNESS OF PARAN
W. Hasma
SINAI
Taba
Ezion-geber
Ain Hawarah
Abu Zeneimeh
Serabit el-Khadim
Nuweiba
Ain Khadra
Gulf of Suez
WILDERNESS OF SIN
Gulf of Aqaba
MIDIAN
W. Feiran
J. Serbal
Rephidim
Ras Safsaf
J. Musa
W. Nasb
J. Katarina
Dahab
el-Khrob
Hala el-Bedr
MI. 0 10 20 30 40
KM. 0 10 20 30 40 50 60

linguistically possible), one finds mentioned here three of the places along the route of the Israelite Exodus, and they even are listed in the same order. This strongly suggests that the road taken by the Israelites was an established, traditional artery. Second, this text provides some clues regarding the locations of Htm and Migdol. Htm must be situated to the south of Tjeku; Migdol most likely should be positioned at the eastern fringes of the Egyptian frontier, because the Egyptian officer forsook the hunt when notified the slaves had passed the fortifications there.

If the foregoing are correct inferences, it follows that Etham could not have been located at Sile, where it is traditionally sought, and that Pi Hahiroth could not have been situated adjacent to Lake Menzaleh. Certainly Sile possessed a well-known fortress, which seems to be the basis for identifying it with Htm ("fortress"), but an entire network of Egyptian fortresses is now known to have existed during this period (see Map 25). Furthermore, if Etham were really the fortress at Sile, then the Israelites would have been following the "Way to the Land of the Philistines." But we are explicitly told that God directed them *not* to take this route lest, confronted with warfare, they decide to return to Egypt (Ex. 13:17). The transportation artery to Philistia surely would have been blocked to Israelite passage, as it was the preeminent Egyptian military route. The reliefs of Seti I (c. 1300 B.C.) depict a series of fortresses protecting that highway, showing that the Egyptians could readily have stemmed any Israelite movement in that direction. In God's providence, then, He led Israel instead "by the Way of the Wilderness towards the Red Sea" which, as will become apparent below, I identify with the Way (of the Wilderness) to Shur (i.e., Darb el-Shur, which joins Egypt and central Palestine via Beersheba and Hebron).

The precise location of Pi Hahiroth remains a mystery. Were it possible to identify the ethnic derivation of the name itself, its approximate location might have been determined. For a Semitic origin would almost certainly presume a northeastern delta location, whereas an Egyptian word origin could be suggestive of a wider geographic horizon. On the one hand, some scholars since the archaeologist W. F. Albright have argued that Pi Hahiroth may derive from a verb that means "to dig/cut" (*HRT), and that a location along a canal is therefore implied. Although this initially appears to be a creative suggestion (see below), such an explanation necessarily entails a Semitic origin for the word (*hārash* in Hebrew); this, I suppose, would have to be attributed to Hyksos influence, and it might even be supported by the way in which the Septuagint translates the name in Numbers 33:7-8 (Eirōth).

However, this suggestion is only tentative, and Gardiner noted long ago[17] that the form of Pi Hahiroth conforms perfectly well with Egyptian: *pi-hahiroth*, "house of Hathor" (an Egyptian goddess). Compare Ezekiel 30:17, *pi-beseth*, "house of

Figure 10 Mt. Sinai. On the Plain of Rafah (foreground, north of Sinai) the Israelites may have encamped.

Bastat" (an Egyptian goddess) and Exodus 1:11, *pithom* "house of (A)tum" (an Egyptian god). (See also Exodus 14:2, 9 [Septuagint].) The derivation and therefore of the localization of Pi Hahiroth remains an unsolved riddle.

Be that as it may, pictured on the map is the vestige of an ancient canal, sections of which have been only recently discovered. This canal was operational in the time of the Israelite Exodus and appears to have run to the south of Succoth. Scholars have concluded that it was most unlikely that this canal should have been used in antiquity for navigational or irrigational purposes. They urge instead that it was used as a wall of defense. Because portions of this canal measure nearly 230 feet wide at ground level and about 65 feet in width at the bottom, it clearly would have represented an impenetrable defensive mechanism to foreign armies or fleeing slaves.[18]

After passing through these intermediate towns, Israel eventually pitched its camp beside *'Eruthre Thalassa* ("Red Sea"), as it is called in the Septuagint, or *yam suph* ("Sea of reeds/papyrus"), as it is referred to in the Hebrew text. Because it is used at times in the Old Testament to denote the reeds/papyrus that grow along the Nile (Ex. 2:3; Isa. 19:6), it appears probable that *sûph* was borrowed from the Egyptian word meaning "papyrus" (*twf[y]*). At other times the expression is employed to designate either the Gulf of Suez

Figure 11 Aerial view of Egypt, Red Sea, and Sinai peninsula. Dead Sea is visible in background.

(Num. 33:10-11) or the Gulf of Aqaba (Num. 14:25; 21:4; 1 Kings 9:26).

Now for two reasons it appears likely to me that the body of water at which the miracle occurred was one of the marshy lakes situated east of the delta area. First, papyrus does not grow in the deep waters of the Gulfs; second, a New Kingdom text speaks of the area between Tanis/Ra'amses and a line created by the intermittent marshes from Lake Menzaleh to Lake Timsah as "the land of papyrus par excellence." (The traditional rendition "Red Sea" in English Bibles ultimately derives from the Septuagint via the Latin Vulgate.) But it is of interest to note that Luther's heavy reliance upon the Hebrew text here led him to use the German *Schilfmeer* ("Sea of reeds"). From north to south, the intermittent bodies of water included Lake Menzaleh, Lake Ballah, Lake Timsah, and the Bitter Lakes.

Based on all the foregoing considerations, taken together with the probable route created by the locations determined for Ra'amses and Succoth, it seems reasonable to suggest that the divine event (cf. Ps. 77:19-20) occurred at or near Lake Timsah, where the Way of the Wilderness to Shur intersected this line of lakes. Alternatively, the crossing may have occurred at the Great Bitter Lake, although that seems less likely to me. Even though striving to be fiercely biblical, I would stress that I am drawing no certain conclusions from this part of the investigation.

But if certain geographical factors are not yet clear, and if the Bible supplies precious few details concerning the logistics of the miraculous crossing, what *is* plain from Scripture, but often overlooked in discussions of this narrative, is that the crossing took place in a mere eight hours or less (cf. Ex. 14:20, 24, 27). Simply to move in such a short order that vast number of Israelites, who at that point were little more than an organized mob, requires that the magnitude of this miracle was much greater than normally depicted in Christian art or Sunday school literature. It is not inconceivable that a corridor of land as wide as five miles might have been required to accommodate the logistics and timing of the Israelite crossing. Therefore, it may be that part of the canal linked to Lake Timsah was itself incorporated into the miracle. It is no wonder that writers of later Scripture repeatedly cite the Exodus event when they are seeking to establish the paradigm of God's sovereign might.

Having been delivered at the water, Israel was next directed to set out on a course for Mt. Sinai. Few Old Testament geographical questions have been more vigorously debated than the location of Mt. Sinai. Today the sacred mountain is sought in any one of three principal regions: somewhere in northwest Saudi Arabia or south Jordan, somewhere in the northern Sinai peninsula, or somewhere in the awesome granite highlands of southern Sinai.

Advocates of the Saudi Arabian/Jordanian hypothesis argue from two scriptural points: (1) having fled from the pharaoh, Moses took up residence in the land of Midian and became the son-in-law of the priest of Midian (Ex. 2:15-16; 18:1), and (2) Scripture is replete with references to what appears to have been volcanic or earthquake activity associated with the establishment of the Sinaitic covenant (e.g., Ex. 19:18; 24:17; Deut. 4:11-12; 5:22-26; 9:10, 15; 10:4; Judg. 5:5; Ps. 68:8; Hag. 2:6; Heb. 12:18, 29; cf. 1 Kings 19:11-12; Isa. 64:1-3). According to this theory, the land of Midian was situated exclusively in the terrain east of the Gulf of Aqaba. It is further asserted that the geological structure of mountains within the Sinai itself is not conducive to either volcanic or earthquake activity, or at least not to recent activity. Individuals who subscribe to this theory will most likely locate Mt. Sinai at Petra, el-Khrob, or Hala el-Bedr (refer to map for locations). Admittedly, this viewpoint has an extremely long tradition, going back to the third century B.C. when Demetrius, a Jewish historian living in Egypt, made such a claim.[19] Moreover, this view is well represented in early mapmaking efforts of the Promised Land.[20]

Objections to each of the arguments for the Saudi Arabian/Jordanian location have seriously eroded their cogency. First, it is impossible that the Midianites themselves should be confined to only one area prior to the Greco-Roman period. In Genesis 36:35 and 1 Chronicles 1:46, for example, Midianites are said to be residing within the territory of Moab. In Numbers 25:6-7 and Joshua 13:21, they are said to be dwelling in the Mishor region of Transjordan. In Judges 7:25 and 8:18-19, on the other hand, Midianites appear to be living in the wilderness east of Moab and Ammon. In 1 Kings 11:18, Midian must be situated in northern Sinai. In Judges 6:1-6 and 7:1, these people are said to be located inside Canaan itself.

In addition to relating Moses to the Midianites through marriage, biblical tradition also links him to the Kenites in the same way (Judg. 1:16; 4:11). Apparently a Midianite clan or subtribe, the Kenites seem to have represented an itinerant band of smiths, to judge from their name, "[copper]smiths". At times the Kenites were situated inside Canaan itself (Gen. 15:19), and later they may be found either in Galilee (Judg. 4:11; 5:24) or just to the south of Judah (1 Sam. 27:10; 1 Chron. 2:55). Whatever the case, one cannot argue that the Midianites, or their subgroup the Kenites, were confined exclusively to only one region at the time of the biblical Exodus.

The volcano/earthquake argument appears to be no more decisive. First of all, although it is admitted that no recent volcanic activity is attested within Sinai, as recently as 1982 the Sinai peninsula experienced a major earthquake (i.e., measuring more than six points on the Richter scale); its epicenter was near Nuweiba, but it was felt atop J. Musa. But second, the phenomenological language in the relevant Bible passages could be reflective of weather conditions that surrounded Mt. Sinai at the time (cf. Ps. 68:8-10). Alternatively, it may be possible to understand the language of those texts in a dynamic sense; the narratives would then be vividly underscoring the reality of an actual appearance of God—a theophany. There are other theophanic passages in the Old Testament that employ the same kind of terminology without presupposing such volcanic/earthquake activity (e.g., 2 Sam. 22:8-16; Ps. 18:7-15; 89:5-18; 97:1-5; 104:31-32). We remain unconvinced, then, by arguments that seek to locate Mt. Sinai in Saudi Arabia or Jordan.

Advocates of the northern Sinai hypothesis also attempt to anchor their argumentation in Scripture, and they will seek to locate Mt. Sinai at either J. Helal, J. Kharif, J. Sin Bisher, J. Yeleq, J. Magharah, J. Karkom, or Kadesh-barnea itself (see map for locations). To begin with, Moses' request in Exodus 5:3 (cf. 3:18; 8:27) was to travel into the wilderness a journey of three-days' distance; proponents of the northern viewpoint deduce therefore that Mt. Sinai could not have been separated from Goshen by more than a three-day march. According to this criterion, J. Sin Bisher or J. Magharah are proposed as likely candidates, being nearer to Goshen than other suggested sites; each of these is separated from Succoth by approximately 75 airline miles. Second, the two biblical references to the arrival of quail (Ex. 16:13; Num. 11:31-32; cf. Ps. 78:27-31; 105:40) are cited. These passages demonstrate that the Israelites encountered quail in close proximity to Mt. Sinai. Residents of northern Sinai are still easily able to capture exhausted quail that have just completed a protracted leg in their annual migration between southern Europe and Arabia.[21] Third, the Israelite victory over the Amalekites at Rephidim (Ex. 17:8; cf. Deut. 25:17-19) is said to be decisive in favor of the northern location, since this is the region in which the Amalekites are otherwise encountered in Scripture. And finally, there are certain Old Testament poetic passages that seem to be supporting such a northern location (Deut. 33:2; Judg. 5:4; Hab. 3:3, 7).

Taken as a whole, these arguments appear rather impressive, but individually they can be regarded as inconclusive. The three-day argument is hypothetical and ultimately collapses under its own weight. It presupposes a certain interpretation of the expression "three-days," over against being construed either as a loose period of time or as a specimen of Oriental bargaining. It also requires that the destination involved in Moses' request was Mt. Sinai, though this is never stated in the text. Although Sin Bisher or Magharah are closer to Goshen than other locations suggested, 75 miles is still too great a distance to cover in a mere three-day period. Itinerary texts from the Mosaic period stipulate that caravans were able to cover no more than about 20-23 miles per day. With the Exodus, however, the size and background of the group, when combined with the factors of accompanying women and children and flocks and herds (Ex. 12:38; 34:3; cf. 17:3; Num. 20:19), eliminate any possibility that as many as 75 miles could have been covered in just three days. The average daily distance maintained by modern bedouin moving from camp to camp is about six miles. And in the end, a total of eight intermediate encampments were actually registered between Israel's deliverance at the sea and the arrival at Mt. Sinai (Num. 33:8-15).

The journey from Goshen to Mt. Sinai took place in the springtime (Ex. 12:18; 19:1), and the trek from Mt. Sinai to Kadesh-barnea occurred about a year later in the springtime (Num. 10:11; 13:20*b*). Anyone who seeks to interpret the quail narratives in terms of natural phenomena, therefore, is obliged to relate them to the *spring* migration of the quail, when they fly from south to north and arrive at Sinai after an extended flight over the waters of the Red Sea. This suggests persuasively that the quail in the biblical narratives had just reached the peninsula (southern), and not the Mediterranean (northern), shore of the Sinai.

I confess that the location of the encounter between the Israelites and Amalekites at Rephidim remains something of a mystery, especially in light of the 1 Samuel 15 narrative. Elsewhere in Scripture the Amalekites seem to be found only in the northern regions, although this is not certain. They may be located in the land of Edom (Gen. 36:16), in the terrain just south of Judah (1 Sam. 27:8), or even as far west as the territory of Shur (1 Sam. 15:7). Not unpredictably, therefore, the Amalekites are commonly regarded as a nomadic people.

Concerning those passages in Deuteronomy, Judges, and Habakkuk that seem to be equating Mt. Sinai with Seir, Paran, Teman, and Edom, one must bear in mind that the texts exhibit a clear poetic structure. On the same grounds, one might with equal justification attempt to argue that Paran must be equated with Seir, Teman, or

Edom. Furthermore, the passages are all addressing the subject of theophany: they each reflect the reality that the God of Israel can save His people from oppression. The common denominator of Sinai, Seir, Paran, Teman, and Edom is simply that they are all located in the same general direction from Canaan.

In addition to this, there are a number of narratives that suggest that Mt. Sinai was separated from Kadesh-barnea by a great distance. We observe in Numbers 33:16-36 that some twenty intermediate stations are recorded in the Israelite itinerary between Mt. Sinai and Kadesh-barnea. Based on Deuteronomy 1:1, it may be that the Numbers 33 narrative is actually only a *selective* itinerary. The same sort of tradition is found in Deuteronomy 1:2, which stipulates that there was an eleven-day march between Sinai and Kadesh-barnea, or in 1 Kings 19:8, which states that it took Elijah forty days to travel from Beersheba to Mt. Sinai. Though the amount of time for travel differs, these biblical narratives concur that Mt. Sinai was separated from Kadesh-barnea by a great distance, which conclusion is fatal to the contention that Mt. Sinai was located in the northern Sinai.

Those who espouse the southern Sinai viewpoint are apt to seek out Mt. Sinai at Ras Safsaf, J. Serbal, J. Katarina, or J. Musa. This position has had a long and very rich tradition: from the environs of the southern Sinai massif (rock outcropping) and near Serbal have been found more than 2,500 Nabatean inscriptions that date as early as the second and third centuries A.D. These clearly attest to the sacral character of the surrounding mountains and indicate they were places of religious pilgrimages.[22] More specifically, the major strand of Christian tradition has been woven around J. Musa ("mountain of Moses"), being traced back to the very beginning of the Byzantine era, even though other southern peaks exceed Musa in elevation. Additional credence must be conferred upon this tradition, as it runs counter to the Byzantine tendency to locate sacred shrines only at places that were accessible to pilgrims.

As further evidence for a southern location, certain sites listed in the Israelite itinerary to Mt. Sinai (Ex. 15:22—19:1) and between Mt. Sinai and Kadesh-barnea (Num. 21; 33; Deut. 1) are suggestive of some modern names, and the locations of two intermediate stations necessarily presuppose a southern route. But before we actually explore this evidence, caution must be urged. Some of the places listed here are not found elsewhere in or outside the Bible, and very few of the names have survived to the present. Now this is not surprising because most of the southern Sinai has never been permanently occupied, and certain of the place names were actually assigned by the Israelites themselves as they were passing through (e.g., Marah in Ex. 15:23; Massah and Meribah in Ex. 17:7). Obviously names given under such circumstances would not have become fixed. And so we must not overstate the case and claim that all, or even many, of the intermediate stations in the Israelites' itinerary can be located with absolute precision.

However, Ezion-geber (Num. 33:35; cf. Deut. 2:8) was indisputably located at Tell el-Kheleifeh, along the shore of the Gulf of Aqaba, and Di-zahab (Deut. 1:1) must surely be reflected in the modern town Dahab, as both names are phonetic equivalents and both have to do with places of gold.[23] Beyond these definite sites, recent discoveries strongly suggest that the station Jotbathah (Num. 33:33), listed as the second stop before Ezion-geber, should be identified with the oasis of Taba, located some seven miles south of Ezion-geber along the eastern side of the peninsula.[24] Beyond this evidence, several authorities seek to situate biblical Dophkah (Num. 33:12) at the site of the ancient mining center in southwestern Sinai, known today as Serabit el-Khadim, where ancient alphabetic inscriptions that date back to the fifteenth century B.C. have been found. Simons has shown, however, that a textual emendation (change made seeking to improve the text) is required for this association to be valid.[25] Because the proposed Scripture emendation lacks textual support, and in the face of the Septuagintal rendering (*Raphkah*), I am skeptical concerning this identification.

It seems that the Ezion-geber/Tell el-Kheleifeh equation itself makes the northern Sinai route impossibly circuitous. For how does one explain a trip from J. Kharif, J. Karkom, J. Helal, J. Yeleq, or even J. Sin Bisher to Ezion-geber if the destination of the itinerary was Kadesh-barnea? Similarly, if either of the identifications suggested for stations along the eastern peninsula would prove to be correct (Di-zahab, Jotbathah), the Saudi Arabian/Jordanian thesis would be rendered geographically incoherent. Therefore I find the traditional, southern Sinai hypothesis to be the most probable one.

Based on this conclusion, I have endeavored to reconstruct a plausible Israelite route to Mt. Sinai, then on the Kadesh-barnea, and finally on to Shittim. It is likely the Israelites followed the coastal road south of Lake Timsah to the mouth of Wadi Feiran, which is a rather broad, gently-climbing corridor across otherwise rugged terrain. From there they emerged into the er-Raha plain immediately north of J. Musa. When departing from Sinai, they probably journeyed southward just past J. Katarina, where they linked up with the Wadi Nasb. By following the course of this wadi to its outlet near Dahab, the Israelites would have been passing a network of oases, the most prominent of which was Bir Nasb. Moreover, with comparative ease they would have been able to pass over the mountain barrier that runs longitudinally along the eastern peninsula and flanks the Gulf of Aqaba. Having arrived at the shoreline (Dahab), they would have trekked north between the mountain and the Gulf, again past a number of oases, including Nuweiba, the largest oasis in the whole of eastern Sinai, until finally they arrived at Ezion-geber. From here, they most likely proceeded in a northwesterly direction toward Kadesh-barnea, the probable road being the one known today as Darb el-Ghaza. It was from Kadesh that the twelve men were dispatched to spy out the land of promise (see Map 26). When the majority of those spies presented a faithless, negative report which was adopted by the whole community, that generation was officially disqualified from possessing its inheritance (Num. 13:1-33).

When the Israelites eventually departed from Kadesh and were en route to Shittim, they were refused passage at Punon across to The King's Highway (Num. 20:14-17), which necessitated a detour of more than 175 miles through imposing landscape, possibly under conditions of torrid heat. This precipitated the "bronze serpent" incident (Num. 21:4-9; cf. John 3:14). Skirting the entire Edomite territory took them once again by Ezion-geber (Deut. 2:8) and then along the desert fringes that flanked a series of Edomite and, farther north, Moabite installations, utilizing a road later called the "Pilgrims' Highway." Finally they approached for a second time The King's Highway (Num. 21:22), where they requested permission to pass through the Amorite territory of Sihon. A battle ensued in which Sihon was defeated. That victory paved the way for Israel finally to complete the third leg in its winding journey, and the wanderers passed by Dibon, Heshbon, and arrived at Abel-shittim (Num. 33:45-49).

Journey of the Spies — MAP 26

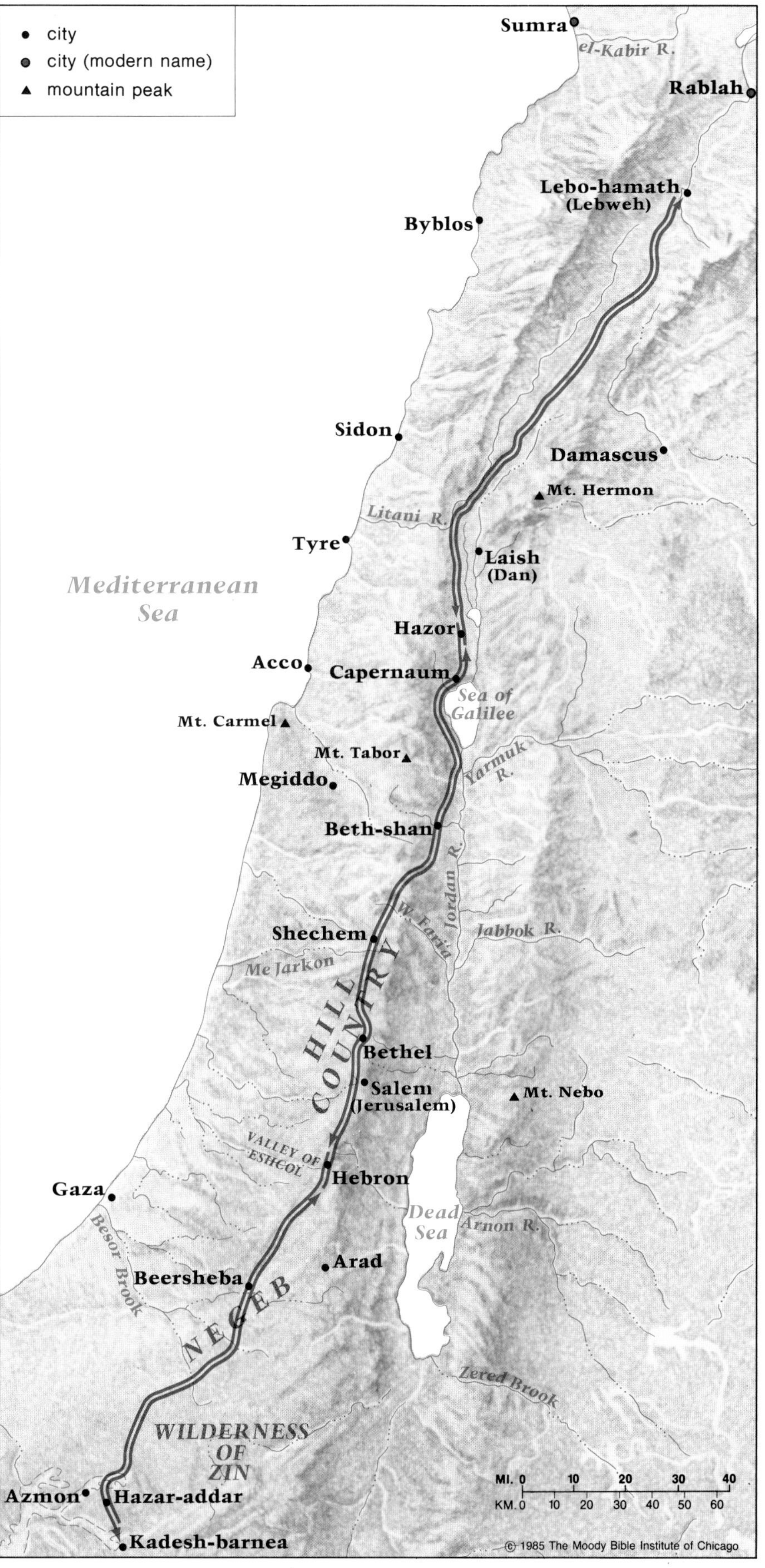

ISRAEL'S CONQUEST OF TRANSJORDAN MAP 27

Though somewhat sparsely settled at the time of Israelite penetration, Transjordan was occupied by Edomite, Moabite, Ammonite, and Amorite kingdoms. The first three of those represented peoples who were distantly related to Israel (Gen. 19:37-38; 36:1). Apparently there were no confrontations between those groups and the Israelites, and the territories of Edom, Moab, and Ammon remained unmolested by Israel at this point. The formidable Amorite kingdoms of Sihon (Heshbon) and Og (Bashan) presented a different challenge. The Israelite itinerary had brought the people to Mattanah where, entering upon the territory of Sihon, a message requesting safe passage was delivered to the Amorite monarch. Sihon adamantly refused and instead mustered his own troops and led them to Jahaz where a battle ensued in which the Amorites were routed, Sihon himself was slain, and Israel gained control of the terrain between the Arnon and Jabbok rivers (Num. 21:21-26).

Following the victory, Moses sent a contingent of troops northward against Amorites dwelling at Jazer. Such maneuvers must have aroused the concern of Og, for the Bashan sovereign marched his army to Edrei, a city guarding his southern frontier, to do battle with Israel (Num. 21:33-35; Deut. 3:4). But Og's fortunes were also dim, and the Israelite army again prevailed. And so all of Transjordan, from Mt. Hermon to the Arnon River, was subdued before the Israelite force (Deut. 3:8), which now returned to bivouac in the plains of Moab, opposite Jericho.

That disturbing proximity of Israelites led Balak, king of Moab, to solicit the services of Balaam, a seer from Mesopotamia. The king desired to secure from him a powerful oracle that would significantly diminish the threat Moab perceived Israel to be. When finally beckoned, Balaam was taken several times to high peaks in the vicinity of Mt. Pisgah, a western promontory in the mountain range of which Mt. Nebo is the summit. From that vantage point overlooking the plains of Moab, Balaam repeatedly tried unsuccessfully to pronounce his curse (Num. 22).

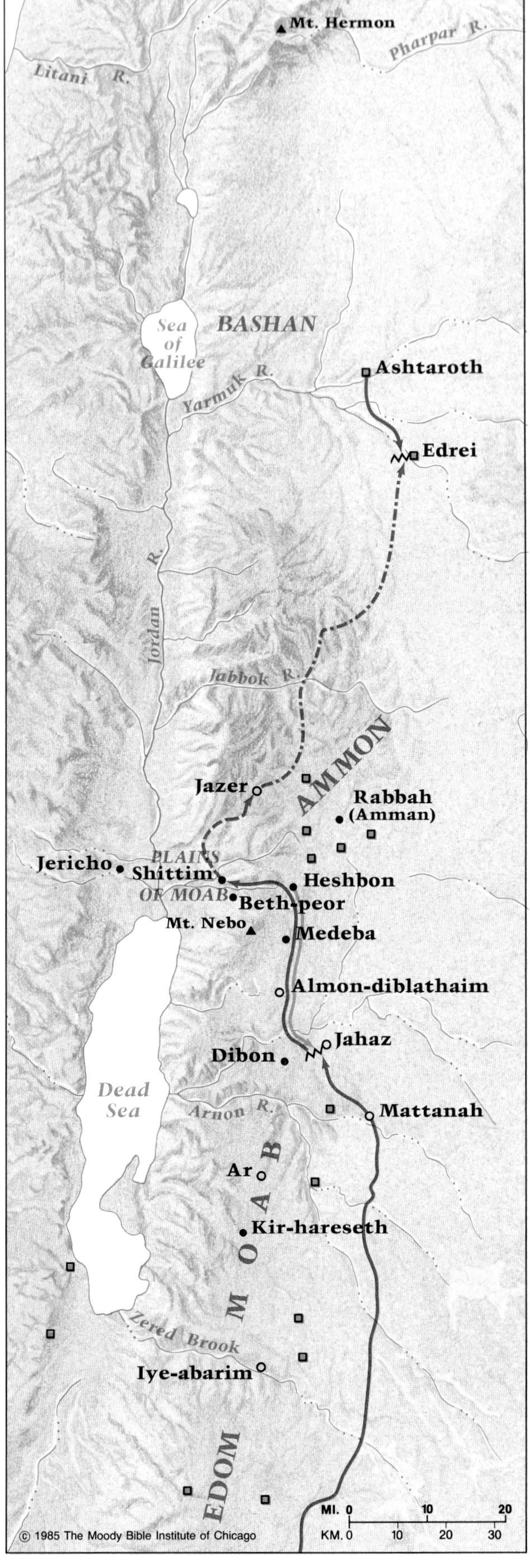

- ● city
- ○ city (uncertain location)
- ▪ enemy fortress
- ▲ mountain peak
- ᴧᴧ clash of forces
- Sihon attacks
- Israelite movements to Jahaz and Shittim
- mission to capture region of Jazer
- mission to capture region of Bashan
- Og of Bashan attacks

THE BATTLES OF JERICHO AND AI/BETHEL

What we call the "biblical conquest" is but a composite of four battles described in the book of Joshua: Jericho (chap. 6), Ai/Bethel (chaps. 7-8), Gibeon-Makkedah (chaps. 9-10), and Hazor (chap. 12). And yet the roster of all kings and territories subjugated by Joshua's forces (chap. 13) indicates that there had to be more than just four battles involved (cf. Map 33). This suggests that the conquest narratives are selective in character, and that those four battles have been included in the text both because they contain significant historical information and because they contribute in a foundational way to the overall theology developed in Joshua (cf. John 20:30).

We cannot discuss fully the theology of the book of Joshua, but briefly I believe it is designed to demonstrate that there is a succession of God's authority and power. That was a sorely-needed message in the wake of the crisis created by Moses' death, and in the wake of subsequent crises in the history of Israel and the church. The early chapters contain a recurring formula central to this theology. At times the people affirmed: "Just as we obeyed Moses in all things, so we will obey you" (1:17; cf. 4:14); at other times God declared: "As I was with Moses, so I will be with you" (1:5; cf. 3:7; 6:27).

Like his predecessor, Joshua was told to take off his shoes, because he was standing on holy ground (5:15; cf. Ex. 3:5).

As the time drew near to invade the western lands, Joshua is shown to have prepared the people of Israel emotionally (1:10-11), strategically (2:1), domestically (4:5-7), and spiritually (5:2-5). At the properly-designated moment, Joshua led a new generation through divided waters, and at precisely the same time in the calendar as their fathers had experienced deliverance at the Red Sea (4:19, 23; cf. Ex. 12:3). The magnitude and timing of this reproduced miracle accredited Joshua as the bona fide successor of Moses. The succession principle is then illustrated throughout the four battles.

Safely dug in at what would become a temporary headquarters in Gilgal, the army of Israel undertook the first of its forays: the conquest of Jericho. Despite its small six-acre size, a combination of factors made Jericho a desirable target. The town had been built at the largest oasis in the region, and water here was otherwise scarce and therefore highly prized. This town moreover represented the gateway to the central Canaanite highlands: three main roads into the interior radiated from Jericho (one to Bethlehem, one to Jerusalem, and one to Bethel).

Then again, not to have taken Jericho might have threatened Joshua's supply line back across the Jordan, for Jericho also represented a gateway to the East. There is some indication that not all the Israelites crossed the river with Joshua. For example, Moses had consented to the request of the tribes of Reuben, Gad, and east-Manasseh who desired Transjordanian inheritance; but he had stipulated that all the fighting men from those

MAP 28

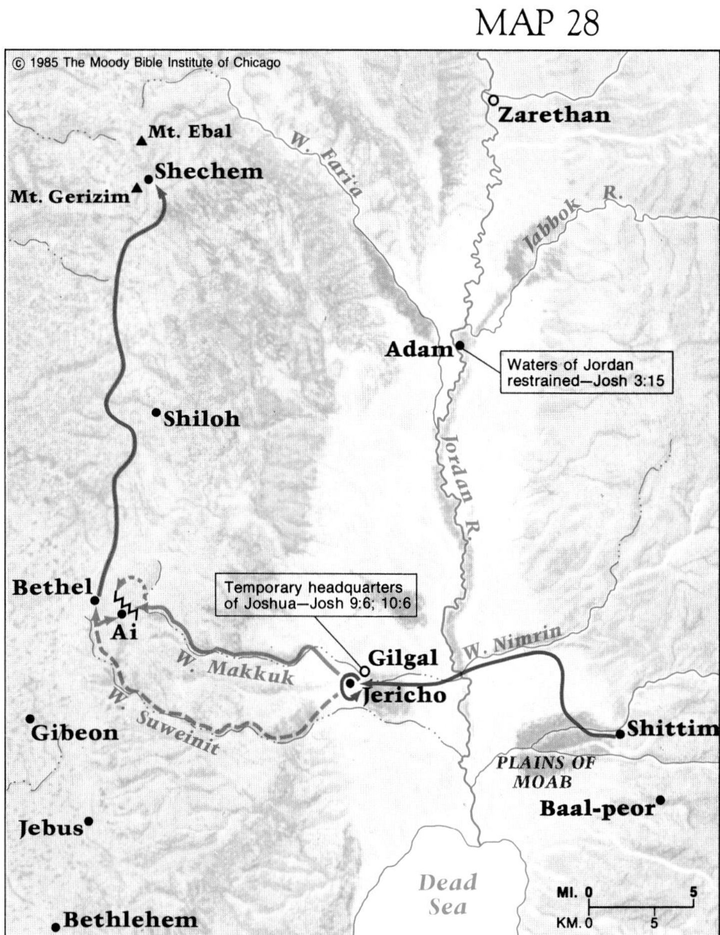

- ● city
- o city (uncertain location)
- ▲ mountain peak
- clash of forces
- Israelites move from Shittim to Jericho and march around the city
- Main Israelite force pitches battle versus Ai, then feigns retreat
- Large ambush force approaches Ai from South
- Small ambush force approaches Ai from North
- Joshua leads Israelites to Shechem to ratify officially the Mosaic covenant with them (Josh 8:30f; 24:1f; cf. Dt 27:4f)

tribes were required to join with their brothers in the contests that still awaited Israel (Num. 32:29). Yet when Joshua crossed the river, he was accompanied by only some 40,000 men from those tribes (Josh. 4:13), whereas the tribes of Reuben and Gad alone were reckoned to have more than 90,000 fighting men (Num. 1:21, 25). But to suggest that the Transjordanian tribesmen reneged on their promise to Moses appears untenable in light of the hearty recommendation Joshua later gave them (Josh. 22:1-6). A possible solution to this situation is that there were Israelites at the outset of the Cisjordanian conquest, especially women and children (cf. Josh. 1:14), who temporarily remained behind in safety. Those people would have formed the mainstay of a supply line to the army and, combined with their flocks and herds, would have needed military protection provided by fighting men from all tribes. Not to have seized Jericho, therefore, carried with it the threat of severing this supply line.

Having tasted victory at Jericho, Joshua set his sights on the central highlands and decided to deploy a minor force to capture the town of Ai, which was near the city of Bethel and was possibly a military outpost of Bethel. That force was bitterly defeated, however, and the first Israelite casualties of the conquest were recorded. Once the sin of Achan, which had caused the defeat, had been uprooted, Joshua prepared a systematic strategy for attacking Ai/Bethel.

First, a large ambush force was secretly deployed between Bethel and Ai (Josh. 8:3). Perhaps this force took up its position by traversing the Wadi Suweinit to the end, which would have placed it immediately south of Bethel but in a well-concealed position. Then, in plain view of the occupants of Ai, Joshua led his main force up close to the town. They encamped overnight on the north side of Ai, with a ravine separating them from the town (8:10-11). Such a vivid description of the topography permits one to identify Joshua's route as the Wadi Makkuk. A main branch of this wadi system flanks the north side of Ai, and from the summit of the town one has practically a bird's-eye view down the descent of Wadi Makkuk in the direction of Jericho.

In the morning, Joshua's force feigned retreat back down the wadi toward the Jordan valley, but not before a small ambush party was deployed to the north of Ai (Josh. 8:11-12). Supposing the maneuver to have been a repeat of the earlier skirmish, the commander of Ai ordered his men to chase the Israelites back down the wadi. But then at Joshua's predetermined signal, both ambush forces unleashed their attack on Bethel and Ai, now unprotected, and finally forced their Canaanite opponents to fight on all fronts (8:18-22). It was a great victory for Joshua, and one that firmly planted Israelite feet atop the central mountain.

Some time thereafter, Joshua led his troops to Shechem, where the Mosaic covenant was officially ratified by a new generation (Josh. 8:30; 24:1-28; cf. Deut. 27).

MIRACLE AT GIBEON

The subjugating of Jericho and Ai/Bethel had paved the way for Joshua's forces to make significant inroads into the Judean highlands. Citizens of four Hivite towns in the vicinity of Gibeon realized their vulnerability and devised a scheme to deceive Joshua into making a treaty with them. When the Amorite kings of the cities of Jerusalem, Hebron, Eglon, Lachish, and Jarmuth discovered the treachery of the Hivites, they determined to attack them immediately (1). Outclassed, the Hivites summoned Joshua's assistance, and he undertook a forced march with his troops through the night in order to arrive at Gibeon by dawn (2). The Amorites were thrown into a panic as the battle ensued, and they fled to the west by way of the ascent at Beth-horon. Passing Aijalon, the enemies made their way to Azekah and Makkedah, where Joshua's army completed its triumph. Whereupon the cities of Libnah, Lachish, Eglon, Hebron, and Debir were assaulted and demolished (3).

Included in this narrative is Joshua's prayer for the sun and moon to stand still respectively at Gibeon and the valley of Aijalon, so that he could be victorious in his battle against the Amorites (Josh. 10:12-14). Few Old Testament passages have excited greater interest or evoked more diverse opinion. Some commentators seek to interpret Joshua's prayer by asking when in the calendar year it occurred. Dates proposed include February 12, July 22, and October 25 or 30. But such ambiguity undermines that approach. It would appear, therefore, to be a line of reasoning that cannot be employed advantageously.

Another critical question posed by Joshua's prayer concerns the nature of his request for the sun to stop. Was he asking the sun to cease *revolving* or *shining?* Did Joshua and his troops need *time* or *shade?* If the former, the rationale for the prayer would have been that the army of Joshua was so dramatically routing the Amorite forces that with the aid of additional time it could have summarily vanquished them. If the latter, the rationale would have been that the army, having undertaken a forced march throughout the preceding night, was in desperate need of relief from the oppressive rays of the sun.

Both verbs in question, translated "be silent/still" and "stayed/stopped" are used elsewhere in the Bible in either of these senses (e.g., 1 Sam. 14:9 and Ps. 131:2; 2 Kings 4:6 and Job 32:16). Both words also are found in Akkadian literature in astronomical contexts, and therefore many evangelical writers since R. D. Wilson[26] have rendered these verbs "obscured/eclipsed" and have pictured a solar eclipse. But there is a chronological problem with that view. We know exactly when solar eclipses that were observable in central Palestine took place between the years 1500-1000 B.C.—August 19, 1157 (8:35 A.M.), September 30, 1131 (12:35 P.M.), and November 23, 1041 (7:40 A.M.). None of those dates correlates even closely with the period of the conquest, no matter which of the two principal dates one assigns the Exodus from Egypt. And therefore, the exact nature of Joshua's request remains somewhat uncertain.

From what location Joshua was likely to have made his request is a third question. Should it have been offered at or near Gibeon/Aijalon, it probably would have been a morning request, owing to the time of the battle's inception and the success portrayed in the narrative as Joshua came "suddenly" upon his foes. Alternatively, should it have been made at or near Azekah/Makkedah, the distances involved urge that it was an afternoon request. It seems to me that Joshua prayed while he was near Gibeon or Aijalon. That is, he entreated God to be at work *where he was,* and not where he had been. Perhaps, then, the verses in question are suggesting that the sun was at Gibeon (i.e., in the east), whereas the moon was waning at Aijalon (i.e., in the west) just after sunrise. Consequentially, I propose that Joshua's request did not entail a suspension of the laws of physics throughout the solar system. The great leader offered his prayer in the morning hours. As such, to have asked for additional sunlight would have been superfluous—he could have expected brilliant sunlight for another six hours or so.

If the Israelite troops needed relief from the sun's heat, God responded to Joshua's prayer in a more striking and dramatic way than even he could have imagined. For the Lord sent not only the much-needed cloud cover to blot out the rays of the sun, but with those same clouds came a hailstorm that killed more of the enemy than Joshua's army did. "And the sun was silent and the moon obscured, so that the nation could avenge its enemies. Is it not written in the Book of Jasher: 'And the sun was obscured in the sky and did not press onward to sunset as on a normal day [note especially *kă + tāmîm*].' And there has not been a day like that day before or since, *in respect to the Lord's heeding the voice of a man*" (italics added).

The event at Gibeon was truly a miracle in that even the forces of nature seemed to be at the

MAP 29

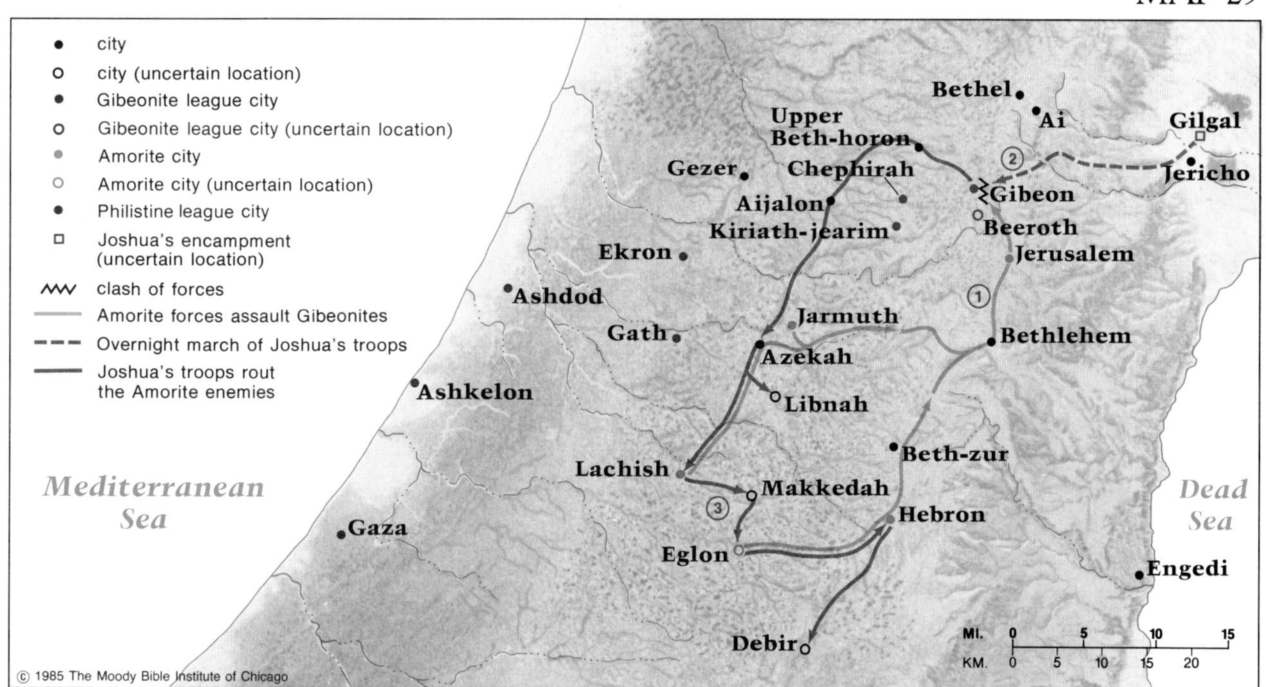

THE CONQUEST OF HAZOR

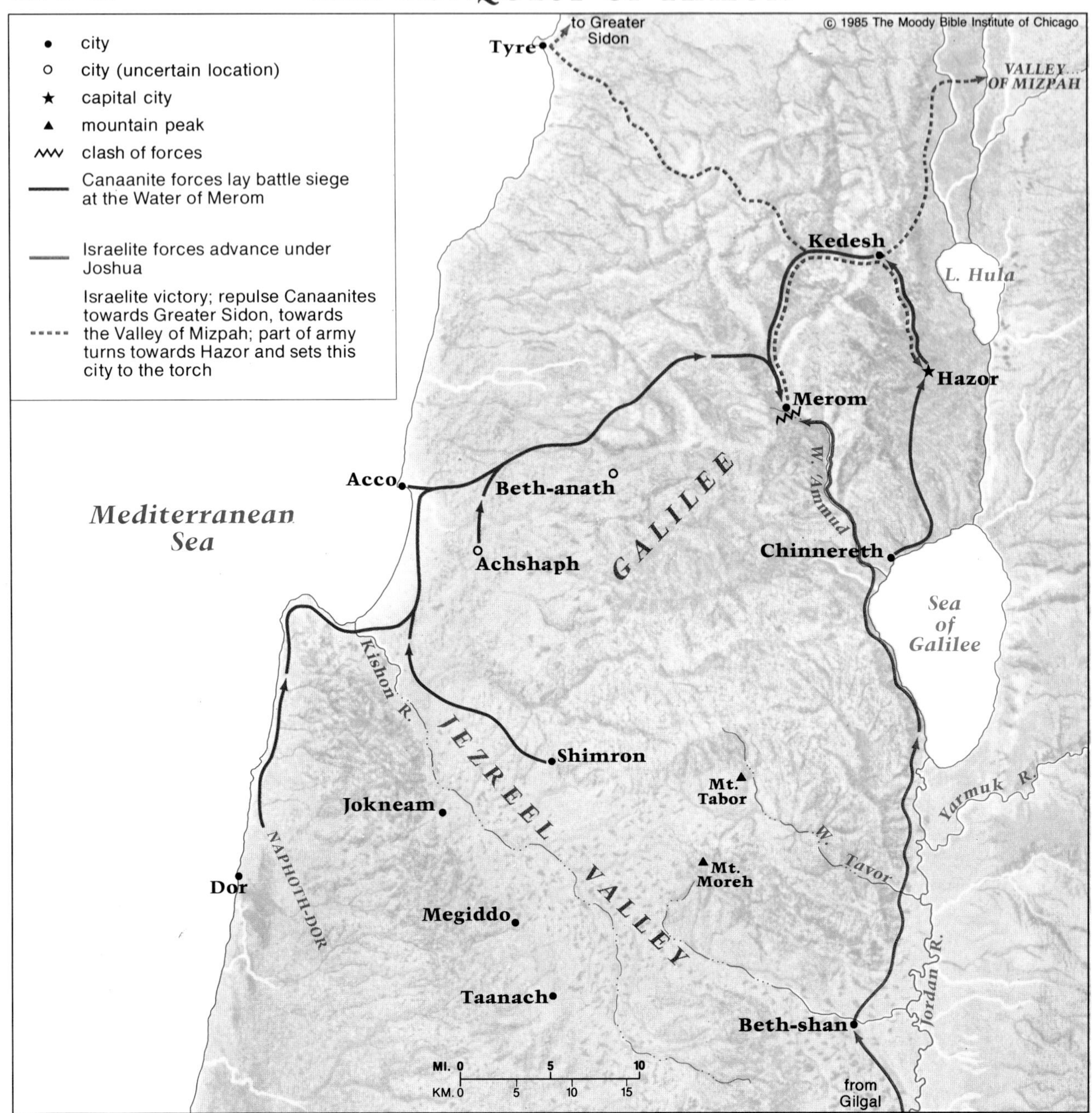

beck and call of one of God's servants. In that sense, the narrative may be likened to a later incident that occurred on the Sea of Galilee, when Jesus calmed even the winds and waves, to the wonderment of His disciples (Matt. 8:23-27).

Israel's first three battles of the conquest were waged against seemingly insignificant opponents. Not so with Hazor. This metropolis was both the largest city of Canaan and the most powerful Canaanite center in Galilee at the time of the conquest. Fortified earlier with massive ramparts of beaten earth, a high, thick, and heavily protected wall, a glacis, and a deep fosse (fortification ditch), the site of Hazor actually comprised two distinct areas in Joshua's day. An upper city, rising from the surrounding plain to an approximate height of 130 feet, incorporated some 30 acres and was surrounded by its own wall. Immediately to the north, a lateral fosse separated this emplacement from a large rectangular enclosure, called the lower city, which itself enveloped an additional 175 acres and was protected on all sides. Archaeological evidence indicates that the lower city reached its zenith precisely in the time of Joshua; demographic estimates suggest that Hazor might have supported a resident population approaching 40,000.

The city, moreover, was a major commercial

and political center. It figured prominently in Bronze Age cuneiform texts from Mari (eighteenth century B.C.) that discuss major emporia throughout the Fertile Crescent in the trade of tin, an essential component in the casting of bronze. The city's importance is also reflected in numerous Egyptian documents of the period, and its role in the Tell el-Amarna letters is of particular significance. This same sort of greatness is attested in the conquest narrative (Josh. 11), where the city is first mentioned in the Bible. Scripture declares (11:10*b*) that Hazor "was the head of all those kingdoms," a description which may be taken to be indicative of its supreme role in Canaanite politics, especially in Galilee.

In the case of the fourth conquest battle, therefore, Joshua's forces were pitted against the strongest possible political and military adversary. What is more, in this case the Israelites were opposed both by the city-state of Hazor and by those territories over which Hazor exercised domination (vv. 1-3). Moreover, the biblical writer (vv. 4-5) seems to go out of his way to emphasize the numerical and technological superiority of the Canaanites: "All these kings joined forces, with all their troops, a great host, in number like the sand that is upon the seashore, with very many horses and chariots." Given the elaborate and detailed descriptions of the strategies employed in the first three battles—marching after the ark around a city day after day, blowing trumpets and shouting (6:3-5); setting of two ambush forces before feigning retreat (8:3-22); undergoing a forced march before routing the enemy through a particular pass and finally destroying them altogether (10:9-23*a*)—the silence of Scripture concerning the strategy used against the Canaanite forces of Hazor is positively arresting. We are informed merely that the confederated Canaanite army was encamped by the waters of Merom and that Joshua came upon them suddenly or unexpectedly. Such meager information makes any reconstruction tentative. Perhaps the Israelite army traversed Wadi 'Ammud, a narrow gorge shut in by high cliffs which runs diagonally from the Sea of Galilee to the immediate environs of Merom. It would have been a risky strategy, and one that took the Israelites through almost impassable terrain, but also it would have allowed Joshua's troops to strike "unexpectedly" (*pit'ōm*).

Whatever the case, the narrow defiles and rugged forests of Merom neutralized the strength and mobility of the Canaanites' chariots, and so the enemy fled towards Sidon and eastward to the Valley of Mizpah where the Israelite victory was concluded. Meanwhile, a contingent of Joshua's army marched directly to Hazor itself, overpowered its residents, and set the city ablaze.

Figure 12 Scene where Israel ratified covenant: Mt. Ebal (right) and Mt. Gerizim (left) with the vale of Shechem in the center.

MAP 31 TRIBAL DISTRIBUTION OF PALESTINE

LEVITIC CITIES AND CITIES OF REFUGE MAP 32

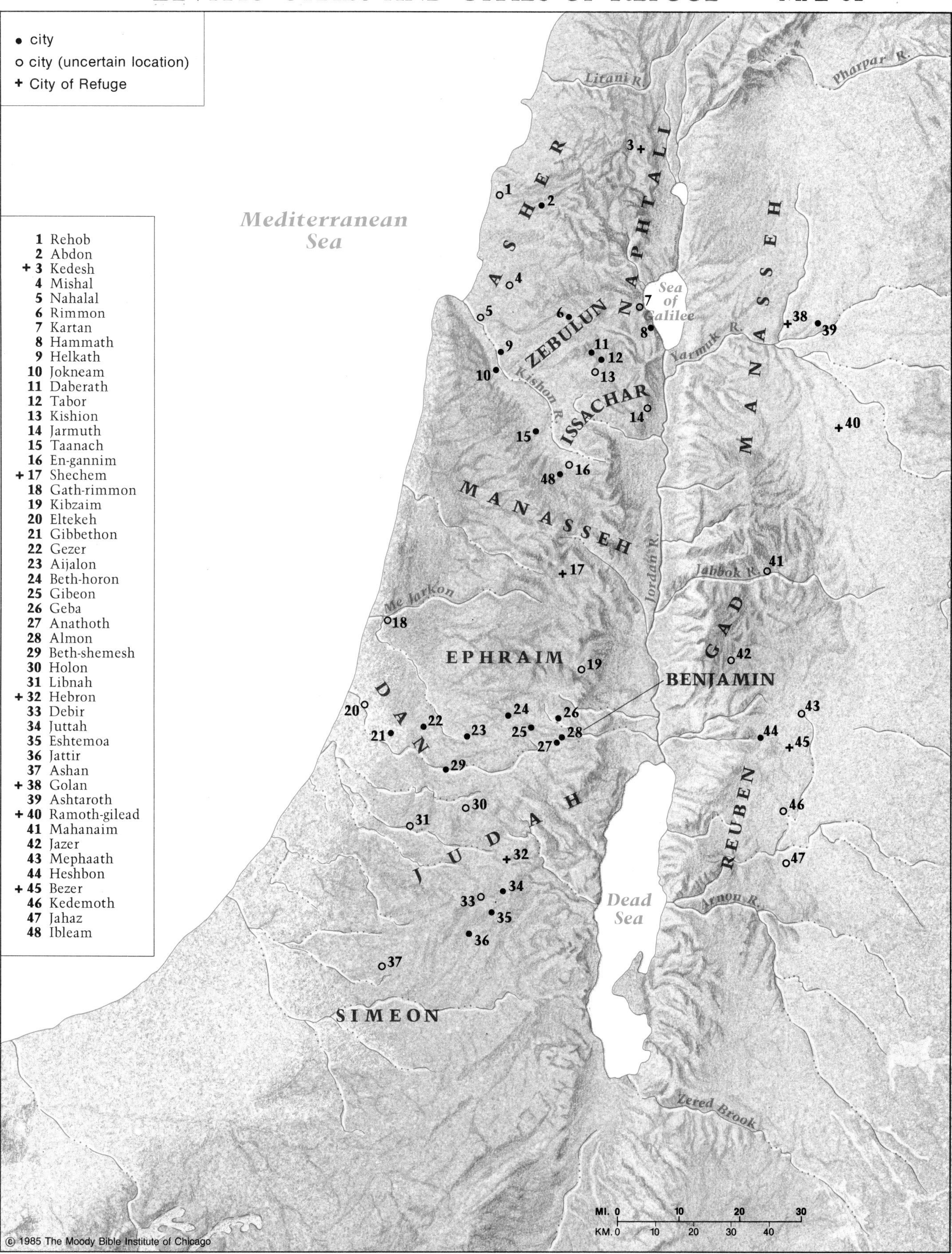

THE CONQUEST ANALYZED

Although at first glance the book of Joshua seems to portray a conquest that was lightning quick, confrontive in nature, and highly successful, a closer look at all the details suggests quite another verdict. True enough, Israel had experienced a string of stunning, even miraculous, successes at Jericho, Ai, Gibeon, and Hazor. However, near the end of Joshua's life there remained huge tracts of the Promised Land still to be possessed. Those included (1) the territories of Philistia (Ekron, Gath, Ashdod, Ashkelon, Gaza), Geshur, and Maacah (from below Mt. Hermon southward) (Josh. 13:1-13; cf. Judg. 3:1-3); (2) strategic cities in the Jezreel valley (Megiddo, Taanach, Ibleam, Endor, and Beth-shan) (Josh. 17:11; cf. Judg. 1:27) and the coastal plain (Aphek, Gezer, and Dor) (Josh. 13:4; 16:10; 17:11; cf. Judg. 1:27, 29); and (3) the city of Jerusalem (Josh. 15:63; cf. Judg. 1:21).

Judges 1 rounds out the grim story of unconquered land by adding that vast stretches of the Phoenician plain (Ahlab, Achzib, Beth-shemesh, Acco, etc.) and the major pass into the Judean heartland (Shaalbim, Aijalon, Har-heres; cf. Gibeon, Josh. 9:3-16) still remained outside Israel's control.

A number of significant geographical factors emerge concerning the territories of the conquest. First, it seems that wherever the Philistines or their allies could run iron chariots—namely, in the Philistine plain (Judg. 1:19) or the Jezreel valley (Josh. 17:16)—the Israelites could not conquer the terrain. But where this technological superiority was neutralized by the rugged mountain highlands of Palestine's interior and Transjordan, Israel carved out its developing kingdom.

Second, there seems to be no record of Egyptian interference during the time of the conquest. That absence of interference is puzzling when one considers that the conquest occurred during a time of relative military strength in Egypt. Yet Egyptian interests in Palestine were merely economic; as long as international caravans could continue to move through Palestine unmolested, Egypt seemingly was unconcerned with internal politics. Perhaps the lack of reference to Egyptian interference can be explained geographically. For reasons just mentioned above, Israel was unable to gain a sizeable foothold in areas adjacent to the international artery of trade (the Great Trunk Road). Geographically, one could then say that Egyptian and Israelite interests in Palestine were mutually exclusive, which could explain why Egypt remained uninvolved during Israel's conquest.

Third, on the central highlands of Map 33 one can observe a close geographical correlation between the territory permanently controlled by Israel and the terrain known today as the West Bank of the country of Jordan. To put it differently, Israel was able to seize during the Six-Day War of 1967 almost exactly the same territory it conquered in the biblical conquest. Here is poignant illustration of how geographic factors can dictate where and how history will occur, the advances of modern military technology notwithstanding.

Figure 13 The terrain of Mt. Gilboa (background) and the fertile Jezreel valley is sharply differentiated.

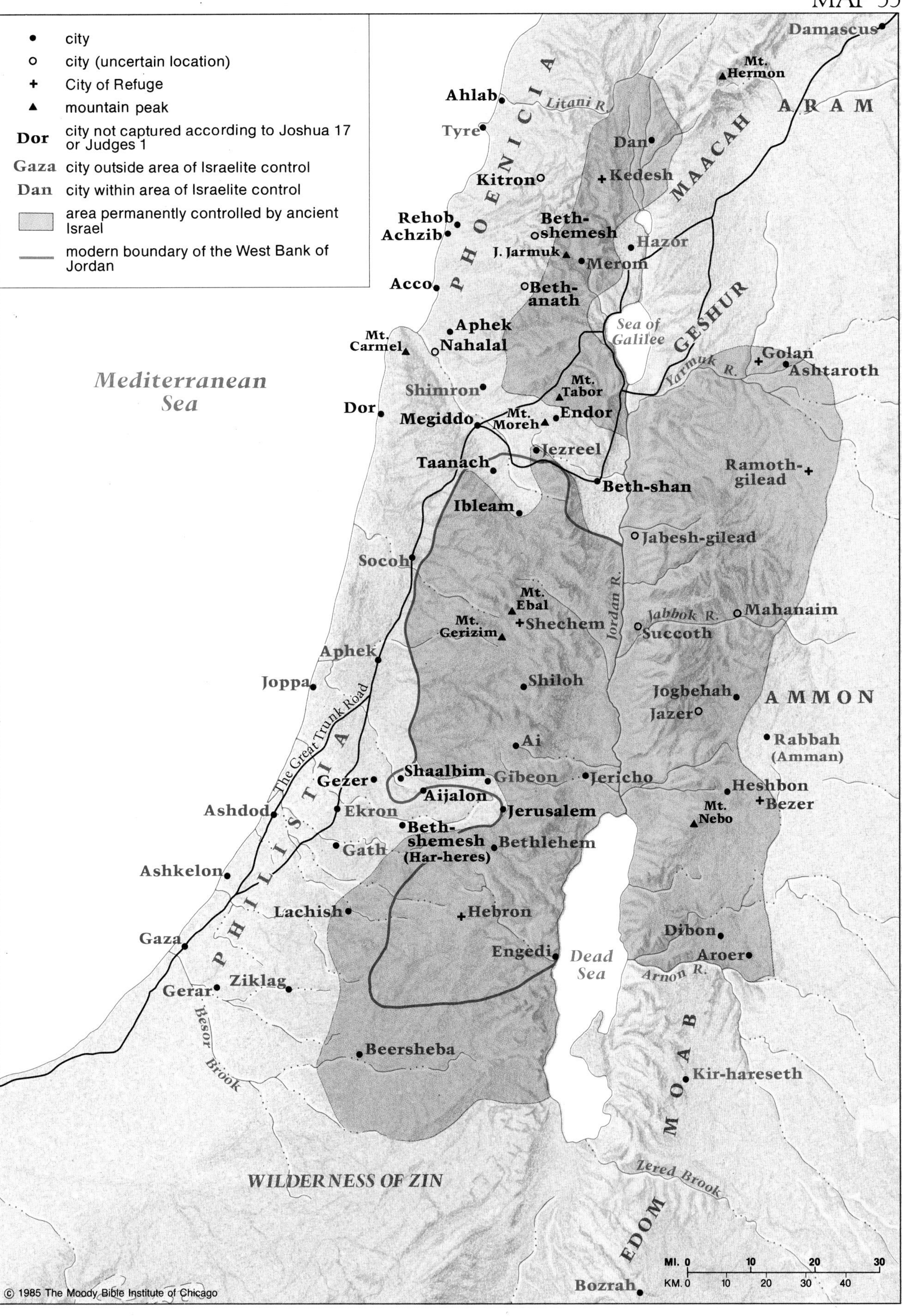
city
city (uncertain location)
City of Refuge
mountain peak
Dor city not captured according to Joshua 17 or Judges 1
Gaza city outside area of Israelite control
Dan city within area of Israelite control
area permanently controlled by ancient Israel
modern boundary of the West Bank of Jordan
Damascus
Mt. Hermon
Ahlab
Litani R.
ARAM
Tyre
PHOENICIA
Dan
MAACAH
Kitron
Kedesh
Rehob
Achzib
Beth-shemesh
Hazor
J. Jarmuk
Merom
Acco
Beth-anath
GESHUR
Sea of Galilee
Aphek
Mt. Carmel
Nahalal
Golan
Ashtaroth
Yarmuk R.
Mediterranean Sea
Shimron
Mt. Tabor
Dor
Megiddo
Mt. Moreh
Endor
Jezreel
Taanach
Beth-shan
Ramoth-gilead
Ibleam
Jabesh-gilead
Socoh
Jordan R.
Mt. Ebal
Jabbok R.
Mahanaim
Mt. Gerizim
Shechem
Succoth
Aphek
Joppa
The Great Trunk Road
Shiloh
Jogbehah
AMMON
Jazer
PHILISTIA
Ai
Rabbah (Amman)
Shaalbim
Gibeon
Jericho
Gezer
Aijalon
Heshbon
Bezer
Ashdod
Ekron
Jerusalem
Mt. Nebo
Beth-shemesh (Har-heres)
Bethlehem
Gath
Ashkelon
Lachish
Hebron
Dibon
Gaza
Engedi
Dead Sea
Aroer
Arnon R.
Gerar
Ziklag
Besor Brook
MOAB
Beersheba
Kir-hareseth
WILDERNESS OF ZIN
Zered Brook
EDOM
MI. 0 10 20 30
KM. 0 10 20 30 40
Bozrah

PERIOD OF THE JUDGES

The era of the judges was one of charismatic leadership in which the Spirit of God would come upon men and women and especially equip them for service (Judg. 3:10; 6:34; 11:29; 14:6; 15:14). The individuals were sometimes characterized by a close relationship to God, and occasionally their exploits were accompanied by the public performance of miracles; at other times, neither holiness nor wonder-working were apparent in their lives. What *is* apparent in the book of Judges is the cyclical formula repeatedly recited there: rebellion, oppression, repentance, deliverance, and peace. Such might give rise to the mistaken impression that "oppression" was a static category. Actually, oppressions could assume a number of forms. They could be military, as in the case of Philistine imperialism, in which Israelite expansion was checked at the perimeter of the mountainous highlands, either adjacent to Judah (Samson) or beside lower Galilee (Shamgar). But oppressions could also take on a political shape, as when certain temporarily-dispossessed Canaanites were able to regroup and retake land previously held by Israel (Deborah/Barak). At other times oppression was an economic category, as illustrated by the Midianites who would seasonally plunder the Israelites' crops and thereby keep them subjugated (Gideon).

Nor must we imagine that all judges functioned in the same way. Deborah's judgeship was legal in character; Gideon's and Jephthah's judgeships were principally military; whereas Samson's bears sociological earmarks. Little is known about the judgeships of Shamgar, Tola, Jair, Ibzan, Elon, and Abdon. In some cases we know the town where they lived or were buried, the length of their tenure, or something of their progeny.

Perhaps the common denominator of all Israelite judges was that they represented dominant figures in a society that was otherwise highly de-

- ● city
- ○ city (uncertain location)
- ★ capital city
- + city of refuge
- □ Israelite encampment
- trip of Levite and concubine to Gibeah where she was sexually abused (19:1–26)
- Israelite main force which attacked Gibeah and feigned retreat (20:1–31)
- Israelite ambush force which smote and burned Gibeah (20:29–39)
- Benjaminite force which attacked, then discovered the real plot and fled towards the wilderness and came to Rimmon where they were vanquished (20:32–48)
- route of Danite migration (18:1–31) (through enlargement but not included thereon)

Figure 14 Effusion of the Jordan River near its headwaters opposite Dan, the site to which the Danites migrated.

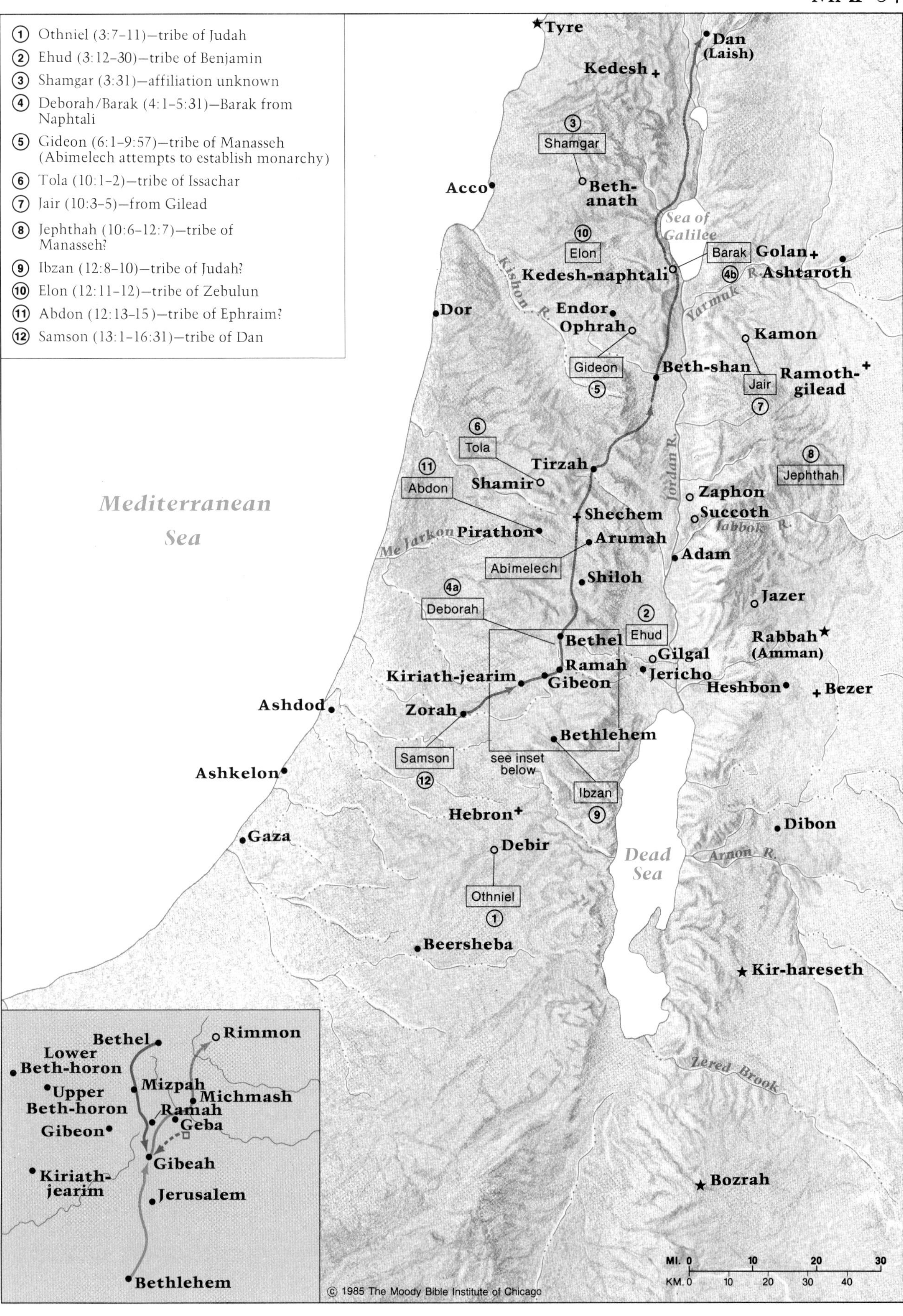

① Othniel (3:7–11)—tribe of Judah
② Ehud (3:12–30)—tribe of Benjamin
③ Shamgar (3:31)—affiliation unknown
④ Deborah/Barak (4:1–5:31)—Barak from Naphtali
⑤ Gideon (6:1–9:57)—tribe of Manasseh (Abimelech attempts to establish monarchy)
⑥ Tola (10:1–2)—tribe of Issachar
⑦ Jair (10:3–5)—from Gilead
⑧ Jephthah (10:6–12:7)—tribe of Manasseh?
⑨ Ibzan (12:8–10)—tribe of Judah?
⑩ Elon (12:11–12)—tribe of Zebulun
⑪ Abdon (12:13–15)—tribe of Ephraim?
⑫ Samson (13:1–16:31)—tribe of Dan
Tyre
Dan (Laish)
Kedesh
Shamgar
Acco
Beth-anath
Sea of Galilee
Elon
Barak
Golan
Ashtaroth
Kedesh-naphtali
Kishon R.
Yarmuk R.
Dor
Endor
Ophrah
Kamon
Gideon
Beth-shan
Jair
Ramoth-gilead
Tola
Tirzah
Jordan R.
Jephthah
Abdon
Shamir
Zaphon
Mediterranean Sea
Shechem
Succoth
Jabbok R.
Me Jarkon
Pirathon
Arumah
Adam
Abimelech
Shiloh
Jazer
Deborah
Ehud
Bethel
Rabbah (Amman)
Gilgal
Ramah
Jericho
Kiriath-jearim
Gibeon
Heshbon
Bezer
Ashdod
Zorah
Bethlehem
Samson
see inset below
Ashkelon
Ibzan
Hebron
Dibon
Gaza
Debir
Dead Sea
Arnon R.
Othniel
Beersheba
Kir-hareseth
Bethel
Rimmon
Lower Beth-horon
Upper Beth-horon
Mizpah
Michmash
Ramah
Geba
Gibeon
Gibeah
Kiriath-jearim
Jerusalem
Bethlehem
Zered Brook
Bozrah
MI. 0 10 20 30
KM. 0 10 20 30 40

centralized, if not anarchistic, and decadent to the core. The two stories of Judges 17-21 (Danite migration, atrocity committed against the Levite's concubine) trumpet loudly the refrain of Israel's total decadence, seen domestically (17:1-4; 19:24-25), morally (19:22, 25; 20:13*b*; 21:20-21), politically (17:6; 18:1; 19:1; 21:25), religiously (17:4-7, 12; 18:4, 30) and culturally (19:11, 15, 18).

Othniel, Ehud, and Samson

Heading the list of judges is Othniel, Caleb's nephew (Judg. 3:9) who later became his son-in-law as a reward for capturing the city of Debir (Josh. 15:15-16). The personal and national identification of the antagonist during the judgeship of Othniel, however, continues to vex biblical scholars. Was he Mesopotamian or Edomite? On the one hand, the name *Cushan-rishathaim,* meaning "Cushan of double-wickedness," is hardly one given by a parent at birth. It may be, therefore, that the biblical writer was intending to assign a pejorative connotation rather than a nomenclature to this oppressor, much as was done later with the son and temporary successor of King Saul. This latter individual is referred to as Ish-baal ("man of Baal") in 1 Samuel but contemptuously as Ish-bosheth ("man of shame") in 1 Chronicles.

On the other hand, Cushan-rishathaim is said to have been king of Aram-naharaim (Judg. 3:8), an expression that elsewhere in Scripture often designates a section of northern Mesopotamia (e.g., Gen. 24:10). But oppressors in the book of Judges normally did not travel from such distant lands as Mesopotamia, and the narratives otherwise fall basically into a south to north sequence (note the arrangement of Judg. 1; some LXX manuscripts place Shamgar's activities [3:31] after those of Samson [16:31]). Also, the judges themselves usually emerged from the locale of each respective oppression. Those factors, taken together with the fact that the Hebrew letters that compose the word Aram (*'rm*) can be sometimes confused with the letters for the word Edom (*'dm*; e.g., 1 Kings 11:15; 2 Kings 16:6; 2 Chron. 20:2; Ezek. 16:57; 27:16), have led some scholars to propose that Cushan-rishathaim actually hailed from Edomite lands. Now admittedly the letters *r/d* are often interchanged in the Hebrew text, hence the reading "Edom" could be obtained with great ease. But no textual support for that reading is adducible. Moreover, such a reading requires one to ignore "naharaim," because that word seems to be meaningless if hyphenated with Edom.

Alternatively, if we bear in mind that Hebrew was originally written without vowels and spaces between words, a more attractive theory suggests itself—the vowelless and undivided letters translated Aram-naharaim (*'rmnhrym*) should have been split after, rather than before, the letter *n*, thus yielding the reading *'rmn hrym,* "mountainous fortress/citadel." That term otherwise serves as an apt description of Edom's impregnable highlands (cf. Isa. 34:13; Amos 1:12). Though contextually appealing to us, this explanation is not certain. So we have graphed two routes for Othniel: one that he might have used against a Mesopotamian foe (**1a**) and another should his enemy have been Edomite (**1b**).

Ehud's call from God was precipitated by a Moabite-Ammonite-Amalekite invasion culminating in a protracted oppression that included an enemy occupation of the "city of palms" (Judg. 3:12-14). Because the Hebrew word for palms is *tamar,* Ehud's skirmish is sometimes placed just south of the Dead Sea at the city of Tamar (cf. Judg. 1:16; 1 Kings 9:18; Ezek. 47:19; 48:28). However, it is possible to equate the "city of palms" with Jericho in Scripture (cf. Deut. 34:3; 2 Chron. 28:15), and further we observe in context the close proximity of Gilgal, a town whose location, though uncertain, cannot be placed to the south of the Dead Sea. Then again, the pivotal role played by the men of the "hill country of Ephraim" at the "fords of the Jordan" forces one to situate the Ehud incident *north* of the Dead Sea. Nor does Joshua's curse on Jericho (Josh. 6:26) presuppose that *Moabites* could not have taken up residence at that location.

Ehud used the occasion of taxpaying to exploit King Eglon's vulnerability (**2**). As the delegation he led was returning home, Ehud decided to return alone to the king with a secret message (**3**). Later, having assassinated Eglon, Ehud fled towards Seirah (**4**) where, in the hill country of Ephraim, he signaled for Israelite assistance. The men who responded followed him to Jericho (**5**) while others passed over to the fords of the Jordan (**6**) and prevented the Moabites from fleeing toward their home (cf. upper inset).

In many respects, Samson stands as a perplexing and enigmatic figure. As a judge, he was without soldier or army and does not even seem to have been responsible for ending the Philistine oppression (cf. 1 Sam. 7). As a person, he displayed a tacit disregard for the values of his parents and the spiritual training inherent in his Nazirite heritage. He was impulsively sensual and even verbally vulgar, and the spiritual catharsis linked with his death does little to modify this assessment. If the book of Judges was written to show a decentralized judgeship that was powerless to prevent recurring apostasy, arguing instead for the office of king ("There was no king in Israel in those days; everyone did whatever was right in his own eyes"), it is understandable that the Samson episode should be the book's final narrative. In unprecedented proportions Samson epitomizes the innate tendencies of his own subjects.

Samson's problems with the Philistines began when he saw a girl from Timnah and demanded that his parents arrange for their marriage (7). Subjected to the enticement of her charms, however, Samson lost the contest of his own wedding riddle. That necessitated a trip to Ashkelon (Judg. 14) to secure garments for his wedding party. But the girl was given in marriage to another, which eventually led Samson to burn out the Philistine wheat fields just before harvest (Judg. 15). The Philistines retaliated and assaulted the men of Judah, who immediately dissociated themselves from Samson and attempted to hand him over to the Philistines at Lehi. But when he was brought to Lehi, Samson broke the ropes that bound him and used an ass's jawbone to exact vengeance upon his foes for a second time (8) (cf. lower inset).

Later, Samson journeyed to Gaza where he stayed with a harlot (9). Thinking that they surely had their enemy this time when told of his whereabouts, the men of Gaza sought to prevent Samson's departure. But in the middle of the night, Samson simply went through the Gaza city wall, taking city gate and bars with him, and fled to the Hebron area (10). Samson's love affair with Delilah would ultimately return him to Gaza though, but in an inglorious manner as the blind slave of the Philistines (11). Not satisfied with his imprisonment after his return to Gaza, the Philistines desired to taunt Samson publicly. So it was that this last judge of Israel had opportunity to avenge himself against his enemies for a third time, though he paid for it that time with his own life.

MAP 35

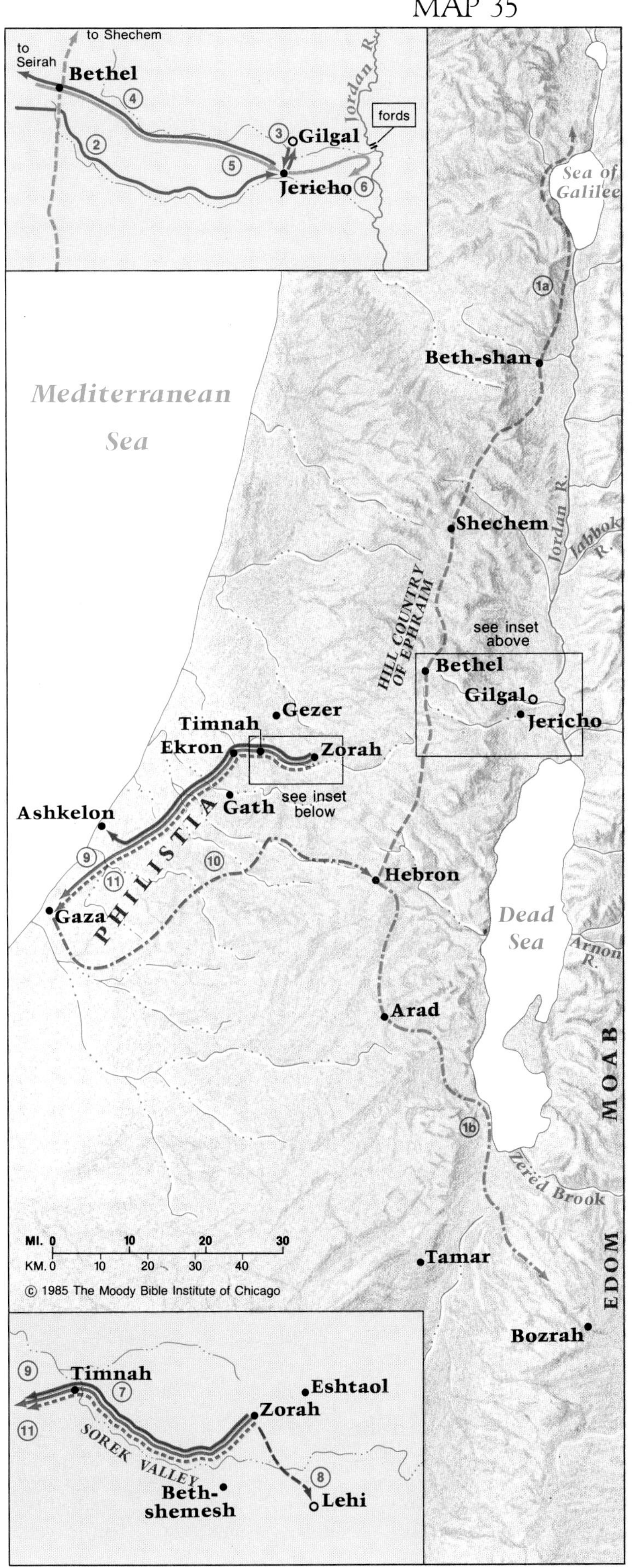

- city
- city (uncertain location)
- Othniel's route against Mesopotamian foe
- Othniel's route against Edomite foe
- Ehud's activities against Moab
- Israelite assistance for Ehud
- Samson travels to Timnah to wed, then to Ashkelon for wedding garments
- Samson's victory at Lehi
- Samson travels to Gaza where he is trapped
- Samson carries city gate to Hebron
- Samson taken prisoner by Philistines to prison at Gaza

MAP 36 DEBORAH-BARAK AND SHAMGAR

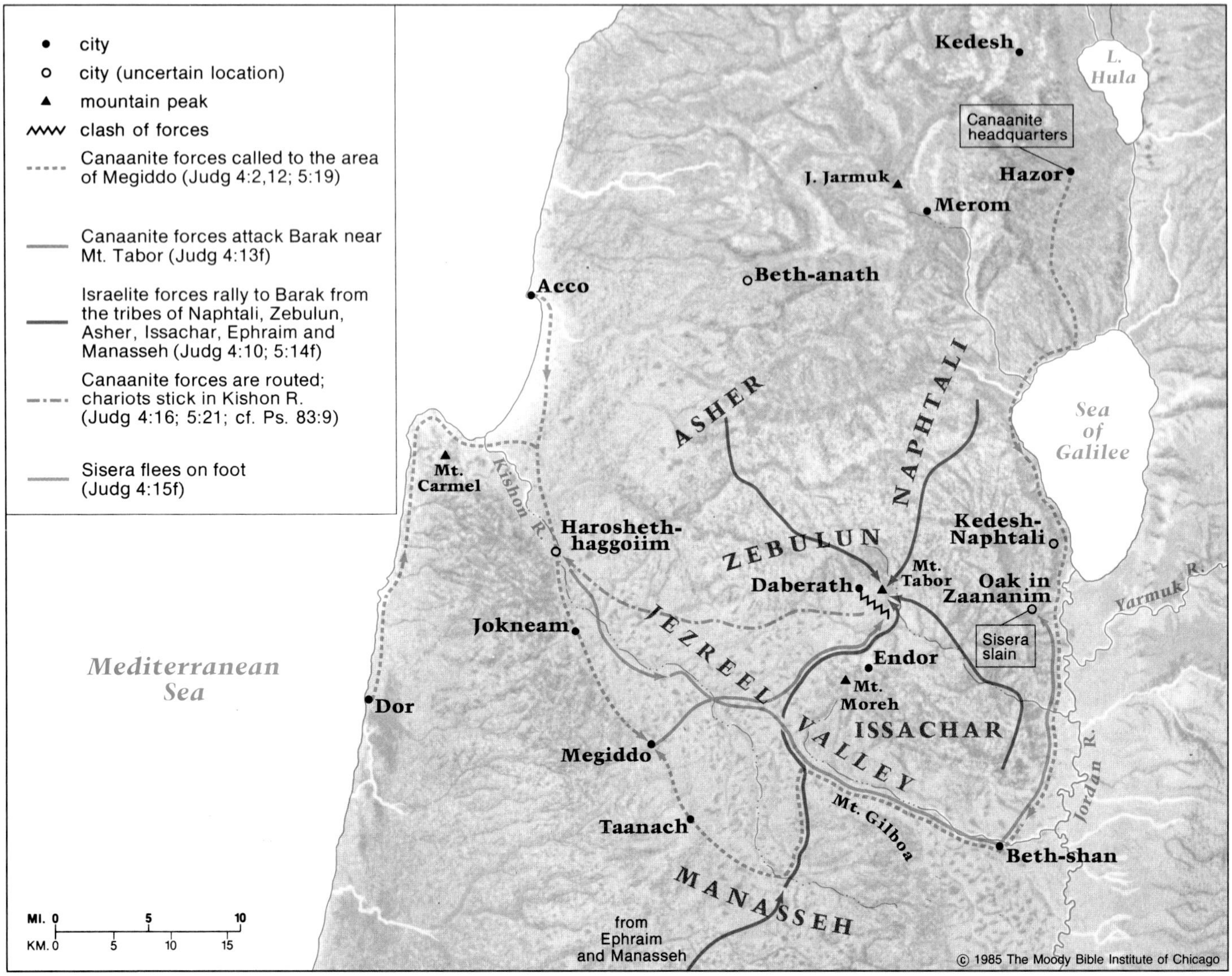

- ● city
- ○ city (uncertain location)
- ▲ mountain peak
- ʌʌʌʌ clash of forces
- ..... Canaanite forces called to the area of Megiddo (Judg 4:2,12; 5:19)
- —— Canaanite forces attack Barak near Mt. Tabor (Judg 4:13f)
- —— Israelite forces rally to Barak from the tribes of Naphtali, Zebulun, Asher, Issachar, Ephraim and Manasseh (Judg 4:10; 5:14f)
- –·–· Canaanite forces are routed; chariots stick in Kishon R. (Judg 4:16; 5:21; cf. Ps. 83:9)
- —— Sisera flees on foot (Judg 4:15f)

Kedesh
L. Hula
Canaanite headquarters
Hazor
J. Jarmuk
Merom
Beth-anath
Acco
ASHER
NAPHTALI
Sea of Galilee
Mt. Carmel
Kishon R.
Harosheth-haggoiim
ZEBULUN
Kedesh-Naphtali
Mt. Tabor
Daberath
Oak in Zaananim
Yarmuk R.
Jokneam
JEZREEL VALLEY
Sisera slain
Endor
Mediterranean Sea
Mt. Moreh
Dor
ISSACHAR
Megiddo
Jordan R.
Taanach
Mt. Gilboa
Beth-shan
MANASSEH
from Ephraim and Manasseh

MI. 0 5 10
KM. 0 5 10 15

Figure 15 Isolated hill of Mt. Tabor, scene of Barak's victory over the Canaanite forces of Sisera.

GIDEON MAP 37

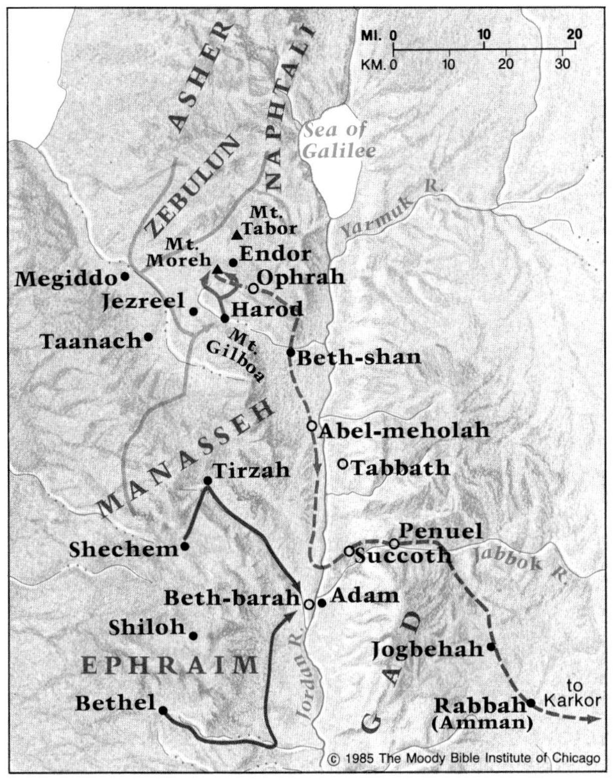

- ● city
- ○ city (uncertain location)
- ▲ mountain peak
- men of Manasseh, Asher, Zebulun and Naphtali form Gideon's army (6:35)
- Gideon's 300 soldiers surround the Midianite camp (7:19f)
- Gideon's forces rout the Midianites as far as Karkor (7:22-23; 8:10f)
- men of Ephraim come to Gideon's assistance (7:24f)

JEPHTHAH MAP 38

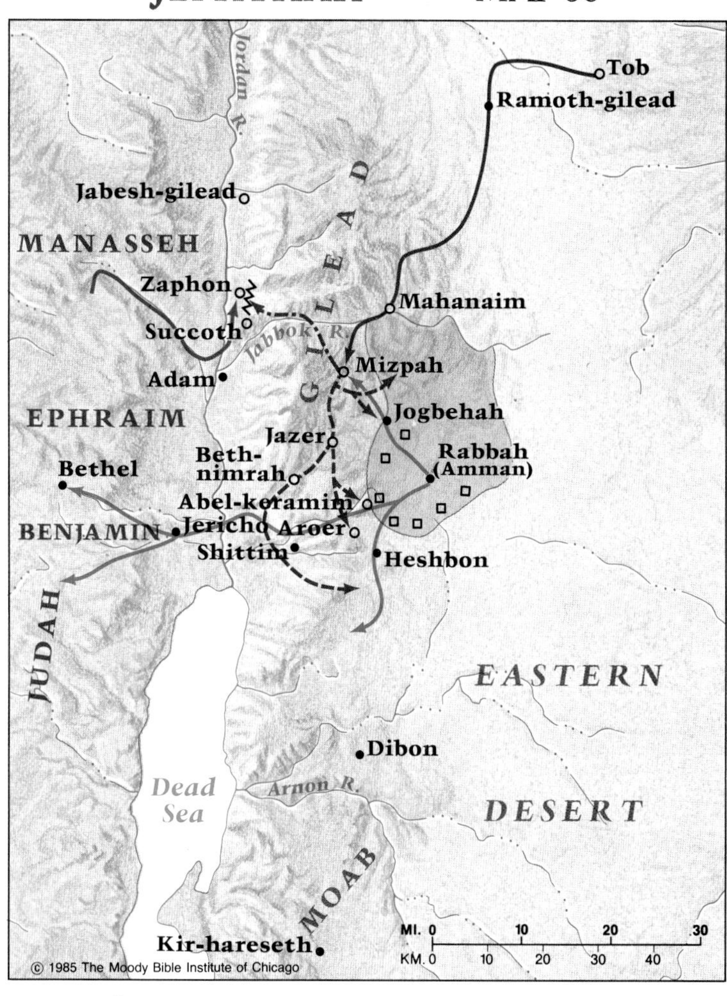

- ● city
- ○ city (uncertain location)
- □ Ammonite Fortress
- clash of forces
- Ammonite oppressive measures against Gilead, Judah, Benjamin, and Ephraim (10:8-9)
- Jephthah brought to Mizpah and appointed judge of Gilead (11:11)
- Jephthah's wars against Ammon (11:29f)
- Men of Ephraim called to arms against Jephthah (12:1f)
- Jephthah routs men of Ephraim (12:4f)
- land of Ammon

The judgeships of Gideon and Jephthah involved confrontation with Transjordanian states that seem to have been well-established by the eleventh century. Capitalizing on the widespread domestication of the camel as a new means of commerce in this era, the Midianites played a vital role in spice and incense trade from the interior of Arabia. But the camel also offered a new means of war (Judg. 6:5; 7:12; 8:21, 26). Gideon's night attack may have been designed to neutralize the superiority and mobility of the enemy; the blowing of horns would have caused the animals to panic and stampede, and the torches could have been used to set Midianites' tents ablaze. The text envisages a campaign that covered considerable territory, if we are to identify the Karkor of 8:10 with Qarqar, a town in the Wadi Sirhan located at the intersection of two important caravan routes (as indicated on the map; cf. 8:11).

In the same period, the Ammonites succeeded in fortifying their borders with a series of massive fortresses, from which they were emboldened to launch strikes against Gilead and even into the regions of Judah, Benjamin and Ephraim (10:8-9; cf. Josh 18:24*a*). Unsuccessful in negotiations, Jephthah led his Gileadite army to victory at Mizpah. Ironically indignant that they had been slighted by Jephthah in not being called to arms (cf. 8:1), the men of Ephraim crossed over [the Jordan] to Zaphon (not "northward," AV; RV) and forced Jephthah into civil war that ended in Ephraimite defeat.

Movements of the Ark

The Philistines and Israelites were each a foreign people who had come to homestead in Canaan at approximately the same time. The Israelites gained control of the mountainous inland terrain while the Philistines came to dominate the coastal plains. It was inevitable that tensions between them should develop, particularly as they both sought to colonize and exploit the rich agricultural valleys of the Shephela that lay between them (cf. Map 42). In the time of Samuel, those tensions gave way to open hostility, and Israel suffered a defeat in the vicinity of Aphek. Realizing the gravity of the situation, the elders of Israel decided to have the Ark of the Covenant carried to the Israelite troops at Ebenezer. Already imbibing in Canaanite theology with its propensity for magic and local gods, the Israelites had come to believe that the presence of God in a battle would magically guarantee victory. Great shouting and rejoicing took place as the ark entered Israel's camp at Ebenezer; so great was the commotion that it was heard by the Philistines, who were encamped across the plain at Aphek. Also Canaanite in their theological persuasions, the Philistines realized the implications of the event. So it was that they were inspired to "acquit themselves like men and fight courageously," because they supposed that they now had to fight both with Israel's army *and* with Israel's God (1 Sam. 4:1-9).

Philistine fervor won the day, producing an outcome of utter defeat for Israel. Israel's army was cut to pieces, Eli's sons Hophni and Phinehas, who had borne the ark, were killed, and, most catastrophic of all, Israel's sacred ark was captured (1). There is some archaeological indication that the shrine city of Shiloh was itself destroyed at that time by the Philistines, a situation possibly reflected in the biblical narratives (Ps. 78:60; Jer. 7:12-15; 26:6-9). What *is* clear is that Shiloh no longer played a significant role as a sanctuary city (cf. role of Nob, 1 Sam. 21:1; 22:9) and that the Philistines were able to establish garrisons in Israel's heartland not far from Shiloh (1 Sam. 10:5; 13:3; cf. 2 Sam. 23:14) (cf. Map 41).

The triumphal Philistines carried their treasure to the city of Ashdod where it was placed in the temple of Dagon (2). But their ecstasy was short-lived. Within days the Philistine god had fallen and broken into pieces before the ark, and an outbreak of "tumors" (possibly the bubonic plague) was reported throughout the Ashdod district. So the ark was taken to the city of Gath, but again an epidemic ensued (3). And when finally the bringing of the ark to the city of Ekron had also brought the same calamity upon that city (4), the Philistines knew the time had come to attempt to placate the ire of the Israelite deity. To that end, they placed the ark, with an accompanying "guilt offering," on a cart drawn by two cows and sent it up the Sorek valley in the direction of Israel, thus ending their seven-month ordeal. In that episode, parenthetically, one sees at its worst the Canaanite doctrine of "local gods."

MAP 39

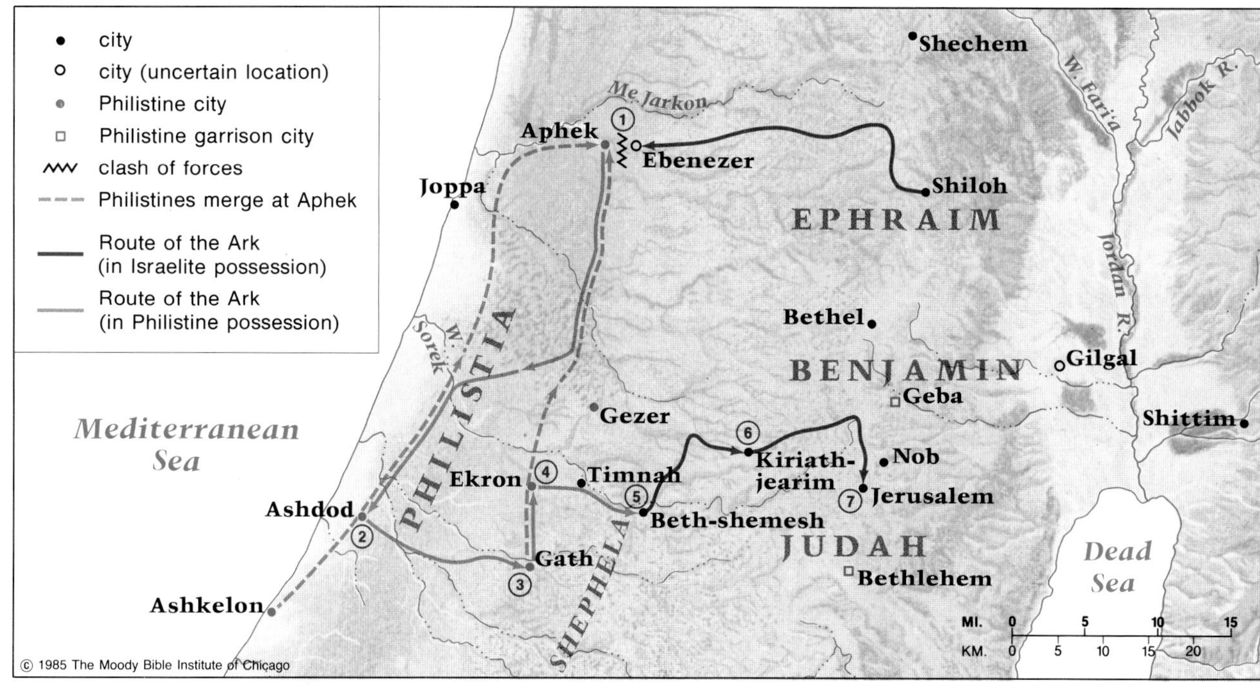

Thus the ark was returned to Israelite hands as it arrived in the fields outside Beth-shemesh at harvest time (5). Here again, possession of that object of Israelite religion was cause for great rejoicing, and a sacrifice of thanksgiving was offered to the Lord. But when some of the citizens of Beth-shemesh dared to look inside the ark, a great number of them were slain, possibly together with their oxen. After that sad incident, the ark was taken by the Israelites and safely stored in the highland town of Kiriath-jearim (6).

For many years (until the time of David) the Ark of the Covenant remained at Kiriath-jearim (2 Sam. 6:1-3; 1 Chron. 13:6-7; 2 Chron. 1:4), although it again may have been taken occasionally into Israelite battle (e.g., 1 Sam. 14:18). But in his enthusiasm to transfer the ark to his new capital at Jerusalem, David neglected to have it carried by the proper personnel, and misfortune again surrounded the object (2 Sam. 6:6). After three months, however, another mission was properly constituted, and the ark came to reside in the holy city (1 Chron. 15:2-15) (7).

It seems reasonable to conclude that the ark remained in Jerusalem for the balance of its existence until, together with the remainder of the Temple complex, it was destroyed by Nebuchadnezzar's troops, although legends abound to the contrary. One apocryphal account says that it was carried away to Babylon (1 Esdras 1:54), whereas another claims that it was removed and hidden by an angel (2 Baruch 6:7), and still another says that the prophet Jeremiah hid it (2 Macc. 2:4). Jeremiah himself declares that the ark will disappear and will be neither remembered nor missed (Jer. 3:16).

Josephus tells us that when Pompey captured the sacred precinct of the Temple, he actually entered the holy of holies to see all that had been unlawful for men to behold.[27] Although he apparently examined many objects, including the golden candlestick, the golden table, numerous vessels and spices, as well as the treasury, there is no mention that Pompey saw an ark, from which some scholars deduce that Judaism's post-exilic worship forms rendered an ark superfluous. Some in fact have related the incident to a proverb that eventually spread throughout much of the Roman Empire: "the Jews are atheists." Whatever the case, it seems that there was no ark in the Temple during the time of Pompey.

American archaeologists digging in the ruins of a synagogue in upper Galilee have recently unearthed what they believe to be a half-ton fragment of an ancient ark of the covenant, possibly dating to the third century A.D. The stone object was more than four feet long and was decorated with lions. It also had a scallop-shell niche, presumably from which an ever-burning lamp was hung.

Figure 16 Fertility of the Sorek valley from Timnah (green mound in foreground) in the direction of Beth-shemesh.

Wars of King Saul

If the book of Judges had underscored how various Israelite tribes were vulnerable to enemy attack, the debacle at Ebenezer vividly demonstrated the same reality, but on a national scale. And so a delegation of elders waited on Samuel, requesting that Israel become like its neighbors and have a king appointed (1 Sam. 8:4-6). Though Samuel was initially somewhat ambivalent, God gave the prophet some divine instructions in the matter, and Saul was eventually selected as the new king. His appointment did not win immediate approval, however (cf. 1 Sam. 10:27; 11:12), and it was not until he had defeated the Ammonite forces of Nahash (1) and had displayed some brilliant strategy in the process of liberating the people of Jabesh-gilead (2), that his appointment was acclaimed nationally (1 Sam. 11:14-15).

But the menace of the Philistines had not yet been addressed. When Jonathan, Saul's son, made a raid on their garrison at Geba (3), the mighty enemy of the west retaliated by moving thousands of horses, chariots, and infantrymen into a position to assault Michmash. At the same time the Philistines sent out raiding parties toward Ophrah, Beth-horon, and in the direction of the Jordan (1 Sam. 13:15*b*-24) (4). Saul's "army" simply "disappeared" before this imposing sight. But again it was Jonathan who exhibited courage. He and his armorbearer stealthily passed over to the Philistine camp outside Michmash, surprised the uncircumcised enemies, and routed them westward through the pass at Aijalon (1 Sam. 14:1-23) (5). Following the temporary reprieve provided by Jonathan's raid, Saul apparently felt at liberty to engage in limited warfare against other opponents: Moab, Ammon, Edom, Zobah, and Amalek (1 Sam. 14:47-48; see Map 41).

But the consolidated Philistine forces soon regrouped and pitched their army in the Jezreel valley at Shunem, at the foot of Mt. Moreh (1 Sam. 28:4*a*) (6). That move would have effectively severed Saul's kingdom and made it impossible for the Judean to maintain even a semblance of control over the Great Trunk Road. Therefore Saul responded to the challenge by leading his forces to a spring near Jezreel (1 Sam. 28:14*b*; 29:1), and the scene for a major confrontation had been set (7). (For the battle of Mt. Gilboa, see Map 44.)

Figure 17 Undulating hills and relative deforestation of Judah, heartland of the kingdom of Saul, David, and Solomon.

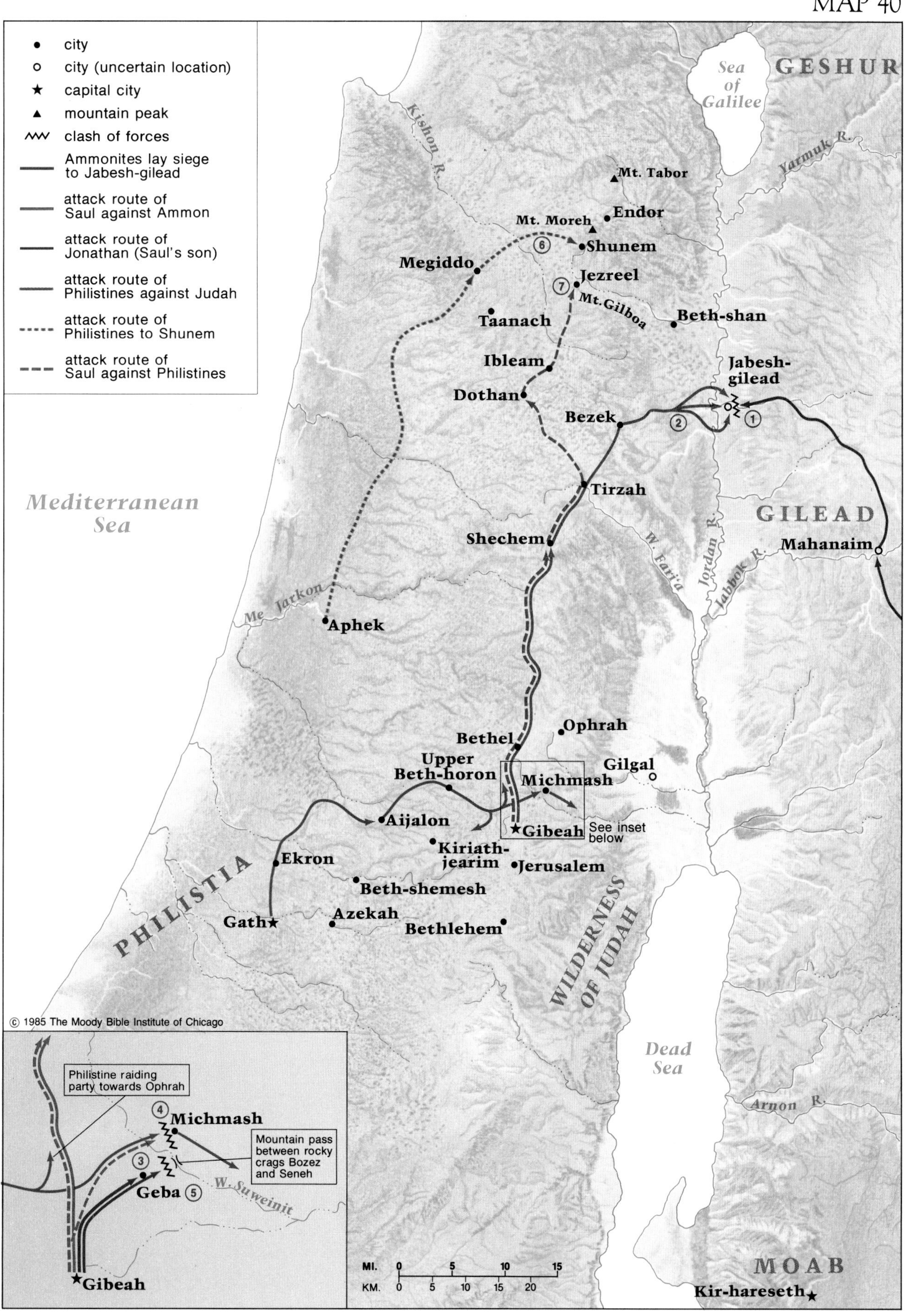
city
city (uncertain location)
capital city
mountain peak
clash of forces
Ammonites lay siege to Jabesh-gilead
attack route of Saul against Ammon
attack route of Jonathan (Saul's son)
attack route of Philistines against Judah
attack route of Philistines to Shunem
attack route of Saul against Philistines
Sea of Galilee
GESHUR
Kishon R.
Yarmuk R.
Mt. Tabor
Endor
Mt. Moreh
Shunem
Megiddo
Jezreel
Mt. Gilboa
Taanach
Beth-shan
Ibleam
Jabesh-gilead
Dothan
Bezek
Tirzah
Mediterranean Sea
GILEAD
Shechem
W. Far'a
Jordan R.
Jabbok R.
Mahanaim
Me Jarkon
Aphek
Ophrah
Bethel
Upper Beth-horon
Gilgal
Michmash
Aijalon
Gibeah
See inset below
Ekron
Kiriath-jearim
Jerusalem
PHILISTIA
Beth-shemesh
Gath
Azekah
Bethlehem
WILDERNESS OF JUDAH
Dead Sea
Arnon R.
MOAB
Kir-hareseth
MI. 0 5 10 15
KM. 0 5 10 15 20
Philistine raiding party towards Ophrah
Michmash
Mountain pass between rocky crags Bozez and Seneh
Geba
W. Suweinit
Gibeah

MAP 41 The Kingdom of Saul

DAVID AND GOLIATH

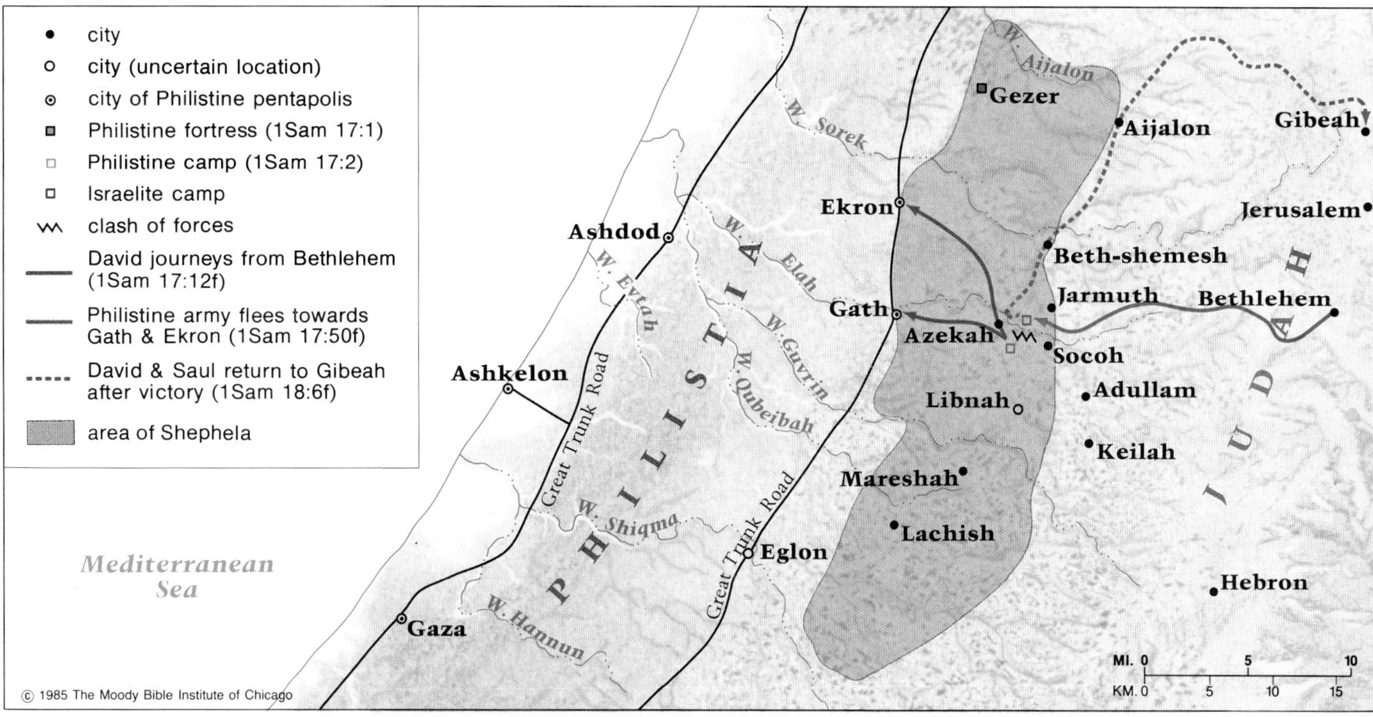

In one of the numerous agricultural wars that Israel and Philistia fought over control of the Shephela, David slew Goliath with a slingshot (1 Sam. 17; cf. 2 Sam. 21:18-22; 1 Chron. 20:4-8); his victory is often dismissed as an allegory. Given the nature of warfare in David's time, however, the narrative might better be taken as an illustration of the skill that ancient slingers possessed and the trust they put in such a weapon. Use of the sling in warfare is amply attested in both the art and literature of Assyria, just as it was used by armed troops of the neo-Hittite city-states, Persia, Greece, and Rome.

As evident from Fig. 18, the Elah valley near Socoh is flanked on either side by higher slopes, which on this occasion served as grandstands from which the camps could observe the contest. A few clues in the narrative and the topography of the area combine to suggest that the Israelites were encamped on the hills to the north (left side of Fig.) while the Philistines' camp was atop the southern crests (right side of Fig.).

Figure 18 The Elah valley near Socoh is aligned on either side by the rolling hills of the Shephela.

DAVID: THE FUGITIVE

"Saul has slain his thousands, and David his ten thousands" (1 Sam. 18:7). In the aftermath of David's stunning victory over Goliath (1 Sam. 17), this is what the women began chanting in the streets of Gibeah. Enraged by the chant and its possible political implications, Saul set out on a course of destroying this young shepherd-turned-soldier. David, for his part, found it necessary to elude Saul's spear on a number of occasions before finally recognizing the extent of the king's personal distress. Perceived as an enemy of Saul's state, David had no choice but to flee for his life and, in that sense, to undertake the life of a fugitive and outlaw, a situation that continued perhaps for as long as a decade, until Saul's inevitable demise atop Mt. Gilboa (1 Sam. 31; see Map 44).

David fled first to the prophet Samuel at Ramah (1 Sam. 19:18) (**1**) where, after a period of time, he was delivered from Saul's hand by Jonathan, Saul's son. He next traveled to Nob (**2**) where Ahimelech the priest provided him with nourishment and gave him Goliath's sword (1 Sam. 21:1-9). Now he journeyed to Gath (1 Sam. 21:10) (**3**) where, through a strange and haunting irony, the aforementioned words of the chanting women actually forced David to feign madness in order to escape a Philistine prison. He fled to Adullam (1 Sam. 22:1) (**4**) where, by this time, some 400 men had joined forces with him (cf. 1 Chron. 12). Apparently sensing that even his family members were not safe from Saul's temper, David took steps to provide for the security of his father and mother; he led them to the safe refuge of Moab (1 Sam. 22:3) (**5**), from where David's own great-grandmother had come (Ruth 4:17, 22). After that, David himself took up residence first along the western shore of the Dead Sea at Masada ("stronghold") (1 Sam. 22:4) (**6**) and later farther inland at the forest of Hereth (1 Sam. 22:5) (**7**). While at Hereth, David learned of the treachery of Saul who had slain Ahimelech for showing loyalty to David. He discovered too that Philistines were plundering the Judean city of Keilah, so he and his men decided to travel there (**8**) and to launch a counteroffensive against the Philistine antagonists (1 Sam. 23:5).

Realizing now that he was a threat to both Saul and the Philistines and possibly fearing Philistine retaliation, David proceeded into the heart of the Judean Negeb, first to the wilderness of Ziph (1 Sam. 23:14) (**9**), and then to the wilderness of Maon (1 Sam. 23:24) (**10**). But Saul was in relentless pursuit, so David moved to the forbidding wilderness of Judea at Engedi (1 Sam. 23:29) (**11**). While staying in this stronghold, David received his first opportunity to slay his rival; but he denied himself that moment of vengeance, feeling that he could not raise his hand against the Lord's anointed with impunity. Knowing full well that his life had been spared, however, Saul gave pretense of abandoning the hunt temporarily, and so David returned south to Masada (1 Sam. 24:22; cf. Ps. 57) (**12**).

Some time later, David re-entered the wilderness of Maon (**13**) and came to the vicinity of the towns of Maon and Carmel, where he met and eventually married Abigail (1 Sam. 25:1-42). But as was the case before when David came to this wilderness, Saul once again was notified of David's presence in the area and was inspired to renew his manhunt. When the king arrived in the wilderness, he is said to have bivouacked on a hill at Hachilah (1 Sam. 26:3; cf. 23:19). During the night, David and his servant stealthily entered Saul's camp and carried off the king's spear, which had been stuck in the ground right beside his head. When at a safe distance, David again reminded Saul that he represented no real threat to the monarch.

After this incident, David traveled once again to Gath (1 Sam. 27:2) (**14**) where he offered his services to Achish, its king, in return for which David was given the city of Ziklag (1 Sam. 27:6) (**15**). Perhaps Achish was seeking to place a buffer between himself and what he perceived to be a growing menace in the direction of Egypt, the marauding tribes of Amalekites, Geshurites, and Gizrites. In any event, David periodically found it necessary to raid some of these regions along the southern frontier of Ziklag (1 Sam. 27:8 (**16**); 30:8-10) (**19**).

The effect of Saul's preoccupation with the threat of David was that he paid insufficient attention to his real foe—the Philistines. Evidence indicates that the Philistines had begun virtually to encircle Saul's kingdom, adding to their control of the coastland and the city of Beth-shan by seizing both the Esdraelon and Jordan valleys. Anticipating a full-scale and final attack on the Judean's forces, the Philistines marshaled their troops at Aphek, the scene of an earlier victory (1 Sam. 4:1-11; see Map 39). Of course the soldiers of Achish were part of this confederation. And so David's array of men marched with them to Aphek (1 Sam. 29:1-3) (**17**), where some of the other Philistine commanders objected to their presence. David and his men therefore returned to their home at Ziklag (1 Sam. 30:1) (**18**). The actual battle between Saul and the Philistines (1 Sam. 31) was lost even before it began; greatly

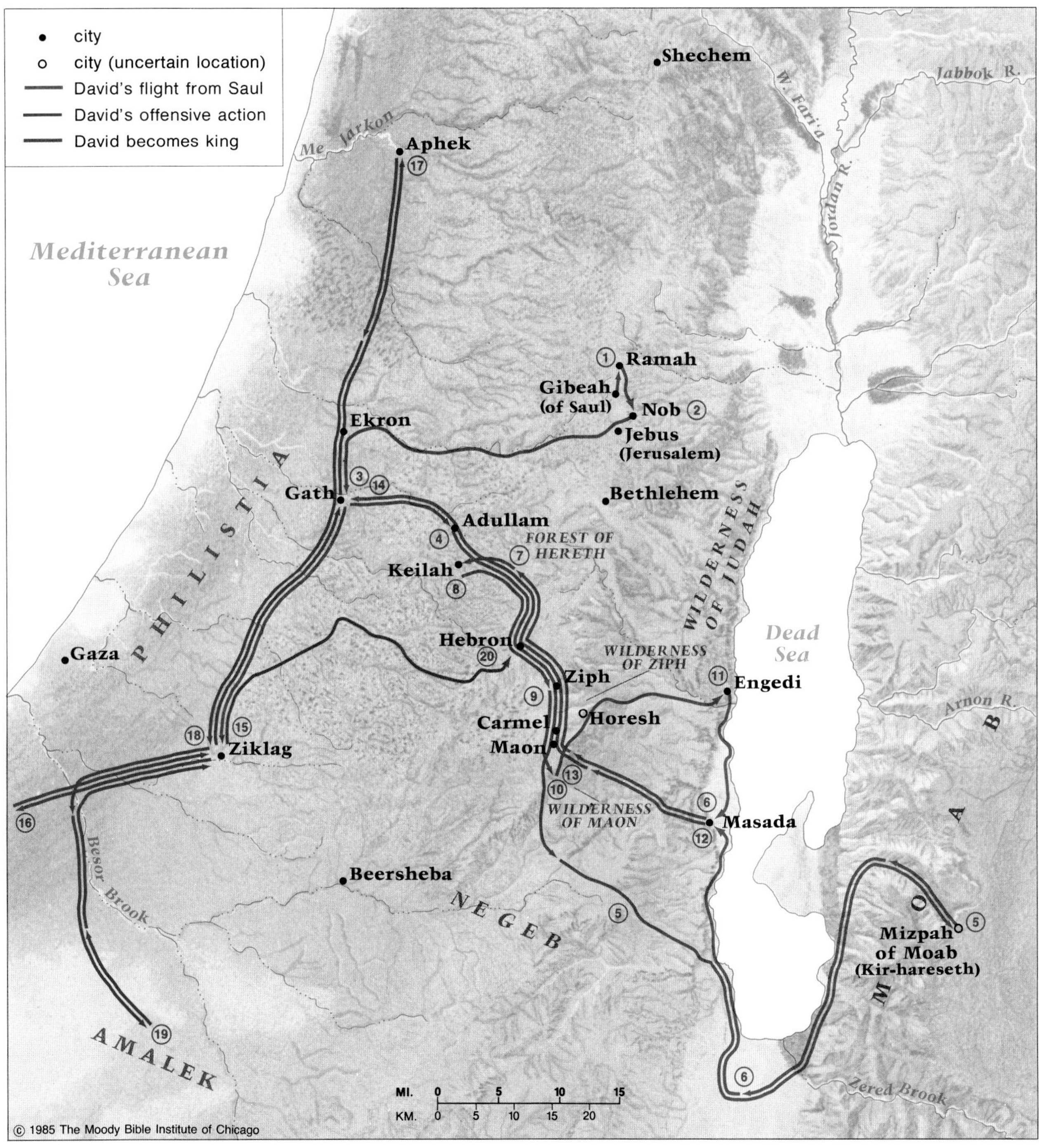

outclassed in manpower and technology and without a positive message from the Lord (1 Sam. 28:6-25), the "battle" of Mt. Gilboa was nothing short of a debacle.

David remained in the Ziklag region for some time; it was there that he was notified concerning the grim details of the deaths of Saul and Jonathan (2 Sam. 1:1-12). After spending an appropriate time in mourning, David inquired of the Lord concerning his options, now that his bid for kingship was uncontested. Informed by his Lord, David set out from Ziklag on a journey that brought him to Hebron (2 Sam. 2:1-4) (20) where he was officially crowned "king of Judah." The former outlaw now reigned!

Many of David's early efforts at Hebron seem to have been directed at healing the breach between Judah and the house of Saul (e.g., 2 Sam. 2:4*b*-7). He publicly distanced himself from the proclaimed murderer of Saul (2 Sam. 1:14-16), and he led the charge to bring the assassinators of Ishbosheth to justice (2 Sam. 4:9-12).

The Battle of Mt. Gilboa

The flow of events that led up to the suicide of Saul atop Mt. Gilboa have been placed into the book of 1 Samuel in a topical, rather than chronological, arrangement. A chronological reconstruction of the events would be as follows. The confederated Philistine armies, determined to effectively slice the country of Israel in half while reinforcing their own hold over the Great Trunk Road, marched from Aphek to Shunem and pitched a battle line against the kingdom of Saul (1 Sam. 28:4; 29:1, 11). Saul responded to that challenge by mobilizing his troops and deploying them on an outlying spur of Mt. Gilboa near Jezreel (1 Sam. 28:4*b*). The Judean king probably realized that the battle was practically lost before it even began. For Saul's army was greatly outclassed in manpower and technology, and the gently rolling terrain around Jezreel would do little to deter the effectiveness of the Philistine chariot force. Moreover, there was the ominous sign of divine judgment: God refused to answer dream, Urim, or prophet, which meant that He had already abandoned Saul. As a consequence of being unable to discern God's will by conventional means, Saul resorted to the extreme measure of necromancy (calling back the dead). Disguised and under cover of darkness, he sought out a witch in the town of Endor and employed her divining powers to conjure up Samuel. But Samuel's words brought Saul neither counsel nor comfort; he prophesied only calamity: "and tomorrow you and your sons will be with me [i.e., dead]; the Lord will also give the army of Israel into the hands of the Philistines" (1 Sam. 28:19).

As the battle ensued on the following day, a Philistine victory was swift and decisive. Saul's army was decimated, and the casualty list included three of his sons (1 Sam. 31:1-2). The king himself had been wounded by an arrow; and wishing to avoid the indignity that his capture necessarily would have entailed, Saul fell on his own sword and died. On the day after the battle, as the Philistine soldiers returned to Gilboa to gather their spoil, they happened upon the body of Saul, which they recognized. Jubilant in their quarry, the Philistines brought Saul's corpse to Beth-shan. This strongly fortified city remained an island of Egyptian domination in the midst of Saul's kingdom (cf. Map 41). At Beth-shan, Saul's decapitated body was impaled on the city wall and his armor was placed inside the temple of Ashtaroth. Archaeology has demonstrated that the worship of Ashtaroth was prominent in Beth-shan during this period. A stone slab depicting that Canaanite fertility goddess has been unearthed among the ruins of a temple at Beth-shan.

As reports spread abroad, some citizens of Jabesh-gilead heard of the desecration against Saul. They remembered with gratitude the fearlessness Saul had demonstrated to them on another day, when he had delivered them from certain disaster (1 Sam. 11:1-7). As a result, a band of men from Jabesh-gilead crossed the Jordan River at night, secretly gathered the remains of Saul and his sons, and carried them back to their city for a decent burial.

When news of the calamity atop Mt. Gilboa reached David at Ziklag, he lamented over the deaths of Saul and Jonathan, his son. "Your glory, O Israel, lies slain on your heights! Oh, how the mighty have fallen! Tell it not in Gath" (2 Sam. 1:19-20*a*).

MAP 44

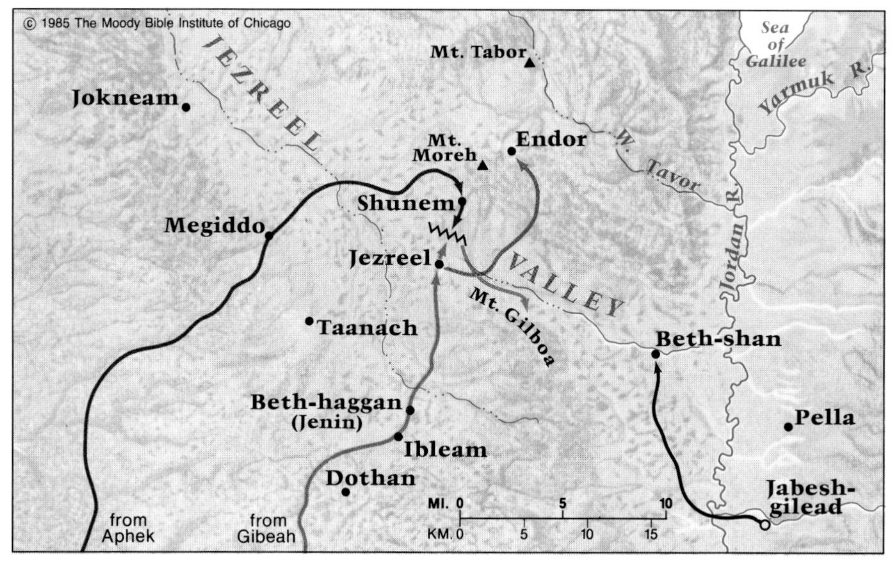

King David's Exploits

During the course of David's thirty-three-year reign at Jerusalem, he converted the city into the nerve center of an empire whose dimensions stretched from Egypt to the vicinity of the Euphrates River. He engaged in considerable building and expansion of the city, and eventually he brought the Ark of the Covenant within its walls, thereby merging for the first time in Israel's history its political and religious capitals (2 Sam. 6:12-19). It only remained for David to make permanent this arrangement, to enshrine Jehovah in Jerusalem forever by building Him a temple. And that is what David aspired to do (2 Sam. 7), but the execution of his dream was reserved for a son of David, because the warrior himself was a man whose hands had shed blood in battle (1 Chron. 28:3).

The main exploits of David occurred early in his reign. Though engaged in what seems to have been minor skirmishes against the Moabites (2 Sam. 8:2; 1 Chron. 18:2) and the Amalekites (2 Sam. 8:12; 1 Chron. 18:11), David's army faced major confrontations with the Philistines, Arameans, Edomites, and the Ammonite-Aramean alliance. Soon after David had seized Jerusalem, the Philistines twice attempted to crush their former vassal (2 Sam. 5:17-20; 1 Chron. 14:8-11; 2 Sam. 5:22-25; 1 Chron. 14:13-16) by proceeding up the Sorek valley and pitching a battle line in the Valley of Rephaim, immediately west of Jerusalem. On one of those incursions, it appears they were successful in capturing Bethlehem (2 Sam. 23:14). On the first of those occasions, David directly confronted his antagonists at the town of Baal-perizim and repelled them back down the valley, capturing some of the Philistines' idols (**1**). In the second instance, however, he flanked their assault and attacked them from the rear, driving them north past Gibeon and Upper Beth-horon as far as Gezer (**2**).

With his western front relatively secure (cf. 2 Sam. 21:15-22), the new king's attention was turned toward Transjordanian opponents. The Aramean city-state of Zobah encompassed much of central Lebanon along Israel's northern frontier. It possessed valuable minerals and rich vineyards and grain fields, and its kings at times displayed aggressive tendencies. It was inevitable, therefore, that Zobah should collide with Israel's monarchy.

David launched a successful strike against Hadadezer, king of Zobah, despite support given the Aramean by Damascus (2 Sam. 8:3-11; 1 Chron. 18:3-10), after which the Israelite carried off spoil from the towns of Berothai, Tibhath, and Cun (**3**). Besides spoils gained, the victory precipitated a friendship treaty between David and the powerful kingdom of Hamath (see Map 46).

After he returned to Jerusalem, David learned of a threat posed by the Edomites who had descended from the heights of their stronghold (most likely at Bozrah) and were encamped in the Valley of Salt, near the southern end of the Dead Sea. Acting swiftly, the Jerusalem monarch led his own troops into that valley and decisively crushed the enemy (2 Sam. 8:13; 1 Chron. 18:12-13) (**4**). That stunning victory, together with the subsequent Edomite retreat to Egypt (1 Kings 11:14-19), paved the way for David's developing kingdom to be extended as far south as the Gulf of Aqaba (see Map 46).

David's problems with the Ammonites arose just after the death of their king, Nahash. Saul's expedition had succeeded in temporarily holding that monarch in check (1 Sam. 11:1-11). But at Nahash's death, when David sent a delegation to his son Hanun to bear condolences, those ambassadors were publicly disgraced at the court in Rabbah (2 Sam. 10:1-5; 1 Chron. 19:1-5). Apparently sensing that David would retaliate for such humiliation, Hanun proceeded to secure the services of a mercenary force from Zobah, Beth-rehob, Maacah, and Tob, which marched southwards toward Rabbah. Meanwhile the Ammonite army itself drew up in battle array at the entrance of its capital city. To meet the challenge, Joab, David's army general, divided the Israelite hosts into two companies: he himself courageously led a contingent of special troops against the Aramean mercenaries while the remainder of the Israelite forces were placed in the charge of Abishai and commanded to attack Rabbah (2 Sam. 10:6-14; 1 Chron. 19:6-15) (**5**). This Israelite victory effectively incorporated the kingdom of Ammon into David's growing domain.

Soon after this victory, Hadadezer of Zobah was emboldened to launch an all-out attack against David. This time he solicited forces from as far away as the Euphrates River and led those combined forces to Helam, northeast of Gilead. Alerted to the new threat, David once again led his troops into Transjordanian assault to meet the challenge. He won a brilliant victory, roundly defeating the Arameans and capturing their horses and chariots. That triumph extensively broadened the northern horizons of David's kingdom. Hadadezer's vassals concluded a peace treaty with David, who installed garrisons in Damascus and came to dominate the terrain more or less up to the Euphrates (2 Sam. 10:15-19; 1 Chron. 19:16-19) (**6**).

God had promised David that one of his sons would build the Temple (2 Sam. 7:12-16). Though in his waning years David might have

MAP 45

city
city (uncertain location)
mountain peak
clash of forces
Philistines confront David in Valley of Rephaim
David repels first Philistine attack
David routs Philistines after second attack
David attacks Hadadezer, king of Zobah
Edomites threaten at Valley of Salt
David crushes Edomites
Ammonites, aided by Aramean mercenaries, challenge David
David's forces conquer Ammonite-Aramean alliance
Hadadezer leads Aramean forces against David
David defeats Aramean alliance at Helam
David expelled from Jerusalem by Absalom; battle ensues
Route of David's census team
Tibhath
Cun
Berothai
ZOBAH
Litani R.
BETH-REHOB
Damascus
Sidon
ARAM
Tyre
Dan
Kedesh
MAACAH
Hazor
Acco
Sea of Galilee
GESHUR
Ashtaroth
Helam
Yarmuk R.
Megiddo
Lo-debar
TOB
Mt. Hauran
Rogelim
Ramoth-gilead
Beth-shan
Mediterranean Sea
Jordan R.
FOREST OF EPHRAIM
GILEAD
Shechem
Mahanaim
Jabbok R.
Aphek
Joab's forces
AMMON
Jazer
Rabbah (Amman)
Abishai's forces
Gezer
Bahurim
Jericho
Aijalon
Jerusalem
Medeba
Gath
see inset below
PHILISTIA
Hebron
GAD
Gaza
Aroer
Dead Sea
Arnon R.
Besor Brook
Beersheba
NEGEB
MOAB
Kir-hareseth
EASTERN DESERT
VALLEY OF SALT
Zered Brook
Bozrah
EDOM
Petra
Upper Beth-horon
Gezer
Aijalon
Gibeon
VALLEY OF REPHAIM
Mt. of Olives
Jerusalem
W. Sorek
Baal-perazim
Bethlehem
Gath
MI. 0 10 20 30 40
KM. 0 10 20 30 40 50 60

cherished that expectation for one of his sons, he became instead the object of intrigue and beleaguered insurrection, stemming ironically from *his sons.* David's eldest surviving son was Absalom, born to the king's wife who had been an Aramean princess of Geshur (2 Sam. 3:3). Absalom had spent three years in exile with his maternal grandfather because he had murdered his half-brother Amnon in retaliation for the rape of Absalom's sister, Tamar (2 Sam. 13:1-38). When he later returned to Jerusalem, Absalom spent some four years gaining the favor of his father's subjects, listening to their grievances, and establishing his own power base, that even included one of David's personal counselors (2 Sam. 15:1-12). When the opportunity seemed right, Absalom attacked Jerusalem and succeeded in temporarily expelling the patriarchal king from his capital (2 Sam. 15:13-30). No stranger to being hunted down, David craftily fled across the Jordan River (2 Sam. 16:5-14) and sought refuge in the secluded inlands around Mahanaim, where he received supplies and assistance from the towns of Rabbah, Lo-debar, and Rogelim (2 Sam. 17:27-29) (7). Meanwhile, back in Jerusalem, to signify the finality of his coup, Absalom publicly engaged in sexual relations with his father's concubines (2 Sam. 16:22). Unfortunately for him, Absalom's delay in the royal city had actually provided David with time to prepare a counteroffensive. And so, when Absalom's troops finally arrived, a battle ensued in the forest of Ephraim, in which Absalom was killed by Joab (2 Sam. 18:1-15). Absalom's usurpation of power had been shortlived.

A final episode that illustrates the extent of David's kingdom is that of his census of the people (2 Sam. 24:1-9). Dispatched under the leadership of Joab, a census team journeyed across the Jordan and began at the city Aroer, located on the border of Moab. From here, the team traveled north to Jazer, near the Ammonite frontier, then it passed through Gilead and Galilee before arriving at Dan. From Dan the census takers went around to Sidon and came to the fortress at Tyre, whereupon they began a southward journey to Judea, closing out their southern trek at Beersheba. At this point, having spent nearly ten months on their mission, the group returned to Jerusalem and reported to the king (8). In David's last hours, another of his sons, Adonijah, attempted to usurp kingship. But this was reserved for another, and David ordered Zadok to anoint Solomon (1 Kings 1:5-10, 32-37).

MAP 47 SOLOMON'S WEALTH AND POWER

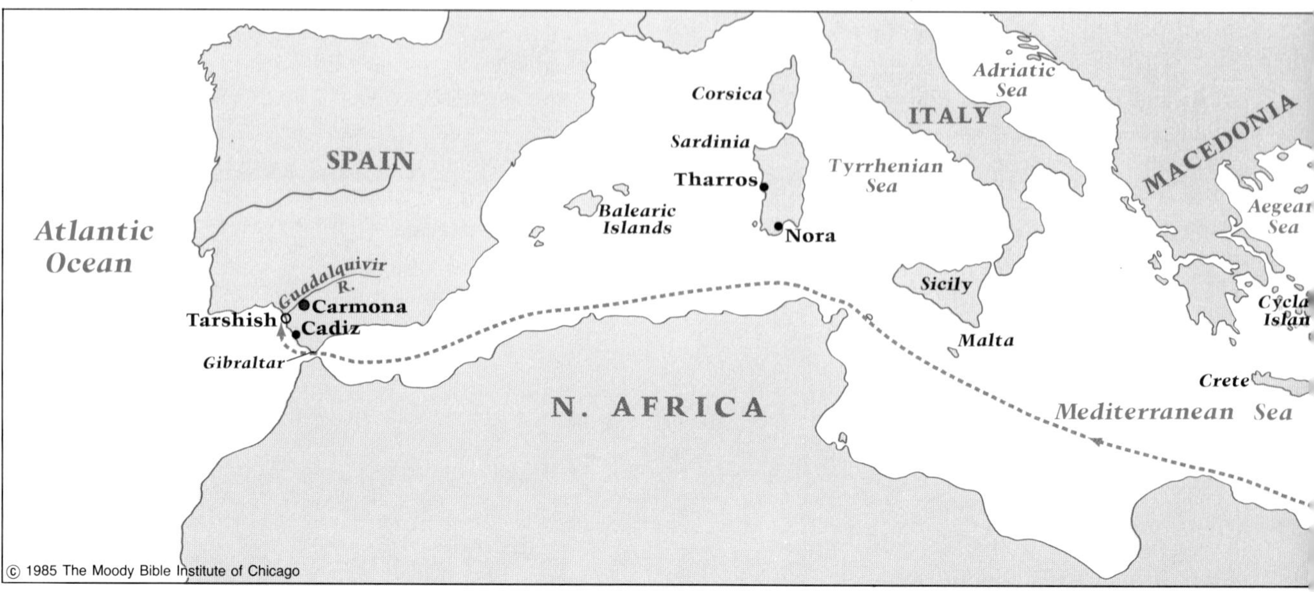

Solomon inherited a kingdom that was extensive and secure. His accession to the throne was not seriously challenged by others, nevertheless he moved quickly against Adonijah, Abiathar, and Joab (1 Kings 2:13-34) to ensure that his kingdom would be safe from within. To guarantee external security, Solomon took wives from many nations surrounding Israel (1 Kings 11:1), including the daughter of a pharaoh (1 Kings 3:1; 9:16). Undoubtedly that marriage paved the way for chariots to be imported from Egypt (1 Kings 10:29), just as his renewed control of Hamath (2 Chron. 8:3; cf. 7:8; 1 Kings 8:65) made it possible to import horses from Kue (Cilicia; 1 Kings 10:28).

Solomon also led Israel into a period of vast commercial expansionism. He revived the alliance with Hiram of Tyre, according to which large quantities of cedar and cypress woods were imported into Israel in exchange for certain staple commodites not found in abundance in Phoenicia (1 Kings 5:10; 2 Chron. 2:16). The location and extent of his domain meant that Solomon was in control of the main trading arteries between Arabia, Africa, and Asia, with all the lucrative benefits of such control. Solomon's domination of those routes probably occasioned the visit from the Queen of Sheba (1 Kings 10:1; 2 Chron. 9:1). But no less important, Solomon's league with Hiram came at the dawn of Phoenician commercial and political expansionism into the Mediterranean world. Present archaeological evidence indicates that by the tenth century B.C., the Phoenicians had expanded into Cyprus and possibly Spain; by the ninth century B.C. their field of commerce reached into parts of North Africa, Crete, Sardinia, and certainly Spain; and by the eighth century B.C., they had colonized Sicily and Malta. Solomon's economic resources and Hiram's technological resources were joined in an effort that would prove to be of immense mutual benefit.

Hiram built two fleets for Solomon: one to sail the Mediterranean, the other to sail the Red Sea (1 Kings 10:22; 2 Chron. 9:21; 1 Kings 9:26; 2 Chron. 8:17-18; cf. 1 Kings 10:11). The Mediterranean fleet sailed as far away as the port of Tarshish and returned once every three years with valuable and unusual commodities: gold, silver, ivory, iron, tin, apes, and peacocks (cf. Jer. 10:9; Ezek. 27:12). The word *tarshish* refers to a place where metal is smelted. It seems probable, therefore, that it became attached to an important and strategic refinery. Through a name similarity, Tarshish has been alternately sought in Cilicia (*Tarsus*) or Sardinia (*Tharros*), but it is almost certain that the city should be sought along the southwestern coast of Spain, on an island near the estuary of the Guadalquivir River. Biblical (e.g., Jonah 1:3) and Assyriological (e.g., Prism of Esarhaddon and Ashurbanipal II.11)[28] references clearly imply that Tarshish was at the farthest end of the Mediterranean. Classical sources[29] seem to interconnect the city with the Guadalquivir.

The following is a reconstructed description of Tarshish from various sixth-century B.C. authors: "Tartessus (i.e., Tarshish) is an illustrious city of Iberia (i.e., Spain-Portugal) which takes its name from the river Bactis (i.e., Guadalquivir) formerly also called Tartessus. This river comes from the Celtic region and has its source in the 'silver mountain'; in its stream it carries, besides silver and tin, a great abundance of gold and bronze. The river Tartessus divides into two arms when it reaches the mouth. Tartessus, the city, stands between the two arms, as on an island."[30]

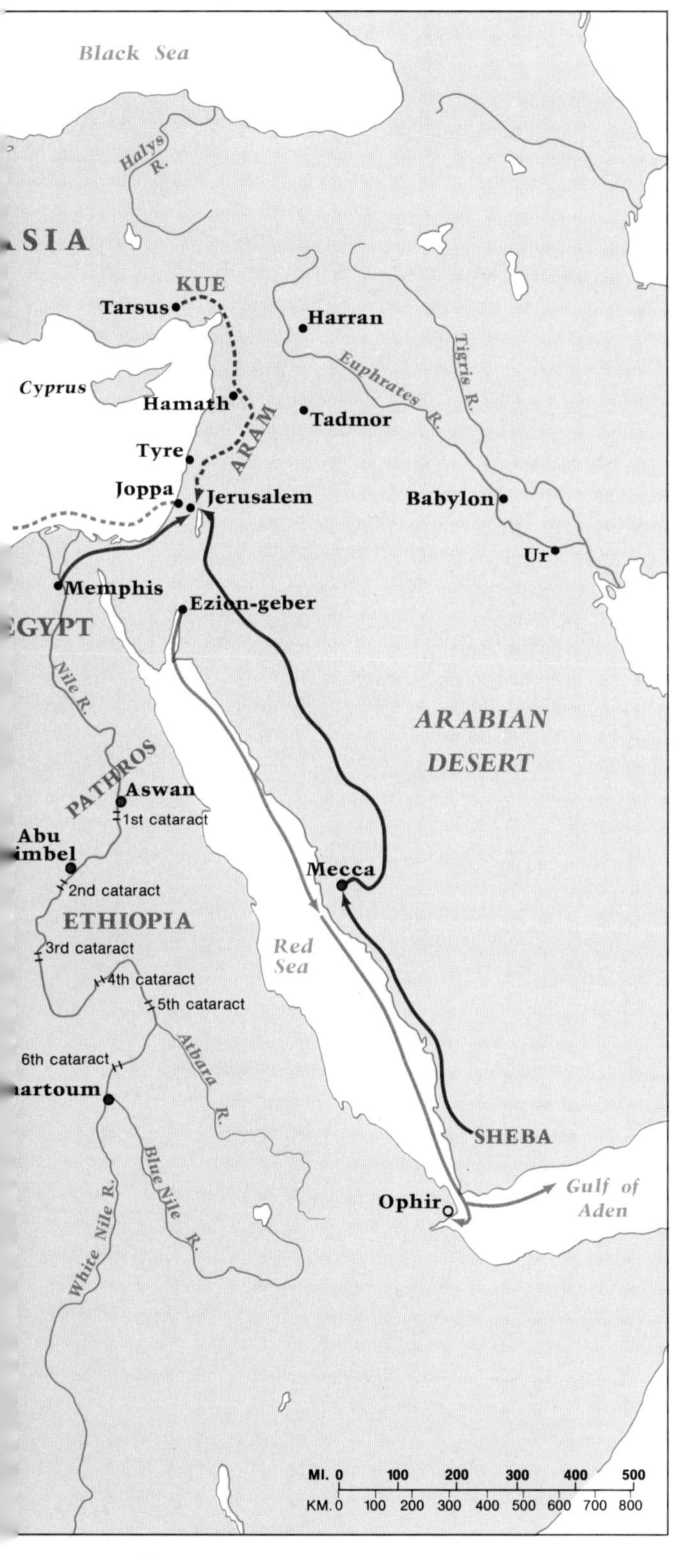

- city
- city (uncertain location)
- city (modern name)
- Solomon's Red Sea fleet
- Solomon's Mediterranean Sea fleet
- Solomon imports chariots from Egypt
- Solomon imports horses from Kue
- Visit of the Queen of Sheba

Traditionally, the city of Cadiz, Spain, is said to have been colonized by Phoenicians in the late twelfth century B.C.[31] Although the historicity of this traditional date has not been accepted by some scholars, a number of Spanish sites supply ample archaeological testimony that the Phoenicians were in the area by the ninth century B.C. at the latest. Tombs found in the vicinity of Carmona contained ivory objects with motifs said to have come directly from Phoenicia. Bronze and silver jugs in the "Samaria design" also have been discovered in the area, as have alabaster jars containing the cartouche of a ninth century B.C. pharaoh. It is not unreasonable to imagine, therefore, that Solomon's Mediterranean fleet sailed as far as Spain, returning with valuable minerals and exotic commodities. Silver, tin, copper, and iron were all native to Spain, gold could have been acquired in the African interior, and lead was available on the island of Sardinia.

Solomon's Red Sea fleet sailed from the port of Ezion-geber on voyages to Ophir, from which it regularly returned with large amounts of gold and rare woods. Based on the supposed linguistic origin of the names of precious imported wood, Ophir has been sought along the western coast of India, about 60 miles north of Bombay. More commonly, however, scholars have situated Ophir either in eastern Africa, along the Gulf of Aden, or somewhere in modern Somaliland. In any event, the historicity of the biblical statements that hail Ophir as a source of gold has recently been confirmed by an ostracon found at T. Qasile (just north of Tel Aviv). That archaeological piece dates to a period just after Solomon and bears the following inscription: "Gold from Ophir for Beth-horon—30 shekels."

The economic effects of Solomon's ventures can hardly be overstated. Opulent affluence of unprecedented proportion was lavished upon Tyre (Ezek. 27:25-27; Zech. 9:3; cf. Isa. 23:8) and Israel. Solomon "made silver as common in Jerusalem as stone, and he made cedar as plentiful as the sycamore of the Shephela" (1 Kings 10:27; 2 Chron. 9:27). Again, "all of King Solomon's drinking vessels were of gold, and all the vessels of the House of the Forest of Lebanon were of pure gold; none was of silver, it was not considered as anything in the days of Solomon" (1 Kings 10:21; cf. 7:47; 2 Chron. 9:20). Besides the revenues generated from caravan taxation, some 666 talents of gold (approximately 21 tons) came to the coffers in Jerusalem annually (1 Kings 10:14; 2 Chron. 9:13). In light of other ancient texts that describe enormous quantities of gold, one need not suppose this to be an impossibly exaggerated figure. Both in a literal and metaphorical sense, then, the Solomonic era became Israel's golden age.

MAP 48 SOLOMON'S ENTERPRISES

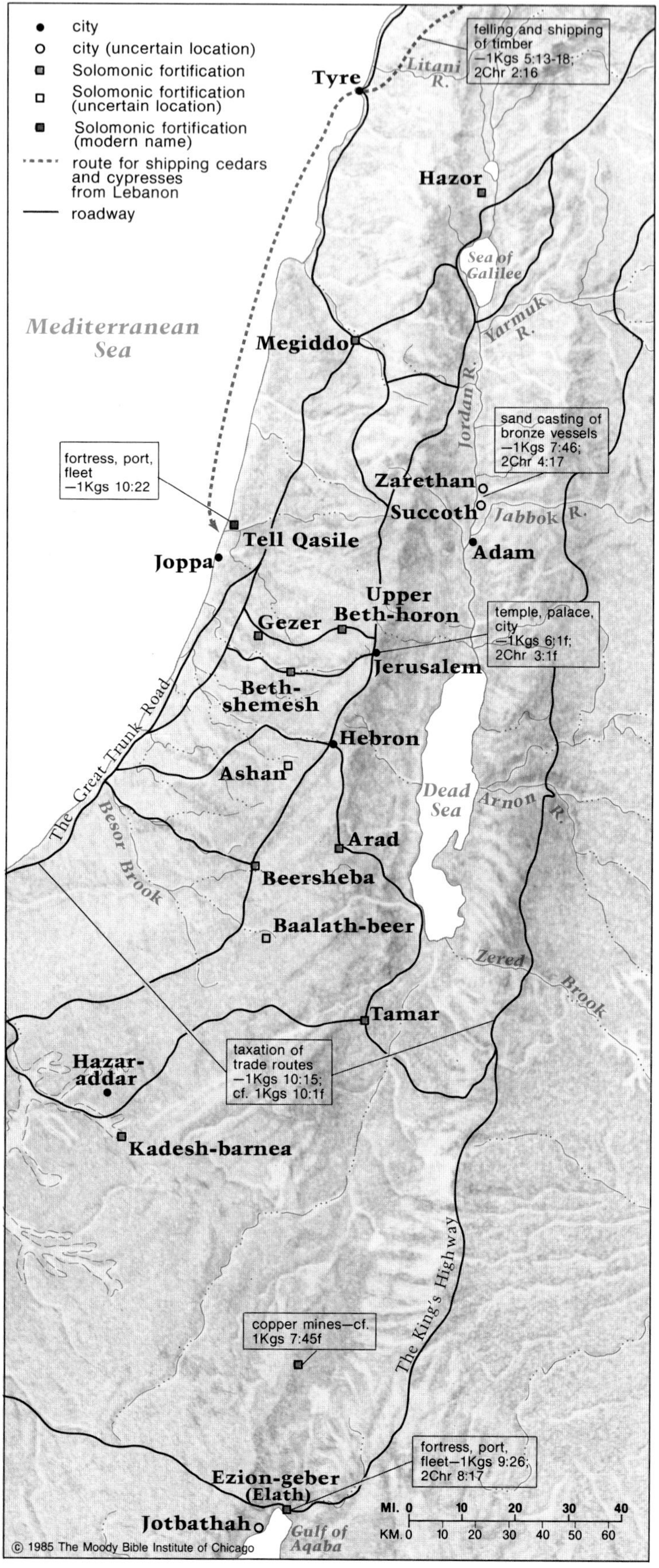

SOLOMON'S BUREAUCRACY

As Solomon's vast standing army and momentous building projects required larger revenue sources than even his commercial ventures could supply, the king was obliged to levy increasingly heavier taxes upon the population of Israel. That was almost in precise fulfilment of what Samuel had predicted when replying to the Israelites' initial request to be like other nations (1 Sam. 8:11-22). One such measure for generating revenue, described in 1 Kings 4:7-19, involved dividing Israel into twelve administrative districts, each with a royal governor and an obligation to furnish provisions for the royal bureaucracy and harem in Jerusalem for one month of a year. Such a system must have been an extremely irritating policy to Solomon's subjects, not only because it would have represented a heavy economic strain upon them, but also because it was grossly unfair (the entire territory of Judah was excused from its demands; cf. 1 Kings 4:19, LXX). Then again, we recall that it was one of those district governors, Jeroboam, who later became the first king over the ten northern tribes as they seceded from the kingdom of Solomon's son Rehoboam because of their displeasure over unfair economic policies (1 Kings 11:26-27; 2 Chron. 10:6-15).

In any case, even with an equivalent number of Israelite tribes and calendar months, Solomon still avoided what would appear to have been a natural criterion in apportioning the new levy. Actually, the redistricting was often done in a way that further obliterated cherished tribal boundaries. That was especially true for districts 1, 3-5, 8-10, divided in a few cases *across* natural geographical or tribal boundaries. A noticeable exception was in district 11, which conformed more or less to the territorial allotment of the tribe of Benjamin. One wonders in fact, in light of the disproportionately small size of that district and the presumed smallness of its population size (cf. Num. 1:36-37), whether Solomon's measure might not have been designed to be particularly repressive against the descendants of Saul. (See also the perimeter of district 2 in light of the Danite migration and the possible accession of part of that region by the tribe of Benjamin, cf. Josh. 16:3*b*-4; but see 18:13-14.) But the Benjamite district was an exception.

Consequently, Solomon's agenda in dividing the administrative districts as he did seems to have included a conscious effort to rid Israel of its cherished tribal heritage, at least to the west of the Jordan River, and an effort to solidify further the monarchistic ideal.

city
city (uncertain location)
Mediterranean Sea
PHOENICIA
ARAM
ASHER
NAPHTALI
LAND OF CABUL
GESHUR
ARGOB
HAVVOTH-JAIR
ISSACHAR
GILEAD
AMMON
BENJAMIN
PHILISTIA
JUDAH
REUBEN
MOAB
EDOM
AMALEK
EASTERN DESERT
Litani R.
Sea of Galilee
Yarmuk R.
Jabbok R.
Jordan R.
Dead Sea
Arnon R.
Zered Brook
Besor Brook
Tyre
Ijon
Dan
Kedesh
Yiron
Hazor
Acco
Cabul
Aphek
Hannathon
Bethlehem
Hammath
Jabneel
Daberath
En-haddah
Jokneam
Dor
Megiddo
Jezreel
Taanach
Beth-shan
Golan
Ashtaroth
Lo-debar
Ramoth-gilead
Ibleam
Abel-meholah
Jabesh-gilead
Hepher
Arubboth
Socoh
Tirzah
Zarethan
Mahanaim
Shechem
Succoth
Adam
Mizpah
Gath-rimmon
Aphek
Joppa
Jazer
Rabbah (Amman)
Upper Beth-horon
Bethel
Mizpah
Naaran
Beth-nimrah
Shaalbim
Gezer
Jericho
Heshbon
Gibeon
Gibeah
Makaz
Jerusalem
Ashdod
Beth-shemesh
Medeba
Gath
Bethlehem
Ashkelon
Libnah
Hebron
Dibon
Gaza
Aroer
Gerar
Beersheba
Kir-hareseth
Tamar
Bozrah
MI. 0 10 20 30
KM. 0 10 20 30 40

A Kingdom Divided

For all his greatness and wisdom, Solomon's oppressive economic policies had brought his once-extensive kingdom to the threshold of collapse. Even before Solomon's death, Arameans were contesting the northernmost sectors of his kingdom (1 Kings 11:23-25), Edomites were breaking away (1 Kings 11:14-22), and the ten northern tribes of Israel were keenly feeling the strain of increasing alienation (1 Kings 4:7-19; 11:26-40). The wise king had actually bequeathed to his son Rehoboam a kingdom that was teetering on the brink.

Rehoboam seems to have done nothing to forestall the inevitable. When a delegation of northern citizens appealed to have their tax burdens lightened, Rehoboam responded by imposing even heavier burdens. It was a desperate gamble for Rehoboam, perhaps one that he was forced to take; it also ignited the flames of anarchy and tribal secession! "What share do we have in David, what part in Jesse's son? To your tents, O Israel! Look after your own house, O David!" (1 Kings 12:16; cf. 2 Sam. 20:1).

One might say that three nations were created from what had been Solomon's territorial domain: Judah (Southern Kingdom), Israel, including the Transjordanian tribes (Northern Kingdom), and Aram (with its city-states of Damascus, Hamath, and Qatna). At the same time, the territories of Ammon, Moab, and Edom were emboldened to disavow loyalties to either Judah or Israel. Politically speaking, both Judah and Israel were left weak and relatively defenseless. In the north especially, nine separate dynasties ruled in the course of only 200 years. Although the borders of those kingdoms periodically may have fluctuated from those depicted on the map, this weak condition persisted down to the destruction of the Northern Kingdom by the Assyrian hordes of Shalmaneser V in August or September 722 B.C. (2 Kings 17:1-6), and the demolition of Jerusalem by the forces of Nebuchadnezzar II in August 587 B.C. (2 Chron. 36:11-21). Between the disintegration of Solomon's monarchy (c. 930-925) and the fall of Jerusalem, the humiliating history of both kingdoms was largely one of foreign assaults and plunderings (cf. Maps 52, 58, 62).

On the economic front, the division of the monarchy produced a strange irony: whereas Rehoboam sought to sustain the economic advantages Judah had enjoyed during the days of Solomon, the schism actually created economic advantages for Israel. Whatever natural resources and access to overseas trade this land possessed would now be controlled mostly by the Northern Kingdom. Most of the large city-states were in the north; the major trade artery, an economic bonanza, crossed the Northern Kingdom but skirted Judah. Such advantages may help explain why Israel was destroyed approximately 135 years before Judah.

And then there was the problem of Jeroboam I. Jeroboam, earlier appointed as an officer in Solomon's adminstration (1 Kings 11:28), became the first king over the disenfranchised Israelites of the north. This monarch quickly and astutely sought to establish his headquarters in Shechem, the spot where an Israelite patriarch had first worshiped Yahweh on the soil of the Promised Land (Gen. 12:6) and where the nation of Israel had officially ratified its covenantal relationship with Yahweh (Josh. 8:30-35; 24:1-28). Yet because Shechem was situated in a vale between Mt. Ebal and Mt. Gerizim and was vulnerable to north-south attack, it proved to be an unfortunate choice as a capital city. The statement that Jeroboam's wife came to Tirzah and that his son died there offers some indication that the capital was moved from Shechem to Tirzah early in Jeroboam's reign (1 Kings 14:17). About thirty-five years after Jeroboam's death, King Omri purchased a high, isolated, and relatively impregnable hill that he converted into the third and final capital city of the northern tribes—Samaria (1 Kings 16:24).

Jeroboam left a permanent legacy to Israel by exploiting another aspect of Israel's tradition to legitimize his own reign. He implemented at the cities of Dan and Bethel a religion of the "golden calves" so that pilgrims would not have to journey southward to Jerusalem to participate in high festival occasions (1 Kings 12:25-33). It seems accurate to characterize Jeroboam's religion, like Aaron's, which he was seeking to emulate (Ex. 32:1-6), as one of *apostasy* (i.e., the undermining or syncretizing of true religion) rather than *idolatry* (i.e., the importing of false religion). Admittedly, however, the golden calf later degenerated into an object of blatant idolatry (Hos. 8:5-6). Whatever the case, his religion included the perversion of Temple, worship, priesthood, feasts, and sacrifices (1 Kings 12:28-33).

It is pertinent to recall that only two of Jeroboam's eighteen successors—Ahab (1 Kings 16:31) and Ahaziah (1 Kings 22:53)—are said to have worshiped Baal, but both of those were related to Jezebel (cf. 1 Kings 18:19). However, Scripture records that fifteen of his successors either followed in the ways of Jeroboam's heterodoxy or tolerated such practices. And unlike their southern neighbors, those who imbibed the theology of Jeroboam were never once visited with revival. Instead, their perversion ultimately contributed to the downfall of the Northern Kingdom (2 Kings 17:21).

city
city (uncertain location)
capital city
sanctuary city
mountain peak
Byblos
Beirut
PHOENICIA
Sidon
Damascus
Mt. Hermon
Litani R.
Tyre
Dan
ARAM
Kedesh
Hazor
Acco
Mt. Carmel
Kishon R.
Sea of Galilee
Mt. Tabor
Ashtaroth
Yarmuk R.
Edrei
Mt. Hauran
Megiddo
Mediterranean Sea
Taanach
Beth-shan
Mt. Gilboa
Ramoth-gilead
Ibleam
Jabesh-gilead
Jordan R.
Tirzah
Samaria
Succoth
Mt. Ebal
Mahanaim
Mt. Gerizim
Shechem
Jabbok R.
Penuel
Aphek
Joppa
Shiloh
ISRAEL
Rabbah (Amman)
Bethel
Jericho
AMMON
Gezer
Ashdod
Aijalon
Jerusalem
Heshbon
Mt. Nebo
Medeba
Gath
Bethlehem
Ashkelon
Mareshah
Gaza
Hebron
Dibon
Dead Sea
Arnon R.
JUDAH
PHILISTIA
Besor Brook
Beersheba
MOAB
Kir-hareseth
W. el-Arish
Zered Brook
EASTERN DESERT
EDOM
Kadesh-barnea
WILDERNESS
MI. 0 10 20 30 40
KM. 0 10 20 30 40 50 60

REHOBOAM'S STRATEGIC CITIES

Rehoboam certainly must have lived to regret the day when he sought to impose his unprecedented tax burden; for the establishment of a northern kingdom under the headship of Jeroboam I carried with it significant and diverse consequences for Solomon's son. There were the obvious adverse effects, political and economic, that would have attended such a vast shrinkage in one's domain. But Jeroboam also represented a military threat: his obvious ties to Shishak, the pharaoh of Egypt, meant that Rehoboam might well expect to be invaded from the south (1 Kings 11:40; 12:2).

It appears probable that in preparation for such an invasion, or perhaps in the immediate aftermath of such an initial invasion, Rehoboam created a fortified defense line designed to cut off all unwanted Egyptian traffic from his kingdom (2 Chron. 11:5-10). Fifteen of the most strategic points in Judah were fortified by the Judean, as every convenient access into Jerusalem had been effectively blockaded (cf. Solomonic fortifications and see Map 48).

The towns of Bethlehem, Etam, and Hebron were located on or immediately adjacent to the Central ridge route (see Map 19), guarding the southern artery to Jerusalem; Ziph and Tekoa protected the two approaches from the wilderness of Judah while Socoh, Adullam, Beth-zur, and Adoraim were fortified to cut off the several inland approaches from Philistia and the Shephela. Finally, Aijalon, Zorah, Azekah, Moresheth-gath, Mareshah, and Lachish represented the front line of defense against an enemy attack via the Great Trunk Road. A comparison of Maps 51 and 42 makes clear the fact that the Philistine cities of Ekron, Gath, and Eglon (all on the Great Trunk Road) remained outside Rehoboam's sphere of control (1 Kings 2:39; Amos 6:2). Moreover, the city of Gezer, given to Solomon as part of his wedding arrangements with the Egyptian pharaoh (1 Kings 9:16-17*a*), was reclaimed at this point by the Egyptians (cf. Shishak inscription).

That none of his fortified cities was located along the border with Israel is an indication of Rehoboam's desire to woo the northern tribes back into his domain. That fleeting ambition died in the next generation, however, with the wars of Baasha and Asa (1 Kings 15:16-24). Map 51 is also helpful in that it clearly defines what were the boundaries of Judah's heartland throughout most of its existence (cf. Maps 3 and 59).

MAP 51

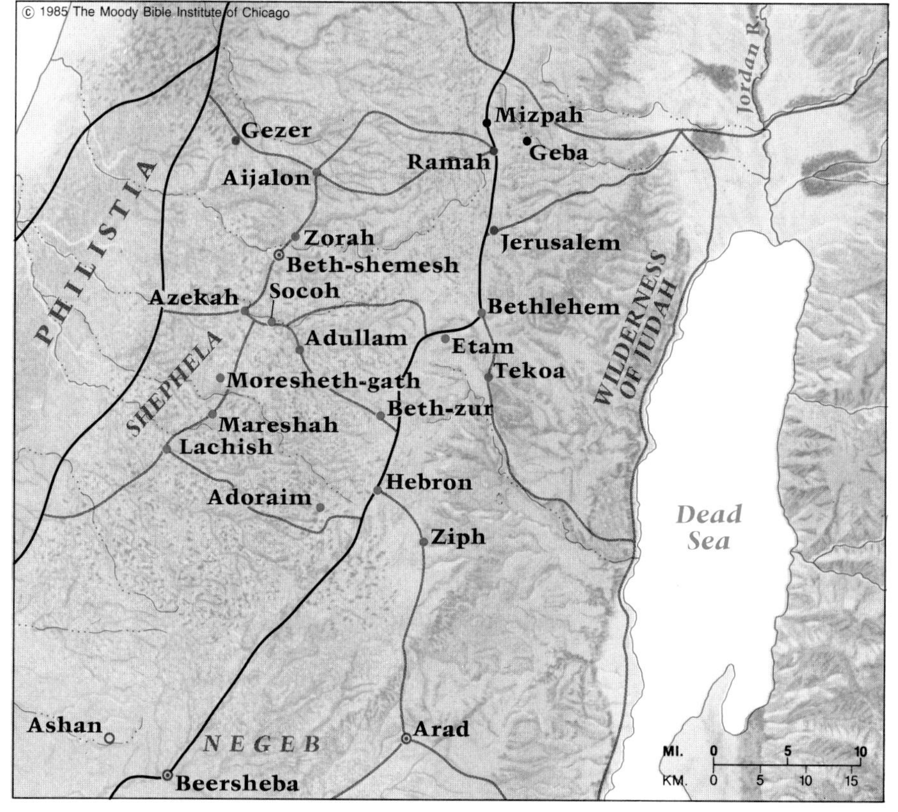

artery
roadway

fortified by Solomon
- city (I Kgs 9:15)
- city (archaeological evidence)
- city (archaeological evidence, but ancient name uncertain)

fortified by Rehoboam (2Chr 11:5-10)
- city

fortified by Baasha (1Kgs 15:17)
- city

fortified by Asa (1Kgs 15:22)
- city

JUDAH AND JERUSALEM BESIEGED

When the Solomonic monarchy was fractured and the kingdoms of Israel and Judah were created, both nations were left weak and militarily vulnerable. "Your country lies desolate," Isaiah declared, "your cities are burned with fire; foreigners devour your land in your very presence; it is desolate, as overthrown by strangers. And the daughter of Zion is left like a booth in a vineyard, like a hut in a cucumber field, like a besieged city" (Isa. 1:7-8). In fact, between the disintegration of the monarchy (930 B.C.) and the fall of Jerusalem to Nebuchadnezzar's Babylonian forces (587 B.C.), the humiliating history of Judah and Jerusalem largely revolved around a series of foreign assaults and plunderings, coming from virtually every quarter (see Map 52).

Almost immediately after the schism of Solomon's realm, Pharaoh Shishak invaded with some 1,200 chariots and 60,000 cavalry (1 Kings 14:25; 2 Chron. 12:2). Shishak's own account inscribed on the wall of the temple of Amon in Karnak says that the Egyptians advanced by way of Gaza to Ekron, where the troops divided. One contingent marched past Gezer and Upper Beth-horon; the other force proceeded up the Sorek valley, past Beth-shemesh, and converged with the first army at Gibeon, a northern suburb of Jerusalem (1). Though the "fortified cities of Judah" had been ravaged, Jerusalem itself was spared an Egyptian onslaught because Rehoboam carried out (to Gibeon) the treasures of the Temple, including the golden shields crafted during the reign of Solomon. (Despite having earlier sheltered Jeroboam from Solomon's wrath (1 Kings 11:40), Shishak now marched into the Northern Kingdom also, attacking Jeroboam's capital cities of Shechem and Tirzah, before crossing the Jordan to seize the town of Penuel, where Jeroboam may have sought temporary refuge. Shishak then captured the cities of Beth-shan, Shunem, and Taanach, before laying siege to Megiddo, the strategic fortress guarding the pass in the Carmel range through which ran the international trade route. When finally seized, Megiddo was converted into an Egyptian military base. A fragment of an inscribed stone (stele) commemorating Shishak's victory has been discovered among the archaeological remains of Megiddo.)

For the first few generations after Solomon, hostilities repeatedly erupted between Israel and Judah concerning their exact borderline. At issue ultimately was the alignment of the tribe of Benjamin, which was claimed by both kingdoms (Jeroboam's altar at Bethel, in Benjamin [cf. Josh. 18:21-22]; Rehoboam's league with Benjamin [cf. 1 Kings 12:21]). During the days of Abijah, an ambush was laid by Jeroboam near Bethel (2 Chron. 13:2) (2). Then during Asa's reign, the Israelite king Baasha was able to press southward as far as Ramah, just five miles from Jerusalem, though he was later repelled (1 Kings 15:16; 2 Chron. 16:1) (3).

A temporary reprieve was gained for Judah when King Asa decisively defeated an Ethiopian league headed by Zerah (2 Chron. 14:9-15; 16:8). In that case, the battle lines were set at the city of Mareshah, about 25 miles southwest of Jerusalem, and the Ethiopians were routed as far as Gerar (4). Then during the days of Jehoshaphat, a Moabite alliance moved through Edom and came to Engedi, from which it followed the Ascent of Ziz and came to the vicinity of Tekoa (2 Chron. 20:1-2), where it was finally repulsed by Jehoshaphat's forces (5).

But Judah's fortunes changed dramatically in Joram's reign. Not only was Edom able to repudiate Judean lordship (2 Kings 8:20-22), but also a confederation of Philistines and Arabs launched an attack on Jerusalem that captured some spoil from the royal city (2 Chron. 21:16-17) (6).

The force of the growing Aramean city-state of Damascus was felt during the days of Joash (2 Kings 12:17-18; cf. 10:32-33). Hazael, king of Damascus, came south and captured the Philistine capital of Gath (7). With this victory under his belt, he set his sights upon Jerusalem, whereupon Joash bribed him by sending him all the gold in the Temple treasury; Jerusalem once again was spared.

Warfare between Israel and Judah was renewed during the time of Judah's Amaziah. In preparation for a military operation against Edom, Amaziah hired some Israelite mercenaries, but then, at the urging of a prophet, he discharged them before actually going into battle (2 Kings 14:7; 2 Chron. 25:5-10). The outraged mercenaries proceeded to loot and murder their way back home. And so, when Amaziah returned in triumph over the Edomites, he requested a face-to-face meeting with King Jehoash of Israel, presumably to take up the matter of the mercenaries' behavior. Unintimidated, Jehoash warned Amaziah to back off, which Amaziah refused to do. Each ruler then mustered his troops and met in battle at the city of Beth-shemesh (8). Amaziah was defeated and taken captive, and Jehoash's troops ascended to Jerusalem, where they broke down part of the city wall and carried off hostages and precious booty.

The sort of grim political refrain just described was muted early in the eighth century B.C. as the two kingdoms experienced something of a renaissance under the leadership of Israel's Jeroboam II and Judah's Uzziah (see Map 56). Seizing upon the advantage that his father had gained against Aram at Aphek (2 Kings 13:17, 24-25), Jeroboam II restored some of Israel's borders that had existed in the days of David and Solomon (2 Kings 14:23-25). Only scant information about those gains is known to us. Amos 6:13-14 refers to capturing the cities of Lo-debar and Karnaim and to establishing a border from Lebo-hamath to the Sea of the Arabah (Dead Sea).

Uzziah's exploits were no less impressive (2 Kings 14:22; 15:1-3; 2 Chron. 26:1-5) (see Map 56). He demolished the walls of the Philistine cities at Gath, Jabneh, and Ashdod; drove south and restored the seacoast city of Elath (Ezion-geber) to Judean control and forestalled the advances of the Meunim; constructed numerous fortresses in the wilderness; and received tribute from the Ammonites. But regrettably with all their newly-discovered influence, Israel and Judah reverted to their former ways of religious syncretism and economic exploitation (cf. Amos, Hosea). God saw to it that their renaissance soon faded.

The kingdom of Judah was severely tested during the days of Ahaz. Early in his reign, a Syro-Ephraimite confederation marched south and laid siege to Jerusalem. Again prisoners and a large amount of booty were carried off (2 Kings 16:5; 2 Chron. 28:5; cf. Isa. 7:1-9) (**9**). As a result, Ahaz contemplated appealing directly to Assyria for support; Isaiah, however, urged him not to do so, pointing out that the confederation would be destroyed within a relatively short time (Isa. 7:8).

Meanwhile, Ahaz's preoccupation with northern threats had made him vulnerable to plunderings from the west and south. The Philistines moved to recover the cities of the Shephela (2 Chron. 28:18) (**10**), while the Edomites were emboldened to invade Judah itself (2 Chron. 28:17) (**11**). Pressed to the limit, Ahaz resorted to the unthinkable: he rejected the advice of Isaiah and appealed to Assyria for assistance (2 Kings 16:7-9). And seizing upon this opportunity of imperialism, Tiglath-pileser III undertook a number of campaigns against Damascus (2 Kings 16:9) and Israel (2 Kings 15:29). In one of those, Tiglath-pileser's army marched southward from Sidon, Tyre, and Acco, passed through the Carmel range, and eventually assaulted and captured the fortress at Gezer (**12**). Archaeological remains from that site amply attest to the destruction, and Tiglath-pileser's artists created a relief on his palace wall at Nimrud that commemorates the victory. After Gezer, the Assyrian monarch decided to take aim at the very individual who had invited him there in the first place (2 Chron. 28:21-22). Being greatly outclassed in technology and manpower, Ahaz was forced to pay a heavy tribute.

Hezekiah came to the throne in Jerusalem when the Assyrian Empire was reaching its zenith under Sennacherib. When this Assyrian ruler became preoccupied with a menace in his neighboring Babylonia, however, Hezekiah decided to rebel (2 Kings 18:7). This laid the foundation for an all-out campaign to the west, which Sennacherib undertook through the coastal cities of Lebanon before razing a number of Canaanite municipalities, including Joppa, Ekron, and especially Lachish. From Lachish, Sennacherib turned his attention to Jerusalem, and, in his own words, he "shut up Hezekiah in Jerusalem like a bird in a cage" (cf. 2 Kings 18:13—19:37; 2 Chron. 32) (**13**). Although Hezekiah was required to pay a huge sum in tribute (2 Kings 18:14-16), God miraculously delivered Jerusalem once again from annihilation.

But by the time the Babylonian kingdom arose some one hundred years later, the limits of God's mercy had been reached. Judah persisted in its evil ways, and Jeremiah even predicted that the Babylonians would be God's agents to bring about Judah's demise (e.g., Jer. 19; 21:3-6). So it was that the mighty hosts of Nebuchadnezzar plundered Judah and eventually demolished Jerusalem, its walls, palace, and Temple. They finally carried off many of Jerusalem's inhabitants into captivity (2 Kings 24:1-4; 25:27; 2 Chron. 36:6-7; Jer. 46:2) (**14**).

Figure 19 From Gethsemane, the Golden Gate is visible.

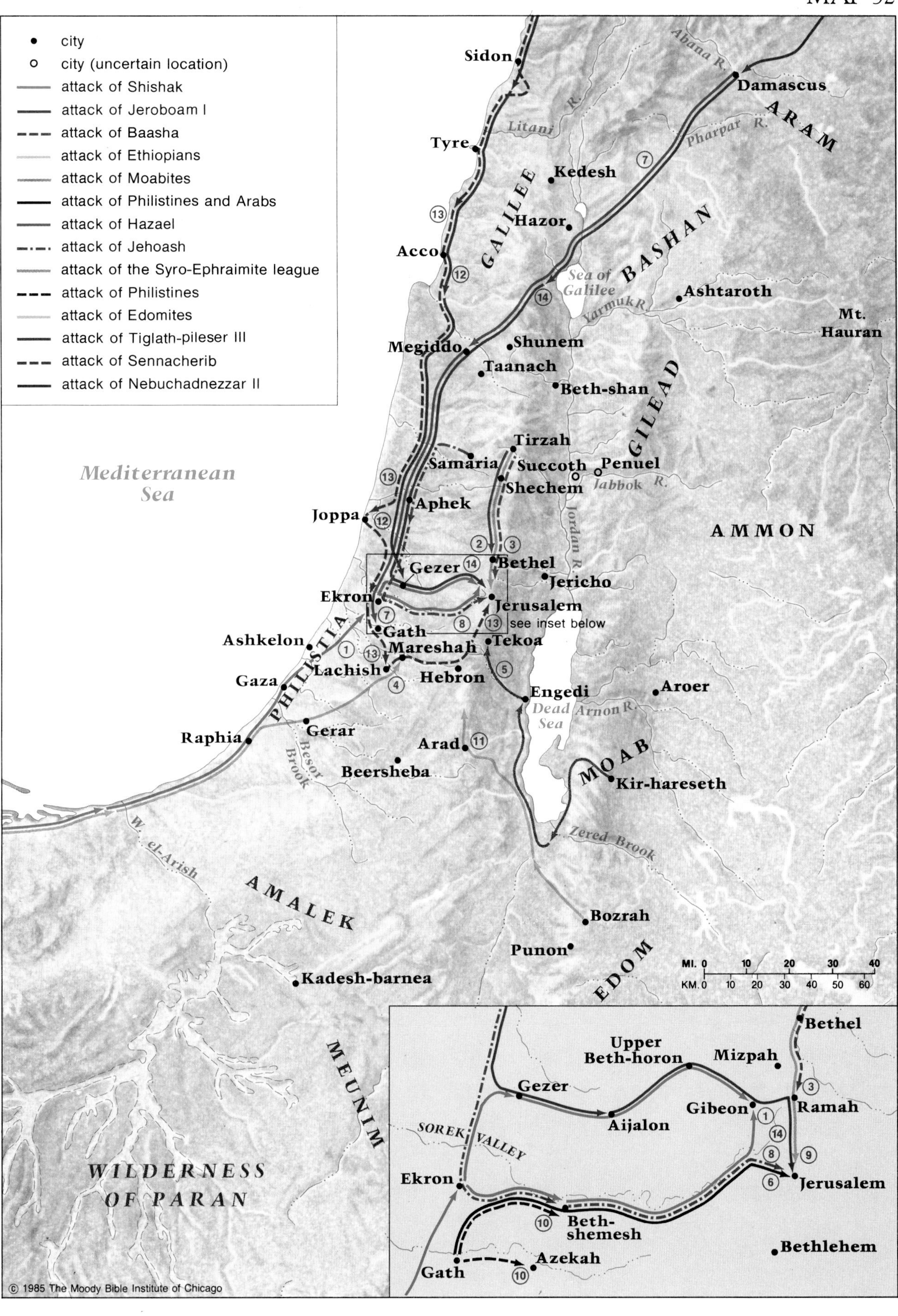

city
city (uncertain location)
attack of Shishak
attack of Jeroboam I
attack of Baasha
attack of Ethiopians
attack of Moabites
attack of Philistines and Arabs
attack of Hazael
attack of Jehoash
attack of the Syro-Ephraimite league
attack of Philistines
attack of Edomites
attack of Tiglath-pileser III
attack of Sennacherib
attack of Nebuchadnezzar II
Sidon
Tyre
Acco
Megiddo
Damascus
ARAM
Kedesh
Hazor
GALILEE
BASHAN
Sea of Galilee
Ashtaroth
Mt. Hauran
Shunem
Taanach
Beth-shan
GILEAD
Tirzah
Samaria
Succoth
Penuel
Shechem
Aphek
Joppa
Mediterranean Sea
AMMON
Bethel
Gezer
Jericho
Ekron
Jerusalem
Gath
see inset below
Ashkelon
Mareshah
Tekoa
Lachish
Hebron
Gaza
Engedi
Aroer
PHILISTIA
Gerar
Raphia
Arad
Beersheba
Dead Sea
MOAB
Kir-hareseth
AMALEK
Bozrah
Punon
EDOM
Kadesh-barnea
MEUNIM
WILDERNESS OF PARAN
Upper Beth-horon
Mizpah
Gibeon
Ramah
Aijalon
SOREK VALLEY
Beth-shemesh
Azekah
Bethlehem

THE BATTLE OF QARQAR

Qarqar was an ancient fortress located on the right (east) bank of the Orontes River, northwest of Hamath. The installation protected Hamath against an enemy approach from the north. In the sixth year of his reign, Shalmaneser III of Assyria fought a battle at Qarqar against a coalition of twelve western kings, including Irhuleni of Hamath, Ben-hadad II of Damascus, and Ahab of Israel, together with minor kings from Byblos, Arvad, Arabia, Ammon and Egypt. Although the kingdom of the Israelite monarch was far from the center of Shalmaneser's campaign, Ahab exercised control over trade routes from Egypt to the north and must have felt threatened by a growing Assyrian expansionism.

The principal source of information concerning this significant battle is Shalmaneser's famous "Monolith Inscription," which was uncovered, together with a relief figure of the king himself, at the modern town of Kurkh, located approximately 75 miles northeast of Harran.[32] According to the Inscription, Shalmaneser marched from Nineveh, his capital, across upper Mesopotamia, received tribute at the cities of Pitru and Sahlala (T. Sahlan) before crossing the Euphrates River at flood stage (probably in June), and collected additional tribute from other municipalities, including Carchemish and Melit (probably Malatya). At that point, he turned southward, marched against Aleppo, and defeated it. Shalmaneser's campaign climaxed in the region of Qarqar, where he pitched a battle line against the confederation. The relative strength of Israel in this confederation is evidenced by Ahab's supplying 2,000 chariots, more than half of the total chariot force, and 10,000 soldiers, about one-sixth of the total infantry. Despite the numerous inscriptions of Shalmaneser that celebrate the Battle of Qarqar as a stunning Assyrian triumph, the outcome of the confrontation remains very much in doubt today. A number of factors indicate that the coalition gained at least a stalemate.

Although the Battle of Qarqar is not mentioned directly in the Bible, it is of supreme importance for Old Testament studies. For during the period in question, Assyrian dates can be fixed with certainty with only a one-year margin of error. Owing precisely to documentary records of this battle, one is able to establish the earliest known exact synchronism between Israelite and Assyrian history and on that basis begin to reconstruct the backbone of an Old Testament chronol-

MAP 53

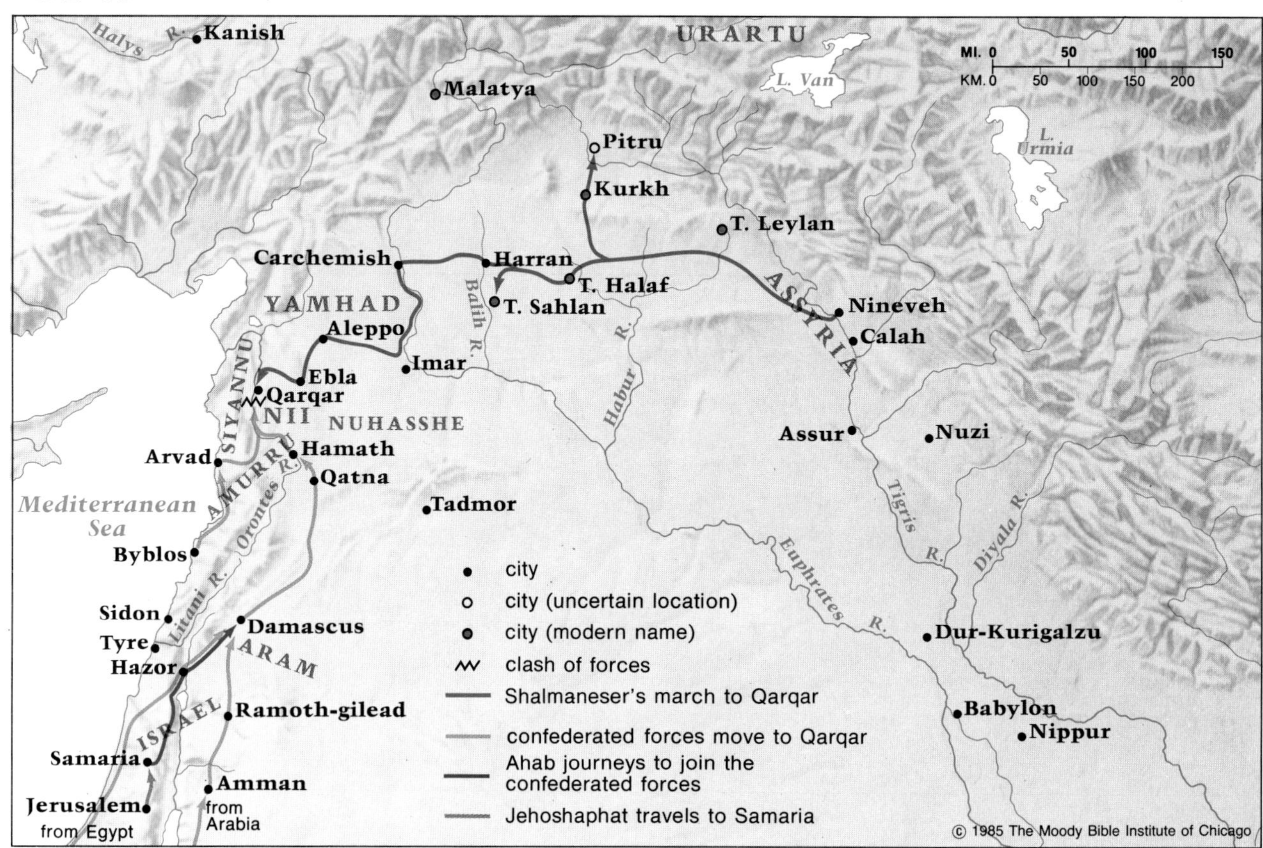

ogy: Assyrian records make it possible to date the Battle of Qarqar to the year 853 B.C. (within one year either way).

Whatever the outcome at Qarqar, the slackening of the Assyrian threat brought Ben-hadad II into renewed collision with his former ally, Ahab, who was now strangely supported by Jehoshaphat, king of Judah (1 Kings 22:1-36; cf. 20:1-34). One wonders, in fact, if perhaps Ben-hadad was emboldened to renew his contest with Ahab because the latter had suffered disproportionately high casualties at Qarqar (cf. 2 Kings 13:7). We note, for instance, that Moab regained its independence from Israel at about this same time (2 Kings 3:4-5; cf. Mesha Inscription, lines 1-9).[33] In any event, the importance of the Ahab/Ben-hadad skirmish lies in the fact that it must have taken place within the same year of Ahab's reign as did the Battle of Qarqar.

This assertion can be sustained by another inscription of Shalmaneser, called the "Black Obelisk." On that stele, the Assyrian monarch heralded the crowning military achievements of the first thirty-one years of his reign. Among other notations, Shalmaneser boasted that in his eighteenth year, he marched to the Senir mountain (Mt. Hermon? cf. Deut. 3:9). From here he first launched an attack into Mt. Hauran, and then he received tribute from the kings of Tyre and Sidon, as well as from Jehu, the son of Omri (cf. Map 58).[34]

Now in the Old Testament, Ahab was succeeded by Ahaziah, who was officially accorded two years of reign (1 Kings 22:51), whereas Ahaziah was followed by Jehoram, whose official length of reign was given as twelve years, before he was murdered by Jehu (2 Kings 3:1). On the surface, this would seem to imply that Ahab's and Jehu's reigns were separated by approximately fourteen years. But one must remember that Israel's kings figured the length of their reigns according to what we today call the nonaccession (antedating) year system. According to that system, a king began to count his first regnal year from the very day he ascended to the throne. His first year therefore corresponded to his accession year, and his second year was figured as commencing with the beginning of a new calendar year, even if the new year should have begun only weeks after the king's accession to the throne. Each king was credited with a whole year for any part of which he reigned. This means, then, that the fourteen years that apparently had separated Ahab and Jehu must actually be collapsed into an interval of only twelve years, because Ahab's last year would have corresponded to Ahaziah's accession (first) year, and Ahaziah's last (second) year would have been coeval with Jehoram's accession (first) year.

Some have attempted to argue that the Battle of Qarqar need not have taken place in the final year of Ahab's reign but that the Judean king might have continued to live for another three or four years after fighting at Qarqar. Were that the case, however, it follows that the accession of Jehu would also have to be put back by three or four years, to about 838 or 837 B.C., which would be impossible if, according to the "Black Obelisk," he paid tribute to Shalmaneser in the latter's eighteenth year (841 B.C.). Alternatively, were one to argue that Jehu might not have paid tribute in the first year of his reign, presuming Jehu's accession to have occurred around 845 or 846, then Ahab's death necessarily would have taken place some twelve years earlier, about 857 or 858, which again would not be possible if Ahab was still alive in 853 to fight at Qarqar. Stated in other terms, the only way that king Jehu could have paid Assyrian tribute in Shalmaneser's eighteenth year (841 B.C.) was that Ahab died during Shalmaneser's sixth year (853 B.C.), and we recall from above that it was in the sixth year of Shalmaneser that the Battle of Qarqar occurred. The date of the Battle of Qarqar, therefore, becomes a cardinal datum in the reconstructing of an Old Testament chronology, especially in the conquest and monarchy periods.

JEHU'S EXPLOITS AGAINST THE HOUSE OF DAVID

MAP 54

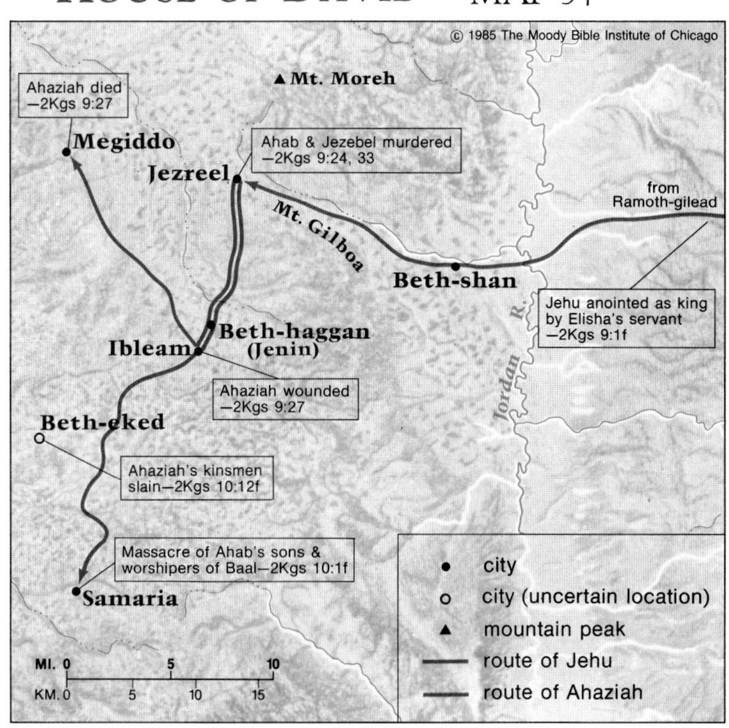

MAP 55 MINISTRIES OF ELIJAH AND ELISHA

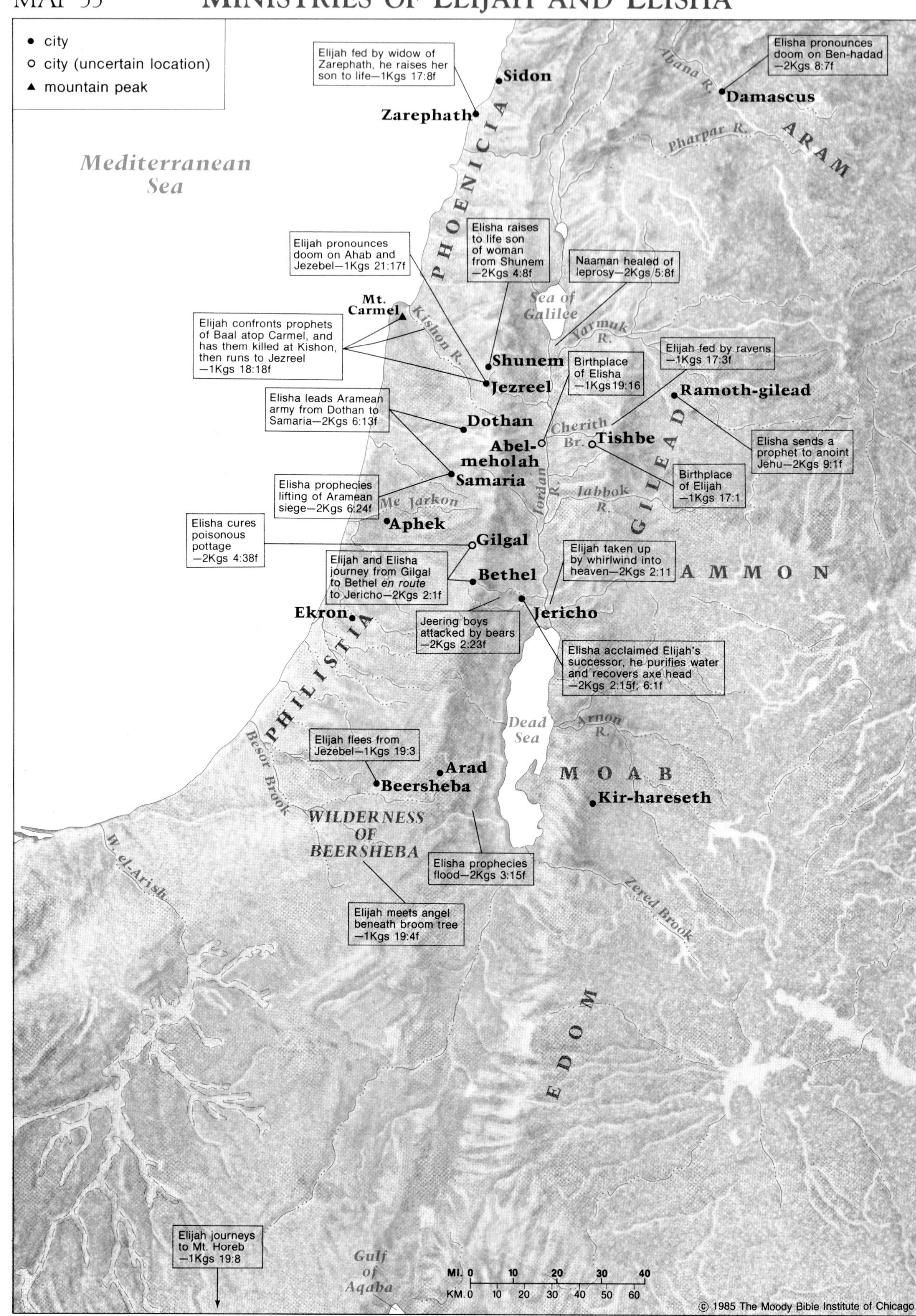

RENAISSANCE IN THE DIVIDED KINGDOM MAP 56

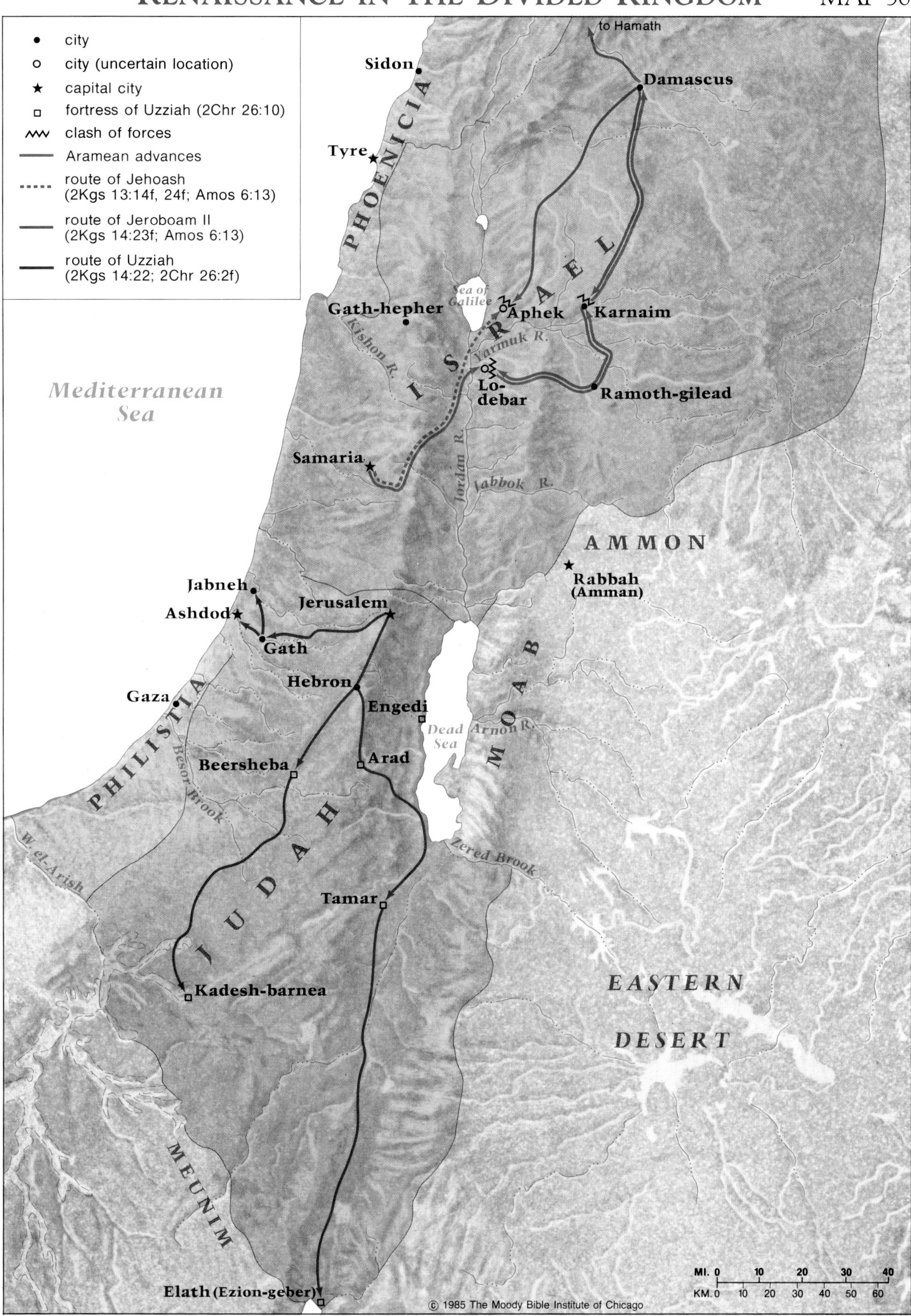

ISRAEL'S PROPHETS

With the foundation of Israel's monarchy came also the virtual eclipse of the office of priest. When Samuel proclaimed that Saul had been deposed from the kingly office (1 Sam. 13:13-15; cf. 15:26-28), the priest's separation from the king was perceived to have been tantamount to the separation of God, and Saul was powerless to respond. Only two generations later, however, king Solomon had garnered sufficient authority to oust Abiathar from his priestly office and to banish him to his hometown (1 Kings 2:26-27). Here is ample illustration of the uncontested authority that the Israelites conferred upon their newly-created office of king.

But with the demise of the priestly office there developed a concomitant new tendency in Israel towards apostasy and idolatry, as Levitical religion lost its central focus around which the life of Israel revolved. And although the prophetic institution had formally existed prior to that time and certainly did not arise merely from national impulse, it was largely this set of circumstances that served as the occasion for God to raise up another cycle of prophetism. It is fair to state that the office of prophet now obtained a more theocratic and public profile, as prophets could advise kings concerning policy or rebuke them concerning sin, while also warn the populace about the abominations of the Canaanites.

Categorization of Israel's prophets is a difficult task, for they came from a diversity of background, tribe, class, and educational distinction. Unlike priests, prophets did not receive their office by birthright, nor did they act according to pattern or prescription (e.g., Isa. 20:1-4; Jer. 13:1-7; 27:1—28:16; Ezek. 4:4-17; 5:1-4; Hos. 1:2-9). They could be officers of the state (e.g., Isaiah) or political outcasts (e.g., Elijah); they could utter predictions (e.g., Micaiah), or futuristic prophecy could play practically no role in their lives (e.g., Jonah). Some performed miracles (e.g., Elisha) while others did not (e.g., Malachi). Some occupied their office for decades (e.g., Jeremiah); others, as far as we know, functioned in that capacity for only months (e.g., Haggai). What Israel's prophets *did* share was a common belief, vision, and function: each had a distinct call of God to the office, each possessed a prophetic awareness of history, and each functioned as a declarer of the Word of God.

MAP 57

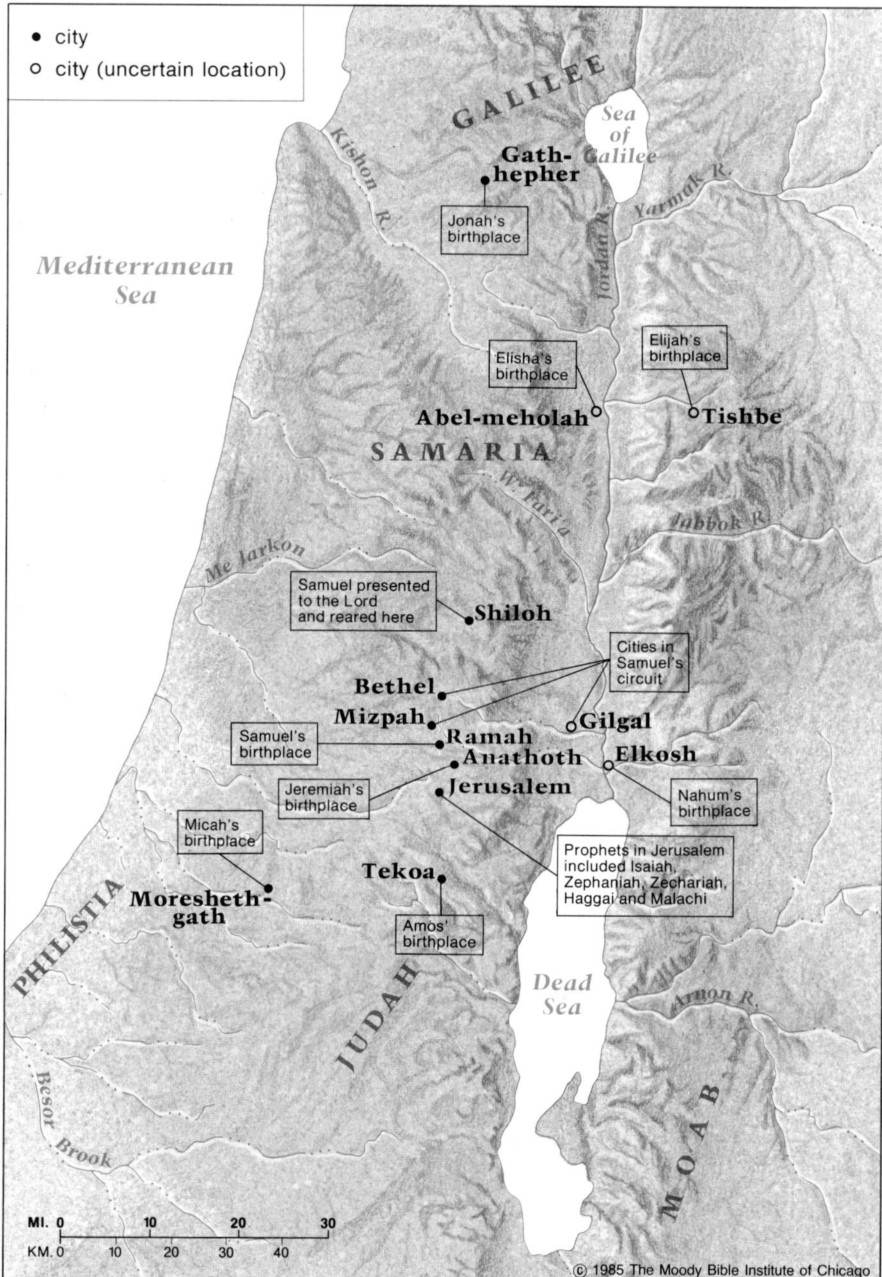

Assyrian Campaigns Against Israel and Judah

MAP 58

Sources for Map 58

A. Assyriological

1. Black Obelisk of Shalmaneser III
2. Assyrian King List
3. Annals of Shalmaneser III, Adad-nirari III, Tiglath-pileser III, Sargon II, Sennacherib
4. Eponym Chronicle
5. Babylonian King List
6. Babylonian Chronicle
7. Miscellaneous sources: monuments, assorted archival materials, palace reliefs, destruction layers from various cities

B. Biblical—2 Kings 15:19-20, 29; 16:7-10; 17:3-6; 18:9—19:37; 1 Chron. 5:6; 2 Chron. 28:20-21; 32:1-23; Isa. 9:1-7; 10:28-32; 20:1-6; 36:1—37:38; Hos. 10:14; Mic. 1:8-16

MAP 59 PALESTINE AFTER NORTHERN KINGDOM

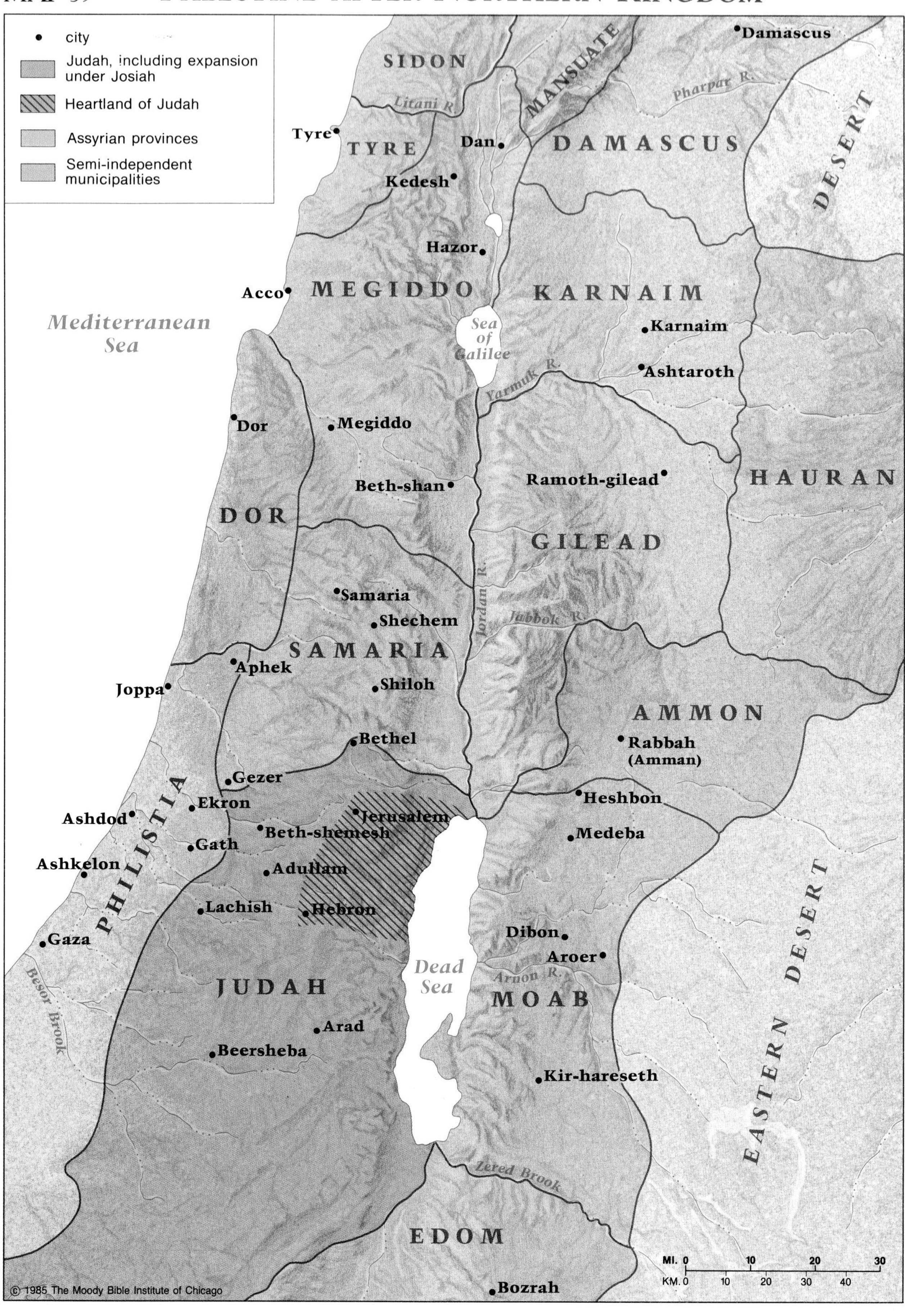

THE ASSYRIAN EMPIRE

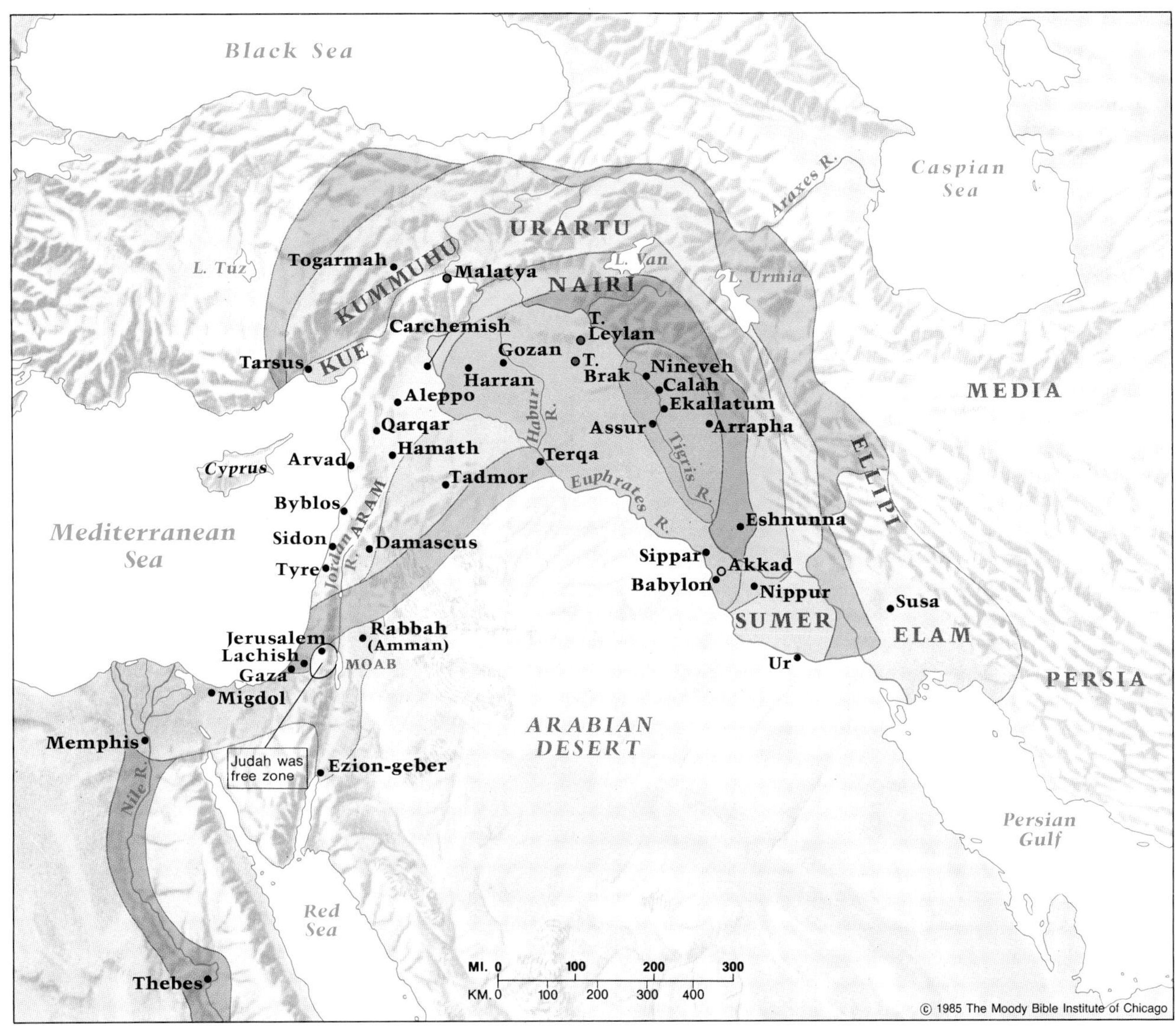

- • city
- ○ city (uncertain location)
- ● city (modern name)
- heartland of Assyrian Kingdom [Assur-uballit I (c. 1350 BC) & Adad-nirari III (c. 750 BC)]
- expansion of Adad-nirari I (c. 1300 BC)
- expansion of Tukulti-ninurta I (c. 1225 BC)
- expansion of Ashurnasirpal II (c. 875 BC)
- expansion of Shalmaneser III (c. 850 BC)
- expansion of Tiglath-pileser III (c. 735 BC)
- expansion of Sargon II (c. 720 BC) & Sennacherib (c. 700 BC)
- expansion of Esarhaddon (c. 675 BC)
- expansion of Ashurbanipal (c. 650 BC)

Assyria's heartland in the days of Ashur-uballit I comprised the plain that straddled the middle Tigris from a point not far from Nineveh, where mountains give way to the Mesopotamian steppe, to a place along the river just west of Eshnunna, where a chain of mountains again interrupts the plain. In the time of Adad-nirari I, the lands of Babylon and Mitanni were added, extending the border to the Euphrates. By the time of Tukulti-ninurta I, the land that arched from Babylon to a point near Carchemish was controlled by Assyria; but after his death, Assyria declined until about the ninth century.

The imperialism described in the Bible began in the time of Ashurnasirpal II, who conquered Nairi, and of Shalmaneser III, who gained control of the Phoenician coast, Aram, and south Lebanon. Tiglath-pileser III seized Bashan and Sumer, and then vanquished the powerful kingdoms of Urartu and Kummuhu. Sargon II fought major wars at Samaria, Babylonia, and along the Median frontier. Later, Esarhaddon gained temporary control of Elam and seized Transjordania, doubtlessly to govern spice and incense trade; he also extended Assyria's dominion into Egypt by sacking Memphis. The empire reached its maximal extent under Ashurbanipal, who captured Thebes.

THE BATTLE OF CARCHEMISH

The Assyrian Empire reached its zenith in the time of King Sennacherib. During his rule an era of *Pax Assyriaca* (Assyrian peace) came to be fully realized. When the Assyrian hordes descended upon Jerusalem in 701 B.C. (2 Kings 18:13—19:37; 2 Chron. 32:1-23; Isa. 36:1—38:22), they had already conquered a territory roughly the size of modern Europe, or approximately equal to all the land bounded by Lake Erie on the north, the city of Atlanta on the south, the Mississippi River on the west, and the Atlantic Ocean on the east. Yet to govern such an expanse in those times meant that imperialistic power was reaching its natural limits. And so Sennacherib and his successors are as much noted for their administrative, domestic, and literary achievements as for their prowess on the battlefield.

The celebrated grandeur of the city of Nineveh—with its walls stretching almost two-and-one-half miles in length, fifteen "metal" city gates, ornate palace, numerous temples, public housing, armory, large plantation with a cotton plant, many zoological gardens, and many other features—owes its existence to Sennacherib. Great engineering skill is reflected in the construction of his new capital. A dam was built on the Tebiltu River, which joined the Tigris right at Nineveh. The dam prevented erosion of the mound on which the city was built, led to the agricultural recovery of what had been marshland, and provided water for a network of canals Sennacherib dug throughout the district.

Efforts to locate new sources of building materials led to the discovery of a plentiful supply of fresh water in the mountains near Bavian. To bring that source of drinking water to his capital, Sennacherib constructed a stone channel more than 50 miles in length. In what is clearly one of the earliest efforts in civil engineering, the Assyrian built at the city of Jerwan, just south of Bavian, a stone aqueduct that spanned a branch of the Gomer River, permitting the newly-found supply of water to continue its southward course toward Nineveh.

Two generations later, Sennacherib's grandson Ashurbanipal channeled literature and learning into Nineveh, as he engaged in the establishment of a large royal library. Embodying more than 25,000 texts and fragments and representing virtually every phase of Mesopotamian society, the library of Ashurbanipal remains the single most important source of Akkadian literature. Included among its remains were the so-called Babylonian flood (*Gilgamesh Epic*) and creation (*Enuma Elish*) stories, the Babylonian Job (*Ludlul bēl nēmeqi*), and the *Descent of Ishtar into Hades*.

Perhaps it was that preoccupation with cultural advancement that made the once mighty Assyrian Empire such an easy prey. Whatever the case, it is clear that within slightly more than a decade (626-612 B.C.), Assyrian dominance, both at home and abroad, was brought to an abrupt end. The individual largely responsible for the rapid demise was Nabopolassar, a Chaldean prince from the region of Bit-Yakin, and the father of Nebuchadnezzar. Having already confederated several diverse political forces within Babylonia, Nabopolassar wrested the city of Babylon from Assyrian control in 626 B.C. Using that city as his command base, the Chaldean gained control of the whole of Babylonia within four years.

Nabopolassar then set his sights on Assyria itself. Though unsuccessful in his initial attempt to overthrow Assur, his troops crushed the former capital in the year 614 B.C. Unfortunately for Assyria, the Medes decided to enter the struggle at that same time. Leading his new confederation, Nabopolassar marched against the citadel at Nineveh later in 614, and in the year 612 B.C. he destroyed this last bastion of Assyrian imperialism. Two years later, with his enemies then rapidly retreating, Nabopolassar expelled the Assyrians from the precincts of Harran.

Most unexpectedly, Pharaoh Necho II endeavored to come to the aid of the retreating Assyrians. Intending to lead his Egyptian army to Carchemish, Necho drove northward. It was then that Josiah, king of Judah, regrettably interjected himself into the shifting balance of political power. Josiah had no affinity whatsoever for Assyrian aggression, and so he sought to intercept the northerly march of Necho at Megiddo. But Josiah's effort proved fatal; being greatly outclassed in manpower and technology, his army was decimated and the king himself was slain in the battle (2 Kings 23:29-30; 2 Chron. 35:20-24).

Josiah's untimely death at the hands of the Egyptians bore profound psychological implications for the covenant community living in Jerusalem at the time, especially because the messianic hopes they fixed on Josiah had led them to believe that Jerusalem would remain secure amidst the political turmoil of the moment. His death also signaled a new wave of Egyptian presence in Jerusalem (e.g., 2 Kings 23:31-37), a presence that would contribute to the pro-Egyptian—pro-Babylonian factionalism that dominated political life during the last twenty years of Judah.

Babylonian forces under the command of Nebuchadnezzar in 607 B.C. laid siege to the city of Carchemish, where for the next two years they repelled every effort on the part of the Assyrian-

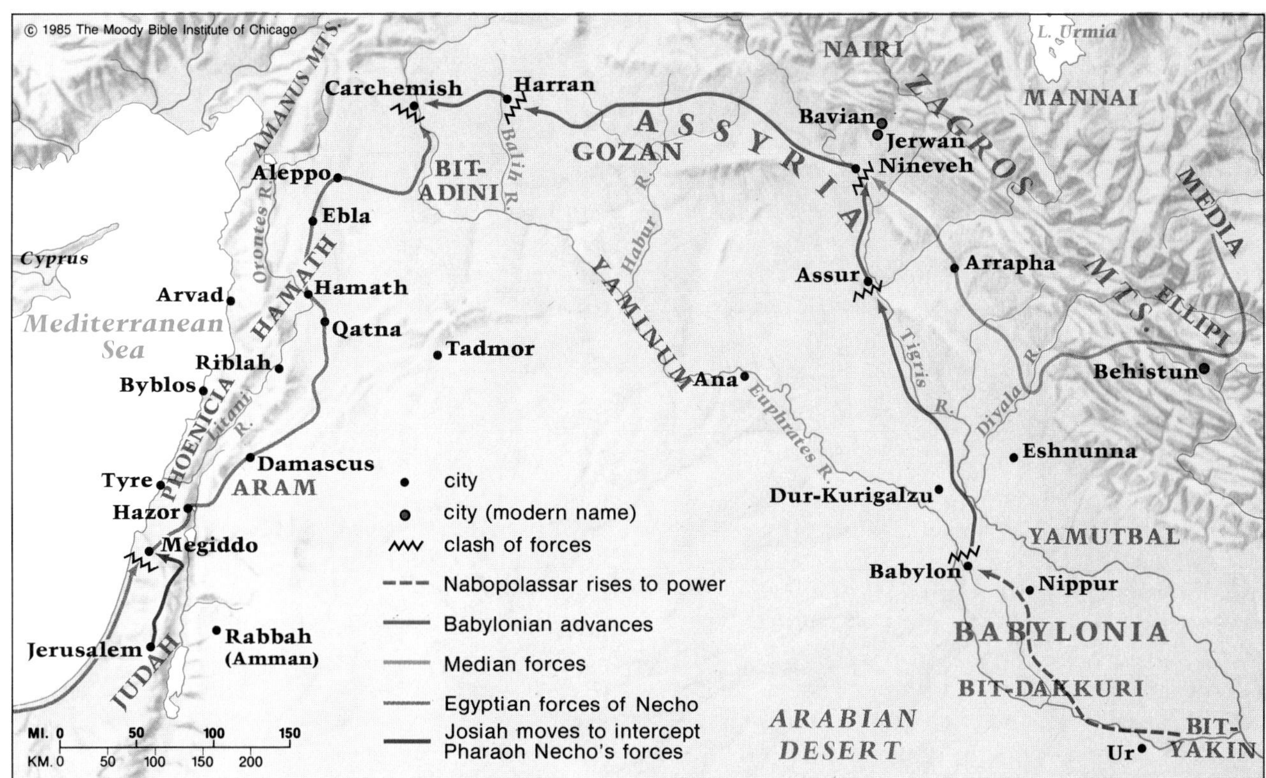

Egyptian coalition to gain Mesopotamian turf. Finally in 605 B.C., in one of the supreme turning-points of Syro-Palestinian history, the two armies collided in full-scale confrontation. Nebuchadnezzar inflicted a sweeping defeat on his foes. Thus perished one of the most remarkable civilizations of the ancient world (cf. Isa. 14:24-27; Nah. 2:1-10; Zeph. 2:13).

Historians often point out a strange irony here: for when in the first Christian century Assyria finally reemerged into history as a Parthian territory known as Adiabene, one of its rulers, Izates, converted to Judaism, was circumcised, and decreed that his royal house should follow suit.[35] The allegiance of the Adiabenians to the Jewish state was demonstrated during the Roman War (A.D. 66-73), when their troops supported the Jews (see Map 75).[36]

Figure 20 The Middle Euphrates River just below its confluence with the Habur River.

JERUSALEM FALLS TO BABYLONIA

Merodach-Baladan II was a Chaldean prince from the tribe of Bit-Yakin (see Map 61) who for about a dozen years just before 700 B.C. succeeded in loosening Babylonia from the grip of Assyrian domination. He was the first native Babylonian ruler to win mention by name in the Old Testament and also the only Babylonian to become king of Babylonia twice, according to the Babylonian King List. After he established himself as king, Merodach-baladan sought to incite rebellion elsewhere in Assyria's empire. Such were his motives in sending a delegation to Hezekiah in Jerusalem (2 Kings 20:12-19; Isa. 39:1-8). Welcomed there by the king, the Babylonian envoys were ushered into the royal treasury and shown all of wealth of Hezekiah's domain. That was the Judean's way of demonstrating to the Babylonians that he represented a worthy ally, one who was quite capable of mustering an army. When Isaiah learned of what Hezekiah had done, however, the prophet warned that it had been a fatal maneuver on the king's part, one that would certainly give Babylonian monarchs an economic incentive to return to Jerusalem, and one that eventually would send Jews into Babylonian captivity. Isaiah's distrust of Merodach-baladan appears to have been well founded: recently-discovered documents from Assyria disclose that Merodach-baladan was a notorious traiter. It was about one hundred years and five generations later when Isaiah's prediction began to be realized, as Nebuchadnezzar made his first advance into Palestine.

Victorious at the Battle of Carchemish (see Map 61), Nebuchadnezzar proceeded into the "land of Hatti" (i.e., Syro-Palestine), all of which was forced to appear before him. That statement in the Babylonian Chronicle may be a little exaggerated, but at the least it probably included the powerful city-states of Damascus and Tyre (1). Then again, that was the time when Jehoiakim became a Babylonian vassal (2 Kings 24:1), and it was possibly then that a contingent of Jews, including Daniel, was carried off into captivity (Dan. 1:1-4) (2). Perhaps because of its Egyptian affiliation, the city of Ashkelon was singled out for particularly harsh treatment during the first campaign; that city was reduced to rubble (cf. 2 Kings 24:7) (3).

About five years later, in December 599 B.C., Nebuchadnezzar launched his second campaign onto Palestinian soil. At first preoccupied with collecting spoil from Arab tribesmen in desert regions, the Babylonian hordes eventually appeared at Jerusalem's gates in December 598 B.C. and initiated a three-month siege. The siege probably corresponded to the three-month tenure of Jehoiachin (2 Kings 24:8-16; Jer. 52:28; *AJ* X.vi.3). Obscurity surrounds the end of Jehoiakim's life. He was taken prisoner by Nebuchadnezzar (2 Chron. 36:6), but apparently he died or was assassinated while still in the Jerusalem area. We do know that this monarch was deprived of a privileged burial plot customarily afforded Davidic royalty (Jer. 22:19). Whatever the case, the Babylonian Chronicle discloses that Jerusalem surrendered on exactly March 15/16, 597 B.C. After that, Zedekiah (Mattaniah), Jehoiachin's uncle, was enthroned as a Babylonian puppet, and a major deportation occurred that included Jehoiachin (2 Kings 24:15) and Ezekiel (*AJ* X.vi.3). Nebuchadnezzar's second campaign had rendered Judah weak and relatively defenseless, and Zedekiah's heartland seems to have been reduced in size (cf. Map 59). Troops from the Edomite kingdom apparently seized the opportunity at that time to do a bit of plundering themselves (Ps. 137:7; Lam. 4:21-22); a letter from that period (found at Arad) refers to the effectiveness of Edomite assaults (4).

The Babylonian's third campaign to Palestine appears to have been brought on by Zedekiah's insubordination and subsequent alignment with Egypt (2 Kings 24:20*b*—25:2). Nebuchadnezzar now systematically destroyed much of Judah, including the cities of Beth-shemesh, Lachish, Beth-zur, Beth-haccherem, and Engedi (5), before turning toward Jerusalem. Archaeological excavation at those sites attests to the ferocity of Nebuchadnezzar's onslaught. City after city capitulated until, in addition to Jerusalem, only Azekah and Lachish remained in Judean hands (Jer. 34:7). An ostracon found in the gate tower of Lachish indicates that signal fires could no longer be seen at Azekah—that city had fallen (6). The destruction layer at Lachish is especially intense. Felled trees were stacked along the perimeter of the wall and set aflame; the fire apparently was so intense that even mortar melted in the wall and later resolidified at the base of the wall. Gaping holes in the walls can still be seen today. Then only Jerusalem remained (7). The city withstood siege for several months, but finally a break was made in the walls in August 587 B.C. (2 Chron. 36:11-21; Jer. 52:4-7, 29; cf. Ezek. 17) (8). With all hope now gone, Zedekiah unsuccessfully attempted to escape into Transjordan (9). Apprehended near Jericho, the monarch was taken captive and eventually deported to Babylonia (2 Kings 25:7; Jer. 52:8-10).

A fourth campaign in the year 582 B.C. was a reprisal for the assassination of the Babylonian governor Gedaliah (Jer. 52:30), although only a few sketchy details are known about the mission.

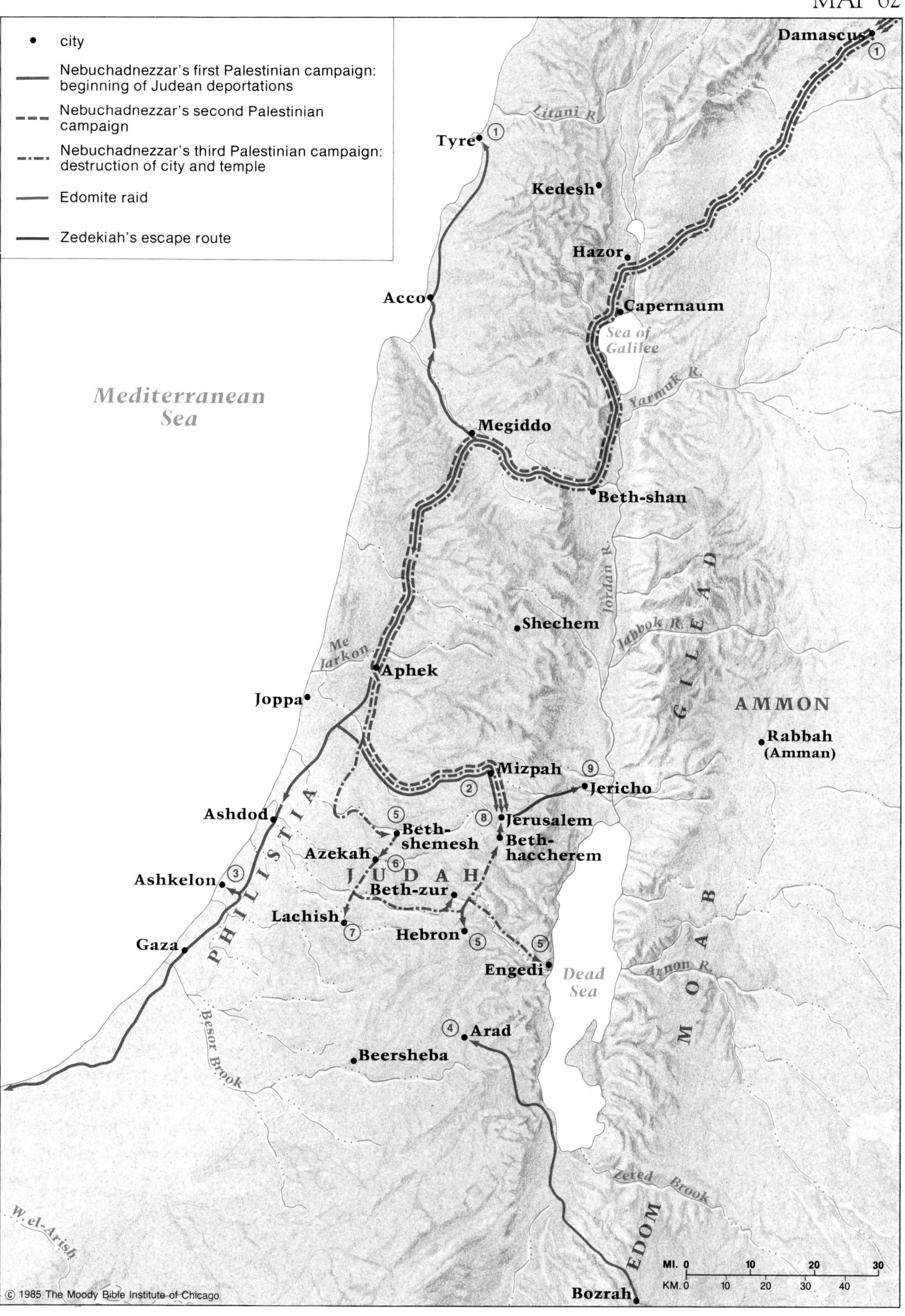
city
Nebuchadnezzar's first Palestinian campaign: beginning of Judean deportations
Nebuchadnezzar's second Palestinian campaign
Nebuchadnezzar's third Palestinian campaign: destruction of city and temple
Edomite raid
Zedekiah's escape route
Damascus
Litani R.
Tyre
Kedesh
Hazor
Acco
Capernaum
Sea of Galilee
Yarmuk R.
Mediterranean Sea
Megiddo
Beth-shan
Jordan R.
Shechem
Jabbok R.
Me Jarkon
Aphek
Joppa
GILEAD
AMMON
Rabbah (Amman)
Mizpah
Jericho
Ashdod
Jerusalem
Beth-shemesh
Beth-haccherem
Azekah
JUDAH
Ashkelon
Beth-zur
Lachish
Hebron
PHILISTIA
Gaza
Engedi
Dead Sea
Arnon R.
MOAB
Besor Brook
Arad
Beersheba
Zered Brook
EDOM
W. el-Arish
Bozrah
MI. 0 10 20 30
KM. 0 10 20 30 40

MAP 63 JEWISH DEPORTATIONS AND RETURNS

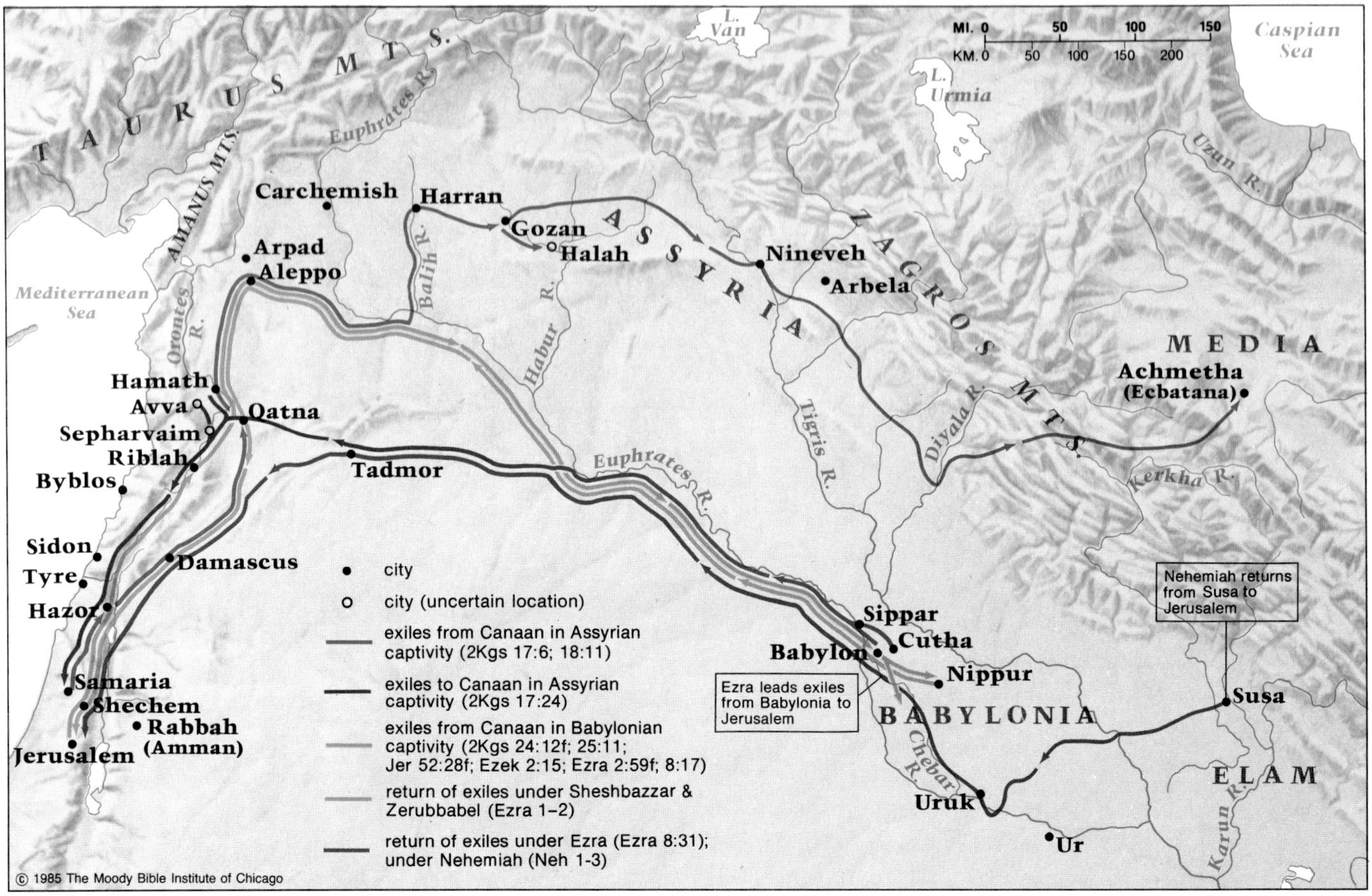

TAURUS MTS.
AMANUS MTS.
L. Van
L. Urmia
Caspian Sea
Mediterranean Sea
Euphrates R.
Balih R.
Habur R.
Orontes R.
Tigris R.
Diyala R.
Uzun R.
Kerkha R.
Karun R.
Chebar R.
ASSYRIA
ZAGROS MTS.
MEDIA
BABYLONIA
ELAM
Carchemish
Harran
Gozan
Halah
Nineveh
Arbela
Arpad
Aleppo
Hamath
Avva
Qatna
Sepharvaim
Riblah
Byblos
Tadmor
Sidon
Tyre
Hazor
Damascus
Samaria
Shechem
Rabbah (Amman)
Jerusalem
Achmetha (Ecbatana)
Sippar
Cutha
Babylon
Nippur
Susa
Uruk
Ur

MI. 0 50 100 150
KM. 0 50 100 150 200

Nehemiah returns from Susa to Jerusalem

Ezra leads exiles from Babylonia to Jerusalem

- • city
- o city (uncertain location)
- exiles from Canaan in Assyrian captivity (2Kgs 17:6; 18:11)
- exiles to Canaan in Assyrian captivity (2Kgs 17:24)
- exiles from Canaan in Babylonian captivity (2Kgs 24:12f; 25:11; Jer 52:28f; Ezek 2:15; Ezra 2:59f; 8:17)
- return of exiles under Sheshbazzar & Zerubbabel (Ezra 1–2)
- return of exiles under Ezra (Ezra 8:31); under Nehemiah (Neh 1-3)

Figure 21 The Israelites were carried into captivity via Wadi Beidan, pictured here from Tirzah in the direction of Shechem.

THE BABYLONIAN KINGDOM

When Nabopolassar's Babylonian-Median confederation succeeded in driving the Assyrians from Nineveh, setting into motion of chain of events that would lead inescapably to the collapse of Assyria, the brilliant strategist directed his efforts towards acquiring as much as possible of the Assyrian Empire. He stationed garrisons of troops near to Nineveh and Calah, and farther north in the Izalla region. But his strenuous efforts to grab land north of Izalla in Urartu were rebuffed by the Scythians, and Nabopolassar had to be content with gaining Kue.

Thus was forged the Babylonian kingdom or, more properly speaking, the Neo-Babylonian (Chaldean) kingdom, in contrast to the Old Babylonian kingdom of Hammurapi. Within a remarkably brief period, Babylon controlled nearly all that had taken Assyria centuries to subjugate. The Babylonian triumph at Carchemish (see Map 61) opened the gates of the Levant and Egypt to Nebuchadnezzar (cf. Map 62), though he appears to have maintained a tenuous hold at best on Egypt, which was constantly fomenting revolt (cf. 2 Kings 25:22-26; Jer. 40:7—41:18; Ezek. 29:6-26).

Meanwhile, the Medes were preoccupied with extending their control northward. Cyaxares overran the kingdom of Urartu and pushed into Asia Minor where he met the Lydians in battle. That foray culminated in a treaty between Media and Lydia establishing their boundary at the Halys River, a treaty negotiated by an ambassador of Nebuchnezzar, Nabonidus. However, a son of Nabonidus, Belshazzar (Dan. 5:22), would meet Medians in less pleasant circumstances, when Cyrus the Mede was hailed in Babylon as a liberator and Jews were permitted to return to their homeland.

MAP 64

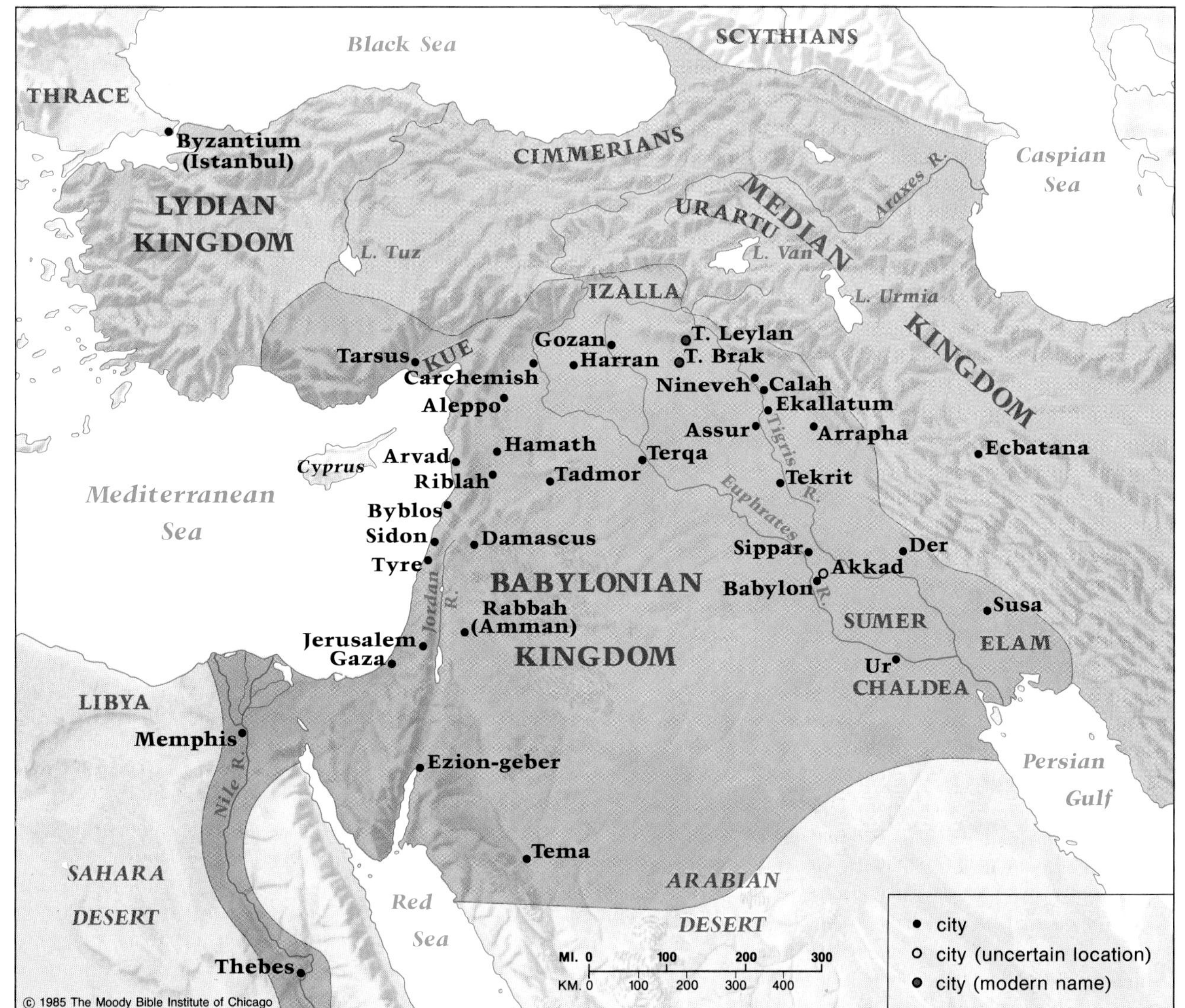

JEREMIAH TAKEN TO EGYPT

"The Lord determined to tear down the walls of the daughter of Zion," Jeremiah mourned. "He marked it off with a measuring line and did not withhold his hand from destroying; he caused ramparts and walls to lament, they languish together" (Lam. 2:8). When Nebuchadnezzar's military machine penetrated the walls of Jerusalem in the late summer of 587 B.C., and began its systematic demolition and burning of the city and Temple (cf. 2 Chron. 36:18-21), Zedekiah, who earlier had been enthroned by Nebuchadnezzar, fled under cover of darkness to find refuge in the Transjordanian highlands. Unsuccessful, he was apprehended near Jericho and taken to Riblah, Nebuchadnezzar's Syrian headquarters, from which he was eventually exiled to Babylonia (2 Kings 25:1-21). With Zedekiah, thousands of families from Judah were also deported.

In Zedekiah's place Babylonian authorities installed one Gedaliah as governor of Judah. He ruled temporarily from the city of Mizpah because Jerusalem had been razed. But just as the governor's efforts to restore Judah were beginning to succeed (Jer. 40:7-12), nationalistic fervor resurfaced when a small band of fanatics came to Mizpah and murdered Gedaliah. Fearing swift and harsh Babylonian reprisal, many Jews began to flee to Egypt (2 Kings 25:22-26). When Jeremiah opposed that move (Jer. 42:7-22), he himself was forcibly taken, together with his scribe Baruch, and brought to the city of Tahpanhes in Egypt. Undaunted, Jeremiah warned the refugees that they could not feel secure even in Egypt, that Nebuchadnezzar's pestilence and destructive zeal would surely come to Egypt (Jer. 43:1—44:30).

Perhaps those warnings contributed to the establishment of Jewish colonies farther upstream along the Nile (cf. Map 85). Whatever the case, Jewish colonization in Egypt became widespread during the Persian period, and Jeremiah sent oracles to his expatriates as far away as Pathros, in Upper Egypt (Jer. 44:1). One important colony in the land of Pathros was located about 500 miles south of Tahpanhes on an island at the first cataract of the Nile, opposite the town of Syene (Aswan; Ezek. 29:10; 30:6) (cf. Map 47). On that island, known today as Elephantine but then as Yeb, were found a few dozen Aramaic papyri dating to the fifth century B.C. Those texts, which are contemporary with the books of Ezra and Nehemiah, provide the earliest extrabiblical documentation for the socio-economic and political life of a Jewish community in or outside Palestine. They also give some valuable insights into Jewish religious life away from Jerusalem's Temple and priesthood.

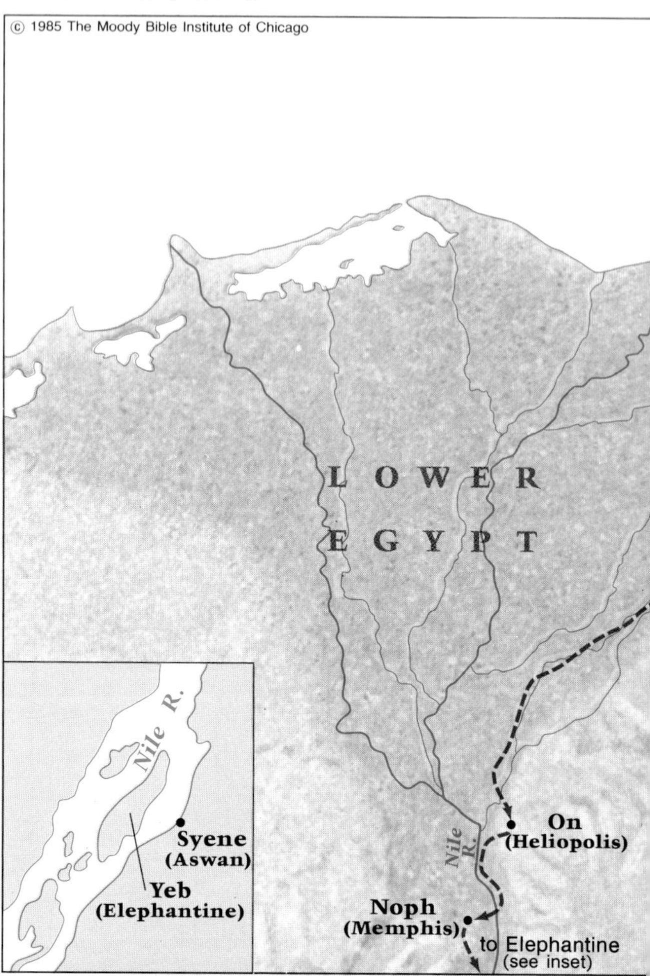

Figure 22 Lying in the midst of the upper Nile River

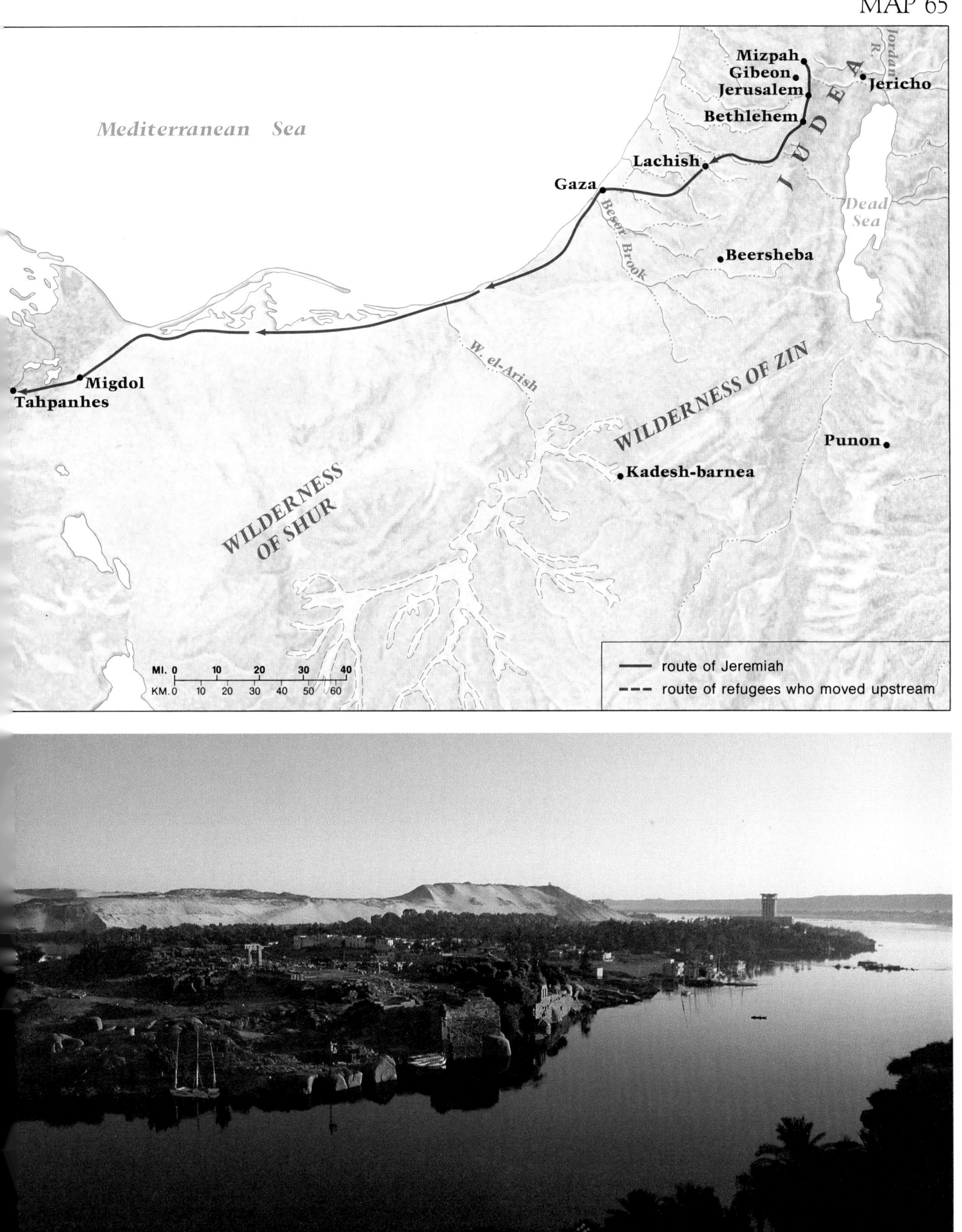

is the lush green island of Elephantine, where a Jewish colony was founded during the days of Ezra and Nehemiah.

MAP 66 EZEKIEL'S VISION OF THE PROMISED LAND

POST-EXILIC JUDEA MAP 67

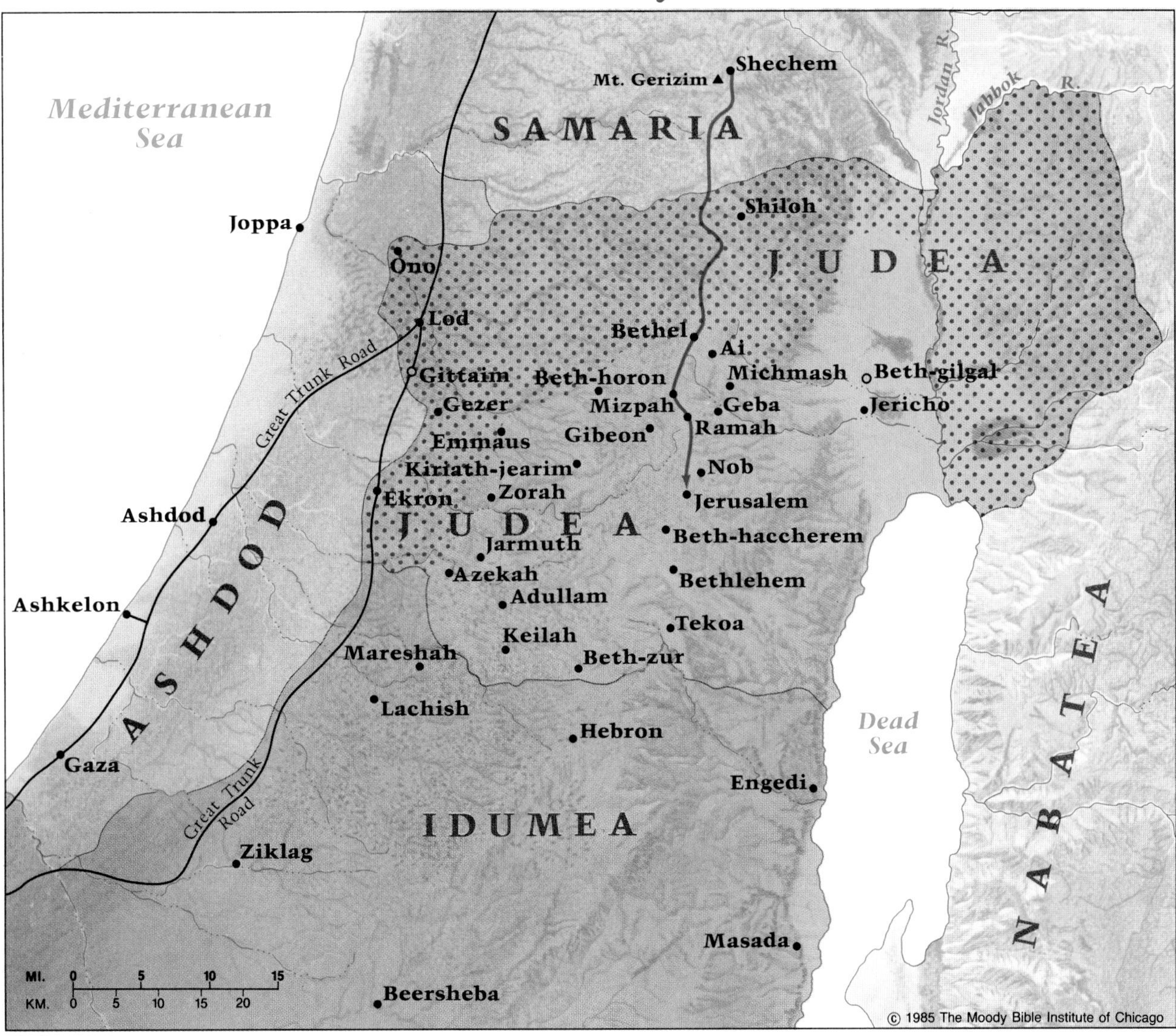

- • city
- ○ city (uncertain location)
- ▲ mountain peak
- —— Samaritans intrude upon rebuilding process (Ezra 4:1f)
- ⁙ area colonized by Jews returning from Babylonian captivity

The year 539 B.C. is one of the most decisive dates in the history of the ancient Near East. First, Semitic influence that had dominated this land mass for hundreds of years—Akkad, Phoenicia, Assyria, Babylonia—came to a conclusion as a succession of new non-Semitic forces—Persia, Greece, Rome—came to solidify western Asia. Secondly, Cyrus's capture of Babylon meant that Jews, like all dispossessed peoples, could finally return to their homes.

The year after Babylon's destruction, Cyrus issued his now-celebrated decree of clemency (Ezra 1:2-4, cf. 6:3; 2 Chron. 36:22-23). Whereupon some 50,000 Jews set out for Judea with Sheshbazzar, a Judean prince who had been appointed provincial governor (Ezra 1:8; 5:14), and Zerubbabel, possibly his nephew (1 Chron. 3:18) and successor (Hag. 1:1). Opposed by Samaritans who wrote letters of accusation, plans of this group to rebuild the Temple were frustrated (Ezra 3:8—4:24). Later (c. 458 B.C.), a second company of Jews returned under Ezra (7:11—8:36), presumably via a dangerous route (Ezra 8:31; see Map 63); this group in turn was followed (c. 444 B.C.) by Nehemiah and his small entourage (Neh. 2:1-11).

For reasons that are not completely clear, most returnees who were not leaders colonized areas around Jerusalem, especially northern areas, and did not occupy the city itself; important in this context were the towns of Beth-gilgal, Bethel, Mizpah, Emmaus, Beth-zur, and especially Lod. Nehemiah (11:1-2) describes measures taken to bring one out of ten individuals to live in the holy city, while the remaining nine-tenths of the population would continue living in the suburbs.

THE PERSIAN EMPIRE

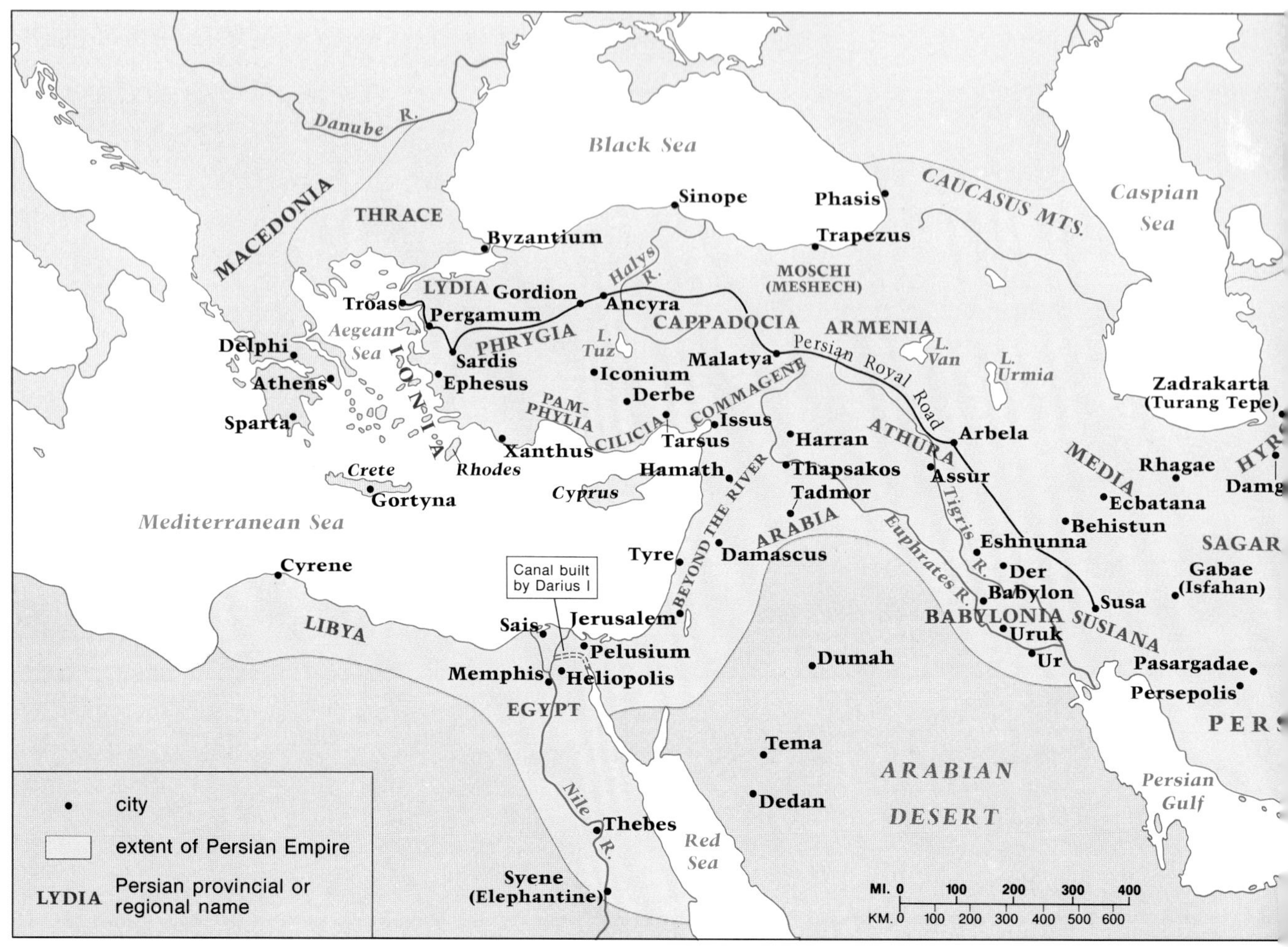

ALEXANDER THE GREAT COMES TO PALESTINE

Philip II of Macedon was one of the greatest reformers of Greek history; before his mysterious death at Pella in 336 B.C., Philip had succeeded in dominating all of the city-states of mainland Greece but Sparta, had conquered all of coastal Thrace to the Black Sea, and had built for himself a power base upon which he intended to wrest Asia Minor from Persia. Philip's noteworthy accomplishments are overshadowed only by those of his extraordinary son Alexander the Great.

As a twenty-year-old claimant to the Macedonian throne in 334 B.C., Alexander set out with a mere 35,000 troops on a much more ambitious mission: Alexander intended to demolish the mighty Persian Empire. Having won a narrow victory near Troy, Alexander liberated the province of Caria and the city of Side before turning inland to winter at Gordion. In the spring, Alexander marched south through the Cilician Gates, through which the apostle Paul would later pass, and re-entered the Cilician plains. In October 333 B.C., the Macedonian's army collided with the Persian forces of Darius III at Issus (in northwest Syria; see Map 70) in one of the most pivotal battles of biblical antiquity. Classical historians Diodorus Siculus and Plutarch relate perhaps with some exaggeration how that with the loss of only 450 soldiers, Alexander's disciplined army killed some 110,000 Persians and captured even Darius's wife and family. The Persian empire had been put on the defensive.

The far-reaching consequence of that victory for biblical history, however, was that the way had now been paved for the Macedonian army to sweep south into Egypt, where eventually Alexander would be hailed as pharaoh. Hence the mighty warrior would set foot on Palestinian soil, and that in turn would ultimately bring Hellenization to Palestinian culture.

Alexander divided his army as he marched south, sending one contingent to seize Damascus, while he himself led the other battalion to Tyre.

There, after a seven-month seige that included building a causeway to the island stronghold, he broke the back of Phoenician commercial imperialism. From Tyre, Alexander's southward procession past Acco, Dora, and Strato's Tower was more or less unimpeded. At one point, Alexander dispatched some troops who were commissioned to sack the city of Samaria. But the strongly-fortified Gaza offered resistance for two months, until finally his troops were able to breach the walls of that citadel.

With Gaza's demise, no further obstacles separated the Macedonian from his African objective. Josephus tells us, however, that instead of marching directly into Egypt, Alexander the Great made his way to Jerusalem where the high priest met him and ushered him into the Temple so that the monarch could offer sacrifice to God. Seeing that Alexander had so honored the Jews, a delegation of Samaritans came to the outskirts of Jerusalem to curry his favor by inviting him to visit their shrine atop Mt. Gerizim. To them, the warrior promised a visitation on his return trip from Egypt.[37]

Occupying Egypt had assured Alexander that his southern flank was secure. With that in mind, the general left Egypt in 331 via Palestine and Damascus and proceeded into Mesopotamia where his second and final encounter with Darius took place at Gaugamela, just east of the Tigris (see Map 70). Though winning the battle, Alexander chose not to pursue Darius, who had retreated in the direction of the Caspian Sea. Rather, he turned south and visited Babylon, Susa, and Persepolis, before passing the Caspian Gates and taking on Persia's northern satrapies from Hyrcania to Bactra and Sogdiana. Then, recrossing the Hindu Kush Mountains, Alexander launched an Indian campaign which he intended should carry him to

MAP 69

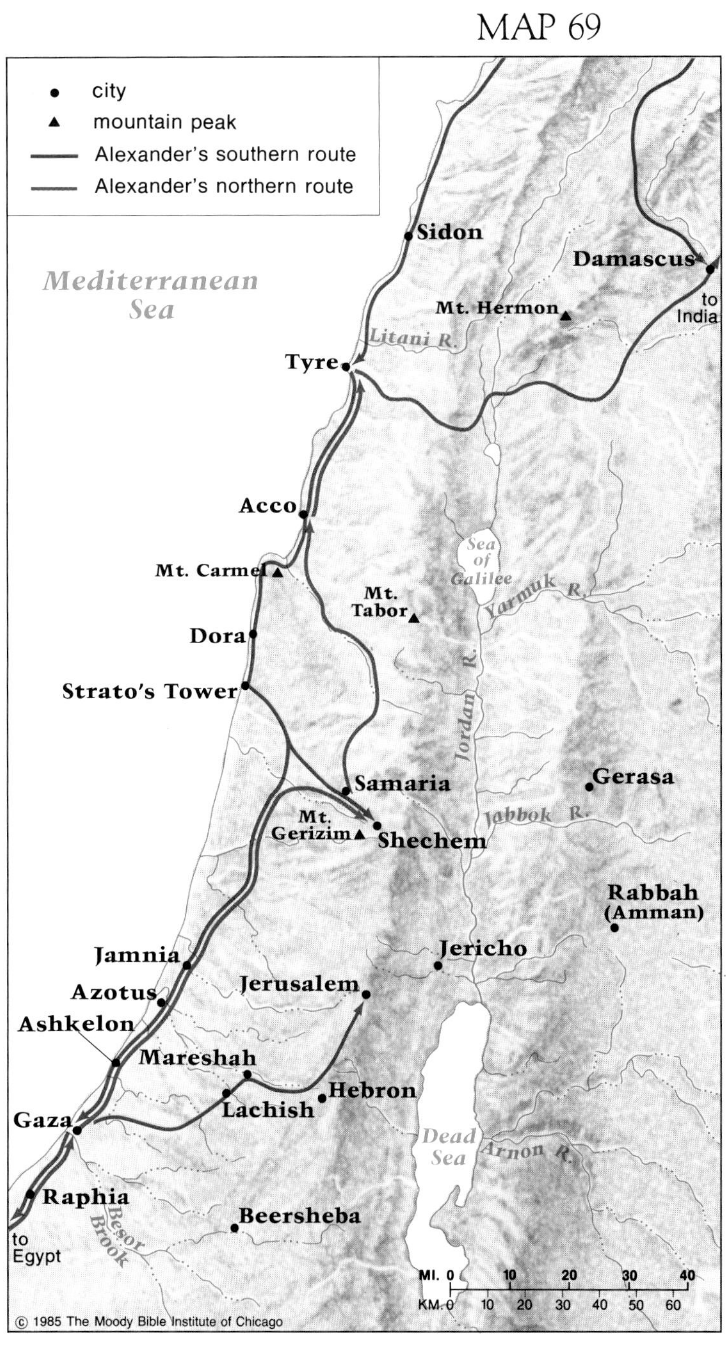

MAP 70 THE GREEK EMPIRE

- city
- mountain pass
- clash of forces
- Alexander's route
- corps of Alexander's force returns to Babylon via Persian Gulf
- extent of Alexandrian Empire

Division of Alexander's Empire at c. 275 BC

- Seleucid kingdom
- Antigonid kingdom
- Ptolemaic kingdom
- minor Hellenistic province

ASIA Alexandrian provincial or regional name

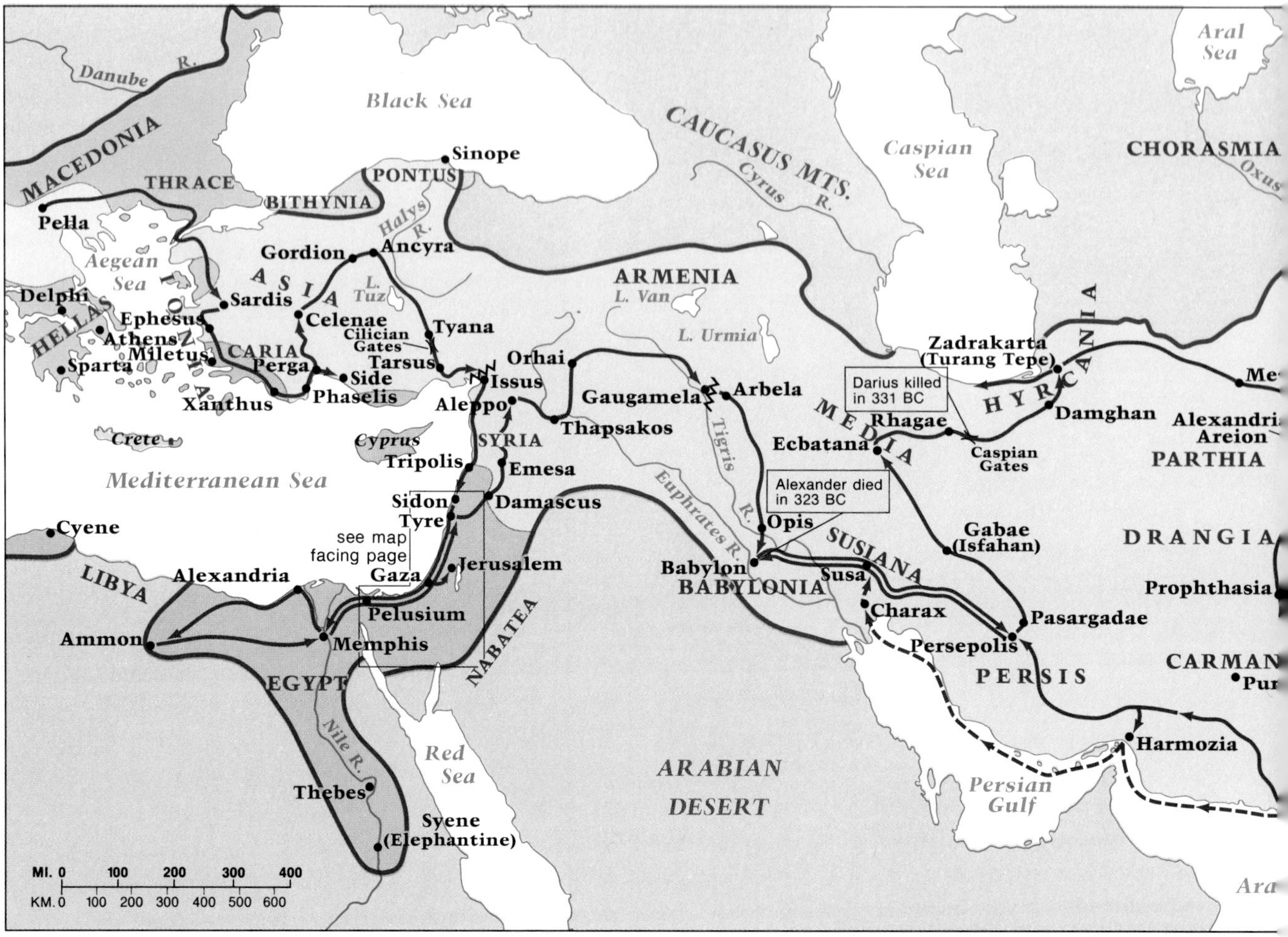

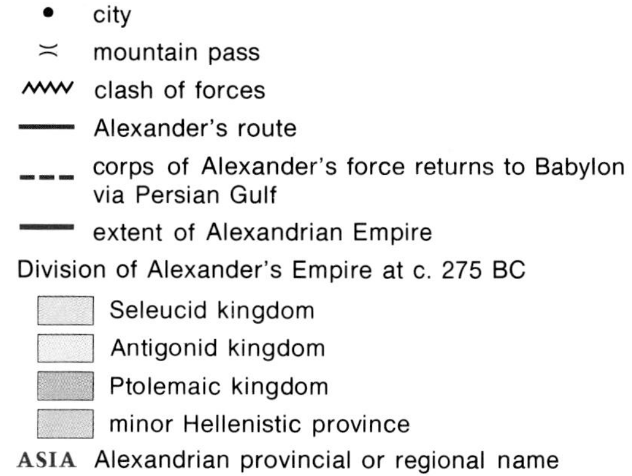

the Ganges River; about one-hundred miles east of the Indus River near Taxila, Alexander won a decisive victory against an Indian prince, despite the latter's use of elephants. But when the Macedonian attempted to plunge still deeper into the Indian interior, his troops mutinied at the Hydaspes River, and the king was forced to turn back. He returned via the Indus valley to the Sea, where a naval corps was dispatched to sail the Persian Gulf to Mesopotamia. Meanwhile, his army trekked across the forbidding plains of Baluchistan to Babylon where, in 323, Alexander died.

The power play that ensued in the immediate aftermath of Alexander's death was bloody and sustained, but by 275 B.C. the number of important rivals had been reduced to three, and the breakup of the Greek empire was then effected. The Seleucid dynasty controlled Mesopotamia, Syria, and most of Asia Minor and Iran. The Antigonid dynasty ruled the territory around Alexander's home, Pella. The Ptolemies exercised rule over Egypt, Cyrene, Palestine, Phoenicia, Cyprus, and coastal parts of Asia Minor. This allotment was soon to change for Palestine, however, and in a most dramatic and profound way.

When the Ptolemaic hold on Palestine was lost to the Seleucids in 198 B.C., the Hellenization of the upper strata of Jewish society was inaugurated. The ensuing tension gave rise inevitably to Jewish factionalism: the more progressive Jews embraced Hellenistic ideology, whereas the more traditional viewed it as a threat to their ancestral religion. But when Antiochus IV (Epiphanes) ascended to the Seleucid throne in 175 B.C., the effort toward Hellenization reached its zenith.

MASSAGETAE
Jaxartes R.
akanda
arkand)
Alexandria Eschate
OGDIANA
hara
BACTRA
Bactra
HINDU KUSH MTS.
Aornus
Cabul
Taxila
Bucephala
ARACHOSIA
dahar
MALLI
Hydaspes R.
Indus R.
ROSIA
Pattala
INDIA
© 1985 The Moody Bible Institute of Chicago
Mediterranean Sea
Sidon
Litani R.
Tyre
Antiochia
Panias
Sea of Galilee
Ptolemais Antiochenes
GALILEE
Sycaminium
Kishon R.
Antiochia (Hippos)
Bucolon Polis
Philoteria
Abila Seleucia
Dora
Itabyrium
Gadara Antiochia Seleucia
Strato's Tower
Narbata
Scythopolis Nysa
Berenice-Pella
Samaria
Gerasa Antiochia-on-Chrysorrhoas
Apollonia
Jordan R.
Jabbok R.
Pegae
SAMARIA
Joppa
PEREA
Port of Jamnia
Philadelphia
Jamnia
Azotus Paralius
Jerusalem Antiochia
Azotus
Ascalon
Marisa
JUDEA
Anthedon
Dead Sea
Arnon R.
Gaza Seleucid Demos
Besor Brook
IDUMEA
Pelusium
W. el-Arish
Zered Brook
NABATEA
town given Greek name
city given Greek name
city given municipal rights by Ptolemies
city given Ptolemaic dynastic name
Antiochia city given Seleucid dynastic name (i.e. underlined)
Gulf of Aqaba
Berenice-Elath
MI. 0 10 20 30 40
KM. 0 10 20 30 40 50 60
© 1985 The Moody Bible Institute of Chicago

The Maccabean Revolt

Antiochus IV constructed at Jerusalem a gymnasium and converted the city into a Hellenistic polis, to be known as Antiochia; the latter measure required a new census. In 168 B.C., he erected in Jerusalem a fortress, called the Akra, and deployed a Syrian legion there. The following year Antiochus issued further decrees against Judaism that were carried out with severity in Jerusalem. The Temple was desecrated and its treasures confiscated. The worship of Yahweh was abolished, and a statue of the Olympian Zeus was installed in the Temple. Outraged at that flagrant perversion, a priest named Mattathias from the town of Modin, about 18 miles northwest of Jerusalem, resolutely refused to offer the prescribed heathen sacrifice. Instead, he killed Antiochus's emissary and fled for his life. When word of that brave action spread throughout Judea, thousands of insurgents, later to be known as the Hasidim ("pious ones"), openly revolted against Syria under the capable leadership of a son of Mattathias, Judas, nicknamed Maccabeus ("mallet-headed").

Judas led his well-trained band of rebels to successive victories at Gophna, Beth-horon, Emmaus, and Beth-zur. Then, laying siege to Jerusalem, they beat back four successive attempts to relieve the Seleucid legion inside the Akra, whereupon a truce was declared. The Hasidim were permitted to occupy the Temple hill, to cleanse the Temple of pagan objects, and to reinstitute sacrifices to Yahweh. Some three years after its profanation by Antiochus, the Temple lamps were again lit in the name of Yahweh. Since that time, Jews have solemnly observed the Feast of Hanukkah ("lights") in memory of the occasion.

With religious purity now within view, Judas set out to achieve political freedom as well. He undertook military expeditions in every direction. In the north, his guerrillas experienced victories at Scythopolis and Dathema; farther north, he invaded the territory of the Itureans. On one occasion, Judas led his men on a three-day march into the Hauran district to relieve the Jewish population inside the city of Bostra. The Maccabean army was able to forge eastward against the Nabateans as far as Jazer. In the south, the Idumean cities of Hebron and Marisa fell. On the coastal plain Judas's forces razed the cities of Azotus and Joppa. His was a far-reaching decision to achieve political freedom, for Judas actually set into motion a chain of events that would culminate a century later when the Roman forces of Pompey would be hailed in Jerusalem as liberators.

In the meanwhile, a Jewish state was created by Judas's successors. Map 73 depicts territories rather permanently incorporated into that newborn state by Judas's two brothers (Jonathan [161-142 B.C.] and Simon [142-134 B.C.]). Afterwards, the torch was carried first by a son of Simon, John Hyrcanus I (134-104 B.C.), followed for a brief moment by Aristobulus I (104-103 B.C.), who subjugated Galilee. Then came Aristobulus's son Alexander Janneus (103-76 B.C.) whose exploits took him as far afield as the plain of Dor, northern Gilead, much of northern Nabatea, and to the threshold of Egypt. However, one of Alexander's sons, John Hyrcanus II, would be obliged to submit to Pompey's dominion.

MAP 72

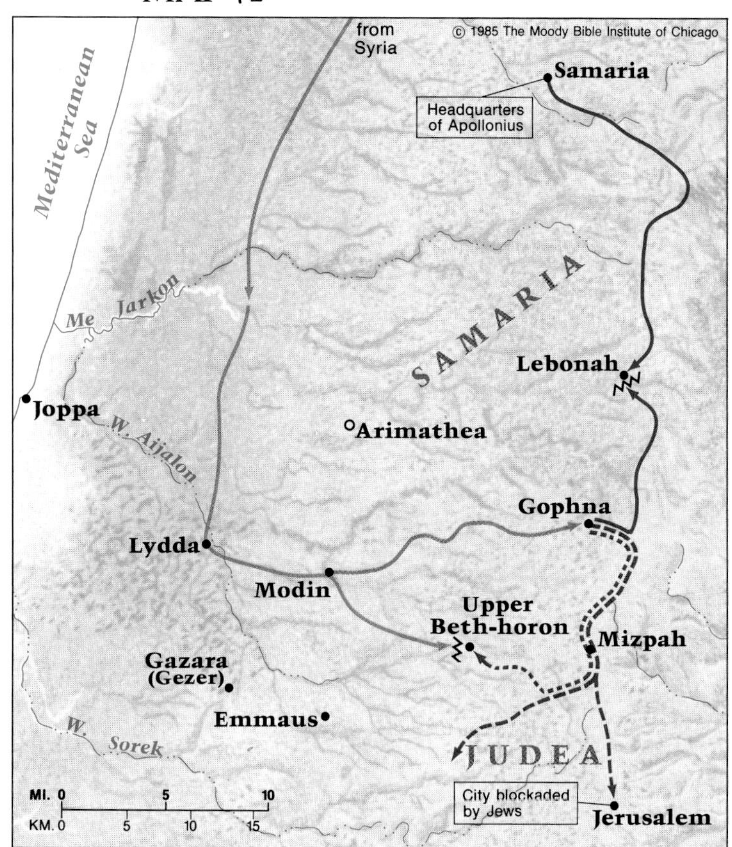

- • city
- o city (uncertain location)
- clash of forces
- Mattathias kills Antiochus' emissary and takes refuge in the hills around Gophna (1Macc 2:1f)
- Apollonius unsuccessfully attempts to quell revolt (1Macc 3:10)
- Judas Maccabeus leads insurgents against Apollonius' forces and slays Apollonius himself (1Macc 3:11f)
- Seron leads Seleucid army from Syria to suppress revolt (1Macc 3:13f)
- Judas' troops surprise Seron as his troops endeavor to navigate the pass at Upper Beth-horon (1Macc 3:16f)
- Judas' troops make nocturnal raids against Syrians in Judea (2Macc 8:1f)

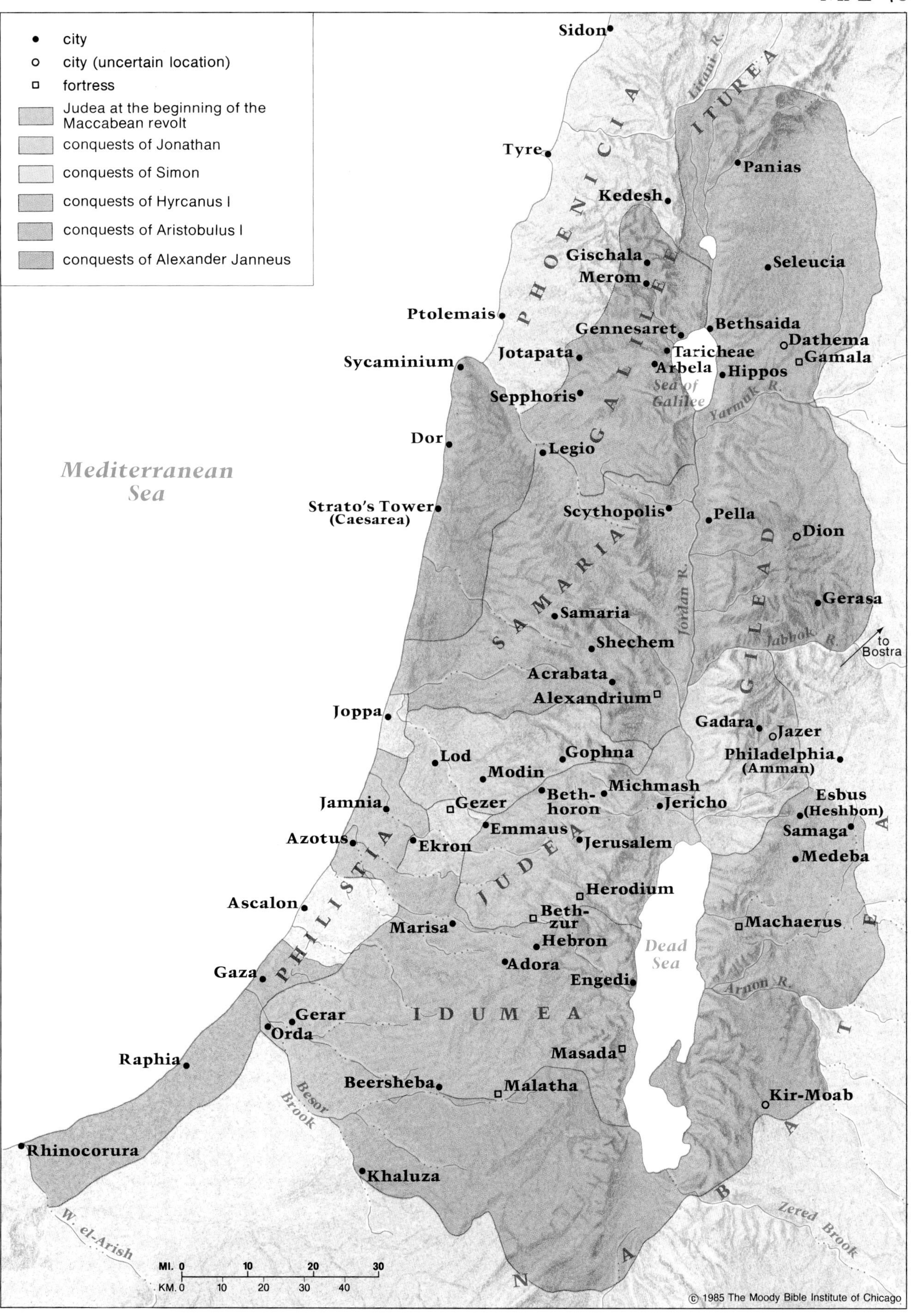

city
city (uncertain location)
fortress
Judea at the beginning of the Maccabean revolt
conquests of Jonathan
conquests of Simon
conquests of Hyrcanus I
conquests of Aristobulus I
conquests of Alexander Janneus
Mediterranean Sea
Sidon
Tyre
PHOENICIA
ITUREA
Litani R.
Panias
Kedesh
Gischala
Merom
Seleucia
Ptolemais
GALILEE
Gennesaret
Bethsaida
Dathema
Taricheae
Gamala
Jotapata
Arbela
Hippos
Sycaminium
Sea of Galilee
Yarmuk R.
Sepphoris
Dor
Legio
Strato's Tower
(Caesarea)
Scythopolis
Pella
Dion
SAMARIA
GILEAD
Jordan R.
Samaria
Gerasa
Shechem
Jabbok R.
to Bostra
Acrabata
Alexandrium
Joppa
Gadara
Jazer
Lod
Gophna
Philadelphia
(Amman)
Modin
Michmash
Jamnia
Gezer
Beth-horon
Jericho
Esbus
(Heshbon)
Azotus
Emmaus
Samaga
Ekron
Jerusalem
Medeba
JUDEA
PHILISTIA
Herodium
Ascalon
Beth-zur
Machaerus
Marisa
Hebron
Dead Sea
Gaza
Adora
Engedi
Arnon R.
IDUMEA
Gerar
Orda
Masada
Raphia
Beersheba
Malatha
Besor Brook
Kir-Moab
Rhinocorura
Khaluza
NABATEA
Zered Brook
W. el-Arish
MI. 0 10 20 30
KM. 0 10 20 30 40
© 1985 The Moody Bible Institute of Chicago

JERUSALEM THROUGH THE AGES

Name. Jerusalem has enjoyed a sacred status with the Jew, Moslem, and Christian alike. Uniquely, it has formed part of the world's thought and literature, and scarcely another city in the world has captivated more religious pilgrims. On the other hand, the meaning of its name has defied the learned, thereby inviting a veritable kaleidoscope of etymological speculation, ranging from "sacred rock" to "complete cloudburst."

The earliest mention of the city occurs in the Egyptian Execration Texts of the late-twentieth and nineteenth century B.C. under a form probably transliterated Urusalimum. In the fourteenth century, it appears in the Abdi-Hepa correspondence from Tell el-Amarna, written *Urusalim*. Later, it is attested in a Sennacherib inscription under the form *Ursalimmu*. It is thus possible to observe that the oldest epigraphic evidence, both Egyptian, West Semitic, and Akkadian, consistently exhibits a form that reflects two transparently Semitic elements—*uru* ("city") and *salim* (a Divine name)—producing a city name with the meaning "the city of (the god) Salim." Hyphenating place names by incorporating divine elements was a common phenomenon in the ancient Near Eastern world, and the god Salim (or Shalem [Akkadian] Shulmanu) is otherwise known to have been a member of the Canaanite pantheon (cf. Ezek. 16:3). Further, one must bear in mind that the Old Testament itself attests that Jerusalem was not originally a Hebrew city. Accordingly, it seems plausible to postulate that the name *Jerusalem* originally translated "the city of (the god) Salim."

In the Hebrew Old Testament, Jerusalem is written *yerushalayim*, whereas in the Aramaic portions the name is rendered *yerushalem*. Here the word seems to be displaying the elements *yarah* ("to found"; cf. Job 38:6) and *shalem* ("a divine name"), yielding the meaning "the foundation of (the god) Shalem." The eloquence of this alteration is reflected in the word "foundation," indicating the permanent home (i.e., in contrast to an impermanent tent; cf. Heb. 11:10) of Shalem. From this, one may deduce that Shalem was the patron deity of the city and that he had given his name to it, an onomastic transference frequently seen in the ancient world.

In the New Testament, Jerusalem translates the two Greek words *Ierousalem* and *Hierosoluma*. The former is simply a Greek transliteration of the Aramaic form; the latter, however, reflects the word *hieros* ("holy"), which represents an instance of Hellenistic paronomasia, but which has correspondence neither with the Semitic root of the name nor with the city's historical reality.

Besides Jerusalem, the city is also called Salem, Jebus, Zion, Moriah, Ariel, the City, Aelia Capitolina, and El-Quds.

Topography. Like Rome, Jerusalem is a city set on hills. A cluster of five hills comprise the denuded quadrilateral land mass roughly one mile long and one-half mile wide, bordered on all sides except the north by deep ravines. Skirting the city on the west and south is the Hinnom valley (Greek, *Gehenna*); hedging Jerusalem on the east is the Kidron valley (cf. Valley of Jehoshaphat, Joel 3:2, 12). Stretching from the modern Damascus Gate in the north to the vicinity of the Siloam Pool, where it converges with the Kidron, was a "Central valley," since the days of Josephus referred to as the Tyropoeon ("cheesemakers") valley. These three principal ravines were connected by a number of lateral valleys, originally segmenting the configuration of the terrain.

East of the Central valley lie three hills. The southernmost, historically known as the southeastern hill, was the site of earliest occupation, undoubtedly because of its more convenient water supply. This was the Jebusite city conquered by David, which was the biblical Zion, in contrast to the modern Mt. Zion (see Map 76). This narrow ridge of land is no more than 60 yards across at the top and encompasses no more than 8 acres; today this area is completely outside the walls of the city. Immediately north of Zion lies the Temple hill, dominated today by the sacred rock on which rests the Moslem Dome of the Rock. Some believe this to be the location of Araunah's threshing floor (2 Sam. 24:18-19) and others aver it to be the site of Moriah (Gen. 22:2; 2 Chron. 3:1). Jerusalem certainly lies a distance of three-days' journey from Beersheba. Separating the Temple hill from the third crest to the east of the Tyropoeon is a lateral valley, called in modern times "St. Anne's valley." Historically known as the northeastern hill, this hill was occupied and named Bezetha ("the new city") in the Roman period when practical necessity dictated that a third northern wall be constructed to accomodate a growing population.

To the west of the Tyropoeon stand the two remaining hills. What is historically known as the southwestern hill was called by Josephus the "upper city," a reference to its higher elevation. Today, the southwestern hill roughly corresponds to the Armenian quarter and is occupied by the citadel of David (built on the foundations of Herod's towers), the Church of St. James, the traditional site of the tomb of David, and the Dormition Abbey. Part of this hill in Old Testament times,

Gareb (Jer. 31:39) was commonly regarded by Protestants until near the end of the nineteenth century as the place of Calvary (see Map 74). The northwestern hill corresponds to the Christian quarter, dominated by the Church of the Holy Sepulchre, built over the traditional site of Golgotha (see maps 75 and 76).

Stationed astride the summit of the Central Spine and located at the axis of the water parting route, which connects Hebron, Bethlehem, Shechem (Nablus) and points north, Jerusalem is commercially central to the country. The lateral roadway through the Judean mountains eastward could not pass south of the city, being blocked by the Dead Sea and its sheer cliffs. The only possibility for this route existed along the crest of the watershed, passing some three to four miles northwest of Jerusalem. Accordingly, Jerusalem lies just off the natural crossroads of Judea.

Not only a city *set* on hills, Jerusalem is also a city *surrounded* by hills. Eastward from the city rises the lofty Olivet summit; southward lie the heights of the Mount of Offense and the Hill of Evil Counsel. West is the alignment of Givat Ram and Mount Menuhot, while the northern horizon is dominated by the summit of Mt. Scopus.

Water always has been in meager supply at Jerusalem. The only natural source of permanent water was the Gihon spring, located in the Kidron just east of the Jebusite fortress conquered by David. Vertical tunnels were burrowed to provide access to the Gihon when Jerusalem lay under siege. And Hezekiah's tunnel was cut through nearly 1,800 feet of hard limestone, allowing the waters of the Gihon to pass through the hill of Zion to the Siloam Pool, *inside* the city wall

Figure 23 South of the Dome of the Rock lies the spur on which rested Old Testament Zion, flanked by the deep gorge of the Kidron valley.

(2 Kings 20:20; 2 Chron. 32:3, 30; cf. Isa. 22:9-11; Sirach 48:17). Farther south, where the Kidron and Hinnom valleys converge, there was another spring, called in the Bible En-rogel. Owing to the lowering of the water table, this source of water ceased to percolate and was subsequently converted into a well. These two sources were clearly insufficient to sustain a sizeable population, and so a vast network of cisterns, reservoirs, and water conduits for supplemental supply had to be devised. In the Herodian period, a number of aqueducts carried water to Jerusalem from points south.[38]

Explorations and Excavations. "Years are required to know Athens, but Jerusalem is exhausted within three months." This imperceptive observation was attributed in 1892 to Ernest Renan, French Hebraist and philosopher. The exploratory activities and archaeological expeditions at Jerusalem, conducted by the five generations that have passed since Renan's remark, conclusively belie his tacit optimism. On the other hand, though no Palestinian city can boast of more excavations, most of Jerusalem's archaeological returns have been substantially fragmentary and chronologically incoherent. This is largely owing to the city's dense contemporary population and sacral character, and to the surprisingly late arrival of modern archaeological technology. In fact, it would be accurate to assert that, while an impressive number of explorations and excavations have been undertaken *at* Jerusalem, never has there been a systematic excavation *of* Jerusalem. Nevertheless, a history of the city's excavations primarily revolves around the axes of four creative periods, accompanied by a host of commendable efforts.

Though modern exploration at Jerusalem appears to date from the surveying of Van Kootwijck (1598-99), followed by the labors of Pococke, Bonomi, Catherwood, and Arundale, it was with the researches of Edward Robinson that the first creative epoch was inaugurated. This American scholar made a series of topographic surveys of profound significance even today, and his activities mark the advent of a flood of literature. Robinson's chief contribution lay in his method: he dared to challenge the time-honored axiom that ecclesiastical traditions provided the primary source for reconstructing a city's history. Instead, he sought to reconstruct Jerusalem's history on the basis of the "unsuspecting evidence of the stones," thereby signaling for the holy city the advent of the archaeological method.

A second creative period commenced in 1864 when the Palestine Exploration Fund launched its first archaeological mission to Jerusalem, through the philanthropic contribution of Lady Burdett-Coutts of London, who wished to improve the sanitary conditions and water supply of the city. Between 1867 and 1870, this modest venture was enlarged as Captain (later Sir) Charles Warren carried out extensive excavations around the Temple area, on the southeastern hill, and in the Tyropoeon valley. Of especial interest was his unearthing of a section of an ancient wall near the southeastern sector of the Temple, a sketch of which adorns the frontispiece of the *Palestine Exploration Fund Quarterly* to this day. While conducting more extensive research within Hezekiah's tunnel, Warren discovered an alternate, archaic shaft connecting the Gihon with a plateau of the southeastern hill. Though not specifically discussed by him, the magnitude of this discovery was considerable for biblical history, as it supplied an entirely reasonable explanation for David's strategy in conquering the city (2 Sam. 5:8). The cartographic materials amassed by Warren and his predecessor Charles Wilson remain the basis of much contemporary topographic research.

In the wake of the much-publicized discoveries of Wilson and Warren came the quests of Conder, Maudsley, and Clermont-Ganneau. In 1881, Guthe conducted additional excavations on the southeastern hill and the Siloam Pool, while Schick reported the discovery of the now-famous Siloam Inscription, which describes how Hezekiah's men dug the channel. At the same time, Bliss and Dickie undertook elaborate excavations of the southern wall, isolating for the first time a wall across the mouth of the Tyropoeon, connecting the southwestern and southeastern hills.

It was with the work of Raymond Weill, however, that the third creative period was begun. Although the area Weill actually excavated on the southeastern hill was comparably small, it was he who first employed the stratigraphic excavation method at Jerusalem. Interrupted in 1914 by the outbreak of World War I, Weill's method already had provided penetrating new insights into Jerusalem's history before the time of David. His labors forever dispelled all doubt that the southeastern hill exercised historical supremacy in earliest times. Following the war, the southeastern hill was again the subject of a campaign by Weill, of a team under the supervision of Macalister and Duncan, and of an expedition led by Crowfoot and Fitzgerald. From 1925 to 1927, Sukenik, Mayer, and Fisher explored north of the city, discovering sections of the "third (Northern) wall" built by Herod Agrippa, grandson of Herod the Great. Later, Iliffe unearthed a cemetery, and Johns excavated the citadel at the Jaffa gate. Johns's unstinting efforts were rewarded with the discovery of walls and towers from the pre-Chris-

OLD TESTAMENT JERUSALEM

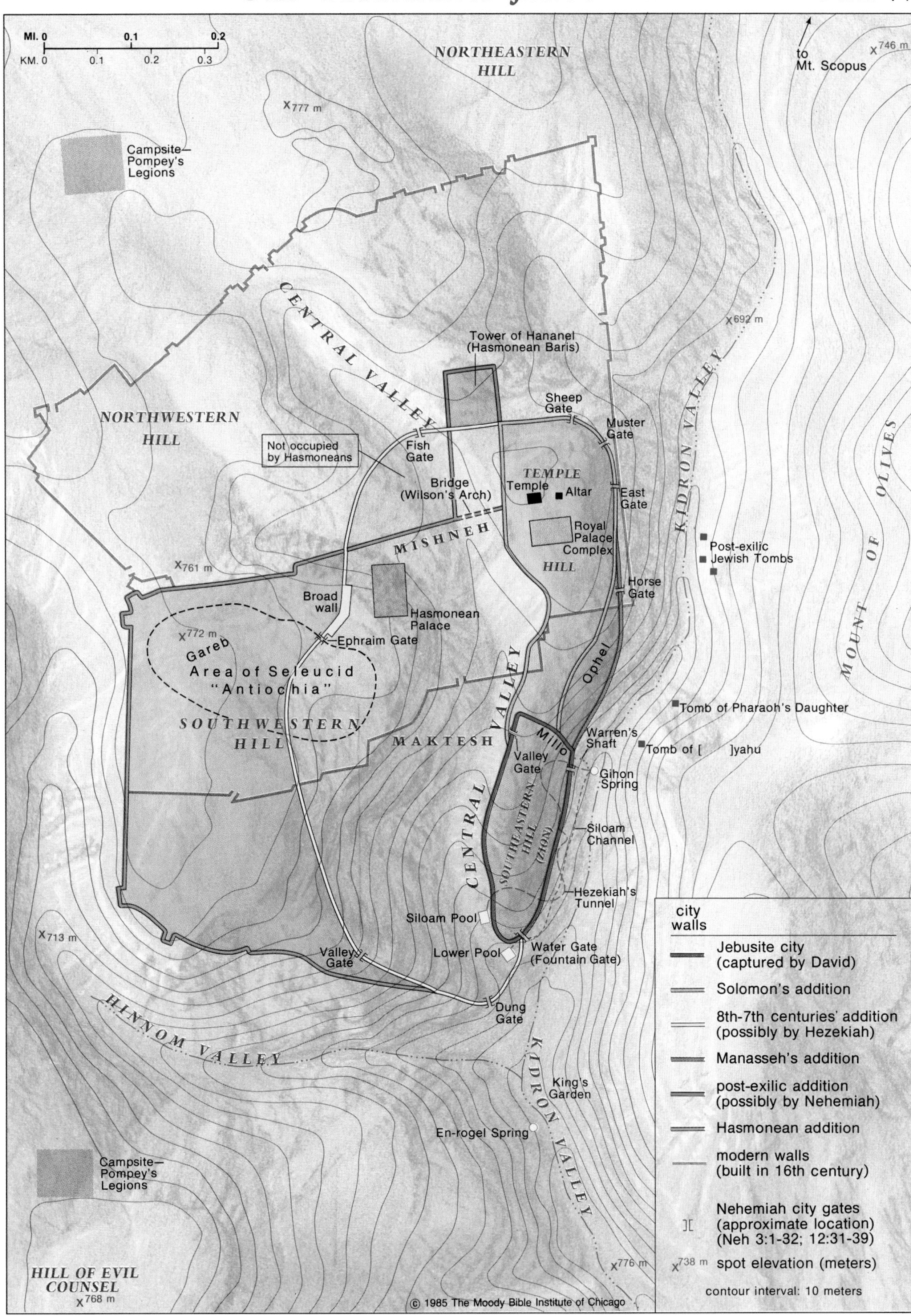

tian era. Just prior to World War II, Hamilton carried out work outside the northeastern wall near St. Stephen's gate; from 1949 to 1953, Testa conducted excavations at Bethphage, where the colt for Jesus' Palm Sunday entry into Jerusalem was obtained (Matt. 21:1-11).

One enters the portals of the fourth creative period with the protracted archaeological expedition under the capable leadership of Kathleen Kenyon. From 1961 to 1967, this British School of Archaeology project explored several regions of Jerusalem, focusing principally upon the southeastern hill near the Gihon, the region of the mouth of the Tyropoeon, the territory immediately south of the Temple area, and the Armenian Gardens just inside the west wall of the present city.

Excavations begun subsequent to the commencement of Kenyon's include Bennett and Hennessy, who toiled in the vicinity of the Damascus gate, and Mazar, whose surveys were conducted primarily along the southern slope of the Temple hill. Since 1968, the Hebrew University, under the direction of Amiran and Eitan, and more recently under Shiloh, has intermittently undertaken archaeological research in and near the city, especially on the east side. During these same years, Israel's Department of Antiquities and Museums has engaged in excavations of what was known prior to the 1967 war as the Jewish Quarter.

History. Ancient flint implements found in the Sorek plain, the plain of the Rephaim, constitute the earliest evidence of the existence of man in the area of Jerusalem. Near the beginning of the fourth millennium B.C., the southeastern hill was first occupied by a sedentary group, a fact evinced from the artifactual remains recovered from graves built on bedrock. By 1800 B.C., the crest of the southeastern hill was walled in rudimentary form (cf. Execration Text references). From the Bible, one discovers that Abraham paid tithes to Melchizedek, king of Salem (Gen. 14:17-20), just as the great patriarch later visited the site of Moriah (Gen. 22:2-9).

In the fifteenth century B.C. or thereabouts, extensive building activities were initiated and measurably improved fortification methods were introduced at Jerusalem. Beginning some 160 feet down the eastern slope of the southeastern hill, the city's occupants undertook to construct platform terraces, engineered to be filled up to the level of the top of the hill. These were reinforced by a series of ribs designed to retain the immense fill that would have been required. At the same time, they erected a strong masonry rampart near the bottom of the slope, below the spot where they had burrowed a vertical shaft to provide access to the waters of the Gihon. At once, this enterprise procured an enlarged land area on the summit, a much stronger and more permanent city wall, and a water access during times of siege. Traces of the northern side of this wall were located by Kenyon; apparently the northern perim-

Figure 24 The western wall of the Temple mount, known as the "wailing wall," is venerated as the most important place of Jewish worship.

eter of this fortress extended to just south of the modern south wall.

Jerusalem fell into Israelite hands when David's band wrested the city from Jebusite control (2 Sam. 5). The capture itself seems to have been effected with remarkable ease, though opinions differ concerning the strategem employed. On the one hand, it is argued that the verb of 2 Sam. 5:8 ("get up") carries the meaning "to touch, to reach" (cf. Ps. 42:7), and connotes that David's men fought their way up the slope as far as the water shaft, so as to cut off the Jebusites from their water access. On the other hand, some of the newer excavations along the eastern slope have tended to strengthen the hypothesis that Joab surreptitiously climbed through the water shaft from the Gihon and took the Jebusites by surprise. Whatever the case, the incorporation of Jerusalem into David's kingdom and its transformation into a royal capital required considerable building of the city. David fortified the Canaanite walls and prepared an extension of the city by the Millo ("filling"; 2 Sam. 5:9; 1 Chron. 11:8), possibly referring to a further bolstering of the Canaanite platform terraces along the northeastern sector of his city. The king also constructed a royal residence in Jerusalem (2 Sam. 5:11). Nehemiah 12:37 suggests that this palace may have lain near the east side of the southeastern hill. It was from a window of this house that Michal saw her husband performing in what she perceived to be an undignified manner (2 Sam. 6:16); from the roof of this palace, David gazed upon Bathsheba as she bathed (2 Sam. 11:1-22), and his son Absalom publicly engaged in sexual intercourse with his father's concubines (2 Sam. 16:21-22).

But by bringing the Ark of the Covenant into Jerusalem (2 Sam. 6:1-2), implying that Yahweh also would be residing there, David displayed his most profound leadership. For in this perceptive act, he merged for the first time in Israel's history its political and religious capitals. Henceforth, Jerusalem would take on the character of a "holy city" and a "royal city"; from now on the city would be known as the "city of David" (e.g., 2 Sam. 5:8) as well as the "city of God" (e.g., Ps. 46:4). Now, adult male Jews would make their pilgrimages *to Jerusalem* to take part in festival seasons. It remained only for David to make permanent this arrangement, to forever enshrine Yahweh in Jerusalem by building Him a temple. And this is what David aspired to do (2 Sam. 7), but God responded that the execution of this dream was reserved for a son of the king (cf. 1 Chron. 28:3).

Solomon inherited a kingdom from his father that was extensive and basically secure. Nevertheless, new and additional military measures were introduced into Jerusalem and the surrounding terrain. He fortified certain key cities and transformed them into military bases where a standing army was deployed (1 Kings 9:15-23; see Map 48). Those bases also accommodated horses and chariots, for it was Solomon who introduced chariot warfare into Israel (1 Kings 4:26; 2 Chron. 9:25). And although his reign was not entirely peaceful, we know of no significant military campaigns that he was obliged to undertake. All of Israel from Dan to Beersheba was said to have enjoyed peace and prosperity during Solomon's tenure (1 Kings 4:25), and this son of David is best remembered for his wisdom (1 Kings 3:16-23; Matt. 12:42), splendor (Matt. 6:28-29), and building.

Solomon was the great Old Testament builder of Jerusalem. His most significant building enterprise was undoubtedly the first Temple. Erected on the summit of Temple hill, this edifice required some seven years in construction (1 Kings 6:1, 38). With a suggested tripartite floor plan, the Temple faced East, the direction of the rising sun. Its interior measured approximately 90 feet in length, some 30 feet in width, and about 45 feet in height. Along the entire front was a portico measuring some 15 feet in depth, with two bronze pillars erected at the center of its front facing (1 Kings 7:15). Surrounding the Temple on the other three were chambers. Following the completion of the Temple, Solomon had the furniture of the Tabernacle, including the ark, moved from Zion (2 Chron. 5:1-5) for the Feast of Tabernacles (Ingathering). This crowning event was climaxed by the coming of the presence of God (1 Kings 8:10).

At the center of the Moslem sacred enclosure, today called Haram esh-Sherif ("the noble sanctuary"), stands the Dome of the Rock Mosque, known also as the Mosque of Omar. Embedded inside this mosque is a large rock long venerated as the spot over which stood the Holy of Holies of the Solomonic Temple. Though such a tradition may be based on fact, nothing definitively dating from the Solomonic era has yet been dug up from the sacred precinct.

Solomon also built Jerusalem's city walls (1 Kings 3:1; 9:15). What this means is that he extended the Canaanite walls to enclose the enlarged land area of his own city. Though it is unlikely that Solomon expanded his city to the south or east, to encompass the Temple required constructing an extension wall to the north. Kenyon corroborates that the area north of the southeastern hill was occupied in the Solomonic era.

Remains of an early occupation on the northern section of the southwestern hill—e.g., the so-called "broad wall" (Neh. 3:8; 12:38)—have been attributed by some writers with a Solomonic extension to the west. Though we consider this rather implausible, and are more likely to attribute this occupation to the time of Hezekiah (cf. the *mishneh* ["Second Quarter," 2 Kings 22:14; 2 Chron. 32:5; 34:22; Neh. 11:9; Zeph. 1:10] and the *maktesh* ["Mortar," i.e., a quarter of the city in which the silversmiths practiced their trade, Zeph. 1:11]), it must be stressed that the position of the city walls depicted here on the Jerusalem maps is largely speculative, based on a modicum of archaeological discovery combined with a description of the walls given by Josephus.[39] Perhaps the two most controversial aspects of the city walls as depicted are (1) the date when the southwestern hill was enclosed and (2) the locations of the second and third northern walls in the New Testament epoch. Whatever the case, not much building went on during the days of the divided monarchy, and the humiliating history of Jerusalem during this period has been shown on Maps 52, 58, and 62. In addition to Hezekiah's building, King Manasseh is said to have constructed an outer wall to the city of David, west of Gihon in the Kidron valley, as far as the entrance of the Fish gate, carrying it round Ophel ("hill, bulge"; presumably located beside David's city and the Temple hill, cf. 2 Chron. 27:3; Neh. 3:26) and raising it to a great height (2 Chron. 33:14).

In 536 B.C., after the fall of Babylon, Cyrus issued his famous proclamation according to which dispossessed peoples could be repatriated (2 Chron. 36:22-23; Ezra 1:1-4). Thereupon, a humble company returned to Jerusalem under the direction of Sheshbazzar (Ezra 1:8), followed shortly thereafter by a small group led by Ezra (Ezra 7:7). And although these groups were permitted to adorn and enrich the Temple, the city remained almost empty and its walls and gates remained broken and dilapidated. Moved by reports of these miserable conditions, Nehemiah decided to leave his post as cupbearer to the king and to go to Jerusalem (Neh. 1:3-4). If the concerns of the earlier returnees focused on the Temple itself, Nehemiah's was upon the city walls. After being in the holy city for three days, he undertook an evening reconnaissance to ascertain the extent of work still required on the walls. His is the most comprehensive description of Jerusalem's post-exilic city walls and topography (Neh. 2:11-16). And spurred on by his energetic enthusiasm, the people completed the task of rebuilding the walls in fifty-two days (Neh. 6:15). Their labors may have included incorporating into Jerusalem the lower of Hanaud (Jer. 31:38; Neh. 3:1; 12:39; Zech. 14:10), known in the Maccabean period as the Baris.

In 332 B.C., Jerusalem, along with the remainder of Judah, peacefully submitted to the army of Alexander the Great (cf. Map 69). In the aftermath of Alexander's death, however, Jerusalem suffered through a series of battles waged between the Ptolemies and Seleucids for Palestinian succession. At first Jerusalem was incorporated into the Ptolemaic kingdom and its economy was stabilized; during the period of comparative prosperity which ensued, the city continued as Judah's administrative center, and Jews were welcomed in Alexandria. But the scene soon changed just after 198 B.C. when Antiochus III crushed the Ptolemaic hold on Palestine and incorporated Jerusalem into the Seleucid domain (see Map 70; for the steps towards Hellenization which precipitated the outbreak of the Maccabean revolt, refer to Maps

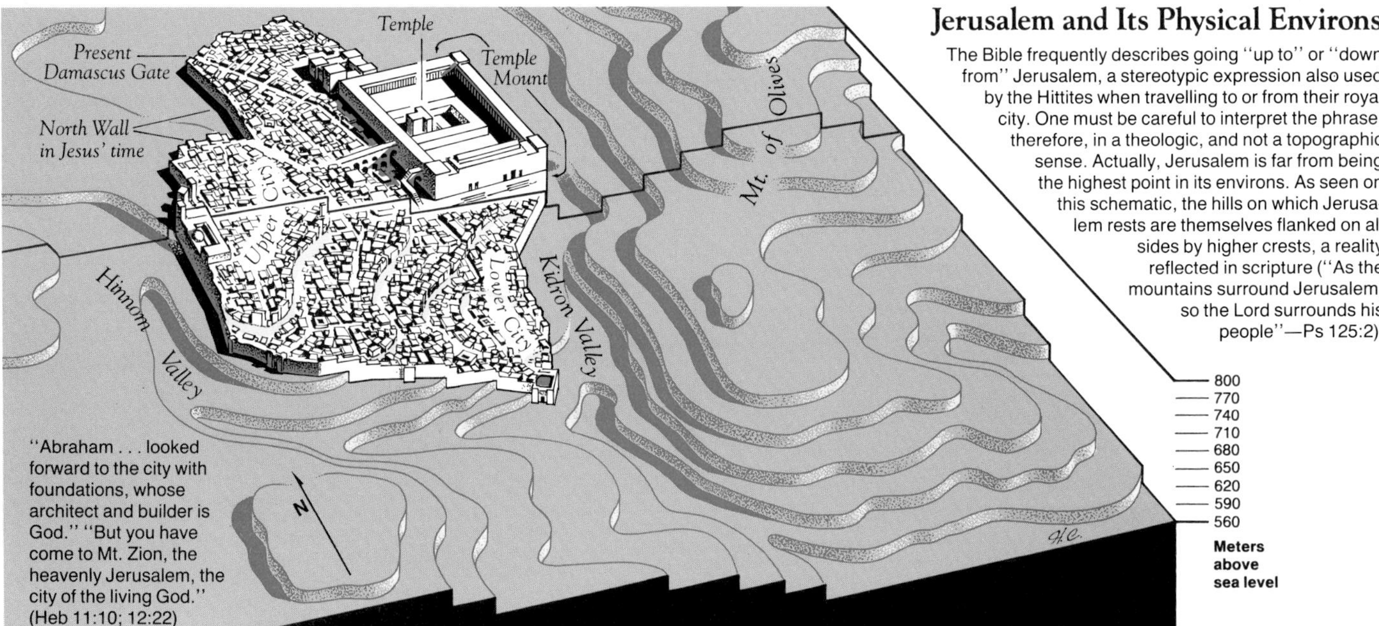

Figure 25 Cross-Sectional Schematic of Jerusalem.

New Testament Jerusalem

MAP 75

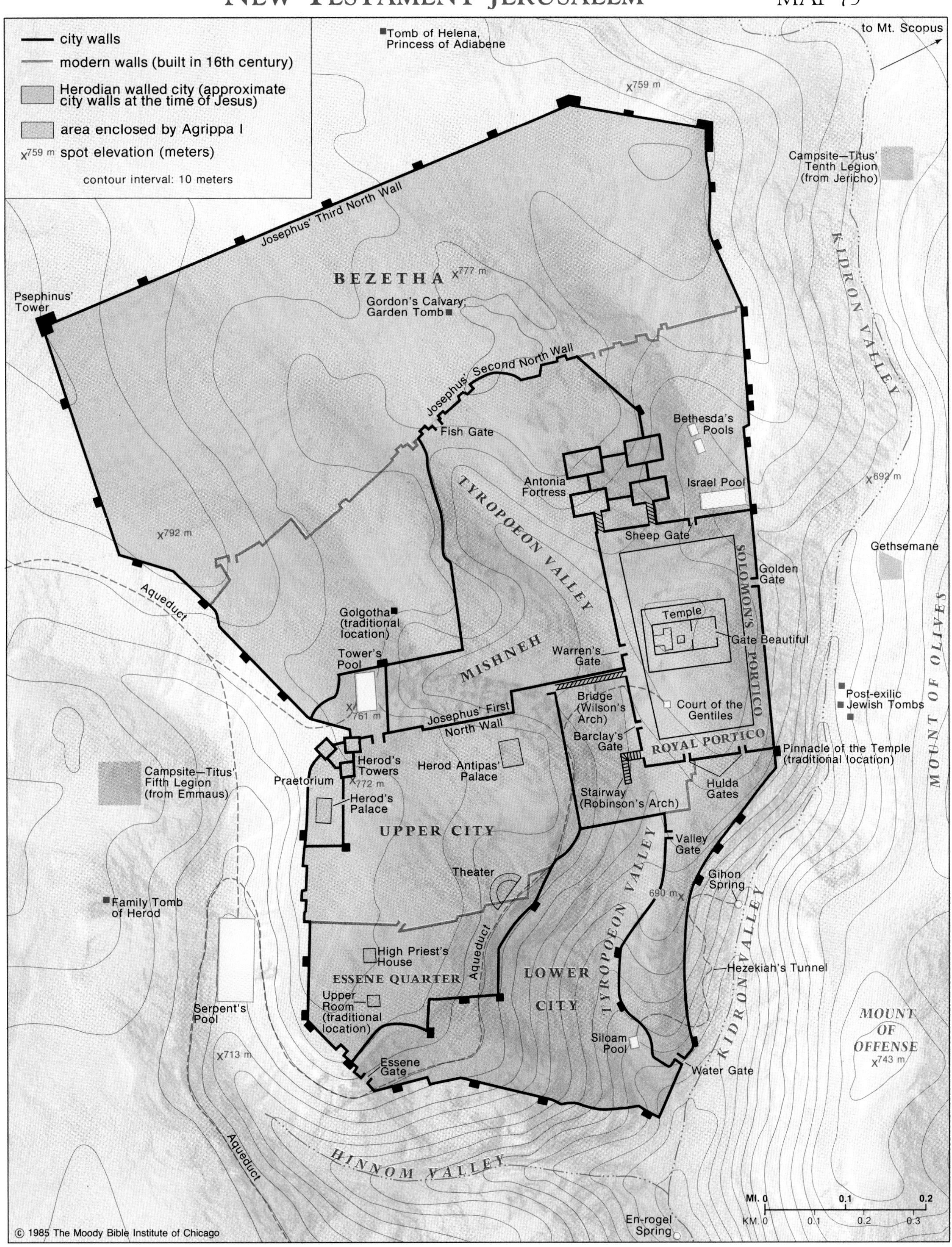

72 and 73 with accompanying text).

A call for national autonomy which had fanned the flames of Maccabean revolt gave way to pleas for law in order in the wake of a sectarian strife concerning who should be the bona fide high priest. Legitimate Maccabean succession had not been a problem until the wife of Alexander Janaeus, Salome Alexandra, assumed the political function of her deceased husband and succeeded in restoring a temporary peace within sectarian ranks. But it was of course unthinkable for all involved that she could assume what had been her husband's sacral role. And so the earmarks for renewed hostilities surfaced at Salome's death. The Pharisees backed Salome's son Hyrcanus II while the Sadducees supported Aristobulus II as legitimate high priest. In the end, a civil war which ensued profited only the Romans. Citizens appealed to Rome, and in the name of law and order, Pompey decided in favor of Hyrcanus. And when the partisans of Aristobulus isolated themselves in the Temple and defied his order, Pompey was forced to lay siege to Jerusalem. In the year 63 B.C., the Temple wall was breached and the Romans broke into the Temple. Pompey simply dissolved the Maccabean syncretism and added Jerusalem to the Roman province of Syria.

Though Pompey had left Hyrcanus in charge of Jerusalem, three times in the next decade Aristobulus or his compatriots attempted to gain control. Throughout these assaults, Hyrcanus was supported by his Roman patron and a wily Idumean (Edomite) named Antipater. At the death of Pompey, Hyrcanus and Antipater aligned themselves with Rome and Julius Caesar whereas a son of Aristobulus, Mattathias Antigonus, found a welcome embrace with the Parthians. When Caesar was assassinated in 44 B.C., Mark Antony established Antipater's two sons—Phasael and Herod—as tetrarchs of Judah. But Roman preoccupation with political affairs outside Palestine would provide Antigonus with his opportunity.

And so in 40 B.C. with the aid of the Parthians, Antigonus attacked and seized Jerusalem, forcing Hyrcanus, Herod, and Antipater to seek refuge in the Maccabean palace. Their doom imminent, they made a futile effort to negotiate a truce. Instead Hyrcanus was taken prisoner, and so Phasael committed suicide. But Herod was able to escape under cover of darkness; he journeyed to Rome where the Senate appointed him to the post "king of the Jews" (cf. Matt. 2:1; et al.). Armed with this new authority, Herod marshaled two Roman legions, and in 37 B.C. he succeeded in forever expelling the Parthians. So began the long and infamous reign of Herod (see Map 78).

Reigning at Jerusalem for thirty-three years (37-34 B.C.), Herod was anything but a passive ruler. Knowing full well how much he was hated by his Jewish constituency, Herod sought to ameliorate his position by providing work, by assessing equitable taxes, and by marrying the Jewess Mariamne. And one cannot deny that Jerusalem largely enjoyed peace and prosperity during his reign.

Herod transformed the external aspect of Jerusalem. He transferred the seat of government to the southwestern hill; here he erected a lavish palace, a xystus (arena) for athletic contests, a theater, and a vast aqueduct network. The Idumean's other building projects concerned the Temple hill. He transformed the old Maccabean fortress (baris) into a much larger structure and named it Antonia, in honor of the triumvir Mark Antony. In the Temple area proper, he enlarged the esplanade on both the north and south sides, giving it a rectangular shape. The Temple's construction was undertaken in 20 B.C., and it was not completed until about A.D. 64, just six years prior to its demolition by Titus (cf. John 2:20). Its dimensions were approximatley 2,500 feet by 1,000 feet, with two concentric courts giving added dimension to the structure. The outer court, called the Gentile court, was the only area where non-Jews might enter. Archaeology has yielded up two Greek inscriptions warning Gentiles not to enter the inner court. The inner court had three subdivisions: one for men, one for women, and one for priests and Levites. Surrounding the Temple hill, a massive wall of huge stones was constructed. A portion of the western perimeter of this wall still stands today, known as the "wailing wall."

Soon after the death of Herod and the banishment of his son, Jerusalem and Judea were made a separate province of the Roman Empire, ruled over by Roman procurators, the fifth of whom was Pontius Pilate. Apart from the visit of Jesus to Jerusalem with His parents (Luke 2:41-52), all associations of Jesus with Jerusalem were contemporary with Pilate.

In the year A.D. 66, full-scale war erupted against Rome (see Map 92 and accompanying text). Initially repelled by the Jewish insurgents in A.D. 70, Titus ordered the construction of a siege wall to blockade the city tightly, weakening its inhabitants through hunger. He then directed a vicious assault upon the Antonia fortress in which his soldiers scaled the wall and entered the Temple precinct, which they burned in a great conflagration. Most of Jerusalem's citizens who had not already died of starvation were killed, though a few were kept as slaves. The city was leveled, except for the three Towers of Herod, which were spared to provide defenses for the tenth Roman legion.

MODERN JERUSALEM

MAP 76

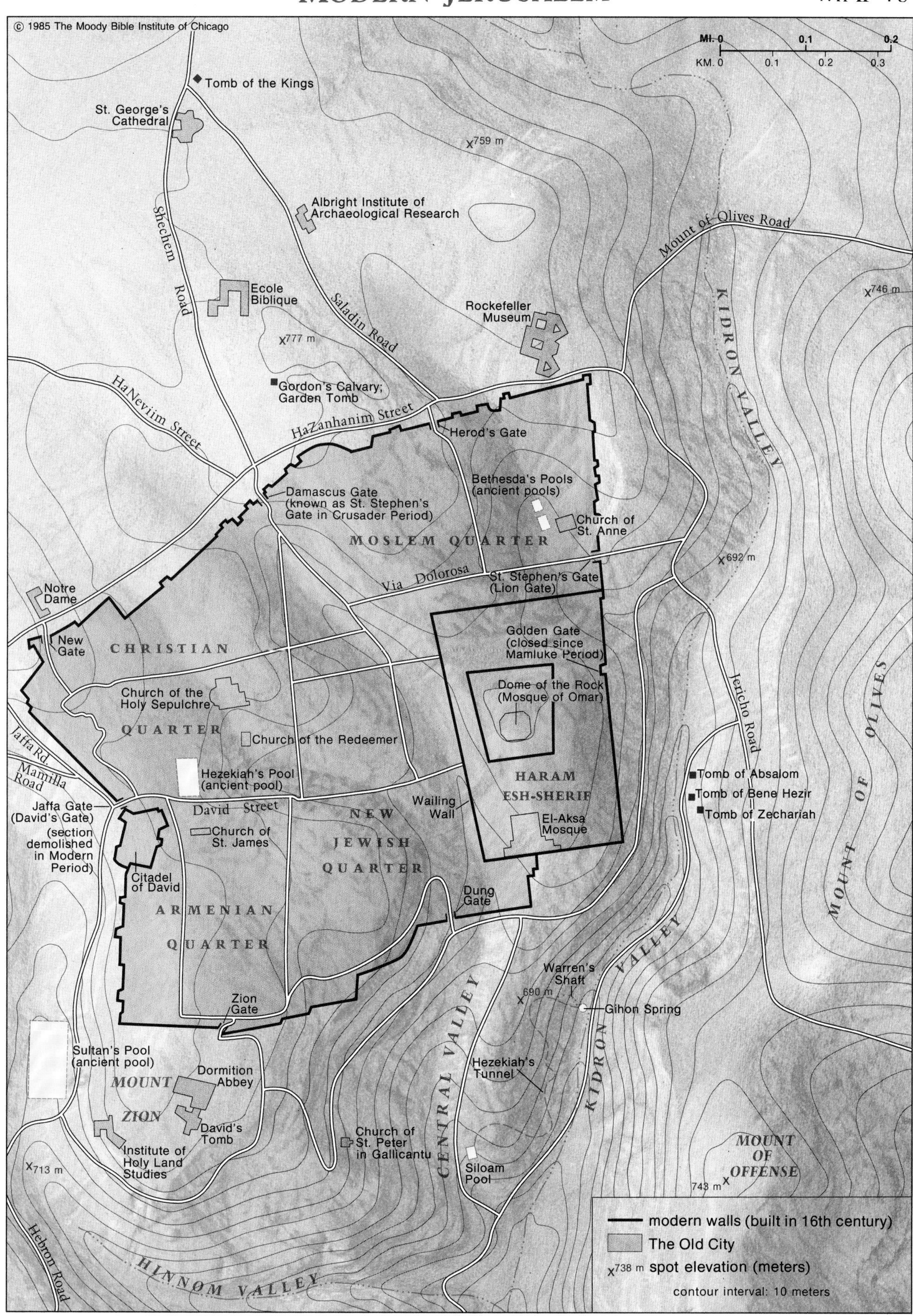

THE ROMAN EMPIRE

"No other state fills so large a place in the history of the world as Rome. It was the achievement of this city to unite all the Mediterranean basin in a great empire under a single government and to unite the nations of this region in many ways. For centuries civilized people from Scotland to Persia paid their taxes into the same treasury, were tried by the same law, were protected by the same armies, and enjoyed a more profound and real peace—the *pax Romana*—than any other time ....

"This achievement was made possible by geography and able diplomacy, generalship, organization, government, and character. The Roman genius, for example, is best shown in the creation of a body of law, which for its completeness and excellence must be considered one of the greatest legislative works of the human race. After many centuries of development, it is true, the empire declined and finally fell into pieces, but from the fragments great modern states, such as England, France, and Italy, have grown, and its civilization in a modified form has passed into modern life."[40]

The expansion of the Roman Empire was a gradual and sometimes involuntary movement. It began as early as c. 240 B.C., when Sicily, Sardinia, and Corsica were annexed. Macedonia, Tripolitania, and Achaia were engulfed by 145 B.C.; but in the next century Rome succeeded in adding Asia, Bithynia and Pontus, Cilicia, Syria,

MAP 77

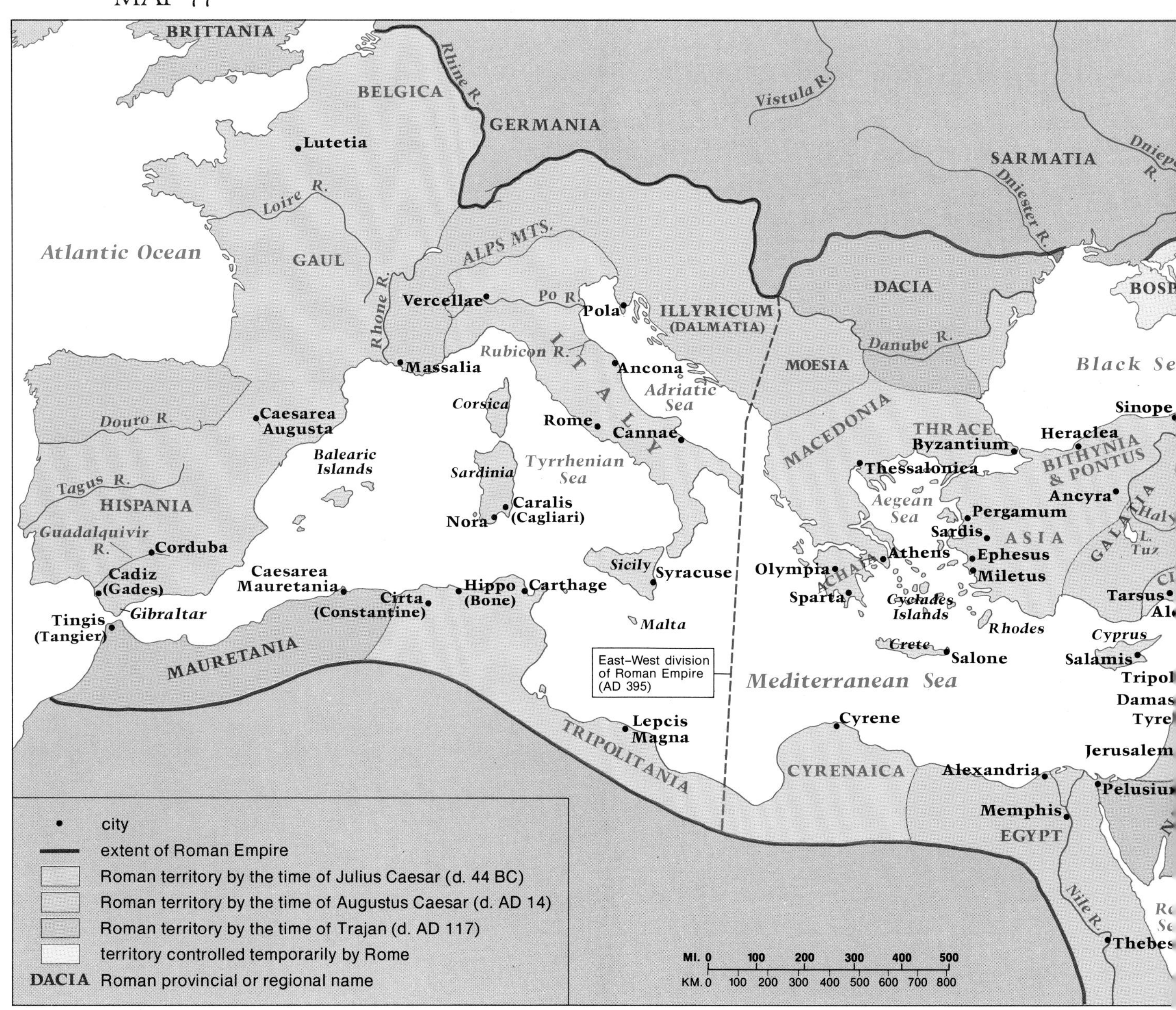

Cyrenaica, Gaul, Belgica, and parts of Hispania. The days of Augustus Caesar saw the provinces of Egypt, Judea, Galatia, Armenia, and Illyricum added to the Empire. Claudius vanquished Mauretania, Brittania, and Dacia; Trajan annexed Nabatea. The mountainous territory between the Black and Caspian seas and the expansive region of Mesopotamia were later acquired, but held only temporarily by Rome.

Historians declare that in the time of the New Testament, Rome could field a minimum of twenty-five legions; when at full strength, each legion included six thousand officers and troops, with an equal number of native auxiliary troops. Many of those troops would be eyewitnesses to the shedding of Jewish blood and even more to the slaughter of Christians.

Rise of Herod the Great

Herod the Great was one of the few non-Roman individuals in the Roman period who achieved extraordinary political status. Appointed "king of the Jews," Herod succeeded in liberating Jerusalem in his 38-37 B.C. campaign, and his control of Judea was complete.

Herod's embellishments of Jerusalem have been discussed (see pp. 163-64). But the Idumean was no less active outside his capital. Having received from Caesar Augustus the hamlet of Strato's Tower, Herod undertook to create a worthy seat of Roman provincial rule, and he named it Caesarea for his patron. Supported in his strug-

Volga R.
Caspian Sea
CAUCASUS MTS.
COLCHIS
IBERIA
ALBANIA
Cyrus R.
Trapezus
ARMENIA
L. Van
L. Urmia
ADIABENE
Arbela
Dura-Europos
Tigris R.
Ecbatana
Euphrates R.
Ctesiphon
Babylon
Susa
Dumah
Persian Gulf
ARABIAN DESERT
© 1985 The Moody Bible Institute of Chicago

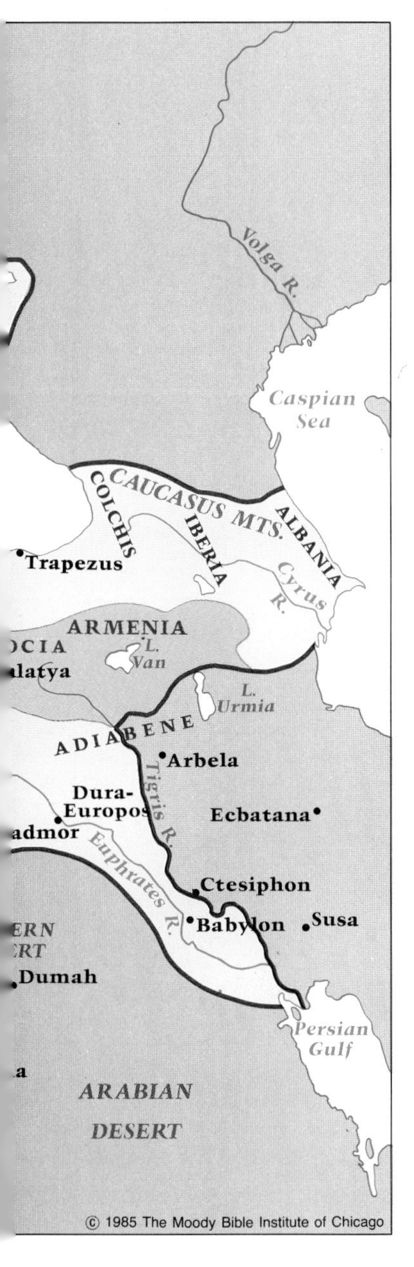

MAP 78

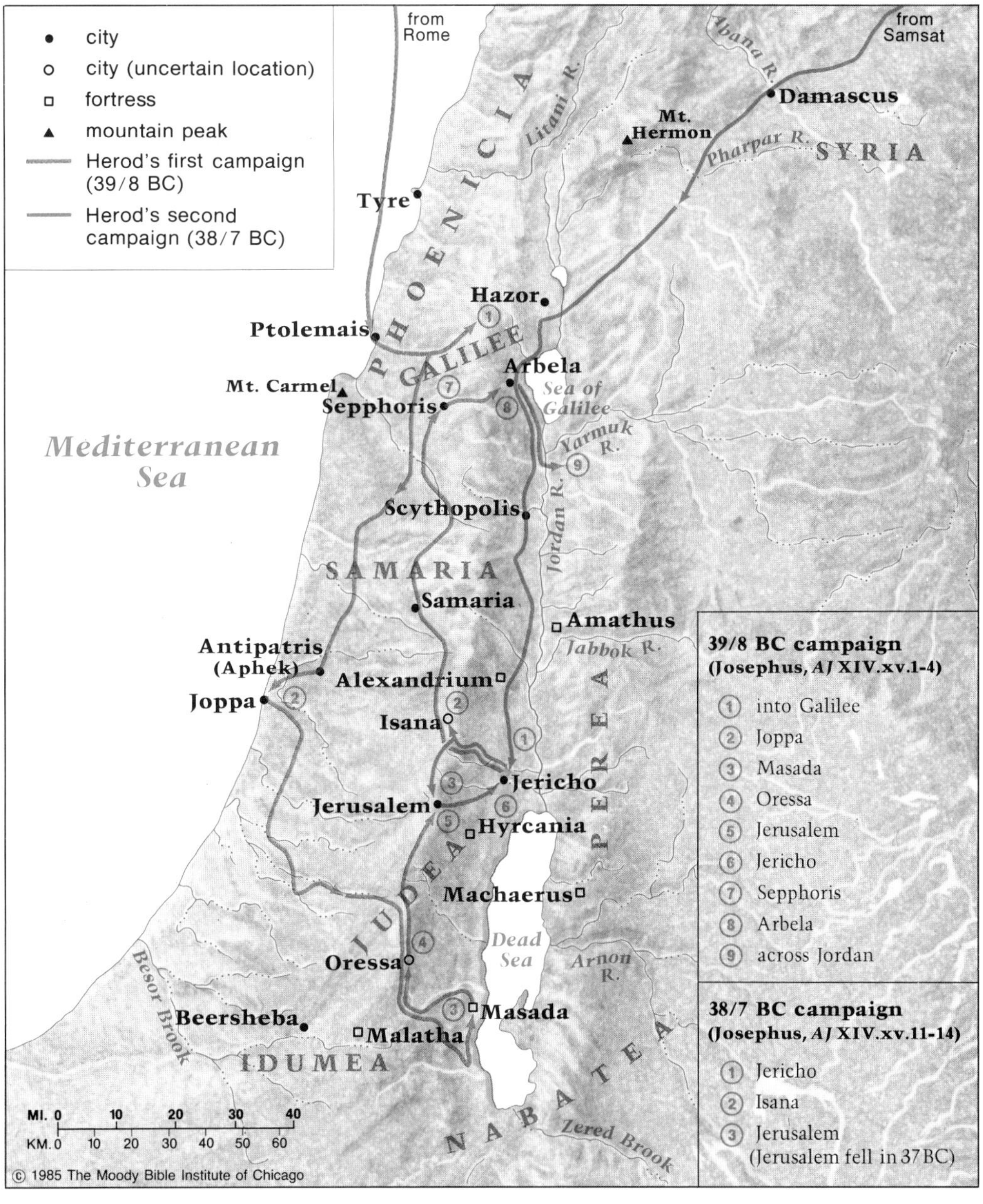
city
city (uncertain location)
fortress
mountain peak
Herod's first campaign (39/8 BC)
Herod's second campaign (38/7 BC)
from Rome
from Samsat
Abana R.
Damascus
Mt. Hermon
Pharpar R.
SYRIA
Litani R.
PHOENICIA
Tyre
Hazor
Ptolemais
GALILEE
Arbela
Mt. Carmel
Sepphoris
Sea of Galilee
Yarmuk R.
Mediterranean Sea
Scythopolis
Jordan R.
SAMARIA
Samaria
Amathus
Jabbok R.
Antipatris (Aphek)
Alexandrium
Joppa
Isana
PEREA
Jericho
Jerusalem
Hyrcania
Machaerus
JUDEA
Dead Sea
Arnon R.
Oressa
Besor Brook
Masada
Beersheba
Malatha
IDUMEA
NABATEA
Zered Brook
MI. 0 10 20 30 40
KM. 0 10 20 30 40 50 60
39/8 BC campaign (Josephus, AJ XIV.xv.1-4)
1 into Galilee
2 Joppa
3 Masada
4 Oressa
5 Jerusalem
6 Jericho
7 Sepphoris
8 Arbela
9 across Jordan
38/7 BC campaign (Josephus, AJ XIV.xv.11-14)
1 Jericho
2 Isana
3 Jerusalem (Jerusalem fell in 37 BC)
© 1985 The Moody Bible Institute of Chicago

KINGDOM OF HEROD THE GREAT

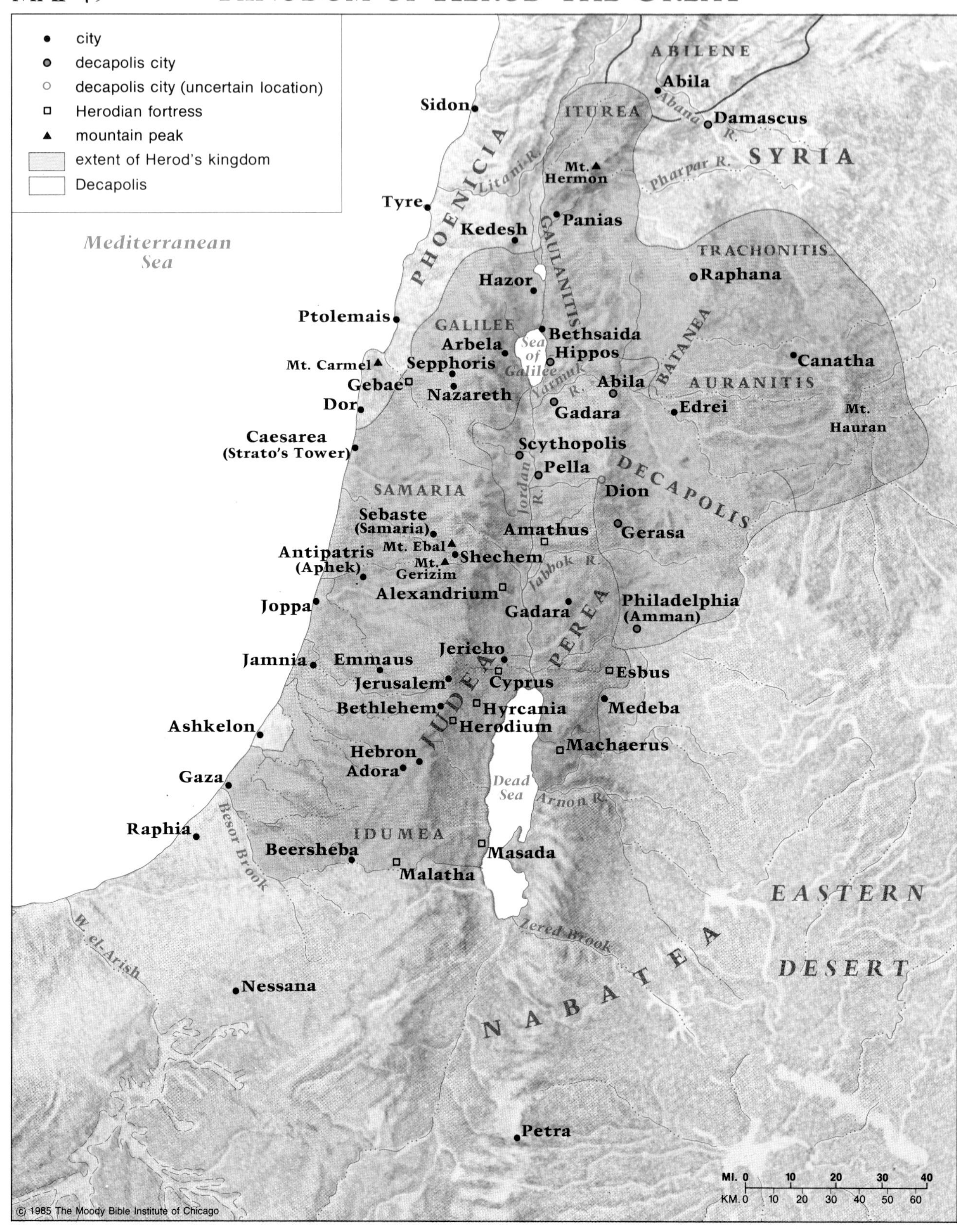

gles to win Judea by the city of Samaria, Herod enlarged and strongly fortified this metropolis in the heartland of his domain, renaming it Sebaste. Herod also constructed or enlarged fortresses throughout his kingdom: Alexandrium, Cyprus, Hyrcania, Herodium, Masada, Malatha, Amathus, Esbus (Heshbon), and Machaerus. Finally, Herod raised an immense shrine at Hebron, over the place memorialized as the burial spot of the patriarchs.

JESUS' EARLY YEARS

Surely even the wrath of men praises God (cf. Ps. 76:10). This appears to be an apt description of the circumstances surrounding the birth of Jesus Christ. We are informed that Caesar Augustus issued a decree for a census to be taken of the whole Roman world, a census that would make it necessary for Joseph, then residing in Nazareth, to journey some seventy miles to the Judean hamlet of Bethlehem to be enrolled there, because he was from David's lineage. So it was that while he was in Bethlehem with his betrothed wife, Mary, that the time of her delivery arrived (Luke 2:1-7) (1). God had used the decree of a Roman Caesar to make possible a scenario in which Jesus would be born in Bethlehem, precisely in fulfilment of what the prophet Micah had foretold so many years before (Mic. 5:2).

Acting according to Mosaic prescription (Lev. 12:2-8), Jesus' parents piously brought Him to Jerusalem about forty days after His birth and presented Him there to be consecrated to the Lord (Luke 2:22-24) (2), after which they returned to Bethlehem. But when magi from the East came to Herod at Jerusalem with the troubling inquiry concerning the whereabouts of a newborn "king of the Jews," they were dispatched to Bethlehem where they found and worshiped the child (Matt. 2:1-11).

Warned of the impending treachery of Herod, Joseph took Mary and Jesus and fled from Bethlehem under the cover of darkness and journeyed to Egypt (Matt. 2:13-14) (3). Later, upon learning of Herod's death, Joseph brought his family out of Egypt, presumably with the intention of returning once again to the environs of Bethlehem. But he discovered that one of Herod's sons had ascended to his father's throne. And so Joseph, directed by God to withdraw to Galilee, brought his wife and son to Nazareth (Matt. 2:19-23) (4).

It was in the sleepy Galilean village of Nazareth that Jesus grew to manhood. At the age of twelve, He was taken for a second time to Jerusalem, this time to celebrate the Passover (5). At the conclusion of the feast, Jesus' parents traveled northward a day's journey, possibly to the vicinity of Lebonah. They supposed He was in the caravan

MAP 80

returning to Galilee but discovered Him missing. Whereupon they returned to Jerusalem and found Jesus in the Temple, sitting among learned teachers who were astonished at His wisdom (Luke 2:41-47). He returned with His parents to Nazareth, though, where He remained for the balance of the "silent years."

Jesus was about thirty years old when He began His public ministry (Luke 3:23). It appears that the public ministry of Jesus and John the Baptist commenced in the fifteenth year of Tiberias Caesar (c. A.D. 27-28) (Luke 3:1). Although John according to tradition had been born in the Judean town of En-karim, just southwest of Jerusalem, his preaching and baptizing efforts were concentrated in the Jordan River valley, in the vicinity of Aenon (John 3:23) and at Bethany beyond the Jordan (John 1:28; cf. 3:26).

John's fervent denunciation of wickedness would earn him imprisonment and eventual decapitation (Matt. 14:1-12; Mark 6:14-29; Luke 3:18-22), which execution possibly took place within the Herodian fortress at Machaerus. But before that, John would baptize Jesus and thereby inaugurate the Lord's public ministry (Matt. 3:13-17; Mark 1:9-11) (6).

JESUS' MOVE TO CAPERNAUM

When Jesus emerged from the wilderness, having successfully undergone a period of temptation (Matt. 4:1-11), He established the headquarters of His Galilean ministry along the northwestern shore of the Sea of Galilee at the city of Capernaum (*kefr nahum*, "village of Nahum"). Though unwalled and small of size, the Capernaum of Jesus' day was nevertheless a prosperous fishing village. This jewel of the Sea of Galilee was located on the border between the domains of Herod Antipas and Philip the tetrarch, and so it had a customs station. Perhaps it was from such duties there that Matthew was called by the Lord (Mark 2:13-14), just as from the same vicinity He called Andrew and Peter from their fishing profession to become fishers of men (Matt. 4:18-20).

MAP 81

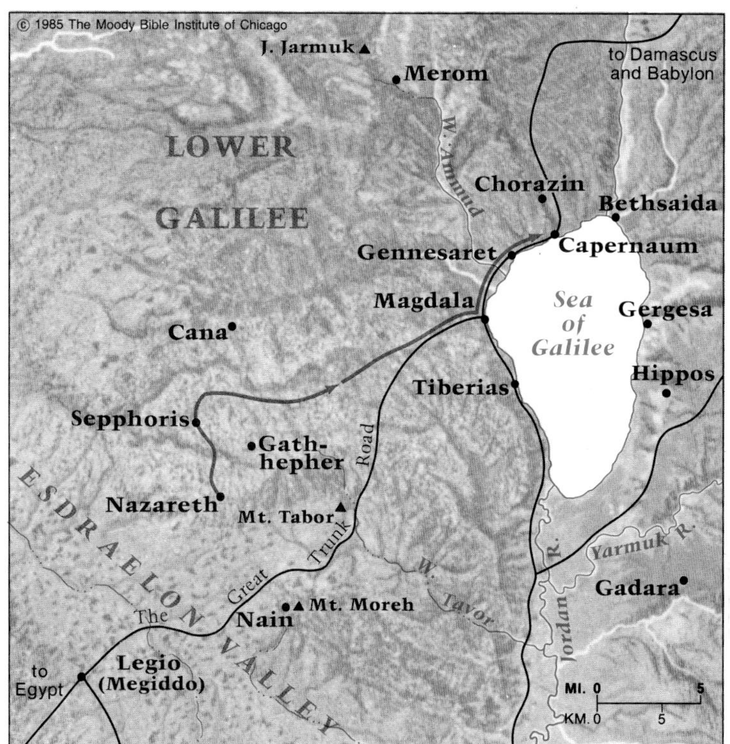

The archaeological remains exhumed from Capernaum have been impressive indeed. These include a synagogue that measures some 65 feet in length. Apparently dating from the third Christian century, the two-storied limestone basilica structure had a gable roof and galleries on three sides for women; benches for the synagogue hierarchy were built into the side walls, and a fountain for ceremonial washings was found in an adjacent portico. The synagogue faces south—in the direction of Jerusalem. The walls of the synagogue galleries were adorned with elaborate ornamentation. Decorations consisted of a frieze picturing a carriage, which is widely interpreted as a depiction of the ark of the law, similar to the Ark of the Covenant. Medallions of leaves encircling various floral and geometic patterns (including the swastika), bunches of grapes, pomegranates, and so forth, also adorned the walls. Immediately to the south of the synagogue has been found an octagonal building now defined as a fifth-century church built over the supposed remains of the apostle Peter's home (cf. Matt. 8:14; Luke 4:38).

Scholars often express puzzlement over Jesus' choice of Capernaum. Did He come to base His ministry in Capernaum because it was not a thoroughly Jewish city? Or did He settle there because this was where His message was readily welcomed? There is undoubtedly a measure of truth in both these ideas, and both differentiated Capernaum from Nazareth, although Christ seems not to have ministered much to the Gentiles of Galilee. But we suggest, moreover, that His reasons for choosing Capernaum may have included geography. Occupied as early as the Early Bronze Age, Capernaum rested astride the international artery of trade (Great Trunk Road) that ultimately linked Egypt and Mesopotamia (see Map 19). Unlike the sleepy, obscure village of Nazareth, Capernaum was at a crucial junction, a conduit if you will, through which coursed a steady stream of humanity from many diverse sectors and countries. Being no isolationist, Jesus perceptively carried His message into Capernaum's alleys and fields, which pulsated with the activities and congestion of internationalism.

One may ponder when considering that the early apostolic movement swept in a northern and western direction from Israel, whereas some of the earliest Christian evidences, and in fact the earliest archaeologically-attested Christian church at Dura-Europos (see Map 93), are to be found in Mesopotamian territory *northeast* of Jerusalem. Ponder, that is, until one realizes that such evidence is but one of the happy consequences of Jesus' astute move to Capernaum.

Many Christians are familiar with the poem entitled "One Solitary Life." This lovely literary piece expounds upon many things that Jesus never did and the many places He never went. But to take another tack, by anchoring His ministry at Capernaum, it became unnecessary for Him to travel great distances, because those who heard and believed His message in Capernaum became instant and far-flung ambassadors, men and women whose vocational travels would carry the message of Christ to the ends of the Roman world.

JESUS' MINISTRY IN GALILEE — MAP 82

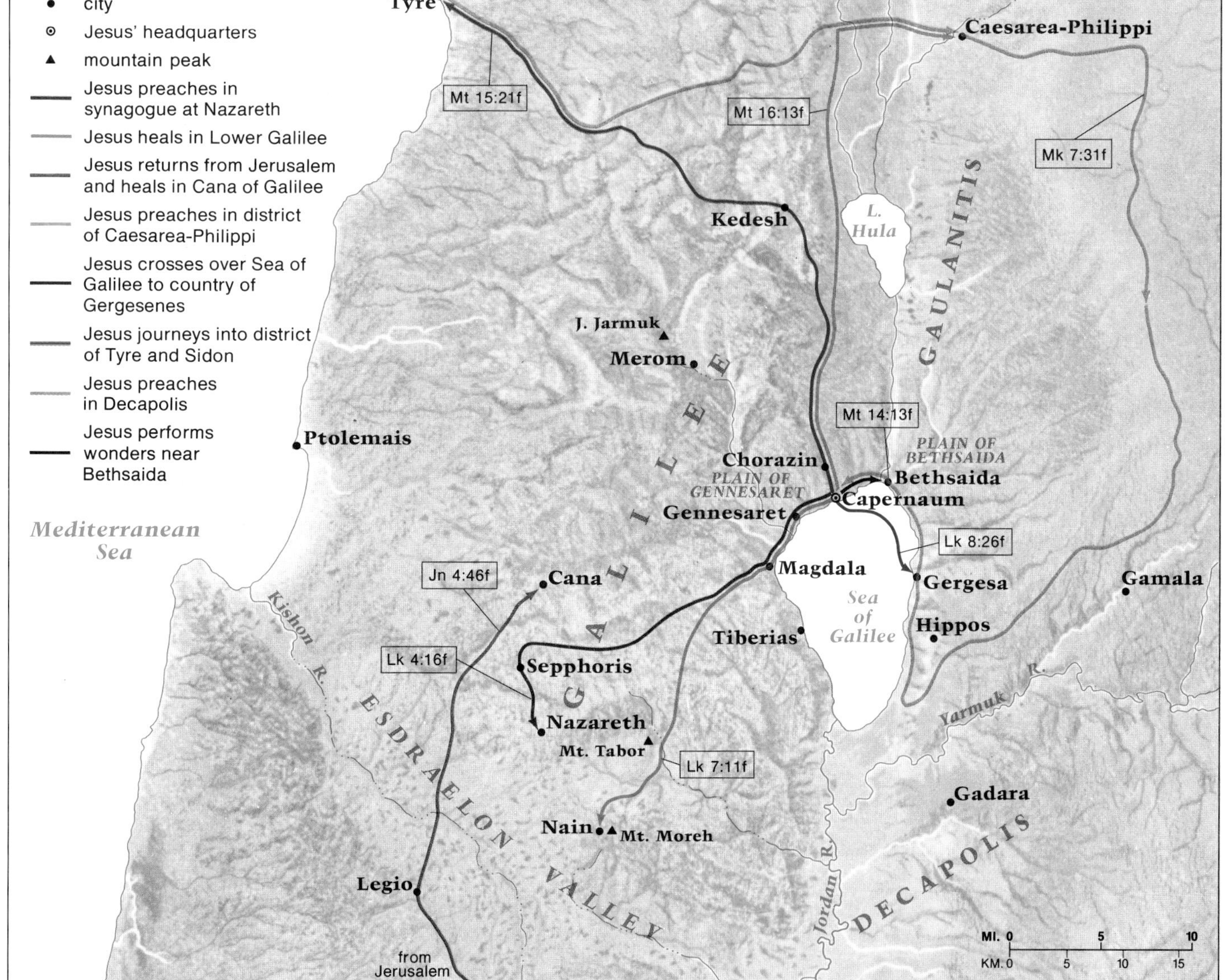

JESUS' MINISTRY IN PALESTINE

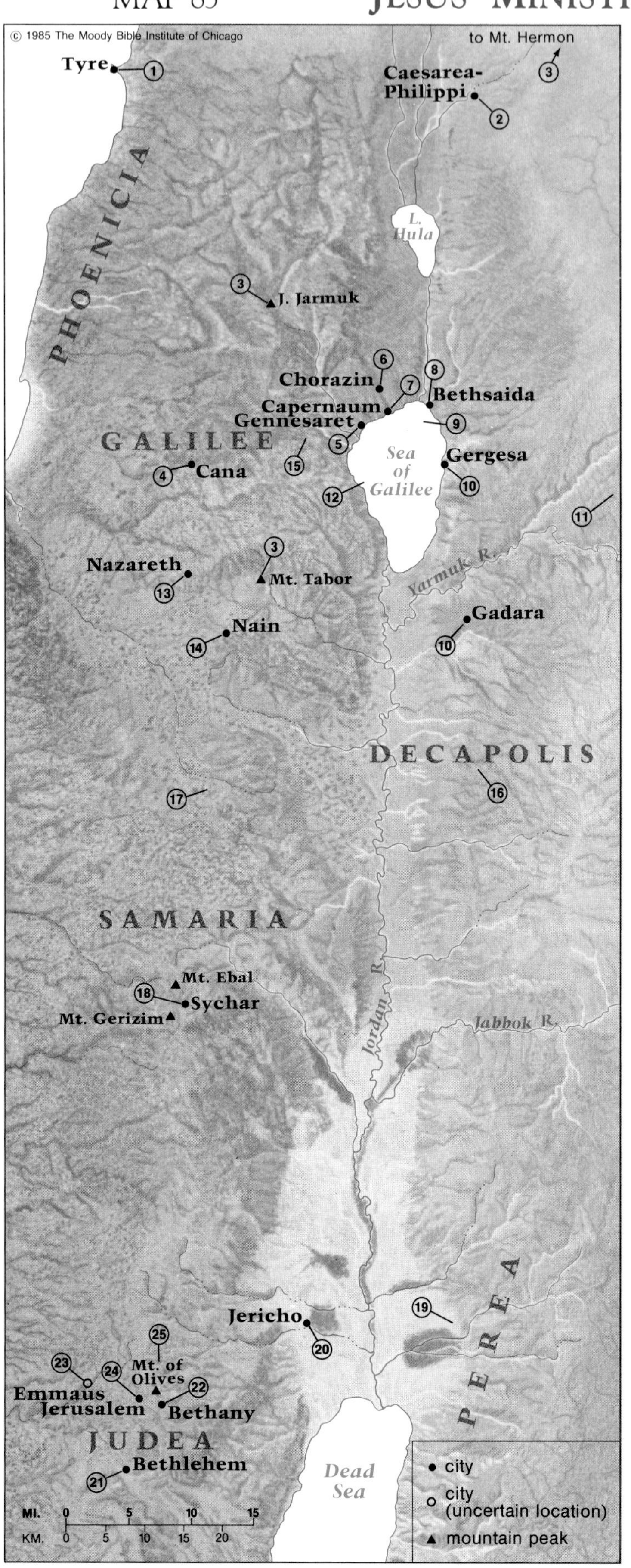

It is impossible to definitively arrange events in the life of Jesus chronologically; hence the present arrangement follows a geographic axis, basically in a north to south order. Because the first gospel book most frequently contains information cited here, synoptic passages are keyed to the book of Matthew, except where not attested there or where more pertinent documentation is available in another gospel.

1. Region of Tyre: Syrophoenician woman's daughter healed—Matt. 15:21-28.
2. Caesarea-Philippi: Peter's great confession—Matt. 16:13-20.
3. Mt. Hermon/Mt. Tabor/J. Jarmuk: (a) possible location of Transfiguration—Matt. 17:1-13; (b) epileptic boy healed nearby—Matt. 17:14-21.
4. Cana of Galilee: (a) water changed to wine—John 2:1-11; (b) Capernaum official's son healed—John 4:46-54.
5. Gennesaret: (a) possible location of feeding of multitudes—Matt. 14:13-21; Matt. 15:32-39; (b) many healings—Mark 6:53-56.
6. Area of Chorazin: (a) judgment pronounced on cities of Chorazin, Bethsaida, and Capernaum—Matt. 11:20-24; (b) possible area of Sermon on Mount—Matt. 5-7.
7. Capernaum: (a) draught of fishes—Luke 5:1-11; (b) demoniac healed—Mark 1:21-28; (c) Sermon on the Mount—Matt. 5-7; (d) Peter's mother-in-law healed—Matt. 8:14-15; (e) centurion's servant healed—Matt. 8:5-13; (f) paralytic healed—Mark 2:1-12; (g) woman with issue of blood healed—Mark 5:25-34; (h) Jairus's daughter raised—Luke 8:40-56; (i) two blind men healed—Matt. 9:27-31; (j) dumb demoniac healed—Matt. 9:32-34; (k) man with withered hand healed—Matt. 12:9-13; (l) blind and dumb demoniac healed—Matt. 12:22-37; (m) tribute provided—Matt. 17:24-27; (n) Bread of Life discourse—John 6:22-59.
8. Bethsaida: (a) possible location of feeding of multitudes—Matt. 14:13-21; Matt. 15:32-39; (b) blind man healed—Mark 8:22-26.
9. Sea of Galilee near Bethsaida: walking on water—Matt. 14:22-33.
10. Gergesa/Gadara: possible location of casting out demons, which enter swine, the swine then rushing down a steep bank and drowning—Luke 8:26-39.

11. Wilderness: temptation—Matt. 4:1-11.

12. Sea of Galilee: storm quieted—Matt. 8:23-27.

13. Nazareth: (a) boyhood home—Matt. 2:19-23; (b) rejected by townspeople—Luke 4:16-30.

14. Nain: widow's son raised—Luke 7:11-17.

15. Galilee: (a) leper cleansed—Mark 1:35-45; (b) post-resurrection appearances—Matt. 28:16-20; cf. John 21:1-22; 1 Cor. 15:7 (disciples).

16. Decapolis: many healings—Matt. 15:29-31; Mark 7:31-37.

17. Between Galilee and Samaria: ten lepers healed—Luke 17:11-19.

18. Sychar: woman at well of Samaria—John 4:1-42.

19. Perea: (a) teachings on marriage—Matt. 19:1-12; (b) possible location of healing of woman with infirmity—Luke 13:10-13; (c) possible location of healing of man with dropsy—Luke 14:1-6.

20. Jericho: (a) Bartimaeus healed—Mark 10:46-52; (b) Zacchaeus converted—Luke 19:1-10.

21. Bethlehem: birthplace—Luke 2:1-20.

22. Bethany: Lazarus raised—John 11:1-44.

23. Emmaus: post-resurrection appearance—Luke 24:13-32 (two men).

24. Jerusalem: (a) discourse with Nicodemus—John 3:1-21; (b) Pool of Bethesda healing—John 5:2-9; (c) woman caught in adultery—John 8:2-11; (d) attempted stoning—John 8:12-59; (e) man blind from birth healed—John 9:1-12; (f) passion week (see Map 75); (g) post-resurrection appearances—John 20:1-18 (Mary Magdalene), 20:19-31 (with and without Thomas).

25. Mt. of Olives: (a) Olivet discourse—Matt. 24:3—25:46; (b) ascension—Acts 1:6-12.

Figure 26 From the site of Jezreel (foreground) Mt. Moreh is visible on the north side of the Jezreel valley. To the west (left) of Mt. Moreh is Nain, where Jesus raised the widow's son.

JESUS' JOURNEYS TO JERUSALEM

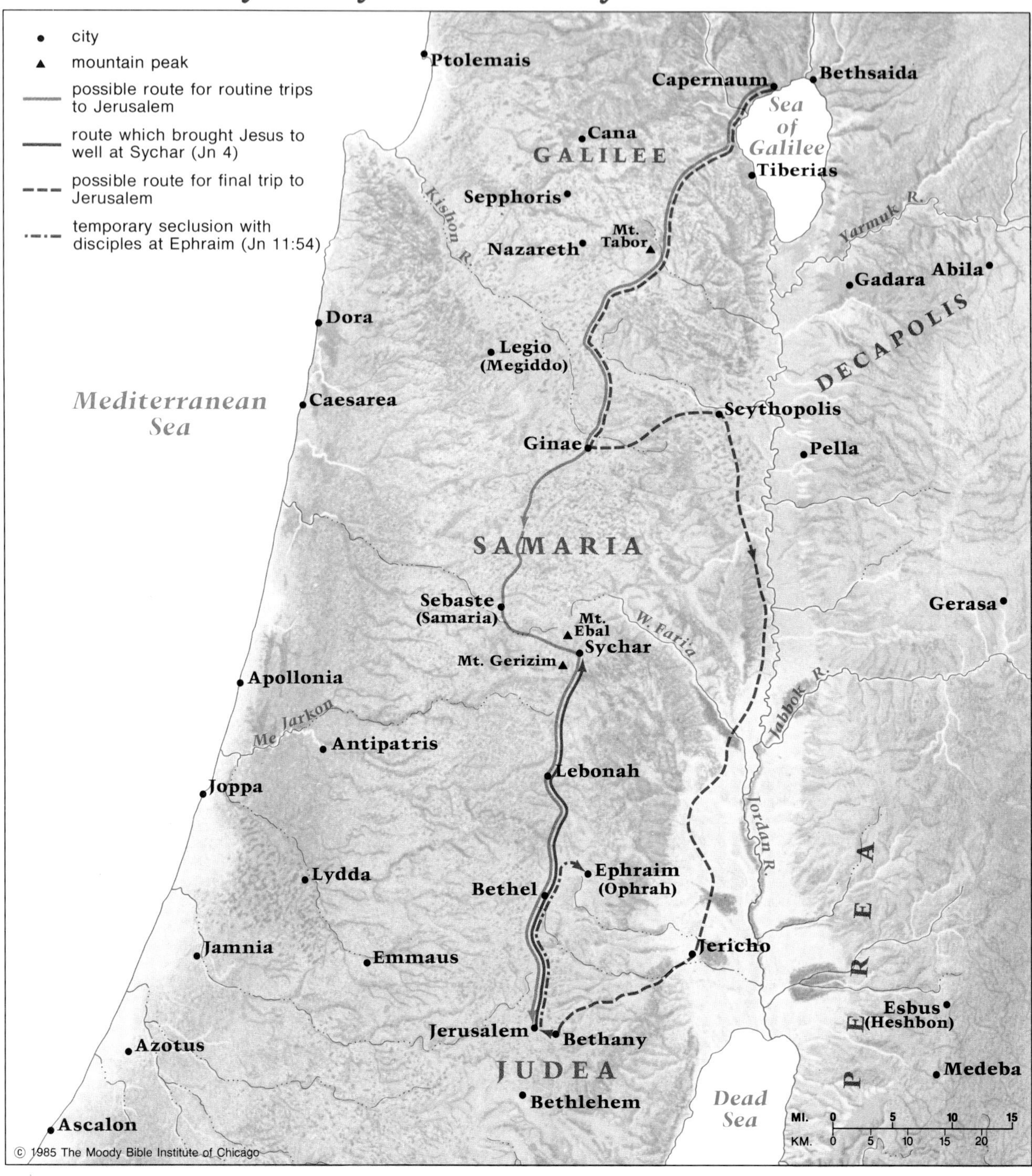

Jesus made numerous trips to Jerusalem during His lifetime; of exactly how many we cannot be sure. The answer may ultimately depend upon the length of Christ's public ministry. Although we are informed that Jesus was approximately thirty years old when He inaugurated His ministry (Luke 3:23), such information concerning the duration of our Lord's labors is nowhere disclosed in the gospels. New Testament scholars traditionally infer that He ministered for about three years, because the gospel of John records His attendance in Jerusalem at three separate Passovers (2:13; 6:4-5; 11:55-56). We must remember, however, that the Bible documents Jesus' attendance at only one Passover before age thirty (Luke 2:41-42), yet that same passage categorically states that Joseph and Mary fastidiously attended the Passover every year. Surely by cultural prescription and personal inclination, Jesus would have accompanied His parents on those occasions. But John tells us that he could not record in his gospel *everything* that Jesus did and said (John 20:30). And then, of course, healthy adult male Jews were required to make pilgrimages to Jerusalem three times annually—Passover, Pentecost, Ingathering. Accordingly, it seems prudent to leave open the question of how many trips Jesus may have made to Jerusalem throughout His ministry.

"It was the custom of the Galileans [in the time of Jesus]," states the historian Josephus, "when they came to the holy city at the festivals, to take their journeys through the country of the Samaritans; at this time there lay, in the road they took, a village that was called Ginae, which was situated in the limits of Samaria and the great plain."[41] The name *Ginae* is reflected in the modern city of Jenin, also located where the Esdraelon valley gives way to the mountains of Samaria. This means that the Jewish pilgrims of Galilee would have utilized a direct route to Jerusalem, passing the cities of Sebaste, Lebonah, and Bethel on the way. One might surmise that Jesus also used the direct route when routinely journeying to the holy city. He certainly returned northward along that route on one occasion; for it was at the well of Sychar that Jesus met with the woman of Samaria and discussed with her the nature of true religion (John 4:3-6).

On what would be His final trip from Galilee to Jerusalem, it appears that Jesus again intended to take the direct route. But He and His disciples were refused passage at a certain Samaritan village (Luke 9:51-56). We are not informed of the identity of that village, but only a few years later a bloody incident took place at Ginae between Samaritans and Jewish pilgrims going to Jerusalem.[42]

This latter episode is at least indicative of the treacherous hostilities that existed between Jews and Samaritans, and it suggests for us why pilgrims normally traveled in caravan style (cf. Luke 2:44).

In any event, Jesus and His disciples were required to take another road and bypass Samaritan territory on the final trip to Jerusalem. That route eventually brought them past the cities of Jericho (Matt. 19:1; 20:29; Mark 10:1, 46) and Bethany (John 11:1). At the latter location, Jesus raised His friend Lazarus from the dead. This miracle engendered such opposition from the religious establishment that Jesus went into temporary seclusion with some disciples at the town of Ephraim (John 11:54), until His time had fully come.

JEWISH DIASPORA AT PENTECOST — MAP 85

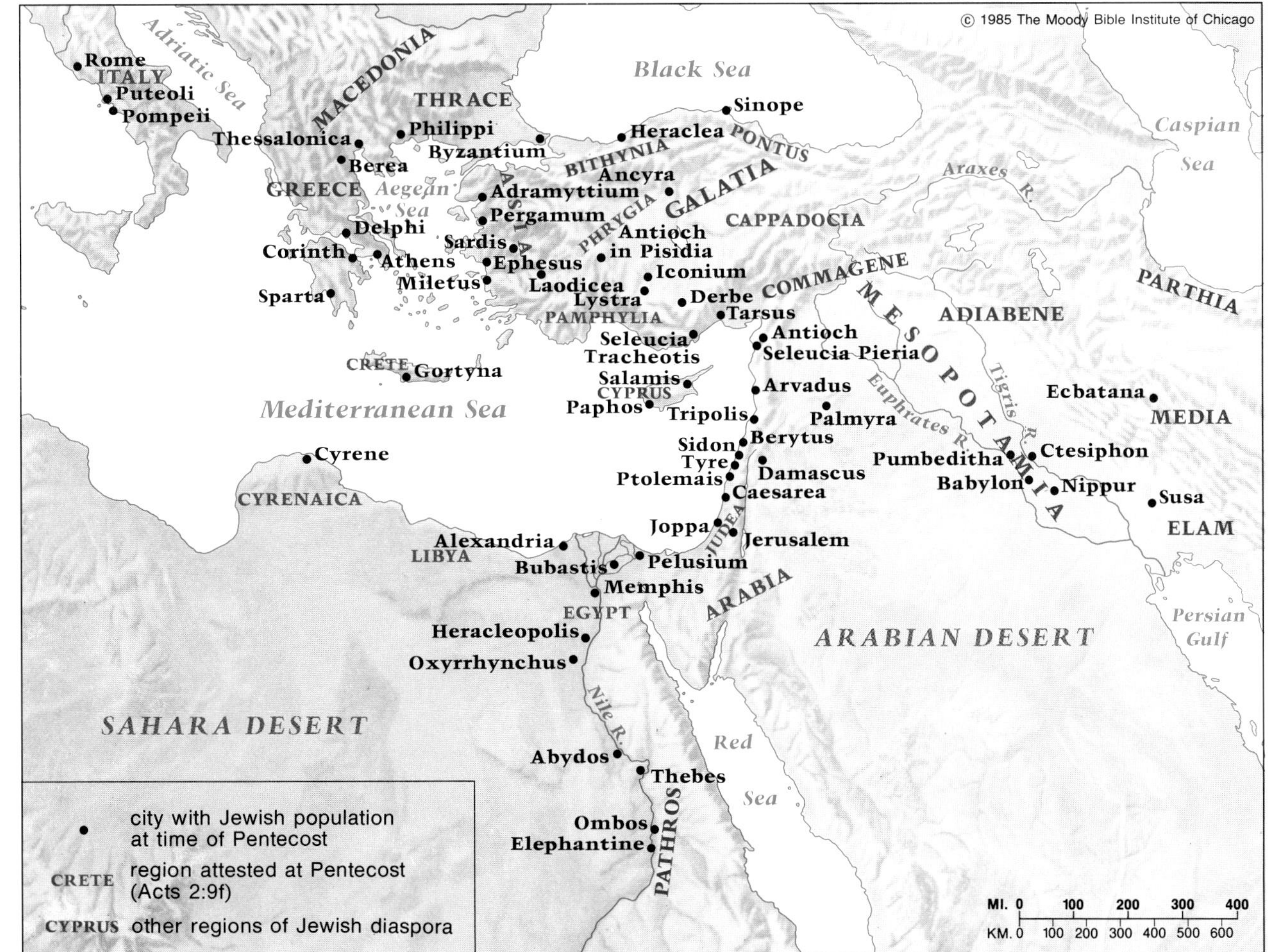

MAP 86 MINISTRY OF PETER AND PHILIP

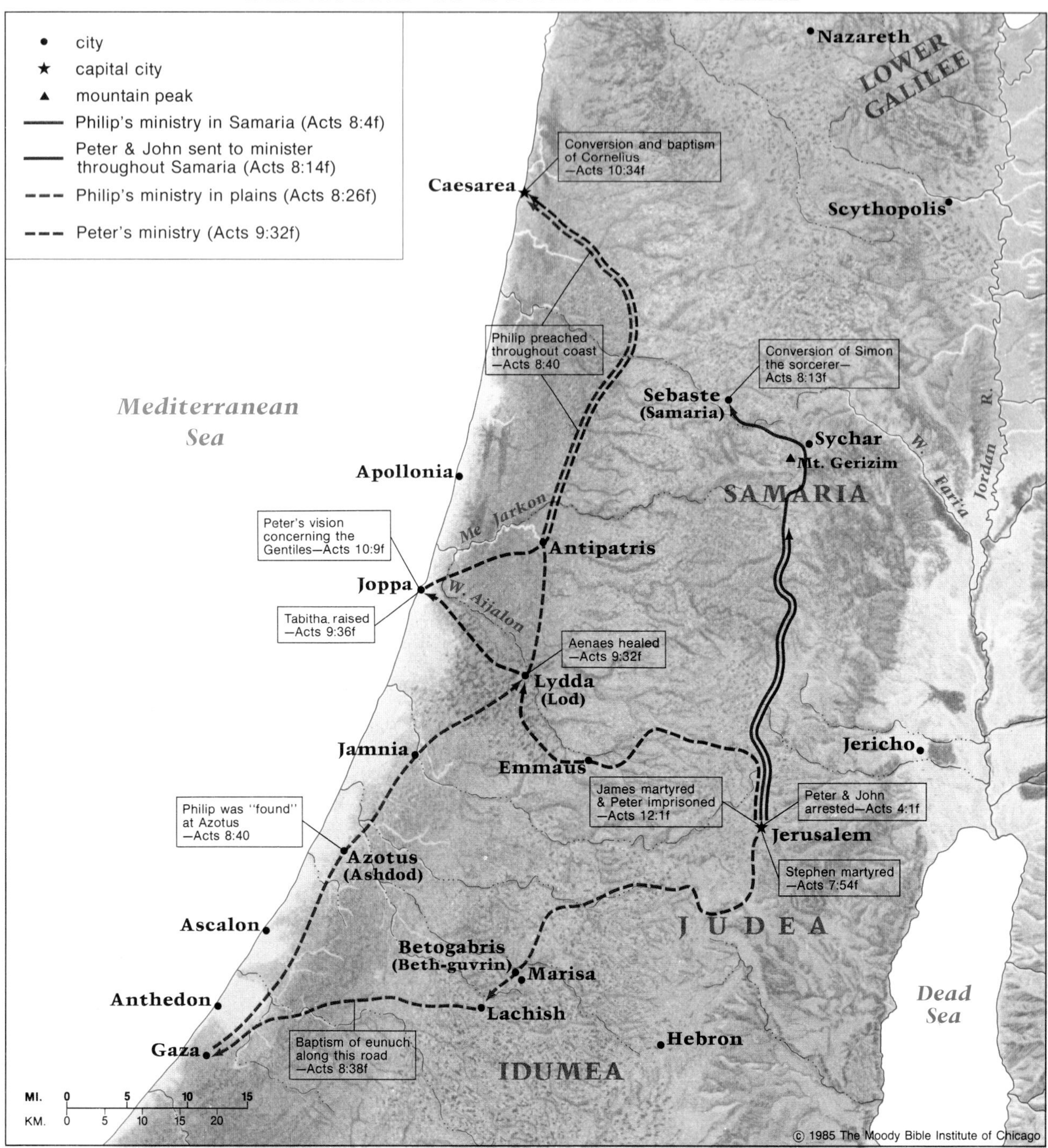

PAUL'S EARLY TRAVELS

The distances traveled by the apostle Paul are nothing short of staggering. In point of fact, the New Testament registers the equivalent of about 13,400 airline miles that the great apostle journeyed; and if one takes into account the circuitous roads he necessarily had to employ at times, the total distance traveled would exceed that figure by a sizeable margin. Moreover, it appears that the New Testament does not document all of Paul's excursions. For example, there seems to have been an unchronicled visit to Corinth (2 Cor. 12:14; 13:1); he refers to shipwrecks of which we have no record (2 Cor. 11:25); and there was his desire to tour Spain (Rom. 15:24, 28), though it is still debated whether or not he ever succeeded in that mission.

Considering the means of transportation available in the Roman world, the average distance traveled in a day, the primitive paths, and rugged, sometimes mountainous terrain over which he had to venture, the sheer expenditure of the apostle's physical energy becomes unfathomable for us. Many of those miles carried Paul through unsafe and hostile environs largely controlled by bandits who eagerly awaited a prey (cf. 2 Cor. 11:26). Accordingly, Paul's commitment to the Lord entailed a spiritual vitality that was inextricably joined to a superlative level of physical stamina and fearless courage.

The following is a list of Paul's journeys, with approximate mileage for each:

1. Acts 9:1-30. Jerusalem-Damascus-(Arabia)-Jerusalem-Tarsus—690 miles (excluding his trip into the desert, the distance of which cannot be calculated [cf. Gal. 1:17-19]; see Map 87).
2. Acts 11:25-26. Tarsus-Antioch—90 miles (see Map 87).
3. Acts 11:30—12:25 (cf. Gal. 2:1-10). Antioch-Jerusalem-Antioch—560 miles (see Map 87).
4. Acts 13:4—14:28. First missionary journey—1,400 miles (see Map 88).
5. Acts 15:12-30. Antioch-Jerusalem-Antioch—560 miles (see Map 87).
6. Acts 15:39—18:22. Second missionary journey—2,800 miles (see Map 88).
7. Acts 18:23—21:17. Third missionary journey—2,700 miles (see Map 89).
8. Acts 27:1—28:16. The apostle journeyed as a prisoner to Rome—2,250 miles (see Map 90).
9. Following a two-year imprisonment (Acts 28:30), the apostle traveled widely throughout the Roman Empire, including Crete (Titus 1:5), Troas (2 Tim. 4:13), Macedonia (1 Tim. 1:3), and Nicopolis (Titus 3:12), before he was imprisoned for a second time in Rome (2 Tim. 1:16-17; 4:6)—2,350 miles (following the shortest possible itinerary).

MAP 87

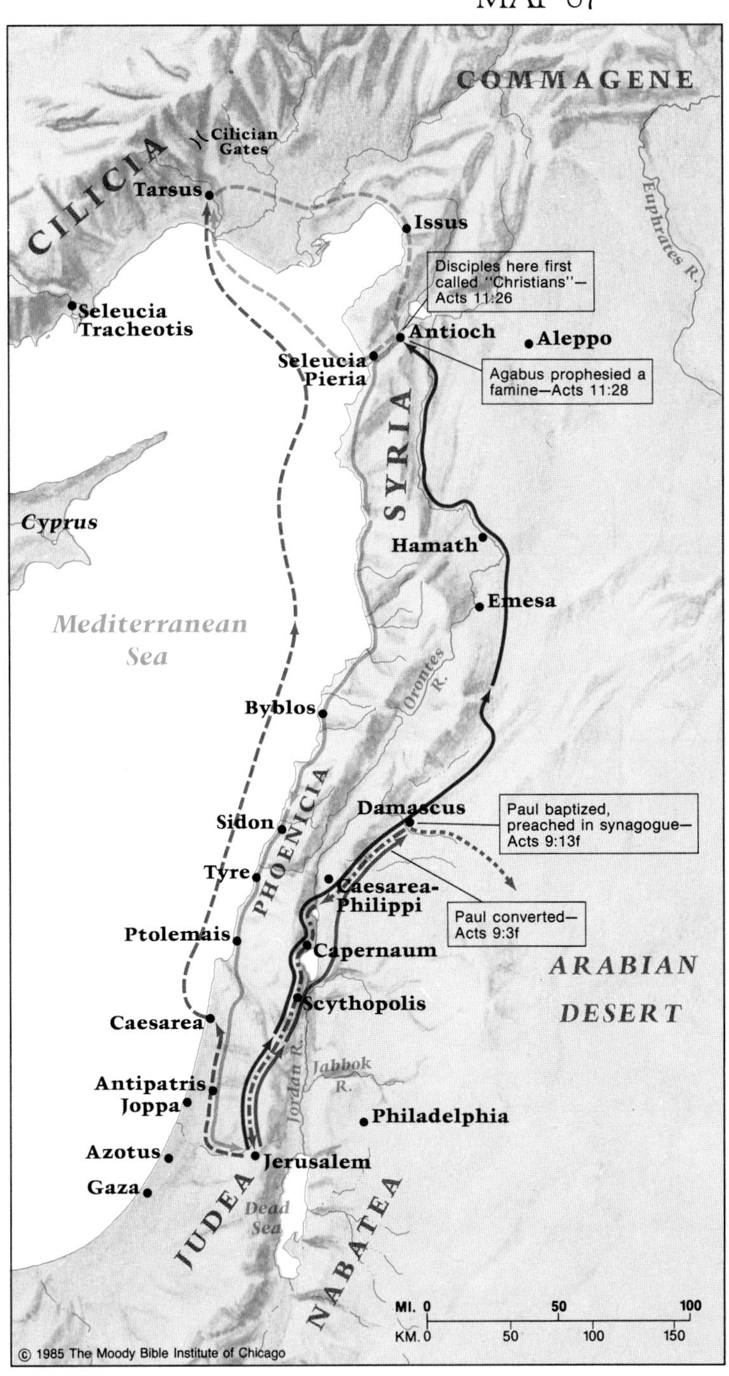

• city

mountain pass

Paul (Saul) commissioned to journey to Damascus and seek out Christians (Acts 9:1f)

Paul spent time in Arabia (Gal 1:17)

Paul returned to Jerusalem and was received by disciples (Acts 9:26f)

Paul fled from Hellenists (Acts 9:28f)

Barnabas journeyed to Tarsus and returned to Antioch with Paul (Acts 11:25f)

Paul & Barnabas sent to Jerusalem with aid for believers amidst famine (Acts 11:29f)

Paul & Barnabas returned to Antioch, joined by John Mark (Acts 12:25)

Paul's Missionary Journeys

To suggest that the story of the early church as told in the book of Acts owes much of its shape to a pagan Macedonian monarch, Seleucus I (Nicator), sounds initially rather far-fetched. Closer inspection of certain details, however, discloses that at the human level this very well may be the case. Seleucus was one of Alexander the Great's foremost generals, who gradually came to rule most of the Asiatic provinces that had been part of Alexander's vast domain. At his inauguration of the Seleucid era, Seleucus founded a number of metropolitan areas, including the city of Antioch. He gave the Jews large tracts of land in the vicinity of Antioch because a large Jewish contingency had assisted him in his victory at the Battle of Ipsus, which opened Asia to his command. More important, however, Seleucus offered citizenship to Jewish individuals, and he granted them privileges equal to those afforded Macedonians and Greeks. Later, as economic and political interests brought Rome to Asia, Antioch became the capital city and military headquarters for the entire Asian province. When other Antiochian citizens implored the Romans to revoke citizenship for Jews, their pleadings went unheeded, strangely enough, and Jews retained their favored status in Antioch.[43]

Therefore, a situation obtained in which Rome was vigorously engaged in crushing Jewish insurrection in Judea and Jerusalem while simultaneously proclaiming free citizenship for Jews residing at Antioch. Not astonishingly, there developed a large and well-established Jewish population in Antioch by the middle of the first Christian century, and the city contained many Greek-speaking synagogues (cf. Acts 6:5). At the same time, because it was the Roman administrative center, Antioch enjoyed a sizeable non-Jewish population with a cosmopolitan and eclectic interest in philosophical and religious inquiry, as well as a high level of public order and police protection. All of those factors combined to create a pervasive atmosphere in Antioch in which the Christian message could be spontaneously received and safely propagated.

Faced with recurring persecution after Stephen's death, early Christians scattered to other regions, including Phoenicia, Cyprus, and Antioch, where they found safe refuge. When some of those early unnamed missionaries proclaimed the Christian gospel in Antioch, great numbers believed and turned to the Lord. As rumors of widespread conversions reached the church in Jerusalem, the elders sent Barnabas to Antioch to report on affairs there. Seeing that the work flourished, Barnabas journeyed to Tarsus, where he located Paul and brought him to the Syrian metropolis to assist in instructing new converts. So strong and effective did that emerging movement become that disciples of Jesus were first called "Christians" at Antioch. Later, when famine spread across parts of western Asia, it was the fellowship at Antioch that sent assistance to the believers in Jerusalem (Acts 11:19-24). Consequently, it comes as no surprise that it was this prominent Christian base that commissioned all three missionary journeys of Paul.

The initial mission saw Paul and Barnabas, supported by John Mark, sail from Seleucia Pieria, the Mediterranean port of Antioch, to Cyprus, where the apostle established a personal ministerial pattern: he preached on the Sabbath in a synagogue, in this case at Salamis (Acts 13:4-5). Having traversed the island as far as Paphos with their message, they were summoned by the Roman proconsul who desired to hear the Word of God. At this point the narrative records the first opposition to the apostle and the first conversion to his message. It seems that a magician named Bar-Jesus, who was a false prophet, sought to confound Paul's message and dissuade the proconsul. But God's messenger withstood him to the face, and Bar-Jesus was smitten with blindness. Seeing what had occurred and being enamored of the gospel, the Roman official became a disciple of Christ.

Paul and his entourage left Cyprus and landed on the mainland of Asia Minor at the inlet of Perga. It was there that John Mark decided to abandon the mission and return to Jerusalem (Acts 13:13). Exactly what motivated Mark to that decision is purely speculative. Perhaps he had growing personal misgivings about working among Gentiles, perhaps he became ill, or perhaps he shrank back from the personal danger that necessarily would have attended travel in the environs of the Taurus Mountains. Whatever the case, Paul and Barnabas proceeded alone to Antioch in Pisidia. That segment of the journey would have taken them to the northern side of the Taurus Mountains. Therefore, they doubtlessly proceeded up the Cestrus (Aksu) River as far as the inland lake district. The dense forestation of the Taurus range coupled with its high altitude made passage any other way impossible.

Again on the Sabbath, Paul preached in the synagogue at Antioch. This time his message so stirred the imagination of his audience that he was invited to speak again on the following Sabbath. On that occasion, however, the apostle was reviled by Jewish leaders, and so he redirected his efforts towards the Gentiles in the region. Many believed Paul's message, a fact that inflamed Jew-

FIRST AND SECOND JOURNEYS

MAP 88

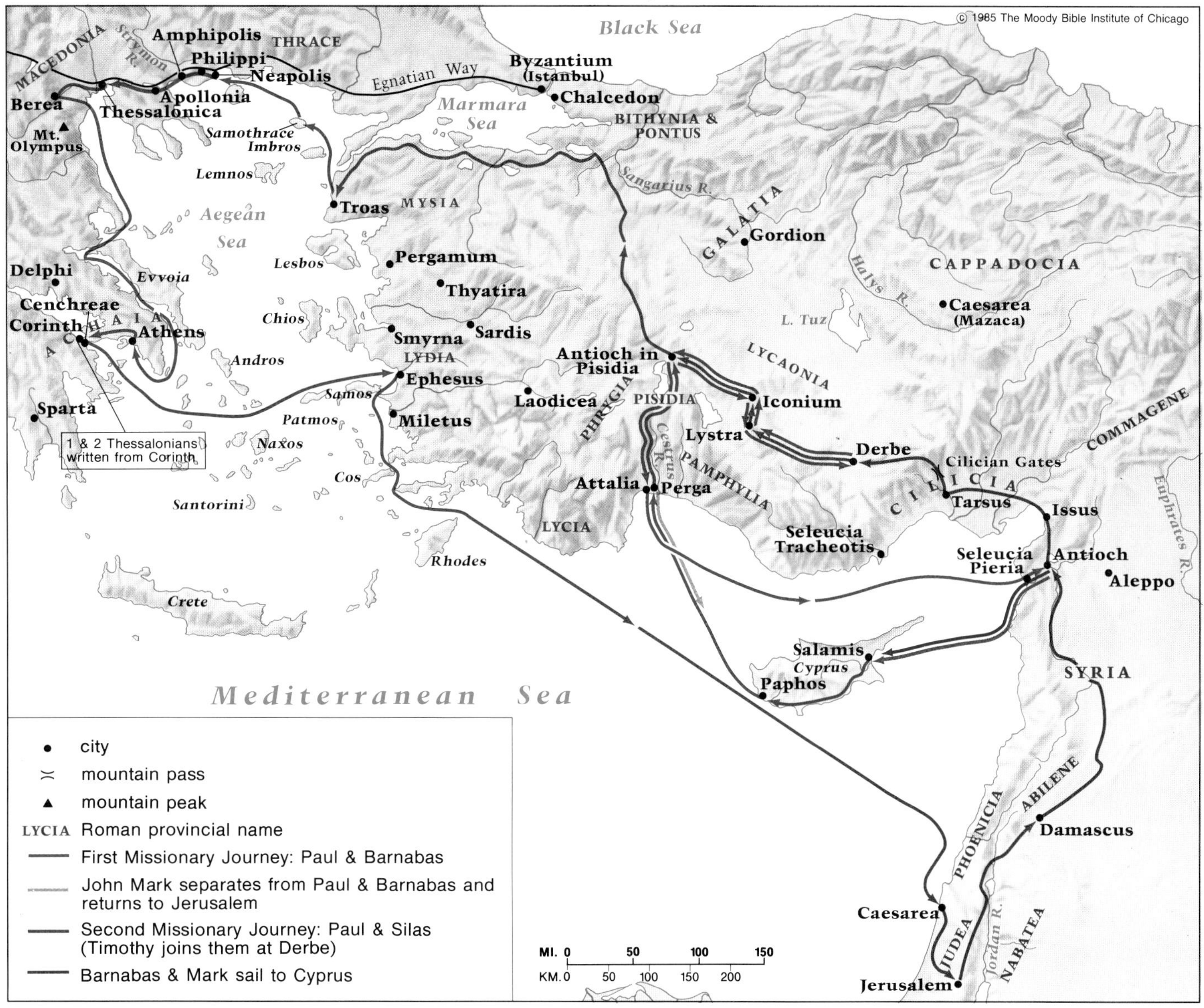

ish hostilities. So the orthodox Jewish leaders insidiously created a disaffection within Antioch, and the two missionaries were driven from the territory (Acts 13:15-50).

Paul and Barnabas then entered the district of Lycaonia where their ministry began at Iconium. In that city, many were captivated by their message, but a plot was contrived to stone them, so they fled to the nearby city of Lystra, an important center of commerce in the eastern Roman world. While they remained there, Paul healed a crippled man; but Jewish zealots from Antioch and Iconium traced the missionaries to Lystra and there persuaded some individuals to help stone Paul. The apostle was dragged out of the city and left for dead (Acts 14:1-19). The final city on the first journey was Derbe, where many disciples were made (Acts 14:20-22). Paul and Barnabas then retraced their steps past Perga to the port city of Attalia, where they boarded a boat and sailed back to Antioch.

After spending some time in Antioch, Paul suggested to Barnabas that they visit their Christian brethren in the cities of the first journey. A sharp disagreement developed between them, however, when Barnabas urged that John Mark accompany them on this second enterprise; Paul, for his part, wanted nothing to do with the idea of taking with them one who earlier had withdrawn from their mission. Therefore, they went their separate ways. Barnabas took Mark and sailed toward Cyprus, his homeland (Acts 4:36), while Paul, relieved of the Cyprian ministry, took Silas and proceeded northward toward Cilicia and Galatia (Acts 15:36-41), passing Issus before coming to his hometown of Tarsus.

A road extended north from Tarsus, and passed the Cilician Gates, a spectacular gorge cut through the Taurus range. Having negotiated that obstacle, Paul and Silas came to Derbe and passed on to Lystra, strengthening believers along the way. In the latter place, they met a young man named Timothy. Timothy's mother and grandmother may have been among Paul's earlier converts at Lystra (2 Tim. 1:5); Timothy himself, in fact, may have become a disciple under Paul's ministry (1 Cor. 4:17; 1 Tim. 1:2). Whatever the case, his reputation among the brethren of the Lycaonian region and his Jewish heritage (his mother was a Jewess) made Timothy a desirable, and eventually an effective, missionary companion of the apostle. So it was that Paul's party, now including Timothy, set out on the Roman road westward, apparently intending to follow the main route toward Ephesus. But when they were "forbidden by the Holy Spirit to speak the word in Asia," they veered north in the direction of Bithynia, passed through the region of Mysia, and came to Troas, a port on the Aegean coast near fabled Troy. It was possibly at Troas that Paul was joined by a Greek physician, Luke, who became his traveling companion and missionary chronicler, and who was also responsible for writing one of the New Testament gospels. It was also at Troas that Paul received a "Macedonian call," an obedient response to which brought the Christian gospel to Europe (Acts 16:1-10).

The missionary sailed from Troas directly to the Macedonian region, spending a night along the way on the island of Samothrace. He passed through the port of Neapolis, a city on the Egnatian Way, en route to Philippi. The Egnatian Way was a transportation artery, the Macedonian extension of the Appian Way, that joined the eastern provinces with Italy. Philippi, the site of Paul's next lengthy stop, was a main center of the Macedonian district. Not more than ten years before the arrival of Paul, the strategic city had been the site of a pivotal battle in the Roman civil war. At Philippi, the forces of Cassius and Marcus Brutus had been decisively defeated by those of Antony and Octavian, which altered the course of the war as a whole and, more important for the expansion of Christianity, led to the creation of an eastern and western sphere within the Roman Empire (cf. Map 77).

Paul sought opportunity to preach on the Sabbath after his arrival at Philippi. His efforts were rewarded when Lydia, a seller of purple goods from the Asian city of Thyatira, believed and was baptized. But when the apostle exorcised the spirit of a slave girl, her owners, who had profited from her strange gift, seized Paul and Silas and had them publicly beaten and imprisoned. But about midnight, as Paul and Silas were praying and singing hymns in the prison, there was a great earthquake, and the missionaries were miraculously delivered from the hands of their enemies. The jailer, supposing that his prisoners had escaped and that he would have to pay the price of their lives with his own, prepared to commit suicide. But Paul called out to him from within the prison, assuring him that not one prisoner had escaped. When the terrified jailer entered Paul's prison cell, he was captivated by the missionary's message and was converted. Whereupon, he took his former prisoners to his home, cared for their physical needs, and was baptized, with all his family.

Figure 27 The Cilician Gates are a series of sharp defiles cut in the Taurus Mts., through which ran the main road from Syria to Asia Minor.

When in the morning the magistrates discovered that they had beaten Roman citizens, they came to Paul and offered their apologies, but requested that he leave Philippi, possibly fearing reprisal if news of the beating were noised abroad (Acts 16).

Paul and his company journeyed along the Egnatian Way as far as the city of Thessalonica, where they found lodging with one Jason. They also found in Thessalonica a synagogue, and there for three successive Sabbaths, Paul mightily expounded the Scriptures concerning Christ. As a result, many believers were added and a church was established. But such a response again aroused the ire of local Jewish leaders, who accused the missionaries of treason and incited a mob to storm the house of Jason. When they were unable to find Paul or Silas inside, the Jews beat Jason himself for harboring the "seditionists." Because of that violent incident and threat of further harm, Paul and his companions left Thessalonica under cover of night and journeyed the short distance to Berea. Their ministry in the synagogue there met with a receptive audience, and it appears that many individuals believed and a sizable church was founded. When news of the Berean ministry reached the ears of some Jews in Thessalonica, however, they came to Berea and sought to harm Paul. Although Silas and Timothy remained behind, presumably to nurture the churches in Macedonia (cf. 1 Thess. 3:1-2), Paul was quickly ushered out of Berea and brought down to the Aegean Sea, where he sailed toward Achaia and Athens (Acts 17:1-15).

As his ship sailed adjacent to the shoreline, Paul might have viewed Mt. Olympus, the mythic home of Zeus, who was the chief god of the Greek pantheon. But it was the myriad of idols composing the entire pantheon that confronted the apostle when he arrived in Athens. Distraught at the bewildering array of deities worshiped in this city, Paul lost no time in debating both in the synagogue and in the Agora (marketplace). On one occasion, he was taken to the Hill of Areopagus, otherwise known as Mars Hill, to deliver a message to some Athenian philosophers. That raised area, located between the Acropolis and the Agora, had been used in bygone days as a seat for the high council of Athens, but by Paul's time it was used only as a forum for philosophical debate. In his eloquent address, which included citations from two Greek poets, Paul sought to argue from a philosophical standpoint that would make his message more attractive to the Greeks. But his ideas concerning resurrection drew sharp criticism, even mocking, from the philosophers, and so Paul left the city of Athens with a few converts but without having founded a church there. The apostle, however, was neither threatened nor dissuaded by the tinge of failure. Rather, he viewed failure as the crucible of progress and triumphantly passed on to the city of Corinth (Acts 17:14—18:1).

Corinth was a sprawling seaport located on the isthmus of Corinth, a narrow neck of land (three-and-a-half miles wide) that offered direct passage between the Aegean and Adriatic seas to merchants and travelers; they could thereby avoid navigating the treacherous Peloponnesus. Nero attempted to build a canal across the Corinthian isthmus, but that did not become a reality until the end of the nineteenth century. As a cosmopolitan center of commerce and trade, Corinth enjoyed lavish prosperity and attracted many unsavory individuals. Such an atmosphere meant that Corinth became a notoriously immoral city (cf. 1 Cor. 5:1; 6:15; 7:1-2). Strabo mentions that more than 1,000 sacred prostitutes were attached to the temple of Aphrodite alone.[44]

When Paul arrived, he met Aquila and Priscilla, who themselves had only recently moved to Corinth from Rome after the emperor Claudius issued an edict requiring all Jews to leave the capital city. They too were tentmakers, or leatherworkers, and Paul quite naturally became their good friend. Perhaps for as many as eighteen months (cf. Acts 18:11), he was their house guest and fellow-worker. During that time, Aquila and Priscilla embraced Christianity. The couple is said to have eventually risked death for Paul (Rom. 16:3-4). But many others also were convinced by Paul's weekly preaching at the synagogue; included among that company were Titius Justus, whose house was next door to the synagogue, and Crispus, an important leader of the synagogue at Corinth. And so, when the message of Christ was reproached by Jewish leaders, the apostle simply moved his base of ministry next door to Titius's house. Incensed, the Jewish authorities fabricated charges against Paul and had him brought before Gallio, proconsul of Achaia, whose name is also attested on an inscription recovered at Delphi. Convinced that the matter was strictly a Jewish problem, however, Gallio refused to adjudicate it. Thus Paul was able to continue his mission in Corinth (Acts 18:1-17).

Nevertheless, after a time, Paul decided to return to Antioch. Accompanied by Aquila and Priscilla, he journeyed across the isthmus to Cenchreae, where he boarded a boat that was headed for Ephesus. When Paul's party arrived in that strategic city, it went to the synagogue where Paul preached. Even though he left Aquila and Priscilla there, Paul himself declined the Ephesians' request to stay on. Instead, he set sail for Caesarea, from which he went up and greeted the church at Jerusalem before undertaking the final leg in the second journey—the trip to Antioch (Acts 18:18-22).

Paul's third missionary journey took him through the regions of Galatia and Phrygia, before he finally arrived at Ephesus. From this it follows that the apostle more or less retraced his earlier steps through the Cilician Gates, past Derbe, Lystra, Iconium, and Antioch in Pisidia, rather than taking the coastal road through Pamphylia and Lycia. Beyond the general statement that Paul was "strengthening all the disciples," we are in the dark about that segment of his trip. At Ephesus, however, he was awaited by his friends Aquila and Priscilla who, since being left there on the second journey, had been engrossed in the ministry. Among other things, they had met a disciple named Apollos whom they had nurtured in Christian doctrine before sending him on to Corinth. But also waiting for Paul at Ephesus was the culture of the city itself. Ephesus was a major metropolis of the eastern Empire, ranked with Alexandria and Antioch. Ephesus was also the home of the goddess Artemis (Roman "Diana"), long venerated as the fertility goddess of all Asia Minor. Her temple at Ephesus was one of the seven wonders of the ancient world.

Paul's success in proclaiming the gospel during his two-to-three year stay in Ephesus (Acts 19:8, 10; 20:31) was felt both in the city and throughout the province. Numerous believers were baptized and many miracles were wrought. His ministry also spanned the Aegean during that same period, when he became aware of problems in the Corinthian church (1 Cor. 1:10-11; 16:8-11). Having dispatched his first epistle to that church, Paul also commissioned Timothy to go to Macedo-

MAP 89 THIRD JOURNEY

nia and doubtless also to Corinth, to report on what progress the church had made there. A mark of Paul's success at Ephesus may be seen in the reaction of a certain Demetrius, who was an Ephesian silversmith. Believing that Paul's message threatened the livelihood of the city's artisans, if not the fabric of the Artemis cult itself, Demetrius summoned other craftsmen in Ephesus and incited them to become riotous in the city. In the ensuing fray, two of Paul's traveling companions, Gaius and Aristarchus, were seized and dragged into the Ephesian theater, a semi-circular stone edifice capable of holding about 24,000 spectators. Although Paul himself was unharmed in that incident, it helped solidify his decision to move on to Macedonia and Greece (Acts 18:23).

Though we cannot be sure, it seems reasonable to infer that Paul revisited the Macedonian brethren in Philippi, Thessalonica, and Berea before coming to Corinth, probably bypassing Athens. It was during his three-month stay in Greece that the apostle penned the Roman epistle (Rom. 15:22-29), in which he expressed the fond hope that he might someday visit Spain (Rom. 15:24, 28). However, he told the Roman believers, he presently had to travel to Jerusalem (Rom. 15:25). It appears that just as Paul was about to set sail for Jerusalem (possibly for Passover, Acts 20:6-16), his life was somehow threatened. Consequently, he traveled overland to Philippi, where he celebrated the Jewish holy days and then caught a freighter and crossed over to Troas in five days. From there, Paul made his way to Assos, where he caught a ship bound for Syria.

Along the way, they stopped at Mitylene, Chios, Samos, and Miletus, Paul having decided to bypass Ephesus. Nevertheless, he could not refrain from calling the Ephesian elders to Miletus where he admonished them, prayed with them, and wept that he would see them no more. His ship then passed on to Cos and Rhodes. In the latter city, Paul might have seen the colossus of Rhodes, a huge bronze statue of the sun god Helios, another one of the seven wonders of the ancient world. From Rhodes, they proceeded to Patara, past Cyprus, and came to Tyre. Taking advantage of the seven-day layover during which the boat was being emptied of its cargo, Paul sought out disciples in that city. Then they passed on and came to Ptolemais and Caesarea, in the latter of which he lodged in the home of Philip the Evangelist (Acts 20:1—21:8).

The Judean prophet Agabus (cf. Acts 11:28) intercepted Paul at Caesarea and implored him not to visit Jerusalem. But Paul had set his face to go to the holy city. Upon his arrival there, he reported to the elders concerning the wondrous ministry that had been begun among the Gentiles. On

TRIP TO ROME — MAP 90

the following day, when in observance of Jewish custom Paul went to the Temple for rites of purification, men from Asia, presumably from Ephesus, recognized him and accused him of desecrating the Temple by bringing a Gentile into the sacred precinct; the missionary statesman was then seized and beaten by the Jews. When the Roman tribune learned of that scuffle, he had Paul arrested and taken to the Antonia where he remained until the commandant was informed of a conspiracy against Paul's life. So, under cover of darkness and with heavy security, Paul was transferred to the provincial prison at Caesarea where he remained incarcerated for two years before appealing as a Roman citizen to the Caesar (Acts 21:15—26:32). The governor of Caesarea, Porcius Festus, could do no other than comply with the apostle's request.

Together with other prisoners, Paul was put aboard a boat from Adramyttium that was setting sail for the Asian coasts (Acts 27:1-2); he was accompanied by Aristarchus from Thessalonica (cf. Acts 19:29; 20:4) and also by Luke. The initial leg of their journey took them past the coast of Cilicia, via Sidon, to Myra in Lycia (Acts 27:3-5), where it became necessary to disembark and board a second vessel, a large cargo ship from Alexandria (Egypt) headed for Italy.

But it was late summer, and the prevailing winds were buffeting westward traffic. Consequently, it was with great difficulty and with some delay that Paul's vessel finally arrived at an island off Cnidus. Sailing from there under the lee of Crete, they were barely able to make shore at Fair Havens. Paul warned not to proceed farther, but the captain sailed on with the intention of wintering at Phoenix (Acts 27:7-12).

Before they could make anchor, however, a fierce northeasterly gale struck and violently drove them towards the open sea. Unable to make Cauda, the sailors feared destruction in the shallows of Syrtis Major. Some fourteen days later, Paul's ship ran aground off the coast of Malta and had to be abandoned (Acts 27:13-44).

Aboard a third vessel, Paul's final leg to Rome was uneventful. After brief stopovers at Syracuse and Rhegium, the Egyptian ship made port at Puteoli, where Paul went ashore. Traveling via the Appian Way en route to Rome, Paul's party passed the Forum of Appius and Three Taverns, where in both places they were met by Christian brethren. Taking courage from them, Paul passed on and came finally to Rome (Acts 28:11-16).

MAP 91 **THE CHURCHES OF ASIA**

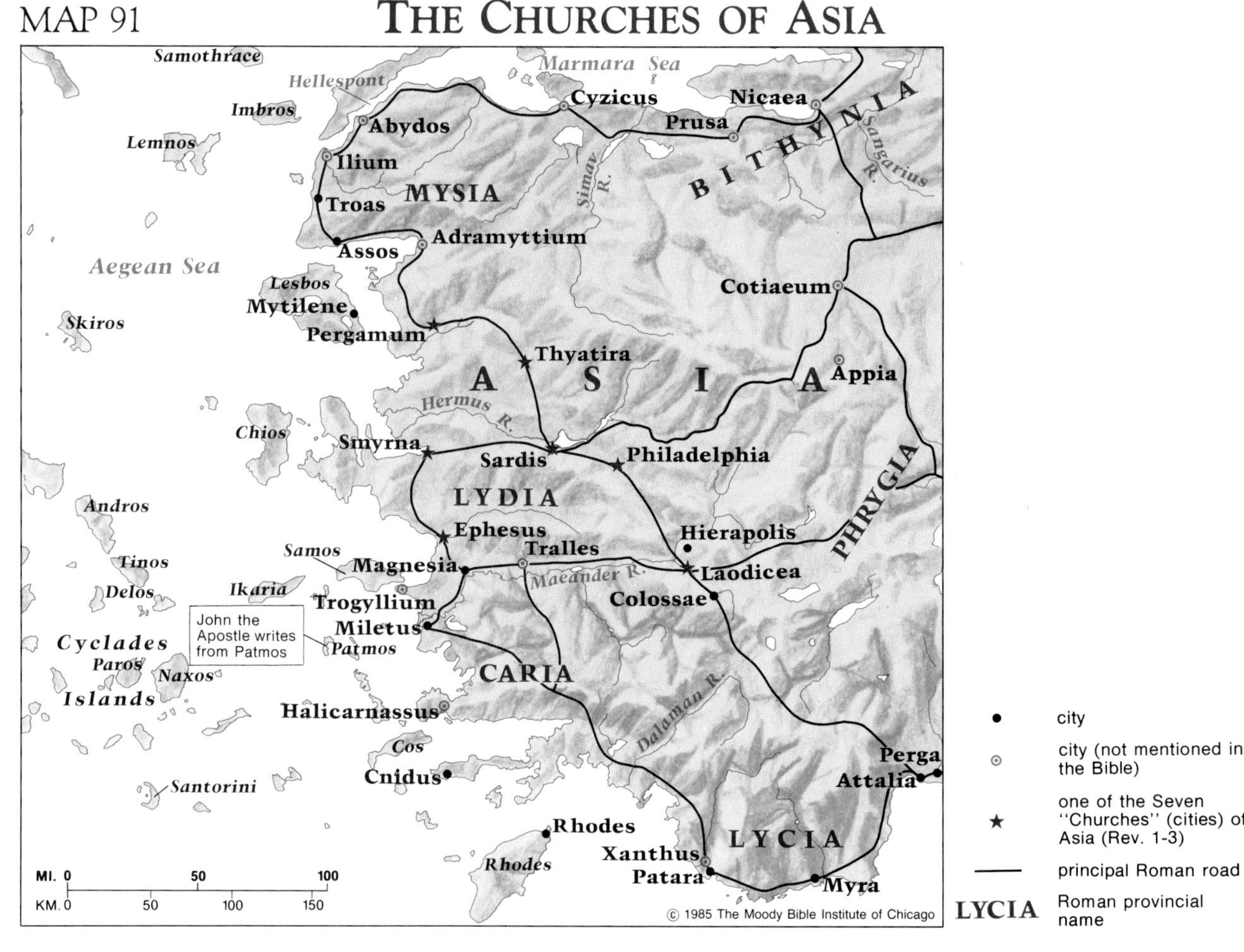

Western Asia Minor is a geographical designation for that peninsula of land bounded on the north by the Marmara Sea and the straits of the Hellespont (Dardanelles), on the south by the Mediterranean, on the west by the Aegean Sea, and on the east by the mountainous plateau of eastern Phrygia. The land mass is tilted down toward the northwest, and extending west from the Phrygian mountains are some outlying crests that naturally segment the terrain and create lateral valleys through which, in New Testament times, the Romans built roadways. Prominent among those was the thoroughfare that entered Phrygia from a point just west of Antioch in Pisidia (see Map 19), ran past Laodicea and then more or less followed the Maeander river valley past Tralles and Magnesia to the western ports of Ephesus and Miletus. An important branch of that route extended north from Laodicea past Philadelphia and Sardis, where one road veered west to Smyrna and another went in the direction of Thyatira, Pergamum, Adramyttium, and Troas.

Together with the opening or enlarging of roads there commenced a rebuilding program of Western Asian cities that were either along or had access to the road system. Sardis, Miletus, Cyzicus, and Pergamum were vastly refurbished in this period; Ephesus was beautified and transformed into the official seat of Roman authority; Smyrna was adorned with paved streets, and Laodicea prospered with its textile industries.

The book of the Revelation is addressed by the apostle John to "the seven churches of Asia" (Rev. 1:4, 11). That these seven churches were particularly selected by the apostle and that the message to them was arranged in a certain sequence may be owing precisely to geographical considerations. The seven churches without exception were situated on principal Roman roads that carried, among others, postal carriers. Arriving at Ephesus from the island of Patmos, a carrier could go north to Smryna and Pergamum (the northern leg on a secondary road); from thence he could turn east and proceed directly along the Roman artery past Thyatira, Sardis, Philadelphia, and Laodicea.

ROME VS. JEWS, A.D. 66-74

A combination of Hellenistic secularism, Roman politics, and Jewish ideology created a strange alchemy in Palestinian culture throughout the first Christian century. The Roman procurators, on the one hand, were sometimes cruel and defiant, sometimes corrupt or contemptuous of Jewish religious practices, but always eager to impose an excessive tax burden. Jewish sectarianism, for its part, had long been a breeding ground for voices of insurrection and resistance movements. Within Judaism's establishment, increasingly bold and bitterly resentful sounds could be heard concerning Rome's tyrannical imperialism. Then there was the Jewish nationalist group, called Zealots, that was committed to the creation of a Jewish state at any price. Suspicions fanned animosities, covert intrigue often gave way to open hostility—an atmosphere had been created in Judea in which revolution was imminent.

It was a series of confrontations occurring in rapid succession during the spring and summer of A.D. 66 that ignited the explosion of revolt. At Caesarea, Jewish anger was violently inflamed when an unscrupulous individual offered a "pagan" sacrifice at the entrance of the synagogue, thus desecrating that house of worship. When Jewish authorities attempted to halt the offense, a cry of violence rose from the people of Caesarea, and the Jews were obliged instead to steal away rather quickly to a nearby town.

Swift Jewish retaliation for the Caesarean affront came in the form of a theological edict: all sacrifices of foreigners, including those brought for the Caesar himself, would be refused in Jerusalem, and Jewish countrymen alone would be permitted to enter the sacred precincts of the Temple. Soon thereafter, the Roman procurator Gessius Florus (probably as an act of reprisal) appeared in Jerusalem and demanded an exorbitant payment from the Temple treasury. When the Jews endeavored to rebuke the procurator for his outrageous demand, they provoked his rage instead. Florus ordered his troops to murder and plunder at will, and Jewish citizens were subjected to rape, public whipping, looting, and crucifixion; there were about 3,600 Jewish casualties, including children.

Jerusalem at once erupted into revolt. Jewish insurgents swarmed through the streets, overpowering the Roman soldiers and driving them from the upper city by force. Whereupon, the insurgents set fire to the house of the high priest, perceived to have been solicitous of Rome, as well as the Hasmonean palace of Agrippa II (cf. Map 75). They torched official archives, destroying all records of debts and debtors, and finally they assaulted and burned the Roman Antonia. Meanwhile, other rebels occupied the fortresses of Masada, Machaerus, and Cyprus, only to return to Jerusalem with a cache of armaments for their allies there.

When word of the outbreak came to the governor of Syria, Cestius Gallus, he immediately set out with his Twelfth Imperial Legion toward Jerusalem. But while attempting to ascend through the pass at Beth-horon, Gallus' veteran forces were ambushed by the guerilla tactics at which the freedom fighters had become quite adept. Although the legionnaires finally arrived at Jerusalem, they were unsuccessful in breaching its walls and were forced to disengage. Rome had lost an imperial eagle, some siege equipment, and the better part of a rear guard; the Jews had regained national autonomy.[45] The newly-founded Jewish government prepared for a full-scale Roman counteroffensive by dividing its territory into seven military districts and assigning a commander to each. Command of the Galilean district was given to a priest named Joseph, whom we know today as the historian Josephus Flavius.

When told of the calamity in Palestine, the emperor Nero ordered his leading general, Vespasian, to mobilize three legions in order to suppress the Jewish menace once and for all. Upon arriving at Ptolemais in the spring of A.D. 67, Vespasian mapped out a skillful and deliberate strategy to gain an ever-tightening grip on the center of the revolt—Jerusalem. The Roman tactician began his systematic dismembering of the Jewish rebellion by attacking Galilee. His forces swept into Sepphoris without resistance, as Josephus' troops retreated to Jotapata where they were forced to surrender forty-seven days later (1). Vespasian next moved to isolate Galilee altogether. He dispatched a secondary force to quell an uprising atop Mt. Gerizim (2), while his main army went from Caesarea across the Jezreel valley, past Scythopolis and Tiberias, to Taricheae. There a bloody naval and infantry battle took place.

The general then subdued the strong fortress at Gamala (3), after which he dispatched his son Titus with the command to vanquish the revolutionaries at Gischala (4). With those actions and a few minor forays against Japhia and Mt. Tabor, Vespasian had succeeded both in silencing the rebellion in Galilee and in severing its life-line to Babylonia. But before the onset of winter, he moved also to secure the Mediterranean front and the transportation artery to Egypt. Joppa fell before a land and sea attack (5), and the cities of Jamnia and Azotus were brought under Roman control (6).[46]

MAP 92

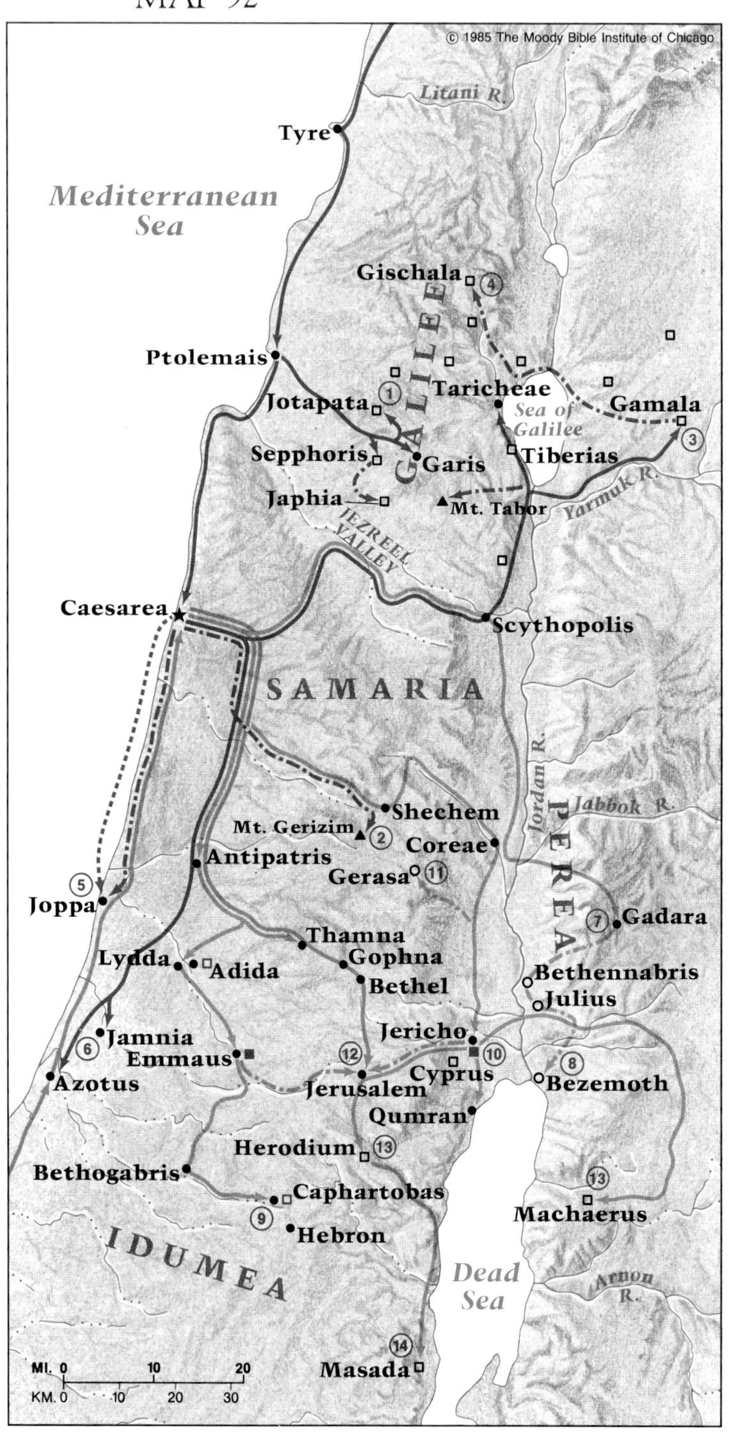

- • city
- ○ city (uncertain location)
- ★ capital city
- □ fortress
- ▲ mountain peak
- ■ Roman legion stationed here
- □ Roman garrison stationed here
- Vespasian's 67 campaign — main army
- Vespasian's 67 campaign — secondary army
- Vespasian's 67 campaign — water attack
- Vespasian's 68 campaign — main army
- Vespasian's 68 campaign — secondary army
- Titus' 70 campaign — main army
- Titus' 70 campaign — supporting army
- Roman operations after destruction of Jerusalem

Vespasian's A.D. 68 campaign was no less skillfully contrived. While tightening his stranglehold on Jerusalem all the more, he moved quickly to subjugate Perea. When his forces had seized Gadara (7), he returned to Caesarea with his main army while a secondary force swept southward as far as Bezemoth (8). Thus all major Transjordanian resistance, apart from Machaerus, had been effectively muted. Vespasian at that point embarked on a mission against the Idumeans. He subdued Antipatris, Thamna, Lydda, and Emmaus, where he positioned a legion of soldiers. Marching on south, his troops captured Betogabris and Caphartobas, where again a garrison of Vespasian's men was stationed to harass the Idumeans (9). His main army then backtracked toward Samaria and stationed an additional garrison at Adida. Vespasian at that point proceeded past Coreae and captured the city of Jericho, where he stationed another Roman legion (10). Roman legions now blocked the only major highway from Jerusalem to the lofty Transjordanian interior and one of the major roadways from the holy city to the Mediterranean Sea. At the same time, a contingent of troops was sent to seize the city Gerasa (11).[47]

But by the spring of A.D. 70, Vespasian had ascended to the imperial throne in Rome, and it was his son Titus who was destined to subdue the remaining strongholds of Jewish resistance. Marching from Alexandria via Caesarea, Titus approached Jerusalem from the north with two Roman legions, while the legions that had been stationed at Emmaus and Jericho advanced toward the city in a pincers movement (12). Thus on this occasion, in the face of such incomparable military odds, the nerve center for the Jewish revolt was forced to capitulate. Following the collapse of Jerusalem in August A.D. 70 (see Map 75), infantry forces were sent to seize the bastions of Herodium and Machaerus (13). Finally in A.D. 74, Roman garrisons under the command of Silva, an ambitious general, succeeded in battering through the walls of the last Jewish holdout position at Masada, and Nero's goal of destroying Jewish rebellion was finally realized (14).[48]

Figure 28 The mesa of Masada with Lisan peninsula and Dead Sea (background). West (right) of Masada is vestige of the Roman ramp.

"One of the most amazing and significant facts of history is that within five centuries of its birth Christianity won the professed allegiance of the overwhelming majority of the population of the Roman Empire and even the support of the Roman state. Beginning as a seemingly obscure sect of Judaism, one of scores, even hundreds of religions and religious groups which were competing within that realm, revering as its central figure one who had been put to death by the machinery of Rome, and in spite of having been long proscribed by that government and eventually having the full weight of the state thrown against it, Christianity proved so far the victor that the Empire sought alliance with it and to be a Roman citizen became almost identical with being a Christian."[49] Jesus' admonition to "go into all the world and preach the gospel" had been taken seriously indeed; far from least among the factors that played a vital role in the rapid spread of Christianity was a zealous apostolic response to the Great Commission.

There were environmental factors emanating from the Roman Empire, of course, that also contributed to the rapid growth of the gospel. First, lands within the Empire were bequeathed an era of peace, and commerce flourished and travel became more accessible, and a great deal safer, than ever before. Highways built for commerce or Roman legions served also the messengers of the cross. Important too was the Greek language, widely used across the Empire by Jews and Gentiles alike. This meant that Christianity could articulate its thought and doctrines in readily understandable forms. But persecution also emanated from the Empire, a testimony to the effectiveness of early missionary activities and apologetic writings. The most famous of those persecutions took place in Rome in A.D. 64 under the Emperor Nero. According to the *Annals* of Tacitus, Nero, having been accused of giving the order to set fire to Rome, which laid waste two-thirds of the city, sought to shift the blame to Christians, who had spoken of a fiery end of the world. To distract suspicions from his own pyromaniacal act, Nero afflicted Christians with relentless passion and ingenious brutality. Some Christians were wrapped in the hides of wild beasts, only to be torn to pieces by dogs. Others, declares Tacitus, fastened to crosses, were soaked with a flammable liquid and set on fire, to light Nero's gardens. Such persecutions and the subsequent round of persecutions under Domitian (A.D. 95), together with greatly intensified hostility in Jerusalem from Jewish authorities, triggered a widespread movement of Christians to safer environs.[50]

Emerging as dominant Christian centers were the cities of Antioch, from which Paul's missionary enterprises were spawned, and Pella (see Map 94), where many Christians fled for safety in the wake of the outbreak of the first Jewish revolt (A.D. 66). In Mesopotamia there were two major centers, one at Edessa, where at a very early date Christianity was made the official religion, and the other at Dura-Europos, where the earliest known Christian house-church has been excavated by archaeologists. In North Africa there emerged two important centers of Christian theology and scholarship—Alexandria and Carthage. Alexandria was the home of Athanasius, who so ably defended the trinitarian doctrine and the doctrine of the Person of Christ, just as it was the base of Origen, who wrote the first systematic treatise of Christian theology and gave to the church the Hexapla (six parallel translations of the Bible). Carthage is where the influential apologist Tertullian preached and wrote.

The preeminent Christian center in Europe

THE SPREAD OF

CHRISTIANITY THROUGHOUT THE ROMAN WORLD MAP 93

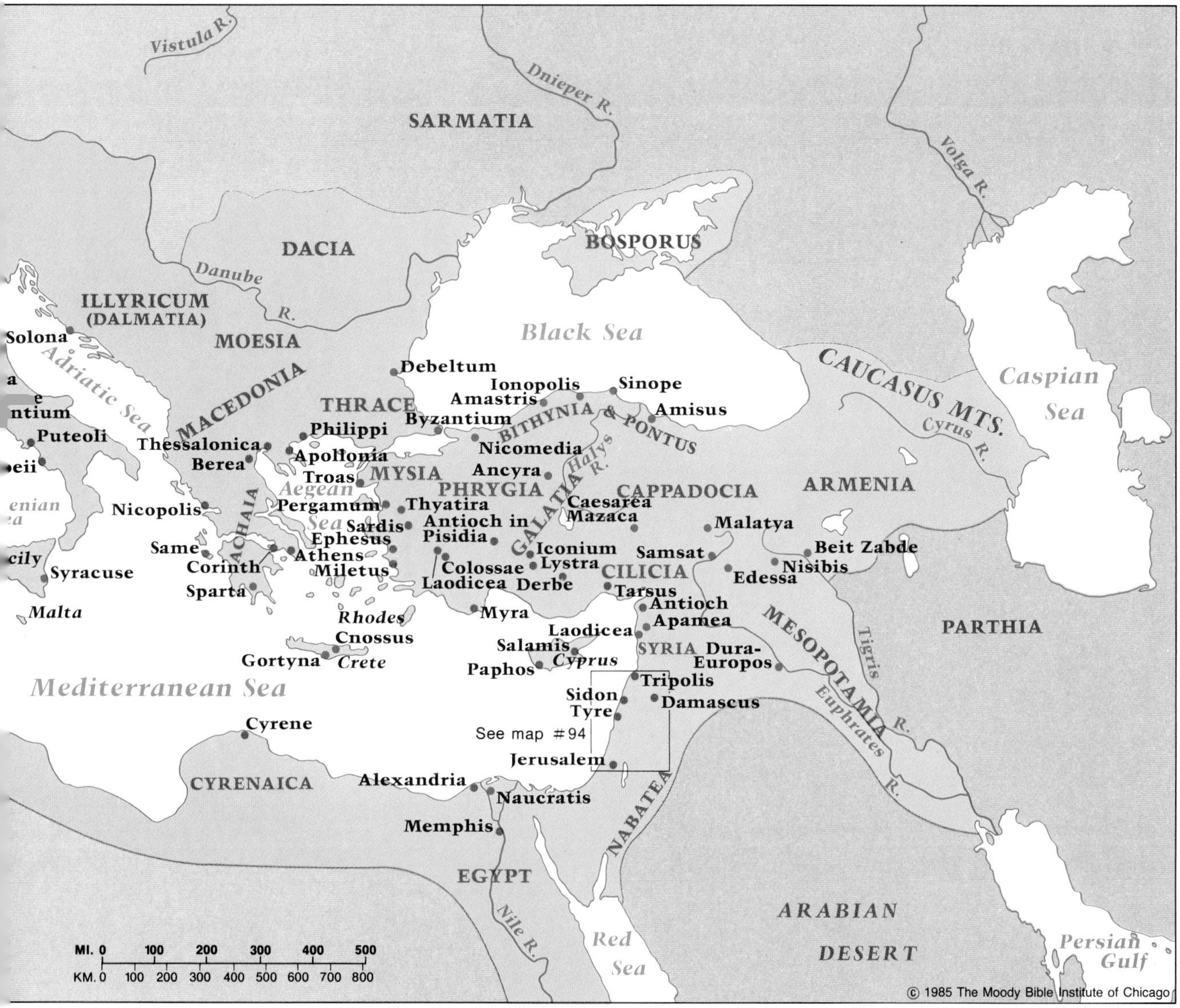

Vistula R.
Dnieper R.
SARMATIA
Volga R.
DACIA
BOSPORUS
Danube R.
ILLYRICUM (DALMATIA)
Solona
MOESIA
Black Sea
CAUCASUS MTS.
Caspian Sea
Cyrus R.
Adriatic Sea
MACEDONIA
Debeltum
Ionopolis
Sinope
Amastris
Amisus
THRACE
Byzantium
BITHYNIA & PONTUS
Puteoli
Thessalonica
Philippi
Apollonia
Nicomedia
Berea
Troas
MYSIA
Ancyra
Halys R.
ARMENIA
Aegean Sea
PHRYGIA
GALATIA
CAPPADOCIA
Caesarea Mazaca
Nicopolis
Pergamum
Thyatira
Sardis
Antioch in Pisidia
Malatya
Ephesus
ACHAIA
Same
Athens
Iconium
Samsat
Beit Zabde
Corinth
Miletus
Colossae
Lystra
CILICIA
Nisibis
Syracuse
Sparta
Laodicea
Derbe
Edessa
Tarsus
Malta
Rhodes
Myra
Antioch
Apamea
MESOPOTAMIA
PARTHIA
Tigris R.
Cnossus
Laodicea
Salamis
SYRIA
Dura-Europos
Gortyna
Crete
Cyprus
Paphos
Tripolis
Mediterranean Sea
Sidon
Damascus
Euphrates R.
Tyre
Cyrene
See map #94
Jerusalem
CYRENAICA
Alexandria
Naucratis
Memphis
NABATEA
EGYPT
Nile R.
Red Sea
ARABIAN DESERT
Persian Gulf
MI. 0 100 200 300 400 500
KM. 0 100 200 300 400 500 600 700 800

was Rome, located at the heart of the Empire. In the time of Eusebius, the church of Rome had 1 bishop, 46 presbyters, 7 deacons, 42 acolytes, 50 readers, exorcists, and doorkeepers, plus 1,500 widows and poor persons under its care. Ascendancy was also conferred upon Lyons during the days of Irenaeus's celebrated bishopric there.

Figure 29 Ruins of Dura-Europos (along the Euphrates River), where the earliest archaeologically-attested Christian church has been found.

MAP 94 EARLY CHRISTIAN COMMUNITIES

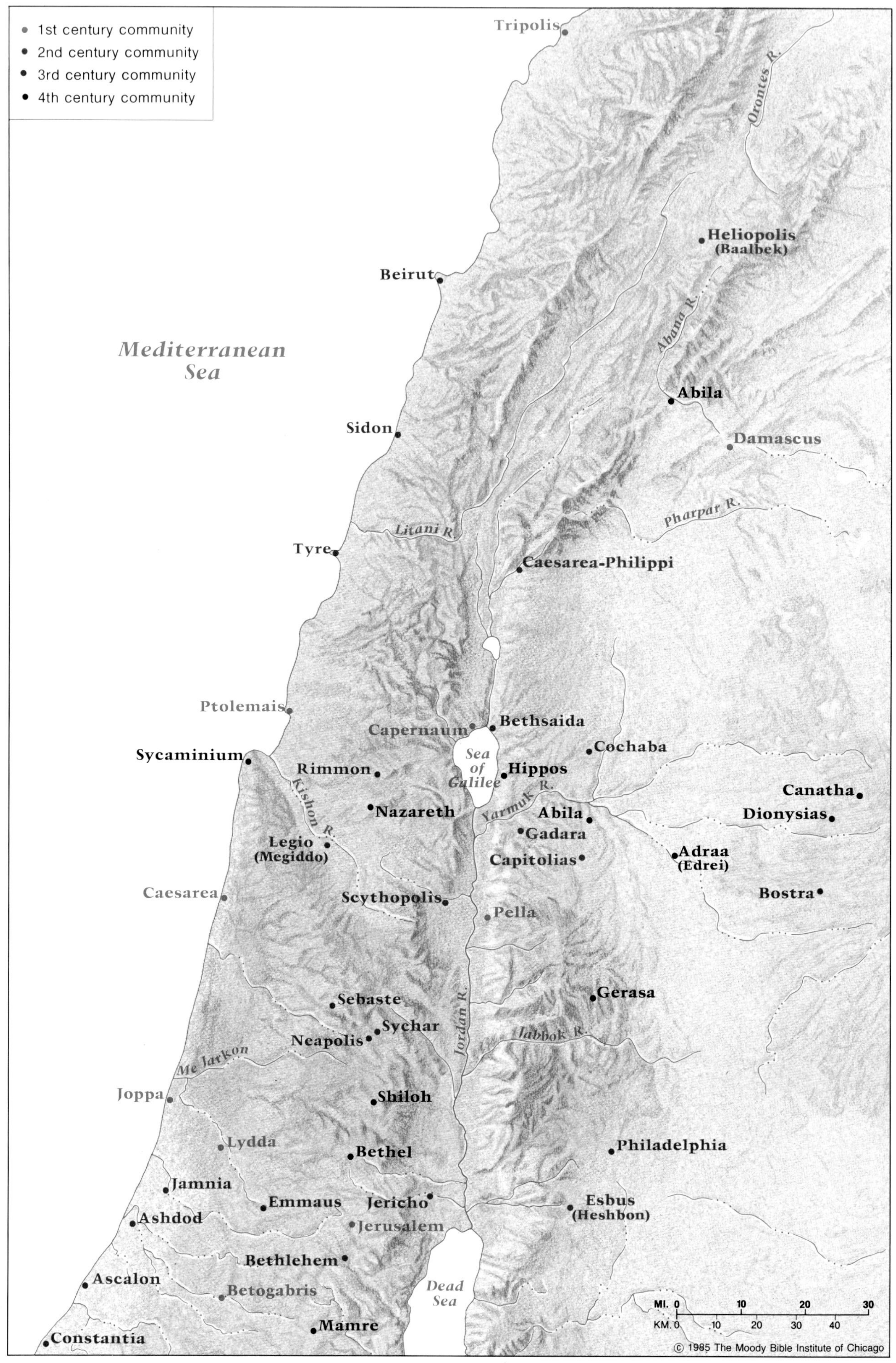

DEVELOPMENT OF MODERN ISRAEL

Notes for Chapter 2

1. E.g., 51.V.68-69.
2. A recension of the Samaritan Pentateuch renders Gihon (v. 13) as "Askoph," which is the ancient name of the Kerkha River.
3. A verbal description of the family tree of Noah, perhaps based on similar genealogical tables unearthed in Mesopotamian archaeology.
4. The names of Noah's sons are assigned a meaning having to do with climate; for example, Ham is construed to mean "hot," so the Hamites are classified as those nations that live nearest the equator.
5. The chapter is designed to demonstrate that the Hebrews (i.e., Eberites) were related to the major nations of the world.
6. The chapter presents a complete anthropological register of mankind.
7. The "70" nations of the descendants of Noah represent the dispersal of the whole of humanity (cf. numerical values of 7 and 10 in the Old Testament).
8. The nations have been classified according to their degree of friendship or animosity towards Israel.
9. The table puts into verbal form the contents of an early map of the world (Mesopotamian, Phoenician [cf. Jubilees 8-9], Herodotus, Strabo).
10. Behistun trilingual inscription equates Gimirraya and Saka.
11. But see LXX and SP.
12. The letter *ś* before a *d/t* changes to *l* in the Babylonian language beginning at about the fifteenth century B.C.
13. The *ś* sound was pronounced in a way that led the Septuagint translators to correlate it with their *l* sound.
14. W. W. Hallo and W.K. Simpson, *The Ancient Near East: A History*, 1971, p. 251.
15. See M. Bietak, *Tell el-Dab'a* II, pp. 28-43.
16. Papyrus Anastasi V; consult *ANET*, p. 259*b*.
17. A. H. Gardiner, "The Geography of the Exodus," *Recueil d'études égyptologiques dédiées à la memoire de Jean-François Champollion*, 1922, pp. 213-14.
18. W. H. Shea, "A Date for the Recently Discovered Eastern Canal of Egypt," *BASOR* 226 (1977): 31-38.
19. See deVaux, p. 435.
20. Consult H. M. Z. Meyer, *Ancient Maps of the Holy Land*, numbers 14 and 15, although Map 26 places the mountain at a position close to J. Helal (cf. Gal. 4:25).
21. Cf. Herodotus 2.77.
22. B. Rothenberg and Y. Aharoni, *God's Wilderness: Discoveries in Sinai*, 1961, p. 170.
23. Abel, *Geographie*, 2:307; Aharoni, p. 200; deVaux, p. 116.
24. Aharoni, pp. 199-200; Rothenberg and Aharoni, pp. 162-63, 185-89.
25. Simons, p. 252, 428. To *Mfkt*, i.e., the Egyptian name for "turquoise" mined at Serabit el-Khadim; cf. Gardiner, *Egyptian Grammar*, p. 568*a*.
26. R. D. Wilson, "Understanding 'The Sun Stood Still,'" *PTR* 16 (1918): 46-54
27. AJ XIV.iv.4.
28. Cf. *ANET*, p. 290.
29. E.g., Strabo, III.ii.11, 14; Herodotus, I.163; IV.152.
30. A. Schulten, *Avieni Ora Maritima*, 135.
31. Pliny, XVI.216; Velleius Paterculus I.ii.4; Strabo, II.v.5.
32. For the relief, see *ANEP*, p. 153, number 443; for a translation of this campaign, consult *ANET*, pp. 278-97.
33. Consult *ANET*, p. 320.
34. For the text, see *ANET*, p. 280; for the picture showing Jehu lying prostrate before Shalmaneser, refer to *ANEP*, p. 122, number 355.
35. AJ XX.ii.1-iv.3.
36. *Wars* II.xix.2.
37. AJ.XI.xi.5-6.
38. Cf. A. Mazar, *Jerusalem Revealed*, pp. 79-84.
39. *Wars* V.iv.1-2.
40. G. Sinnigen and C. A. Robinson, Jr., *Ancient History from Prehistoric Times to the Death of Justinian*, New York: Macmillan, 1981, p. 323.
41. *AJ* XX.vi.1.
42. *AJ* XX.vi.1.
43. Cf. *AJ*, XII.iii.1.
44. *Geog* VIII.vi.20.
45. *Wars* II.xiv. 5-xviii.9.
46. *Wars* III.vi.1-IV.iii.14.
47. *Wars* IV.vii.3-ix.1.
48. *Wars* V.i.1-VII.xi.5.
49. K. S. Latourette, *A History of Christianity*, New York, 1953, p. 65.
50. Tacitus *Annals*, XV. 38-44.

3
The History of Biblical Mapmaking

Introduction to Mapmaking

"Of the making of maps there is no end, and no known beginning." This axiom is vividly illustrated in the history of Near Eastern mapmaking, including Palestine, which represents a long and extremely fascinating subject. For example, during the first fifty years after Johann Gutenberg (1400-1468) inaugurated the age of printing with his invention of moveable type, no fewer than fifty books wholly or partly devoted to geography were published. Most maps presented in those volumes portrayed whole continents or parts of them, and maps of single countries were only rarely published. Despite that, more than a quarter of all the maps in those books were specially prepared maps of the Bible lands. Throughout the two centuries following Gutenberg, practically every renowned cartographer produced maps of Palestine.

But the story of mapmaking is much older. More than three thousand years before Gutenberg, and long before the age of travel and exploration launched by the quests of Christopher Columbus and Ferdinand Magellan, ancient Near Eastern man was already producing maps. Sometimes his maps were scratched onto clay tablets (cf. Ezek. 4:1) or inscribed in stone or bronze; at other times they were painted on papyrus scrolls or emblazoned on limestone walls of tombs or inside coffins. Some maps reflected those practical concerns of economics, warfare, or travel, whereas others represented cosmological speculations or nationalistic propaganda. His maps could be oriented toward north, or east, or south, or west, while elsewhere they were composed without reference to a compass point. Space regrettably limits our discussion of this engaging topic, but a pertinent bibliography of mapmaking of Bible lands has been supplied.[1]

Ancient Mapmaking

The oldest map known today that still exists in its original form was found in the archaeological excavations of Nuzi, in northern Iraq. Inscribed on a clay tablet that can be dated epigraphically to approximately 2300 B.C., the map depicts a river or irrigation channel and two mountain ranges. Among other printed matter on the map there are found a few city names, but little more. Therefore, uncertainty prevails concerning just what the map portrays and what its original purpose was. From inscriptions on the tablet, it has been suggested that this map may be picturing a large estate near Nuzi.

Figure 30 The Nippur City Map

The site of Nippur, the famed cultural and religious center of ancient Sumerian civilization, is located about midway between Baghdad and the Persian Gulf. From Nippur comes what is today the oldest city map known, dating to about 1500 B.C. (Fig. 30). The map depicts Nippur in the Old Babylonian period and is meant to be oriented with northwest at the top. From the upper left (west) to the lower left (south) corners of the tablet run two parallel lines which, according to the inscription contained inside them, represent the Euphrates River. Aligning the Euphrates from the first bend in the river to the bottom of the tablet is the southwestern city wall, shown on the map with two narrow parallel lines. Also visible are the southeastern walls and a portion of the northeastern wall, but the eastern and northeastern sectors of the city wall are lost in the brokenness of the tablet. Just inside the southern point of the city walls a large house may be seen. East of that house is pictured some kind of storehouse, and on the eastern edge of the tablet are found two temples, presumably the home of Nippur's patron deity, Enlil. An interior canal, called in the tablet the Idshauru Canal, runs vertically through the city and divides the storehouse and the temples. That is most probably the canal known today as the Shatt el-Nil Canal.

The southeast wall is shown breached by three gates. Between the aforementioned house and storehouse is found the "Nanna gate" (Nanna was the Sumerian moon god); between the storehouse and Idshauru Canal, the "Uruk (Erech) gate" is positioned; and below the temple another gate is situated, this time labeled the "Ur gate." The position of the latter two gates and the direction of the respective cities to which they led permits one to orient this map. Also visible are three gates that breached the wall aligning the Euphrates. From north to south these are labeled the "Unclean gate," "Lofty gate," and "Great Gate." Finally, the northwest wall was breached by one gate, adjacent to where the wall juts out and crosses over the Idshauru Canal. Immediately outside the walls on the top and bottom of the tablet is pictured some kind of terrace or wall reinforcement, and a moat is presented just beyond that. At the very top of the map, there is located a canal that presumably intersected with the Euphrates at a point west of the city.

A tablet commonly known today as the "Babylonian Map of the World" was found among the ruins of the city of Sippar, about 25 miles south of Baghdad (Fig. 31). The tablet is datable to the seventh or sixth century B.C., but a note at the end of the text says it was copied from an earlier tablet. The map pictures the world as a disc surrounded by or floating in a circle of water called the "Bitter River." At the top of the world, just inside the river, is presented the segment of a circle, which is labeled "mountains" and probably represents the Taurus Mountains of eastern Turkey. Running south from those mountains and from the edge of the "Bitter River," two parallel lines delineate the Euphrates River. The river runs practically to the bottom of the world where it intersects a horizontal band, the right wing of which is marked "marsh" and the left wing of which is marked "outflow." To the right of the marsh is a double curving line that bears an unintelligible inscription. Further north, a rectangle labeled on the right "Babylon" is drawn across the Euphrates to demarcate the Babylonian capital. Surrounding Babylon are eight cities/districts in the form of small circles. Some of these have only a dot in the center whereas others are simply marked "city," but two are identifiably labeled: Assyria is found immediately east of Babylon (it is actually *north* of Babylon!), and the city of Der is placed southeast of Babylon. Three other geographic regions are marked: (1) Bit-Yakin, a powerful Chaldean tribe from which Merodach-baladan hailed, is placed just above the outflow of the Euphrates; (2) Habban, the homeland of a Kassite tribal group from Iran, is placed (wrongly) to the west of Babylon; and (3) Urartu, an independent kingdom located between the Black and Caspian seas, is placed relatively correctly to the north of Assyria. The inclusion of these three particular regions dates the composition of the map.

Beyond the Bitter River lie eight irregularly-

Figure 31 The Babylonian Map of the World

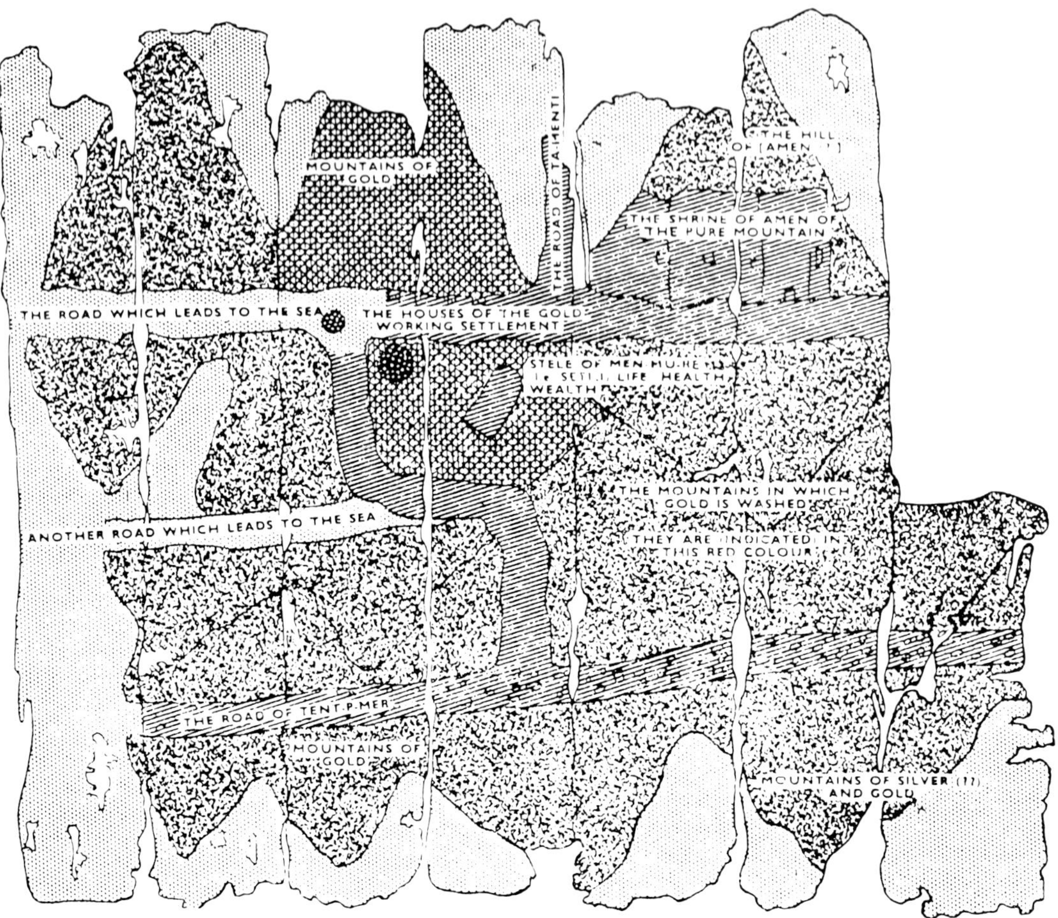

Figure 32 The Egyptian Papyrus Map

spaced triangular "regions." Four of those are legible and bear a name that refers to distant regions or islands that sometimes served as the home of strange or legendary figures. Between the triangles is written a note: "six (or seven) *bērū* in between." (A *bēru* is a Babylonian unit of time or linear measurement.) On the reverse of the tablet, the eight regions are described, though the text remains somewhat obscure. The term used for "region" seems to have had a special mythological significance (e.g., Gilgamesh Epic, tablet 11). The inscription includes the names of certain mythological monsters that in other Babylonian texts are imagined as inhabiting the underworld. Elsewhere some of those are mentioned as primeval monsters who march at the command of Tiamat, the arch adversary of the god Marduk (e.g., Babylonian Epic of Creation, tablet 4). A final paragraph summarizes "all eight 'regions' of the four quarters of the earth." The expression "four quarters" corresponds to the four quarters of a compass, and is one of the regular Babylonian words for *universe*, again tending to indicate a mythological or cosmological context. It may be, then, that this tablet actually represents a visual and verbal piece of Babylonian propaganda: like the Babylonian Epic of Creation *(Enuma Elish)*, this tablet might have been designed to demonstrate the centrality of Babylon in the world as well as the supremacy of the Marduk cult in the Babylonian pantheon (see below for Nippur and Jerusalem as the center of the world).[2]

Earliest Egyptian cartographic efforts seem to have been preoccupied with providing aid to the deceased on their journey to the Egyptian afterworld, though a mural relief depicting an expedition to the land of Punt during the time of Queen Hatshepsut (c. 1475 B.C.) is exposed on a wall of her palace at Luxor. The oldest Egyptian map, prepared under pharaoh Ramses II (c. 1300 B.C.), is written on a papyrus now on display in Turin, Italy. An English reproduction of the papyrus map is found here (Fig. 32). Originally discovered in the shaft of a gold mine, the papyrus deals with metalworking and shows two parallel valleys between mountains in which gold was mined or worked. It locates a stele of the pharaoh and the mountainous shrine of an Egyptian deity. According to some, the map depicts a portion of the Wadi Hammamat, which essentially runs on a lateral axis between the area of Thebes and the Red Sea, bordering on the Nubian desert. Be that as it may, the Nubian desert has yielded up more than one hundred such gold mines from antiquity, and many of them were equipped with washing tables and querns (primitive hand mills for grinding grain). It is presumable that the map as pictured here is actually upside down, because the two roads leading to the sea (Red Sea?) are headed off to the west.

Classical to Medieval Mapmaking

Biblical mapmaking took a quantum leap forward in the classical period, owing to the great scientific advances in math and astronomy, as well as in philosophical speculation. Strabo, in fact, asserts that geography was a concern of the philosopher and that Homer was the first geographer (*Geog* I.1, 11). Despite that assertion, we possess no classical maps from the Homeric age, though maps from the period are referred to in classical written sources. The oldest classical map which we possess today is a lovely sketch map of the world produced by Herodotus (484-420 B.C.). The "father of history," has offered detailed accounts of his own travels. He sometimes included materials (e.g., IV. 16-116) that have enabled later individuals to reconstruct a map of the world of his time. Sharing the tradition of his culture, Herodotus's world included the three continents of Europe, Asia, and Libya, and extended as far east as the Indus River, the eastern frontier of the Persian Empire. What today is known as the Indian Ocean, Persian Gulf, and Red Sea is all called by Herodotus the "Red Sea." West of Libya and Europe is the Atlantic Ocean, and enclosed by the three continents are the Mediterranean Sea (*Mare Internum*), Black Sea (*Pontus Euxinus*), and Caspian Sea (*Mare Hyrcanum*).

At the same time, theoretical geographic speculation had begun by the fourth century B.C. By the time of the Greek astronomer Eudoxus (391-338 B.C.), a spherical earth was taken as a firmly established datum. Eudoxus's work was the source for Aristotle's treatise "The Sky," which later became part of Columbus's inspiration to sail west to India. However, it was the brilliant Greek mathematician and astronomer from Alexandria, Eratosthenes (c. 195 B.C.) who might properly be called the "father of geography," for he coined and defined the word *geography*. That scientist made important observations on Near Eastern geography, from Egypt and the Mediterranean as far east as the Tigris River and the Persian Gulf. Moreover, Eratosthenes' astronomical observations supplied him with data with which he was able to calculate the total circumference of the earth. His critical and enduring discovery in turn would pave the way (1) for a world map in the shape of a globe and (2) for the development of a global grid

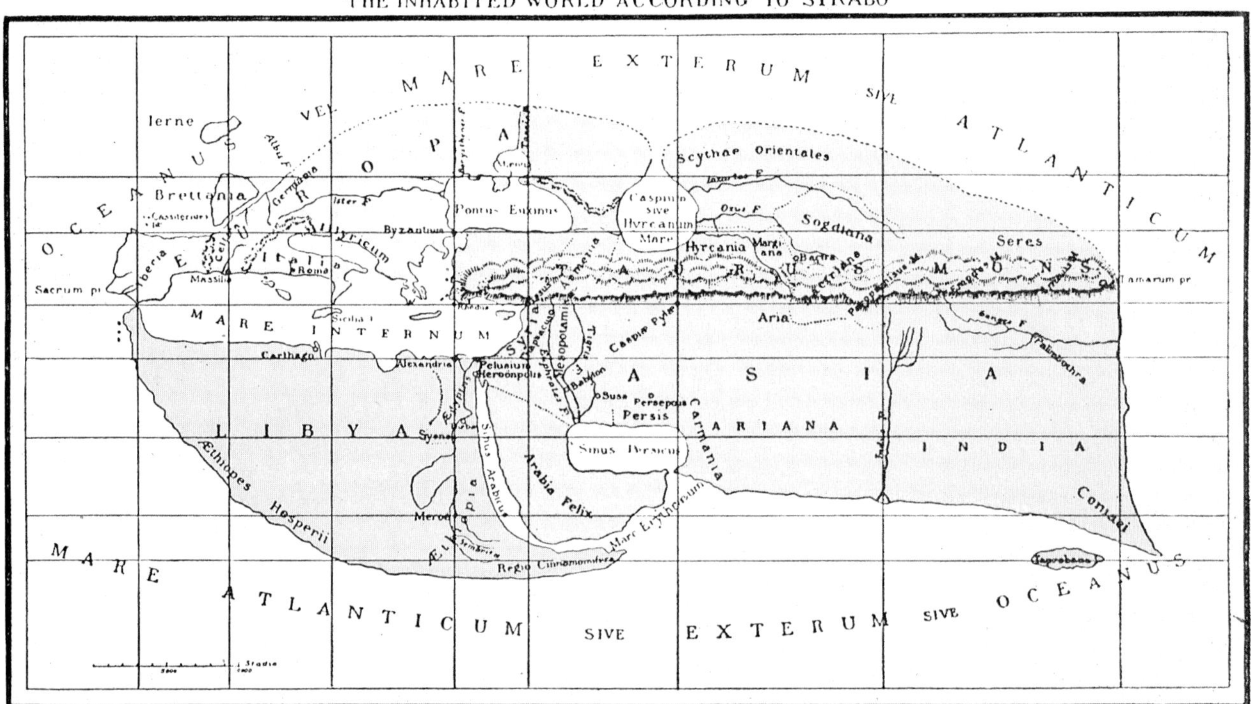

Figure 33 The Map of Strabo's World

system of 360 degrees north/south latitudes and east/west meridians.

Most of the preceding information concerning the classical period comes from the works of Strabo (64 B.C.-c. A.D. 25), who was a world traveler and also spent a large part of his life in Alexandria where he no doubt studied mathematics, astronomy, and history. Near the inception of the Christian era, Strabo undertook the ambitious project of writing a geographical encyclopedia of the inhabited world. In the end, his writing comprised a seventeen-book treatise that supplied elaborate and extensive geographic information. Book sixteen of the *Geography* describes his impressions and observations while traveling through Egypt, Palestine, and Mesopotamia. Like Herodotus before him, Strabo's world contained the three continents of Libya, Asia, and Europe (Fig. 33).

But perhaps the apex of classical mapmaking was achieved through the pioneering, innovative research of Claudius Ptolemaeus, who worked in Alexandria from A.D. 127-145. Having already composed textbooks on mathematics and astronomy, Ptolemaeus set out to prepare a comprehensive, scientific guide for the compilation of maps based on the projection and grid of the known surface of the earth. His highly-technical *Guide to Geography*, which actually constituted his chief contribution to mapmaking, was predicated on the novel idea of a *north* orientation and was commonly regarded as cartography's high water mark almost to the time of Christopher Columbus (Fig. 34). Indisputably, it was the canonization of Ptolemaic ideas that propelled Arab geographers into control of medieval cartography. And even some thirteen centuries after Ptolemaeus's death, maps influenced by his ideas were employed by Columbus when he sailed west to India.

Meanwhile, an impetus for Christian mapmaking efforts was achieved through the research and writing of Eusebius (c. A.D. 263-c. A.D. 339), the eminent church historian and Bishop of Caesarea who was also confidant to the Emperor Constantine. His *Onomasticon* records in alphabetical order all the principal place-names occurring in the Bible, together with the corresponding Greek or contemporary name, and succinct indication of the mileage and direction from some better-known point in the area. Though it remains a matter of dispute whether the bishop ever actually made a map of Palestine from his own records, the localizations of the Medeba map (see next paragraph) were based almost entirely on the *Onomasticon*, as were certain Roman road maps and Christian pilgrim maps. Jerome translated the *Onomasticon* into Latin about A.D. 400, and numerous subsequent manuscripts of this translation have been made over the years, some-

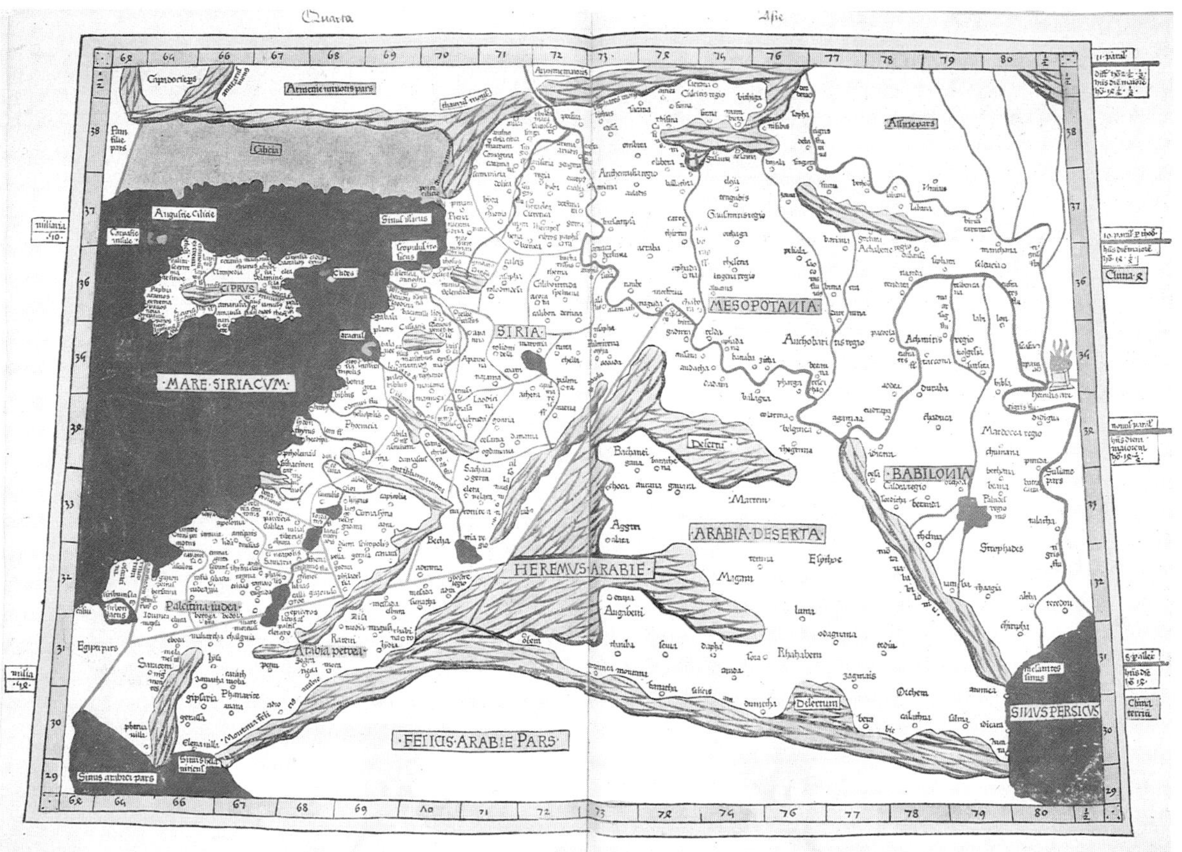

Figure 34 The Ptolemaeus Map

times with an accompanying map of Palestine as part of the manuscript.

About 100 years ago in the small Jordanian town of Medeba (Num. 21:30; Josh. 13:9, 16; 1 Chron. 19:7; Isa. 15:2; cf. 1 Macc. 9:36; Mesha stele), located approximately 20 miles southwest of Amman, a multi-colored mosaic map was uncovered among the ruins of a floor in a Greek Orthodox church. The Medeba map dates from the early sixth century A.D., and remains the earliest original depiction of the Holy Land (Fig. 35). Stretching some 39 feet from north to south and having an east orientation, the Medeba map extends from Salem (located near Beth-shan) to the mouth of the Nile delta, though it is interrupted by a number of lacunas. A study of the source material combined with a few small side fragments, however, has led scholars to the inference that the original map spanned approximately 88 feet from north to south, covering the area between Byblos-Hamath-Damascus and Alexandria, Egypt, while extending west from Kerak in Moab as far as the Mediterranean coast. Oriented toward the east, the center of the map is dominated by the Jordan River and the Dead Sea. A fish at the mouth of the Jordan is pictured swimming away from the Dead Sea, perhaps depicting the lack of marine life in the Sea. In the valley beside the Jordan, a lion is chasing a gazelle. Above the Dead Sea (east) are pictured the towering mountains of Moab. Once again, pride of place is given the city of Jerusalem, highlighting the landscape between the Dead Sea and the Mediterranean at a disproportionately large scale. Encompassing the Holy City is a wall, complete with gates and towers on the north side. Within the city are pictured certain churches and Roman imperial structures.

It is necessary to acknowledge a dual tendency in early Christian exegesis that was to prove disastrous to cartography for no less than a millennium. First, the scholarly efforts and promising methodology of on-site survey developed by Eusebius became suffocated by "established ecclesiastical tradition," and not until the time of Napoleon were scientific surveys of the Holy Land resumed. Secondly, the affirmation of Ezekiel 5:5, that Jerusalem was the "center of the earth" (Judg. 9:37; Ps. 74:12; Ezek. 38:12; cf. Jub. 8:19; Enoch 26:1; Josephus *Wars* III.iii.5; Jewish midrash)[3] was converted into a veritable dogma of the church, and it was literally put into practice by Christian cartographers. Admittedly, the same kind of ideologic distortion had been practiced earlier by the Sumerians who believed that their beloved Nippur was the "bond of heaven and earth" (*dur.an.ki*), that is, the "center of the universe," or by the Babylonians who elevated their capital city to the same lofty heights (see above, Fig. 31). As is

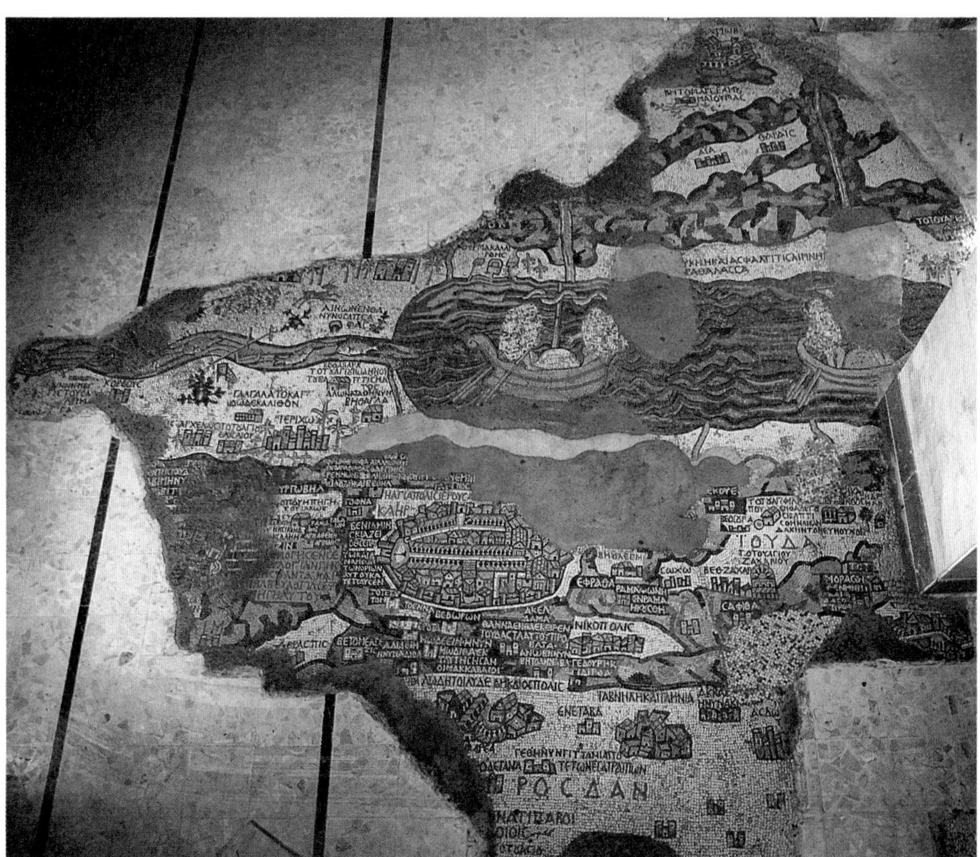

Figure 35 The Medeba Map

obvious from a contemporary perspective, these unfortunate tendencies within the church plunged Christian efforts of mapping the Holy Land into a hopeless quagmire. Medieval maps of Bible lands lack scale and grid and frequently show direction incorrectly, ignoring as they do the cartographic framework that had been worked out by Eratosthenes or Ptolemaeus. Oftentimes, medieval maps allot as much as twenty percent of the land mass of the entire world to a depiction of the Holy Land. They normally portray the earth as a flat circle with Jerusalem at the center. Dating from about 1250 is a particularly striking specimen of such a map, originally attached to a Latin manuscript of the book of Psalms (Fig. 36). The three continents known at the time are drawn on the map: Europe (below, left), Africa (right), and Asia (above). To the right (south) of the Holy City is Mt. Zion ("m. sion") and Bethlehem ("belehem"), and above (east) is the Brook Kidron ("torrens cedron"). Above the Kidron is the Jordan River, which flows out of Mt. Lebanon ("m. libans"). The Jordan enters the Sea of Galilee, in which a fish is sketched; on its banks, the cities of Bethsaida and Tiberias are found. From the Sea of Galilee, the water is pictured running to the Dead Sea ("mare mortuum"). Beside the Jordan's exit from the Sea of Galilee, a mountain is depicted, with an accompanying inscription: "a high mountain where Satan tempted the Lord" ("mons excelsus ubi diabolus staruit [sic] D(omi)n(u)m"). Southwest of Jerusalem is shown the Nile, which divides into the seven distributaries of the delta.

Medieval maps also depict the earth as a square or rectangle, perhaps in accordance with the statement of Revelation 7:1 concerning the four winds of the earth (cf. Isa. 11:12; Ezek. 7:2). In one case, the world is represented in the shape of a three-leaf clover with a picture of Jerusalem in the center, shown at a greatly enlarged scale (Fig. 37). Once again, the three continents radiate from the city of Jerusalem. Also of particular interest on the clover leaf map is what is found in the lower left corner: "America: the New Land." America had been discovered about 90 years before this map was published in 1580.

Figure 36 Jerusalem at the Center of the World Map (Psalms)

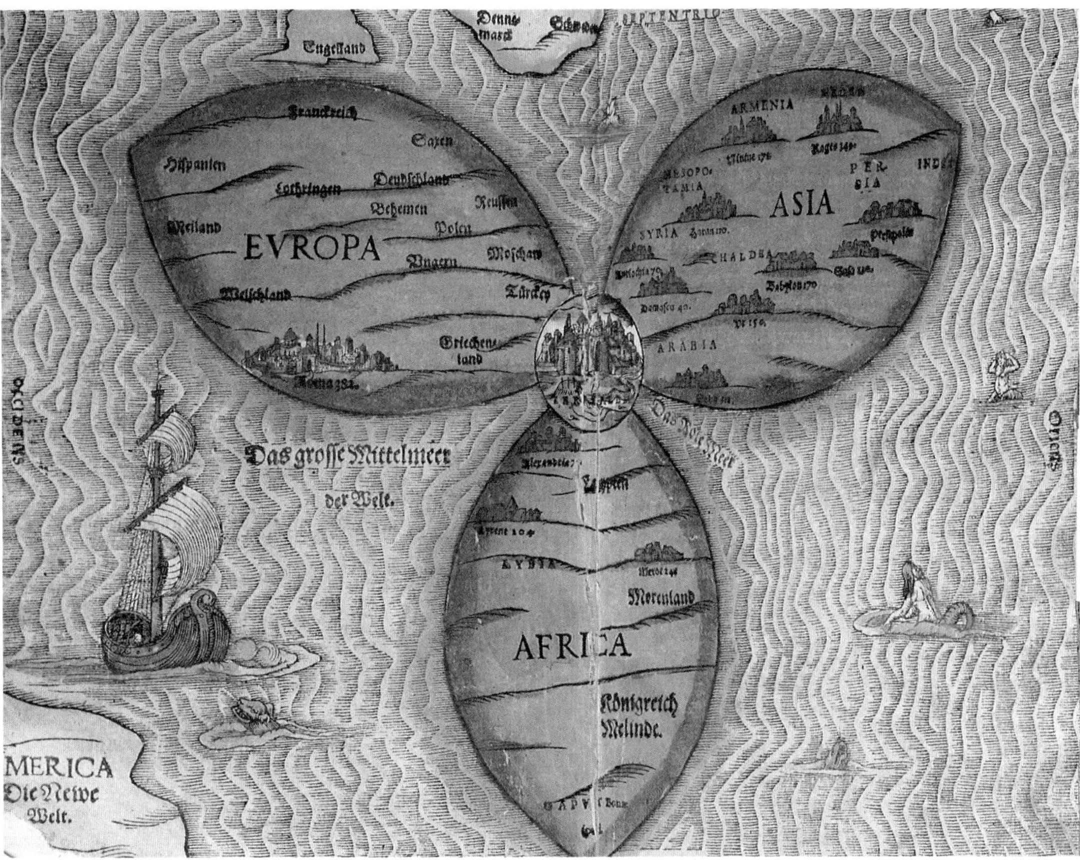

Figure 37 Jerusalem at the Center of the World Map (clover leaf)

EARLY MODERN TO CONTEMPORARY MAPMAKING

Early modern and contemporary cartography benefited greatly from the oceanic voyages and scientific achievements of Christopher Columbus, Ferdinand Magellan, and Vasco da Gama. Moreover, the labors of Gerhard Kremer (1512-1594) were seminal to cartographic advances in the modern period. Kremer was a Flemish mathematician of German extraction who, in his earlier days as an instrument maker, constructed large globes of the world. Kremer adopted the Latin form of his surname (Mercator) and produced a number of noteworthy maps between 1537 and 1547, including one of Palestine. Mercator was the first mapmaker to use the word *atlas* for a collection of maps. In 1578, he published a critical edition of 27 maps of Ptolemaeus. But Mercator's crowning achievement may be seen in his 1569 publication of a map of the world. In that map the meridians are straight lines parallel to one another, and the latitudes are also parallel but at compensated distances from the equator, so that the degrees of both retain the same ratio they would have on a sphere. Though Mercator was not the first to incorporate such projection, "Mercator projection" was named after him because he was the first to put it into a navigational manual, which allowed a compass course to be charted on a straight line making the same angle with all the meridians. The precision of Mercator projection began almost immediately to influence the scale, shape, and grid of Palestinian maps. Because of that precision, it is still widely used today.

The dramatic effect of Mercator's innovations on later mapmaking efforts can hardly be overstated; largely for the same reason, Dutch cartography is said to have dominated the Renaissance and post-Renaissance periods. In 1600, Mercator's cartographic business passed from his family to Jodocus Hondius, who published a number of revised editions of "Mercator's Atlas." In 1657, Jan Jansson, whose sister had married Mercator's son Henricus, took over the business. Included among the numerous atlases published by Jansson is a particularly attractive engraving of some early patriarchal movements (Fig. 38). The left side of this map is dominated by the island of Cyprus, the Mediterranean Sea (Mare Magnum quod Nouissimum), and the Nile River with its delta. On the right of the map are depicted the land of Mesopotamia and the Tigris and Euphrates rivers. Beginning at the city of Ur in lower Mesopotamia (Chaldea), Abraham's migration to Harran (Charan) is shown. Stretching from Harran across the northern segments of the Arabian Desert is a route titled "The way which Jacob took when with his family and flock he fled from the presence of his father-in-law Laban to his native land" (Via quam Iacob ivit quando cum Familia et grege coram facie soceri Laban ad patriam fugeret). Passing by Ammonite territory and entering the land of Canaan (Terra Chanaan) just south of the Sea of Galilee, this route ends at Mt. Gerizim (Gerizim mons) and the city of Shechem (Sichem). The names of numerous nomadic or pastoral groups encountered in the Promised Land by the Israelites are listed there; from north to south, these include the Kadmonites (Cedmonaei), Girgashites (Gergessaei), Kenizzites (Cenezaei), Perizzites (Pheresaei), Jebusites (Jebusaei), Hittites (Hethaei), Amorites (Amorrhaei), Amalekites (Amalechaei), Kenites (Cinaei), and Horites (Chorraei). The wavy line to the south of Canaan is a depiction of the route of the Israelite Exodus from Egypt. Following the tradition of medieval mapmakers, and in accordance with the translation of the Septuagint, this map delineates the Exodus to have occurred at the Red Sea (Mare Rubrum). Continuing, the route meanders through the Sinai and circles the mountains of Edom before skirting the Valley of Woodlands, Salt, and the Dead Sea.

Palestinian mapmaking advances in the modern period also have been spawned by the surveys and cartographic details amassed by individuals such as Ulrich Seetzen, Edward Robinson, W. F. Lynch, Charles Conder and H. H. Kitchener, F. M. Abel, Alois Musil, Gustaf Dalman, W. F. Albright, and Nelson Glueck. Since 1948, Israeli cartography has taken great strides forward, due in no small measure to the unstinting labor and erudition of Benjamin Mazar and Yohanan Aharoni. The quality of that work is seen today in the vividly clear and exquisitely detailed maps of the Survey of Israel. The Survey has produced a series of 26 maps of the whole of Israel, on a scale of 1:100,000, together with a series of some maps of the Sinai, at the same scale. Those maps have served as the cartographic backbone for the depictions contained within this atlas.

A final ingredient in the initiatives of the modern period has been the scientific breakthroughs in photography and space exploration.

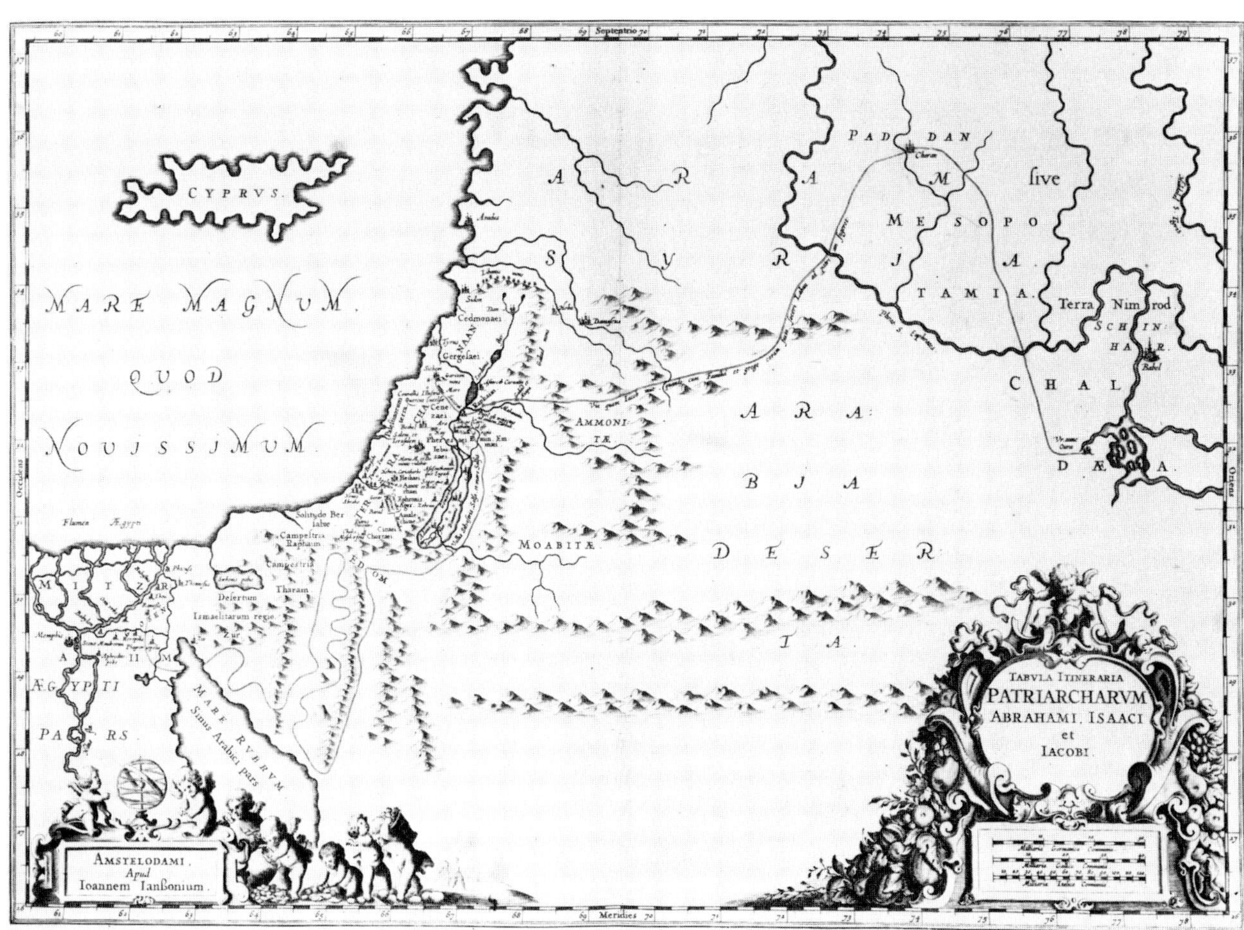

Figure 38 The Early Israelites' Travels Map

Figure 39 The NASA Composite Map of Israel

Such achievements provide for the first time in history the possibility of seeing the entire landscape of Israel in a single view, as is shown here in the breathtaking photography of NASA (Fig. 39).

This is a multi-spectral image composite of three photographs taken from Landsat-1, January 1, 1973; the photo includes parts of Lebanon, Syria, Jordan, and Israel. Pictured at the extreme top, the city of Beirut is located on the point of land jutting out into the Mediterranean. Snow is visible on the mountain peaks to the northeast and southeast of Beirut, the latter of which is Mt. Hermon. Between these snow-capped crests, in the shaded area, is located the Beqa' Valley, a longitudinal extension of the Jordan Rift Valley. As this Rift Valley continues its southward course, clearly etched into the center of the picture are the Sea of Galilee, Jordan River, and Dead Sea (with the Lisan peninsula protruding from its southeastern shore). South of the Dead Sea in the direction of the Red Sea, the cleavage of the Wadi Arabah is plainly visible, as are the mountainous heights of Edom that crowd it on the east flank. The basaltic terrain to the east and northeast of the Sea of Galilee shows dark on this picture. Slightly north of the basalt, a lateral river that seems to flow into an area of reddish hue may be seen; this is the Abana River and the oasis of Damascus. Equally vivid is the appearance of some of Jordan's water systems. The Yarmuk system, depicted in light tones, flows out of the southern reaches of the basaltic area and joins with the Jordan River just south of the Sea of Galilee. The Arnon system, pictured in dark, flows westward and enters the Dead Sea above the Lisan peninsula. Various gravels and desert sands of the Negeb and southern Jordan seem to predominate respectively the southwestern and southeastern extremities of the photograph.

Notes for Chapter 3

1. E. Unger, "Ancient Babylonian Maps and Plans," *Antiquity* 9 (1935): 311-22; H. Fischer, "Geschichte der Kartographie von Palastina," *ZDPV* 62 (1939): 169-89; ibid., 63 (1940): 1-111; W. W. Hallo, "The Road to Emar," *JCS* 18 (1964): 57-88; H. M. Z. Meyer, *Ancient Maps of the Holy Land*, 3d ed., enlarged 1965; Z. Vilnay, *The Holy Land in Old Prints and Maps*, 2d ed., 1965; *Atlas of Israel*, 2d (English) ed., 1970; I. V. Schattner, "Maps of Ereṣ Israel," *Encyclopaedia Judaica* 11 (1973), cols. 918-32; R. North, *A History of Biblical Map Making* (1979); K. Nebenzahl, *Mapping the Promised Land: Images of Terra Sancta Through Two Millennia* (forthcoming).
2. I am indebted to C. B. F. Walker of the British Museum for part of the description of this map. Conceptually speaking, the Babylonian map must be studied in conjunction with a multi-colored, eight-pointed star mural discovered at Tuleilat el-Ghassul, a site opposite Jericho located about two miles north-east of the Dead Sea. Doubtlessly, however, this latter item considerably antedates the Babylonian map and was not itself designed as a map.
3. A. Jellinek, *Sammlung kleiner Midraschim u. vermischter Abhandlungen aus der älteren jüdischen Literatur* 5 (Vienna, 1873): 63: "God created the world like an embryo. Just as the embryo begins at the navel and continues to grow from that point, so too the world. The Holy One, blessed be He, began the world from its navel. From there it was stretched hither and yon. Where is its navel? Jerusalem. And its (i.e., Jerusalem's) navel itself? The altar." (Translation follows D. Sperling, *IDBSupp*, 622.)

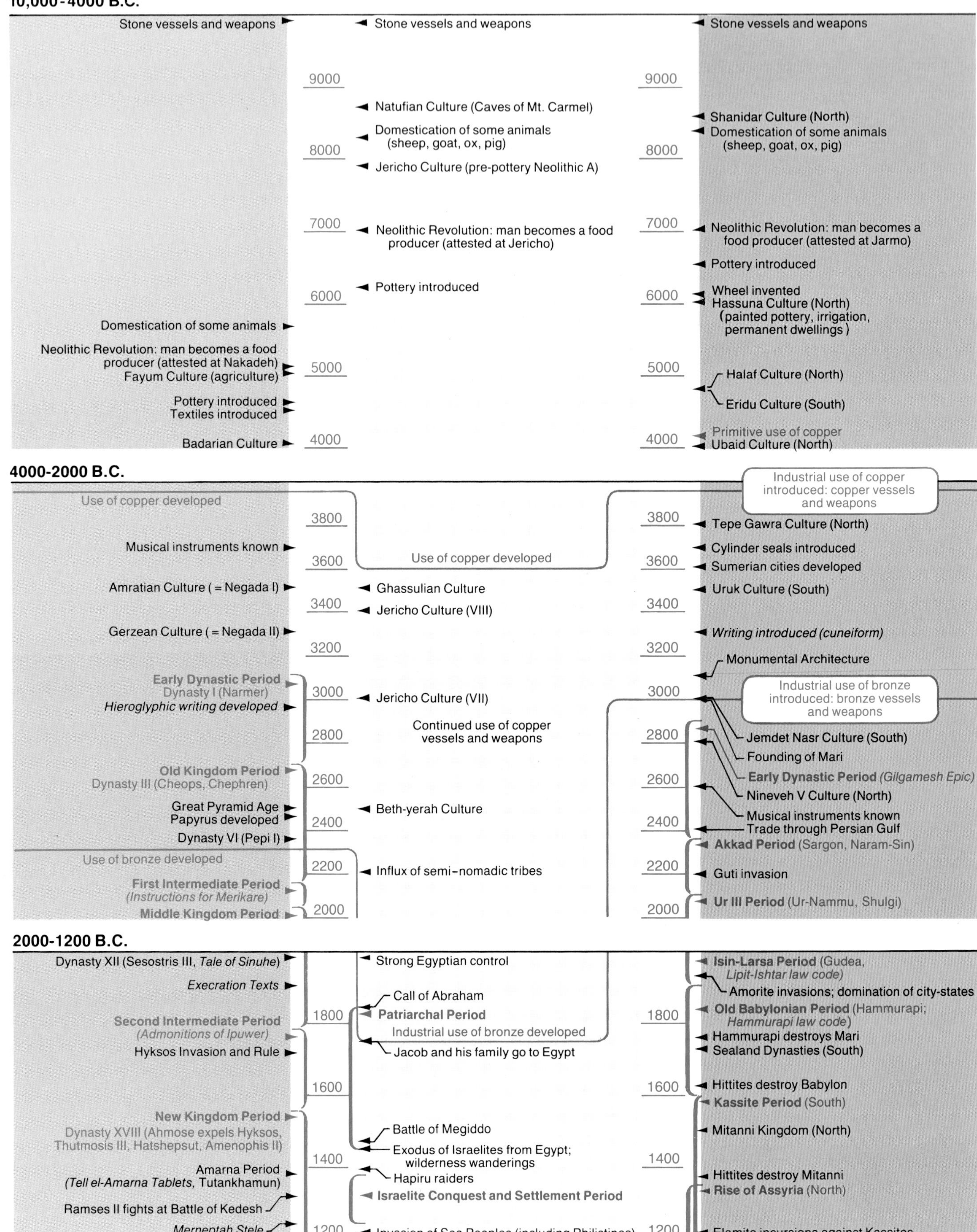

Egypt
Palestine
Mesopotamia
10,000-4000 B.C.
Stone vessels and weapons
Stone vessels and weapons
Stone vessels and weapons
9000
9000
Natufian Culture (Caves of Mt. Carmel)
Shanidar Culture (North)
Domestication of some animals (sheep, goat, ox, pig)
Domestication of some animals (sheep, goat, ox, pig)
8000
8000
Jericho Culture (pre-pottery Neolithic A)
7000
Neolithic Revolution: man becomes a food producer (attested at Jericho)
7000
Neolithic Revolution: man becomes a food producer (attested at Jarmo)
Pottery introduced
Pottery introduced
6000
6000
Wheel invented
Hassuna Culture (North) (painted pottery, irrigation, permanent dwellings)
Domestication of some animals
Neolithic Revolution: man becomes a food producer (attested at Nakadeh)
Fayum Culture (agriculture)
5000
5000
Halaf Culture (North)
Eridu Culture (South)
Pottery introduced
Textiles introduced
Badarian Culture
4000
4000
Primitive use of copper
Ubaid Culture (North)
4000-2000 B.C.
Industrial use of copper introduced: copper vessels and weapons
Use of copper developed
3800
3800
Tepe Gawra Culture (North)
Musical instruments known
Cylinder seals introduced
3600
Use of copper developed
3600
Sumerian cities developed
Amratian Culture (= Negada I)
Ghassulian Culture
Uruk Culture (South)
3400
Jericho Culture (VIII)
3400
Gerzean Culture (= Negada II)
Writing introduced (cuneiform)
3200
3200
Monumental Architecture
Early Dynastic Period
Dynasty I (Narmer)
Hieroglyphic writing developed
3000
Jericho Culture (VII)
3000
Industrial use of bronze introduced: bronze vessels and weapons
2800
Continued use of copper vessels and weapons
2800
Jemdet Nasr Culture (South)
Founding of Mari
Old Kingdom Period
Dynasty III (Cheops, Chephren)
2600
2600
Early Dynastic Period (Gilgamesh Epic)
Nineveh V Culture (North)
Great Pyramid Age
Papyrus developed
Beth-yerah Culture
2400
2400
Musical instruments known
Trade through Persian Gulf
Dynasty VI (Pepi I)
Akkad Period (Sargon, Naram-Sin)
Use of bronze developed
2200
Influx of semi-nomadic tribes
2200
Guti invasion
First Intermediate Period
(Instructions for Merikare)
Middle Kingdom Period
2000
2000
Ur III Period (Ur-Nammu, Shulgi)
2000-1200 B.C.
Dynasty XII (Sesostris III, Tale of Sinuhe)
Strong Egyptian control
Isin-Larsa Period (Gudea, Lipit-Ishtar law code)
Execration Texts
Amorite invasions; domination of city-states
Call of Abraham
Second Intermediate Period
(Admonitions of Ipuwer)
1800
Patriarchal Period
1800
Old Babylonian Period (Hammurapi; Hammurapi law code)
Industrial use of bronze developed
Hammurapi destroys Mari
Hyksos Invasion and Rule
Jacob and his family go to Egypt
Sealand Dynasties (South)
1600
1600
Hittites destroy Babylon
New Kingdom Period
Kassite Period (South)
Dynasty XVIII (Ahmose expels Hyksos, Thutmosis III, Hatshepsut, Amenophis II)
Battle of Megiddo
Mitanni Kingdom (North)
Exodus of Israelites from Egypt; wilderness wanderings
1400
1400
Amarna Period
(Tell el-Amarna Tablets, Tutankhamun)
Hapiru raiders
Hittites destroy Mitanni
Israelite Conquest and Settlement Period
Rise of Assyria (North)
Ramses II fights at Battle of Kedesh
Merneptah Stele
1200
Invasion of Sea Peoples (including Philistines)
1200
Elamite incursions against Kassites

10,000-4000 B.C.

Date	Syria	Asia Minor	Greece/Rome
	Stone vessels and weapons	Stone vessels and weapons	
9000			
	Mureybet Culture	Belbasi Culture	
8000			
7000	Neolithic Revolution: man becomes a food producer (attested at Ugarit and T. Judeida)	Neolithic Revolution: man becomes a food producer (attested at Çatal Hüyük)	
	Ugarit Culture (V-C)		Neolithic Revolution: man becomes a food producer (attested at Nea Nicomedia)
	Pottery introduced		
6000			
		Hacilar Culture Pottery introduced	
5000	Painted pottery	Painted pottery	
4000			

4000-2000 B.C.

Date	Syria	Asia Minor	Greece/Rome
3800	Ugarit Culture (III-C)		
	Use of copper developed		
3600		Use of copper developed	
	Carchemish Culture		
3400			Cretan ships in Mediterranean
3200	Founding of Byblos		
	Writing developed		
3000	Ugarit Culture (III-B)	Founding of Troy	Use of bronze developed (Crete)
	Use of bronze developed		
	Egyptian influence attested at Byblos	Troy Culture (II)	
2800	Amuq G Culture	Use of bronze developed	
2600			
	Founding of Tyre and Sidon Khirbet Kerak Culture		Minoan Civilization on Crete
2400	Ebla Culture		Greeks invade Balkan peninsula
2200	Amorite Expansionism		
		Hittites enter Anatolia	
2000			

2000-1200 B.C.

Date	Syria	Asia Minor	Greece/Rome
		Assyrian Colonies	Middle Minoan Culture
1800	Development of Hurrian city-states	Assyrian Colonies destroyed (*karum* Ib)	Use of bronze developed (Italy)
	Aramean Expansion (Damascus, Hamath)		*Minoan Linear A*
1600		Old Hittite Kingdom (Hattushilish, Murshilish, Suppiluilmash)	
	Alphabetic writing attested at Ugarit Hittite incursion (destruction of Aleppo)	Industrial use of iron introduced: iron implements and weapons	Eruption of Santorini Island (Minoan Civilization destroyed on Crete) Mycenean Culture (Greece)
	Mitanni Dominion		
1400	Hapiru raiders	*Hittite Hieroglyphic Writing*	*Minoan Linear B*
	Battle of Kedesh	Hittite Kingdom Muwataliash fights at Battle of Kedesh	
1200	Invasion of Sea Peoples: Alalakh, Carchemish, Aleppo, Ugarit and Tyre destroyed	Hittite Kingdom destroyed by Sea Peoples	Trojan War: fall of Troy

Egypt | Palestine | Mesopotamia

1200 B.C.-800 B.C.

Date	Egypt	Palestine	Mesopotamia
	Invasion of Sea Peoples; repelled by Ramses III	Philistines settle in southwestern plains	Use of iron developed
	Use of iron developed	Use of iron developed	End of Kassite domination and rise of Sealand Dynasties (South)
1100	End of New Kingdom Period	**Period of Judges**	Tiglath-pileser I
	Third Intermediate Period (*Journey of Wen-Amun*)	Samuel Saul	
1000		**United Kingdom** David	
		Solomon	
	Shishak invades Jerusalem, Judah and Samaria		
900		**Divided Kingdom**	**Period of Assyrian Empire**
		Elijah's ministry Elisha's ministry	Shalmaneser III
800	Libyan dynasties		

800-400 B.C.

Date	Egypt	Palestine	Mesopotamia
			Tiglath-pileser III
			Shalmaneser V Merodach-baladan II sends delegation to Jerusalem
700	Fall of Raphia to Sargon II Nubian dynasty	Fall of Samaria to Shalmaneser V: Assyrian deportations	Sennacherib
	Fall of Memphis to Esarhaddon: Period of Assyrian domination Fall of Thebes to Ashurbanipal	Hezekiah faces Sennacherib's Assyrian hordes Isaiah	Rise of neo-Babylonians (Nabopolassar; Nebuchadnezzar II)
	Saite Period		Fall of Asshur, Nineveh, and Harran to Nebuchadnezzar
600	Necho II marches across Palestine to Carchemish	Death of Josiah at Battle of Megiddo	Nebuchadnezzar victorious at Carchemish
	Tacit submission to Babylonian control	Fall of Jerusalem to Nebuchadnezzar: Babylonian deportations	**Period of neo-Babylonian Empire**
		Jeremiah taken to Egypt	Nabonidus, Belshazzar
		Edict of Cyrus permitting Jews to return to homeland: Zerubbabel leads first return	Cyrus the Great incorporates Babylon into Persian Empire
500	**Late Dynastic Period:** Period of Persian domination	Haggai, Zechariah plead with remnant to complete mission of rebuilding temple	**Period of Persian Empire**
			Darius I suffers defeat at Marathon Xerxes suffers defeat at Salamis
	Jewish colony established on island of Elephantine; *Elephantine papyrii*	Ezra leads second return Nehemiah returns to repair Jerusalem's walls	
400			Artaxerxes II

400-0

Date	Egypt	Palestine	Mesopotamia
		Falls to Alexander the Great: Period of Greek domination	
300	**Period of Greek Domination:** Falls to Alexander the Great	Part of Ptolemaic kingdom	Falls to Alexander the Great Part of Seleucid kingdom
	Writings of Moses translated into Greek at Alexandria		Parthians gain independence
200	Period of Ptolemaic rule	Passes to Seleucid kingdom	
	Antiochus IV invades Egypt	**Maccabean (Hasmonean) Period** Judas Maccabeus leads revolt	**Period of Parthian Empire**
100		Pompey conquers Jerusalem	War with Rome: Passes to Roman control
0	Annexed by Rome	Herod the Great Birth of Jesus	

0-A.D. 100

Date	Egypt	Palestine	Mesopotamia
20	Continued Roman subjugation		
		Jesus' ministry Pontius Pilate: Crucifixion of Jesus	
40			
		Paul's Mission in Asia Minor 1st Jerusalem Council Paul's Mission in Europe	Vologaeses I
60			
		Jewish-Roman Wars Destruction of Jerusalem Destruction of Masada	
80			*Last use of cuneiform writing* (attested at Uruk)
		Jewish religious center at Jamnia	
100			

Syria		Asia Minor		Greece/Rome
1200 B.C.-800 B.C.				
Use of iron developed		Rise of Phrygia and Lydia		
	1100	Phrygia acknowledges vassalage to Tiglath-pileser I	1100	Dorian invasion of Greece
Development of Phoenician alphabet				
Phoenician mercantile expansion and colonization				Ionian settlement in central Greece
	1000		1000	
Hiram of Tyre				Use of iron developed (Italy)
Hadadezer of Zobah				Etruscan settlement in central Italy
Rise of Aramean Damascus		Rise of Melid (Malatya)		
Development of Aramaic script	900		900	
Ben-hadad II of Damascus				Villanovan Culture (Italy)
Battle of Qarqar				
	800		800	
800-400 B.C.				
Assyrian domination		Assyrian domination		
				First Olympiad (traditional date)
				Founding of Rome (traditional date)
Fall of Damascus to Tiglath-pileser III				Homer
				First Greek alphabet texts
	700	Cimmerian invasion: Phrygia destroyed	700	
		Lydian Kingdom (Gyges)		
Fall of Sidon to Esarhaddon				
				Apex of Etruscan culture
				Athenian law codified
Battle of Carchemish	600		600	Invention of coined money
Babylonian domination				
		Treaty between Lydia and Media establishing their boundary at Halys river		
		Croesus of Lydia		Beginning of Peloponnesian league
	500		500	Roman Republic established
Persian domination		Persian domination		
Phoenician's supply fleet for Persian attacks on Greece				Battle of Salamis
				Delian league established in Greece
				Peloponnesian Wars
	400		400	Fall of Athens to Sparta
400-0				
				Socrates' death
Battle of Issus				Philip II of Macedon
Falls to Alexander the Great	300	Falls to Alexander the Great	300	Alexander the Great
Part of Seleucid kingdom		Part of Seleucid kingdom		
				Punic Wars
Antiochus III	200		200	Hannibal in Italy
		Battle of Magnesia		Spain annexed by Rome
Antiochus IV (Epiphanes) forces Hellenization of Judah				Fall of Corinth and Carthage to Rome
	100		100	
		Passes to Roman control		1st Triumvirate
Passes to Roman control				Battle of Actium
	0		0	
0-A.D. 100				
				Tiberias
	20		20	
Continued Roman subjugation		Continued Roman subjugation		
	40		40	Caligula
Paul's mission		Paul's mission		
	60		60	Paul to Rome
				Nero: Rome burns
				Persecution of Christians
				Titus destroys Jerusalem and Judea
	80		80	Eruption of Mt. Vesuvius
				Domitian
	100		100	Trajan

Map Citation Index

In scope, the Map Citation Index is intended to contain all geographical data appearing on the maps, arranged according to map number (not page number). An effort has been made to qualify or further define homonyms when they occur immediately after the name itself. Island names, Israelite tribal names, and region names are also indicated in brackets immediately following the respective entry. A set of parentheses containing bold face grid indicators following an entry refers to that city's placement on the four-page Palestinian city map (No. 15, pp. 56-59). City names preceded by the symbol + are of uncertain location. For abbreviations found in the Index, consult the Table of Abbreviations in the front of this volume.

Index of Scripture

NEW TESTAMENT

Index of Extra-Biblical Literature

APOCRYPHA

OLD TESTAMENT PSEUDEPIGRAPHA

Selected Bibliography

ATLASES

Aharoni, Y., and Avi-Yonah, M. *The Macmillan Bible Atlas* (rev. ed.). New York: Macmillan, 1977.
Atlas of Israel (2d [English] ed.). Jerusalem: Survey of Israel, Ministry of Labour, 1970.
Baly, D., and Tushingham, A. D. *Atlas of the Biblical World.* New York: World, 1971.
Gardner, J. L., gen. ed. *Reader's Digest Atlas of the Bible.* Pleasantville, N. Y.: Reader's Digest Ass'n, 1981.
May, H. G., ed. *Oxford Bible Atlas* (3d ed.). New York: Oxford U., 1984.
Negenman, J. H. *New Atlas of the Bible.* Edited by H. H. Rowley. Translated by H. Hoskins and R. Beckley. Garden City, N. Y.: Doubleday, 1969.

GENERAL REFERENCE WORKS (PHYSICAL GEOGRAPHY)

Abel, F.-M. *Géographie de la Palestine* (2 vols.). Paris: J. Gabalda, 1967 (repr.).
Baly, D. *The Geography of the Bible* (rev. ed.). New York: Harper & Row, 1974.
Dalman, G. *Sacred Sites and Ways.* New York: Macmillan, 1935.
Karmon, Y. *Israel: A Regional Geography.* London: Wiley-Interscience, 1971.
Keel, O., and Küchler, H. *Orte und Landschaften der Bibel.* Zurich: Benziger I, 1984, II, 1982, III (forthcoming).

GENERAL REFERENCE WORKS (REGIONAL GEOGRAPHY)

Orni, E., and Efrat, E. *Geography of Israel* (4th rev. ed.). Jerusalem: Israel Universities, 1980.
Simons, J. *Handbook for the Study of Egyptian Topographical Lists Relating to Western Asia.* Leiden: E. J. Brill, 1937.
Smith, G. A. *The Historical Geography of the Holy Land* (25th rev. ed., repr.). New York: Harper Torchbooks, 1966.
Turner, G. A. *Historical Geography of the Holy Land.* Grand Rapids: Baker, 1973.

GENERAL REFERENCE WORKS (HISTORICAL GEOGRAPHY)

Aharoni, Y. *The Land of the Bible* (rev. ed.). Translated and edited by A. F. Rainey. Philadelphia: Westminster, 1979.
Baly, D. *Geographical Companion to the Bible.* New York: McGraw-Hill, 1963.
Frank, H. T. *Discovering the Biblical World.* Maplewood, N. J.: Hammond, 1975.
Grosvenor, M. B., gen. ed. *Everyday Life in Bible Times.* Washington D.C.: National Geographic, 1976 (repr.).
Simons, J. *The Geographical and Topographical Texts of the Old Testament.* Leiden: E. J. Brill, 1959.

GENERAL REFERENCE WORKS (HISTORY OF ISRAEL)

Bright, J. *A History of Israel* (3d ed.). Philadelphia: Westminster, 1981.
Harrison, R. K. *Old Testament Times.* Grand Rapids: Eerdmans, 1970.
Vaux, R. de. *The Early History of Israel.* Translated by D. Smith. Philadelphia: Westminster, 1978.

GENERAL REFERENCE WORKS (ARCHAEOLOGY)

Aharoni, Y. *The Archaeology and the Land of Israel.* Edited by M. Aharoni. Translated by A. F. Rainey. Philadelphia: Westminster, 1982.
Avi-Yonah, M., gen. ed. *Encyclopedia of Archaeological Excavations in the Holy Land* (4 vols.). Englewood Cliffs, N. J.: Prentice-Hall, 1975-78.

Dornemann, R. H. *The Archaeology of the Transjordan in the Bronze and Iron Ages*. Milwaukee: Milwaukee Public Museum, 1983.

Ellis, R. S. *A Bibliography of Mesopotamian Archaeological Sites*. Wiesbaden, West Germany: Otto Harrassowitz, 1972.

North, R. *Stratigraphia Geobiblica. Biblical Near East Archaeology and Geography*. Rome: Pontifical Biblical Institute, 1970.

Shanks, H., ed. *Recent Archaeology in the Land of Israel*. Washington D.C.: Biblical Archaeology Society, 1984.

Schoville, K. N. *Biblical Archaeology in Focus*. Grand Rapids: Baker, 1978.

Sussmann, A., gen. ed. *Excavations and Surveys in Israel*. Jerusalem: Israel Department of Antiquities and Museums, 1982-.

Thomas, D. W., ed. *Archaeology and Old Testament Study*. Oxford: Clarendon, 1967.

Vogel, E. K. "Bibliography of Holy Land Sites," *HUCA* 42 (1971):1-96.

Vogel, E. K., and Holtzclaw, B. "Bibliography of Holy Land Sites, Part II," *HUCA* 52 (1981):1-92

Yadin, Y., ed. *Jerusalem Revealed: Archaeology in the Holy City 1968-1974*. New Haven: Yale U., 1976.

Yamauchi, E. *The Archaeology of the New Testament Cities in Western Asia Minor*. Grand Rapids: Baker, 1980.

Moody Press, a ministry of the Moody Bible Institute, is designed for education, evangelization, and edification. If we may assist you in knowing more about Christ and the Christian life, please write us without obligation: Moody Press, c/o MLM, Chicago, Illinois 60610